Ethnic Politics and State Power in Africa

Why are some African countries trapped in vicious cycles of ethnic exclusion and civil war, while others experience relative peace? In this groundbreaking book, Philip Roessler addresses this question. Roessler models Africa's weak, ethnically divided states as confronting rulers with a coup–civil war trap—sharing power with ethnic rivals is necessary to underwrite societal peace and prevent civil war, but increases rivals' capabilities to seize sovereign power in a coup d'état. How rulers respond to this strategic trade-off is shown to be a function of their country's ethnic geography and the distribution of threat capabilities it produces. Moving between in-depth case studies of Sudan and the Democratic Republic of the Congo based on years of field work and statistical analyses of powersharing, coups and civil war across sub-Saharan Africa, the book serves as an exemplar of the benefits of mixed methods research for theory-building and testing in comparative politics.

Philip Roessler is an Assistant Professor of Government and Director of the Center for African Development at the College of William and Mary, Virginia. He is an expert on conflict, state building, and development in sub-Saharan Africa with extensive field experience across the region. His book builds on his 2011 *World Politics* article "The Enemy Within", which won the Gregory Luebbert Award from the American Political Science Association for the best article in comparative politics. He is also author of *Why Comrades Go to War: Liberation Politics and the Outbreak of Africa's Deadliest Conflict* (with Harry Verhoeven, 2016).

Ethnic Politics and State Power in Africa

The Logic of the Coup–Civil War Trap

PHILIP ROESSLER

College of William & Mary, Williamsburg, Virginia

 CAMBRIDGE
UNIVERSITY PRESS

CAMBRIDGE
UNIVERSITY PRESS

University Printing House, Cambridge CB2 8BS, United Kingdom

Cambridge University Press is part of the University of Cambridge.

It furthers the University's mission by disseminating knowledge in the pursuit of
education, learning, and research at the highest international levels of excellence.

www.cambridge.org
Information on this title: www.cambridge.org/9781107176072
DOI: 10.1017/9781316809877

First published 2016

Printed in the United States of America by Sheridan Books, Inc.

A catalogue record for this publication is available from the British Library.

ISBN 978-1-107-17607-2 Hardback
ISBN 978-1-316-62821-8 Paperback

Cambridge University Press has no responsibility for the persistence or accuracy of
URLs for external or third-party Internet websites referred to in this publication
and does not guarantee that any content on such websites is, or will remain,
accurate or appropriate.

For Kate and my parents, Anne and Jim

Contents

Figures

Tables

Maps

Preface and Acknowledgments

What causes civil war? This question has been at the forefront of development and foreign policy agendas over the past quarter-century as intrastate conflict remains one of the principal sources of mass violence, displacement, economic destruction, and regional instability. From Syria to Iraq to South Sudan, the scourge of large-scale political violence between the state and its citizens continues.

What underlies this pernicious phenomenon? Poverty?[1] Inequality?[2] Conflict over land and territory?[3] Environmental change?[4] Weak, corrupt, and predatory states?[5] Ethnonationalism?[6]

This book places bargaining over power—the *sine qua non* of civil war—at the center of the analysis. While seemingly an obvious approach, it is surprising the degree to which competition for control of the central government has been marginal to the civil war literature.

[1] Paul Collier, *The Bottom Billion: Why the Poorest Countries Are Failing and What Can Be Done About It* (Oxford: Oxford University Press, 2007).
[2] Frances Stewart, *Horizontal Inequalities and Conflict: Understanding Group Violence in Multiethnic Societies* (New York: Palgrave Macmillan, 2008). Lars-Erik Cederman, Kristian Skrede Gleditsch, and Halvard Buhaug, *Inequality, Grievances, and Civil War* (Cambridge: Cambridge University Press, 2013).
[3] Monica Duffy Toft, *The Geography of Ethnic Violence: Identity, Interests, and the Indivisibility of Territory* (Princeton, NJ: Princeton University Press, 2003).
[4] Thomas F. Homer-Dixon, *Environment, Scarcity, and Violence* (Princeton, NJ: Princeton University Press, 1999).
[5] James D. Fearon and David D. Laitin, "Ethnicity, Insurgency, and Civil War," *American Political Science Review*, 97 (1) (2003): 75–90.
[6] Andreas Wimmer, *Waves of War: Nationalism, State Formation, and Ethnic Exclusion in the Modern World* (Cambridge: Cambridge University Press, 2013).

In focusing on state power, the theoretical approach is fundamentally Hobbesian; civil war is seen as a consequence of the problem of forging order and peace out of anarchy. Hierarchies and anarchies, order and disorder ebb and flow throughout the course of human history. How and why they do so are among the most important puzzles with which social scientists grapple.

In this book, I focus on the anarchic conditions that arose with the dissolution of colonialism in Africa. With the withdrawal of the colonial Leviathan, a fierce competition for control of the extractive institutions left behind by the European imperial powers ensued. In the absence of strong cross-cutting institutions, this high-stakes game for political power often played out along ethnic lines—that is, between different descent-based social groups with shared culture and customs, a common homeland and geographic proximity, and strong norms of reciprocity. The Hobbesian problem confronting African states after independence was how, in the absence of an absolute authority, these strong social groups could forge a political covenant to govern their new countries.

In Africa's newly independent states, rulers recognized that sharing power with ethnic rivals was integral to building peace. Without such alliances, rulers lacked the capabilities to broadcast power beyond their own group, leaving their regimes vulnerable to societally based armed rebellions that they had little capacity to effectively defeat. But sharing power risked opening the door for their rivals to seize sovereign power for themselves in a coup d'état. Overall, then, this book's central argument is that the withdrawal of the colonial Leviathans, and the weak ethnically divided states they left behind, confronted Africa's postcolonial rulers with a coup–civil war trap.[7] The post-World War II international system worsened the strategic uncertainty dominating politics in these regimes by granting sovereign recognition to any group that controlled the capital city, no matter how they came to power and how much control they had outside the capital.

One of the devastating implications that follows from this theoretical framework is that civil war represents the consequence of a strategic choice by rulers, backed by their coethnics, to coup-proof their regimes from their ethnic rivals. With their rivals unable to credibly commit not to exploit their access to the central government to seize sovereign power for themselves, rulers are tempted to choose exclusion as a strategy to

[7] That the coup–civil war trap has also plagued Ethiopia and Liberia after the breakdown of ethnocratic rule illustrates that this political phenomenon is not only a legacy of European colonialism.

consolidate their hold on power and trade the clear and present danger of the coup d'état today for the uncertain risk of a distant, future civil war. This helps to account for the intractability of civil wars in many African states: they result not from miscalculation or greed but rather follow a clear strategic logic and are deemed the least threatening option for the political interests of the ruling group.

The upshot of this, however, is that as the *strategic* costs of civil war increase, choosing ethnopolitical exclusion becomes less appealing. And it suggests, counterintuitively, that strong civil war, or threat, capabilities, in which rival groups can mobilize a rebellion that can credibly threaten the capital *even* when they are excluded from state power, may help to induce powersharing. The empirical evidence demonstrates exactly this. Powersharing is significantly more likely to be self-enforcing when the ruling group *and* a given rival are endowed with strong threat capabilities due to their size and proximity to the capital. Under such conditions, rulers and the opposition are more likely to choose powersharing and reluctantly trade executive authority via coups—which do not significantly alter the relative distribution of power—than accept a mutually costly total war for control of the state.

This finding, however, points to another pernicious legacy of colonial rule—it tended to create unusually large and unusually divided states. Thus, for rulers of Sudan, Chad or the Democratic Republic of the Congo (DRC), three of Africa's most notorious conflict-affected, failed states, their countries' ethnic geography reduces incentives for powersharing with peripheral groups, whose remoteness renders them strategically impotent and gives them little leverage to hold their rulers accountable.

What is the way out of this vicious trap? Deeply rooted in the sociopolitical foundations of the African state, overcoming the coup–civil war trap will not occur overnight. Instead, it will require significant changes over time along three key dimensions: (1) the rules of the game; (2) the structure of the state; and (3) the basis of societal mobilization. Yet, over the past two decades, there has been significant change across all three dimensions. For example, on the changing rules of the game, the African Union no longer recognizes groups that come to power via coups and elections are now the modal source of political change. On the changing structure of the state, a number of African regimes, backed by renewed external investment, especially from China, in big infrastructural projects, have sought to strengthen the state's capacity to broadcast its power into the periphery. Finally, on the changing basis of social mobilization, urbanization, technological diffusion, and generational change are strengthening interethnic social ties and bases of trust, while leading an increasing number of individuals to reject political appeals along ethnic lines. This broadening of social identification and social movements increases society's capabilities to hold incumbents to account if they violate the letter or spirit of constitutionalism.

The significance of these changes should not be underestimated; at the same time, they have a long way to go before the coup–civil war trap is rendered obsolete. For now, coups still remain a viable instrument of political change, if not a path to sovereign power, despite the anti-coup rules of the African Union; electoral rigging and other malfeasance undermine the institutional constraints posed by elections; despite significant investments in infrastructure, the political topography of the African state does not look vastly different than at independence; and, finally, political mobilization along ethnic lines remains the dominant mode of politics in many countries. Until institutional, structural, and social change is consolidated, the pernicious consequences of the coup–civil war trap will remain a key source of state failure and large-scale political violence, as was tragically demonstrated in South Sudan at the end of 2013—the case that opens the book.

* * *

The seeds for this book project were planted long ago when I was an undergraduate student at Indiana University and ended up spending three summers working in western Kenya. My time in Kenya had two profound influences on me: it inspired an interest in both the politics of the African state and civil war. With Sudan's civil war between the government and the Sudan People's Liberation Army (SPLA) still raging at the time and spilling over into Kenya, I developed a fascination with Kenya's troubled northern neighbor. Each summer I was in Kenya I would make my way up to the United Nations Operation Lifeline Sudan base camp in Lokichogio, northwest Kenya. There I hoped to hitch a ride on an aid flight into South Sudan with the goal of learning firsthand from South Sudanese about the long-running conflict. It would take me three years of trying, but I finally made it into South Sudan—only to end up in western Mayom County in Unity State on the day before Khartoum launched one of its final counteroffensives to clear the oil fields ahead of the peace talks getting under way in Kenya. To this day I remain grateful to the people of the village of Keriel who hosted me and kept me safe as we fled for four days together to Bahr el Ghazal; the sight of their bodies getting smaller and smaller as I was safely lifted out of the area by a food aid flight remains seared into my memory. And it is my hope that, in whatever small way, this book contributes to ending and preventing war and the suffering it causes.

Witnessing the devastating consequences of civil war in South Sudan reaffirmed my interest in the subject and profoundly shaped the course of my Ph.D. at the University of Maryland. At Maryland I was extremely fortunate to study under the guidance of Mark Lichbach, whose formidable theoretical understanding of conflict provided the perfect balance to what I was learning firsthand in the field. At Maryland I also benefited from the guidance of a number of faculty members, including Virginia Haufler, Christian Davenport, Jillian Schwedler, Ernest Wilson, Fred Alford, and, especially, Marc Morjé Howard. As mentor, coauthor, and friend, Marc opened many doors for me while instilling in me the value of mixed-methods research and the importance of family–academic balance.

At Maryland, I also had the opportunity to work for the International Crisis Group as part of the original "dream team" of interns John Prendergast assembled to work on Sudan and other African countries. I would work as a consultant for the Crisis Group at various points throughout my graduate student career and would benefit immensely from the friendship and intellectual support of JP, John Norris, Colin Thomas-Jensen, and, especially, Suliman Baldo and Dave Mozersky. (I remain indebted to Dave for a number of things, but especially for helping from Nairobi to extricate me from the aforementioned trouble I ran into in Mayom County.)

As I was formulating my thesis on the link between political authority in weak states and civil war, Darfur erupted into large-scale political violence. Despite also facing high levels of political and economic marginalization from the central government and intermittent cycles of communal conflict, Darfur had never produced the kind of sustained antigovernment rebellions seen in South Sudan. The puzzle for me was why not and why now. Supported by a David L. Boren Fellowship from the National Security Education Program and subsequent support from a Dissertation Improvement Grant from the National Science Foundation, I set back out to Sudan. I sought to accomplish two things: (1) to better understand the political causes of the civil war in Darfur and (2) to situate it in comparative perspective. In doing so, I became fascinated as to why, a decade before the outbreak of the Darfur civil war, the Sudanese government, also led by Omar al-Bashir, faced and effectively defeated a rebellion in Darfur but failed spectacularly to do so in 2002 and 2003. Same underlying structural conditions, two rebellions, two radically different outcomes. The existing civil war literature could not account for this variation.

In addressing this puzzle I conducted semi-structured interviews with hundreds of Sudanese (many interviewees multiple times) from the top echelon of the Islamic Movement, Islamist cadres, military officers, tribal elders in Darfur, leaders of Darfur's rebel movements, rank-and-file members of the rebellions, opposition politicians, journalists, civil society activists, academics, and international observers. (Among the internationals, I am particularly grateful to Janice Elmore, Opheera McDoom, and the African Union Mission in Sudan for the assistance they provided me.) With Khartoum as a base, I made several trips to all three of Darfur's states as well as to Eritrea (where most of the rebel leadership was based at the time), Chad, and Abuja, Nigeria, where the Darfur peace talks were being held.

Despite its reputation to the outside world, Sudan is an incredibly hospitable place to work, as many know who have conducted research in the country. Beyond the famous hospitality, generosity, and sense of humor of the Sudanese, there exists a culture of support and encouragement for educational pursuits and endeavors (sadly a thing that too few Sudanese are able to embark upon). This spirit was evidenced in Sudanese from all walks of life from the *amjad* drivers in Khartoum, with whom I incessantly discussed the split in Al-Harakat Al-Islamiyya between Bashir and Turabi, to the Darfurians who opened their offices and doors to me to dissect the roots of the devastating civil war in their homeland, which I know could often invoke painful memories.

In Sudan, the following people were especially gracious and patient in helping me understand the complexities of Sudanese politics: Atta el-Battahani, Ali Shammar, Abul Ghasim Seif El Din, Abdallah Adam Khatir, Sayeed al-Khateeb, General Ibrahim Suleiman, Idriss Yusef, Jibril Abdullah, Qutbi al-Mahdi, Mohammed Hassan al-Amin, Mohamed Suliman Khatir, Sharif Mohamedein, Abdel-Rahim Hamdi, and especially Hamid Ali Nour, who generously served as what amounted to my personal tutor on Sudanese politics. I will always fondly remember our sessions over sweet Sudanese tea. For their friendship and for showing me Sudanese life beyond the political realm, including trips down the Nile River to Crocodile Island, I am grateful to Hassan Salah and Mubarak Mahgoub. I also would like to thank Anwar Idris and Mamoon Mohammed Abdallah for superb research assistance with translation and in the newspaper archives, respectively. Outside of Sudan, I am thankful to Ali al-Haj for taking the time to extensively meet me several times to discuss the rise and fall of Sudan's Islamic Movement as well as Professor Abdelwahab El-Affendi for sharing his unparalleled knowledge of the Movement. Last but not least I am exceptionally grateful to Abdulghani Idris from whom I gained a deeper understanding of the Islamic

Movement and broader Sudanese political history and whose sense of humor, compassion, and friendship uplift all who know him.

Having derived an original interpretation of the Darfur civil war and the building blocks of a generalizable theory of civil war in weak states, I then had the wonderful opportunity to further develop and expand the project on fellowships from Stanford University and Oxford University. Both institutions represent incredible intellectual environments and connected me to fellow scholars who would profoundly shape the development of the book. At Stanford, where I was a predoctoral fellow at the Center for International Security and Cooperation (CISAC), I am deeply appreciative to Lynn Eden, the Associate Director for Research, for overseeing the fellowship program and investing in each of us. At Stanford, I tried to absorb as much knowledge as I could from Jim Fearon, David Laitin, Jeremy Weinsten, Michael McFaul, and David Abernethy. Coming to Stanford with Darfur's sandy soil virtually still on my shoes, their incisive questioning and feedback helped crystallize what at that time were still raw ideas. I am pretty sure it was in one of our lunch conversations that Jim Fearon elegantly summed up my interpretation of the Darfur civil war as a ruler choosing to substitute civil war risk for coup risk. Beyond pushing me to take the project to the next level, I learned from these distinguished scholars the meaning of academic collegiality and mentorship.

After Stanford, I moved to Oxford, where I received an Andrew Mellon Postdoctoral Fellowship in the Department of Politics and International Relations. At Oxford I would be surrounded by a wonderful group of Africanists and political scientists—Nancy Bermeo, Dave Anderson, Adrienne LeBas, Nic Cheeseman, Phil Clark, Anke Hoeffler, and Ricardo Soares de Oliveira—from whose friendship and intellectual support I immensely benefited (with special thanks to Adrienne who is a kindred spirit for many of us in our Africanist cohort). My time at Oxford coincided with the publication of the Ethnic Power Relations (EPR) dataset by Andreas Wimmer, Lars-Erik Cederman, and Brian Min. I wish to thank Andreas for sharing the dataset and offering valuable feedback and encouragement at the early stages of this project. The dataset provided an invaluable opportunity to empirically test the existence of a coup–civil war trade-off in postcolonial Africa if I could generate data on the ethnicity of coup conspirators and rebels. So I set off to the enchanting Rhodes House Library to scour its Commonwealth and African Collections for detailed information on all of Africa's postcolonial conflicts. Indispensable to this endeavor was the Africa Contemporary Record and the Historical Dictionary series, especially the volumes by Samuel Decalo. I am grateful to the staff at the Rhodes House Library for their assistance. This research would be published in *World Politics* in 2011 under the title, "The Enemy Within: Personal Rule, Coups and Civil War." This forms the basis of parts of Chapters 4 and 8 in this book.

At Oxford I received two grants from the John Fell OUP Fund that proved instrumental to the project's advancement. The grants allowed me to conduct additional field research in Sudan and critically also in Chad. (In N'djamena I benefited immensely from the assistance of Dr. Siddick Adam Issa, who not only introduced me to a number of key players but whose own insights into the Darfur conflict and Chad–Sudan relations were quite valuable.) The research grants from the John Fell OUP Fund also enabled me to qualitatively test my coup-proofing theory of civil war on a second case. One of the most intriguing possibilities was the Democratic Republic of the Congo and the war that would break out there in August 1998—Africa's Great War. The quantitative analysis pointed to the DRC case as a paradigmatic example of a co-conspirator civil war, but few seemed to study it in this way. The prospect of delving into the massively complex case of the DRC, a country in which I had never worked, was daunting to say the least. But then I met Harry Verhoeven.

As I was pondering adding the Congo case, I gave a lecture at the Sudan Programme, a forum for discussing Sudan at St. Antony's College under the inimitable stewardship of Ahmed Al-Shahi, the prominent social anthropologist on northern Sudan, who would become a good friend and supporter during my time at Oxford. It was after that lecture that I met Harry, a D.Phil. student in politics at Oxford at the time. Aptly described by our mutual friend, Phil Clark, as a "one-man juggernaut," given the depth and breadth of his intellect and scholarship and the dynamism of his personality, Harry had lived and worked in Kinshasa as an intern in the Belgian Embassy some two years earlier and expressed enthusiasm in the merits of adding the DRC to the project. At that moment our collaboration was born, and we set off to work together on applying the coup–civil war trap to the post-Mobutu order in the DRC. From the Holy See in Rome (where we were graciously received by Frank De Coninck, the former Belgian Ambassador to Congo, who was serving as Ambassador to the Vatican at the time) to Kinshasa to Kigali, we tracked down and interviewed as many of the protagonists and other stakeholders involved in the overthrow of Mobutu and the outbreak of Africa's Great War. It proved an incredible physical and intellectual journey, punctuated by the nightly mad dash across the Boulevard du 30 Juin to O'Poeta, trips to the Congo river, and intense interviews on the banks of Lake Kivu, in the back bar at the Sultani Hotel, and in nondescript offices in Kigali. Harry's theoretical insights, encyclopedic knowledge of Congo and the region, and unparalleled skills in winning and then executing elite-level interviews strengthened this book immensely. Chapter 9 is a product of our incredible collaboration. Unable to contain all of our research and theoretical insights on Africa's Great War in a single chapter or paper, we have since coauthored *Why Comrades Go to War: Liberation Politics and the Outbreak of Africa's Deadliest Conflict* (2016).

After Oxford, I joined the Department of Government at the College of William & Mary (W&M), another wonderful academic institution and intellectual environment and the perfect place to complete the book project. Being surrounded by both supportive and smart colleagues has helped me to see this book to the finish line. At W&M I would like to thank the former chair of the Government Department, John McGlennon, for his steadfast support of my research and my need to make field trips to Sudan, Congo, Angola, and elsewhere in sub-Saharan Africa. I am also grateful to the College's Faculty Summer Grant Program, which funded summer work on the book manuscript.

At the end of my second year at W&M, the Institute for the Theory and Practice of International Relations (ITPIR) sponsored and hosted a book workshop for me. The book workshop proved invaluable and easily the best day of my young academic career. Filled with positive energy and careful and constructive discussion of debates I had had in my own head for some time, the book workshop strengthened the manuscript immeasurably. I am deeply appreciative to ITPIR and its indomitable director, Mike Tierney, for organizing and holding the workshop. As our colleague Simon Stow describes him, Mike produces a Steve Jobsesque "reality distortion field" that inspires and brings out the best of all of us at W&M; for his inspiration and generous provision of public goods, we are grateful.

For their generous participation and insightful feedback and suggestions, I owe deep thanks to Will Reno, Alex de Waal, and David Cunningham as well as to my colleagues at W&M: Mike, Steve Hanson, Sue Peterson, Paul Manna, Paula Pickering, Maurits van der Veen, Cullen Hendrix, and Dave Ohls.

Beyond the incredible feedback on the existing draft, the book workshop also helped to solidify a collaboration with Dave Ohls. Dave has a razor-sharp mind. It was his intuition that as the costs of civil war and coup converge such that rulers gain no strategic advantage from exclusion then powersharing becomes more likely that motivated the threat-capabilities theory of powersharing. Armed with this insight, we set out to identify the conditions that lead rivals to choose powersharing. Chapter 10 summarizes the results of that collaboration. We have fully developed and tested that argument in different form and with additional data in our stand-alone paper, "Self-Enforcing Powersharing in Weak States."

Beyond my colleagues, special recognition is also due to a remarkable group of W&M students who helped in various stages on the book: Luke Elias, Michael Hibshman, Logan Ferrell, Kyle Titlow, and Nadia Ilunga. Luke and Logan took extensive notes at the book workshop; both think with incredible clarity and have offered insightful reflections on the book's theoretical model. Moreover, debriefing with Luke after the workshop helped me to get my head around the hundreds of different comments and suggestions to come out of the workshop. Michael contributed valuable research assistance that helped to strengthen Chapter 10, especially on the dynamics of durable powersharing and the coup trap in Ghana. Meanwhile, Kyle significantly advanced the geospatial analysis in this book, not only in helping to calculate the threat-capabilities' scores used in the analysis in Chapter 10 but also in producing a number of excellent maps, including the ones that formed the basis of the maps in this book. Finally, I am extremely grateful to Nadia Ilunga for excellent research assistance both at W&M and in Kinshasa and for the wonderful hospitality of her family.

Throughout this project's duration, I also benefited from feedback at research presentations at Stanford, Oxford, Maryland, and W&M, and also at Yale University, University of Chicago, American University, St. Andrews University, and London School of Economics as well as at several of the annual meetings of the American Political Science Association. In addition, discussions with the following scholars proved useful at various stages throughout this project: Macartan Humphreys, Dan Slater, Stathis Kalyvas, Scott Straus, Lars-Erik Cederman, Julia Choucair Vizoso, Kristen Harkness, Jack Paine, and, especially, Rob Blair, who offered a set of very useful comments at my talk at Yale.

Such an endeavor and project is impossible, however, without a core base of support that can sustain one throughout its entirety, from the time in the field to the data collection and analysis to the writing and rewriting. I am blessed to have a wonderful group of friends and family without whom I would neither have initiated nor completed this project. I wish I could name and thank each individually.

In my first summer trip to Kenya I traveled with my dear friend Justin; from breaking my malaria-induced fever as we rushed to the hospital to our nightly conversations by kerosene lamp, he was and remains a great friend. For instilling in us a scientific outlook and Roessler family values, Grandma and Grandpa Ocre. For embodying those family values much better than I have, my unwavering and selfless sister and brother, Lisa and Steve. For the motivation to study the human condition, the inspiration to ask big questions about how the world works, and the fortitude to go out and tackle them, I wish to thank our parents, Anne and Jim. The love, support, and devotion they give to all of us—and now our children and their grandchildren—are beyond words.

Finally, to my dearest Kate. This project coincided with our young lives together. Your dad, Greg, was the first person from home I talked to when I finally made it out of Mayom County. Our engagement in the Maasai Mara occurred in the middle of my dissertation field research; our wedding was only a few weeks after I *finally* "finished" that field research. Fellowships at Stanford and Oxford led to our adventures in California and England and unforgettable trips with your sisters, Kim and Kristen. Our time at Oxford ended with the birth of Lucy, while Lena's birth in Williamsburg came just on the heels of my book workshop and Libby's a few months before I finally put the book to rest. That we have shared this experience together—and that you so generously allowed our experience to be shared with the labors of such a project—and that it has been punctuated by so many wonderful memories—not the least the births and first years of our wonderful daughters, Lucy, Lena, and Libby—mean so much to me. Without your patience, understanding, and intellectual support, this book would not be what it is.

Abbreviations

AU	African Union
CAR	Central African Republic
DLF	Darfur Liberation Front
DRC	Democratic Republic of the Congo
ECOWAS	Economic Community of West African States
EPR	Ethnic Power Relations
EPRDF	Ethiopian People's Revolutionary Democratic Front
FAC	Forces Armées Congolaises
FAN	Forces Armées du Nord
ICC	International Criminal Court
ICF	Islamic Charter Front
IGAD	Intergovernmental Authority on Development
ISIS	Islamic State of Iraq and Syria
KUSU	Khartoum University Student Union
NCP	National Congress Party
NIF	National Islamic Front
NISS	National Intelligence and Security Service
NPFL	National Patriotic Front of Liberia
NUP	National Unionist Party
OAU	Organization of African Unity
PAIC	Popular Arab and Islamic Conference
PRC	People's Redemption Council
PSC	Peace and Security Council
RCC	Revolutionary Command Council
RPA	Rwandan Patriotic Army
RPF	Rwandan Patriotic Front
RUF	Revolutionary United Front
SAF	Sudanese Armed Forces

SCP	Sudanese Communist Party
SFDA	Sudan Federal Democratic Alliance
SLA	Sudan Liberation Army
SPLA	Sudan People's Liberation Army
SPLM	Sudan People's Liberation Movement
UNLA	Uganda National Liberation Army

I

Introduction

I.I THE PURGE: JUBA, DECEMBER 2013

The fighting erupted late on Sunday night, ten days before Christmas, within the headquarters of South Sudan's Presidential Republican Guard. The next morning, with the violence spreading, South Sudan's president, Salva Kiir, clad in full military fatigues, held a press conference in which he accused Riek Machar, his former vice president, of triggering the bloodshed in an attempted coup d'état. Reviving memories of a coup Machar attempted some twenty-two years ago against Dr. John Garang, then leader of the SPLA and eventual hero of South Sudan's independence, President Kiir declared, "My fellow citizens, let me reiterate my statement [from] a few days ago in which I said that my government is not and will not allow the incidents of 1991 to repeat themselves again. This prophet of doom continues to persistently pursue his actions of the past and I have to tell you that I will not allow or tolerate such incidences once again in our new nation."[1]

The general consensus, however, conflicts with Kiir's telling of events.[2] Many claim that what triggered the violence was not a coup attempt but

---

[1] South Sudan TV, "President Salva Kiir Announced Foil a Coup Attempt Led by Riek Machar," December 16, 2013. Available at www.youtube.com/watch?v=boLU20O5JDI (accessed August 21, 2016).

[2] For example, as noted South Sudan expert Douglas H. Johnson writes, "while the government of South Sudan has kept to this version of events, they have presented little concrete evidence to support their claim of a plot, and few friendly governments have accepted it unequivocally. Instead there was strong international pressure for the release of the eleven detainees." Douglas H. Johnson, "Briefing: The Crisis in South Sudan," *African Affairs*, 113 (451) (2014): 300–309. Riek Machar claims that in a closed-door IGAD (Intergovernmental Authority on Development) summit in Addis Ababa in June 2014, Yoweri Museveni, President of Uganda and one of Salva Kiir's strongest regional allies,

the incumbent's analogue—a *purge*.[3] Fearing the very event he claimed to have faced,[4] Salva Kiir sought to selectively disarm those loyal to Riek Machar within the presidential guard. When they resisted, all caution was thrown to the wind, and Salva Kiir sought to liquidate Riek Machar and his supporters. Machar's house was obliterated; perceived Machar loyalists in the Presidential Republican Guard were killed; and a witch hunt ensued in Juba to round up and kill men of the same ethnic background as Machar.[5] Moreover, a group of ten high-ranking officials within the Sudan People's Liberation Movement (SPLM), including the wife of Dr. John Garang, Rebecca Garang, and the secretary general of the party, Pagan Amum, were arrested and held incommunicado on allegations they were party to the coup conspiracy.

The purge failed to kill Riek Machar, but it did neutralize his capability to seize power from within. Having disarmed or killed Machar's forces in the presidential guard, disrupted his political network within

acknowledged there was no coup. See "Museveni Dismisses Kiir's Claims Coup Attempt Sparked Conflict," *Sudan Tribune*, June 11, 2014. Available at www.sudantribune.com/spip.php?article51319 (accessed August 21, 2016).

[3] One of the strongest counters to Salva Kiir's telling of events was by Dr. Peter Adwok Nyaba, former minister for higher education in the government of South Sudan, 2011–2013, and then a member of the Sudan People's Liberation Movement (SPLM) leadership council. See Dr. Peter Adwok Nyaba, "It Wasn't a Coup: Salva Kiir Shot Himself in the Foot," *South Sudan Nation*, December 20, 2013. Available at www.southsudannation.com/it-wasnt-a-coup-salva-kiir-shot-himself-in-the-foot (accessed August 21, 2016). Rebecca Garang corroborated Nyaba's account of the events on December 15: "Rebecca Nyandeng Garanga Reveals All: How Salva Kiir's 'Private Army' Prompted the Current Conflict," *London Evening Post*, January 25, 2014. Available at www.thelondoneveningpost.com/exclusive-rebecca-nyandeng-garang-reveals-all-how-salva-kiirs-private-army-prompted-the-current-conflict (accessed August 21, 2016). Kiir loyalists insist that the disarmament of the Nuer in the presidential guard was only initiated to stop a coup that was under way.

[4] Salva Kiir's fears were not completely unfounded, of course. Riek Machar had made it abundantly clear he was going after Salva Kiir's seat. While Machar seemed to be pursuing a nonviolent path to sovereign power through the ruling party, the SPLM, it is not beyond the realm of possibility, given his track record for the use of force to make political gains, that he would have done so through a coup, especially as Salva Kiir prevented open competition through the SPLM. On the link between the intra-party politics and the events of December 15, see Philip Roessler. "Why South Sudan Has Exploded in Violence," *Washington Post*, December 24, 2013. Available at www.washingtonpost.com/blogs/monkey-cage/wp/2013/12/24/why-south-sudan-has-exploded-in-violence (accessed August 21, 2016).

[5] "S. Sudan Presidential Guards Raid House of ex-VP Machar," *Sudan Tribune*, December 17, 2013. Available at www.sudantribune.com/spip.php?article49217 (accessed August 21, 2016). Human Rights Watch, "South Sudan: Ethnic Targeting, Widespread Killings," January 16, 2014. Available at www.hrw.org/news/2014/01/16/south-sudan-ethnic-targeting-widespread-killings (accessed August 21, 2016).

Juba, overcome resistance by Nuer soldiers within the SPLA headquarters, and forced the former vice president to flee to the bush, Salva Kiir and his inner circle eliminated the clear and present danger of the coup d'état from the "prophet of doom." But Kiir's preemptive strike came at a steep price: full-scale civil war.

The problem for Kiir was the state he retained control of was extremely weak. Having been born out of decades of devastating and destructive war against Khartoum, South Sudan lacked the hardware (e.g., roads and other infrastructure) and software (e.g., impersonal bureaucracy) necessary for the central government to broadcast power over its population and territory. Instead, its authority and control emanated from a set of informal alliances between Big Men—powerful individuals who sat atop of and were embedded in a network of followers and were able to produce violence to gain control of scarce resources.[6] These alliances were critical for the people of South Sudan to wrestle independence from Khartoum. For years, interethnic fighting within South Sudan weakened the region's capacity to gain full concessions from the government of Sudan. The SPLA was only able to formally extract the right of separation from Khartoum after Riek Machar was reintegrated back into the rebel movement as number three in command behind Garang and Kiir in 2002.[7] The integration of Nuer militia leaders, such as Peter Gatdet, in the SPLA after the signing of the Comprehensive Peace Agreement with Khartoum contributed to a significant reduction of violence in South Sudan.

The pre-Christmas purge in 2013, however, destroyed these fragile alliances and divided the military. Immediately Machar was able to mobilize allies in Unity and Jonglei States against the government. The Fourth Division Commander of the South Sudan Army defected in Unity State and declared himself governor of the oil-rich state.[8] Peter Gatdet, the commander of the Eighth Division, defected and captured the strategic town of Bor in Jonglei State. Less than five days after the purge, the South Sudan government lost control of the two states. Soon they would lose

---

[6] Mats Utas, ed. *African Conflicts and Informal Power: Big Men and Networks* (London: Zed Books, 2012). Douglass Cecil North, John Joseph Wallis, and Barry R. Weingast, *Violence and Social Orders: A Conceptual Framework for Interpreting Recorded Human History* (Cambridge: Cambridge University Press, 2009).

[7] John Young, *The Fate of Sudan: The Origins and Consequences of a Flawed Peace Process* (New York: Zed Books, 2012).

[8] "Unity State's 4th Division Commander Defects, Assumes Governorship," *Sudan Tribune*, December 21, 2013. Available at www.sudantribune.com/spip.php?article49274 (accessed August 21, 2016).

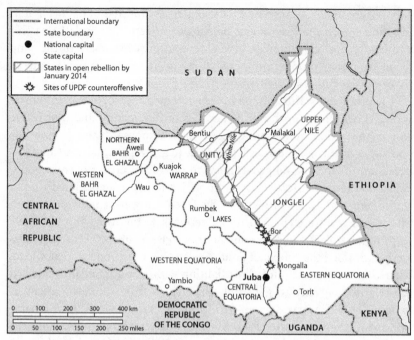

MAP 1.1 The Outbreak of Civil War in South Sudan, December 2013–January 2014

control of a third when Malakal, the capital of Upper Nile State, fell to Machar's forces on Christmas Eve.[9] (See Map 1.1.)

With a significant part of the country in open rebellion, Salva Kiir faced the possibility that Machar and his allies would now march on the national capital, Juba, from Bor.[10] But, as sovereign ruler of South Sudan, a position that he had taken such extreme measures to guard, Kiir possessed two advantages that he put into great effect. First, he controlled the state coffers and could leverage his discretionary authority over patronage to mobilize support against Machar.[11] Most importantly,

[9] "Machar's Forces Capture Upper Nile State Capital, Malakal," *Sudan Tribune*, December 24, 2013. Available at www.sudantribune.com/spip.php?article49320 (accessed August 21, 2016).

[10] The specter of this was real, especially in early January 2014 when the rebel forces managed to make their way down the Bor–Juba road, inducing panic in Juba. For a comprehensive chronology of events in the early part of the conflict, see Small Arms Survey Sudan, "South Sudan Crisis Timeline," June 27, 2014. Available at www.smallarmssurveysudan.org/fileadmin/docs/documents/HSBA-South-Sudan-Crisis-Timeline.pdf (accessed August 21, 2016).

[11] Alex de Waal, "When Kleptocracy Becomes Insolvent: Brute Causes of the Civil War in South Sudan," *African Affairs*, 113 (452) (2014): 347–369.

Kiir was able to elicit the support of the three Equatorian governors of the states around Juba who ramped up recruitment efforts to support the army.[12] Second, he was able to call on other sovereign states to protect his "democratically elected" government from an unconstitutional challenge posed by Riek Machar. Uganda, a strong ally of South Sudan, immediately responded and deployed substantial forces to, at first, protect Juba and the evacuation of foreign nationals, and then to attack opposition forces from both the ground and the air as they marched from Bor all the way to Mongalla.[13] Without the support of the Ugandan military, it remains an open question whether Kiir would have been able to hold Juba.[14] Though Kiir was able to survive in power and reverse some of the big early gains made by the opposition forces, his government was not able to crush the rebellion, and civil war engulfed the new state of South Sudan, leading to tens of thousands of deaths and millions displaced one year into the conflict.

The tragic course of events in newly independent South Sudan illuminates a dynamic that has been at the heart of state failure across postcolonial Africa—what I label as *the coup–civil war trap*. In Africa's weak states, accommodating rival Big Men in the central government is necessary to mobilize support from beyond the ruler's own ethnic base and extend the reach of the state. But doing so lowers the costs rivals face to usurp power in a future coup d'état, in which a given faction or group exploits its partial control of the state, especially the military, to unseat the ruler by force or other unconstitutional means.[15] Excluding rivals weakens their coup-making capabilities but at the cost of increasing the risk of *civil war*—in which a group of violence specialists mobilize a

[12] "Military Mobilisation in E. Equatoria Attracts Excess Recruits," *Sudan Tribune*, February 15, 2014. Available at http://sudantribune.com/spip.php?article49964 (accessed August 21, 2016). Cited in de Waal, "When Kleptocracy Becomes Insolvent," p. 366.

[13] Nicholas Kulish, "South Sudan Recaptures Town from Rebels," *The New York Times*, January 18, 2014. Available at www.nytimes.com/2014/01/19/world/africa/south-sudan-recaptures-strategic-town-from-rebels.html (accessed August 21, 2016).

[14] Ugandan sources suggest this fear motivated the Uganda People's Defence Force (UPDF) to take robust action. Haggai Matsiko, "Inside UPDF's Juba Mission," *The Independent*, June 29, 2014. Available at http://allafrica.com/stories/201406300788.html.

[15] Samuel P. Huntington, *Political Order in Changing Societies* (New Haven, Conn.: Yale University Press, 1968); Edward Luttwak, *Coup d'État: A Practical Handbook* (Harmondsworth: Penguin Press, 1968); Patrick J. McGowan, "African Military Coups d'État, 1956–2001: Frequency, Trends and Distribution," *Journal of Modern African Studies*, 41 (3) (2003): 339–370; Jonathan M. Powell and Clayton L. Thyne, "Global Instances of Coups from 1950 to 2010: A New Dataset," *Journal of Peace Research*, 48 (2) (2011): 249–259.

private military organization from a societal base to challenge the central government and its military.

The coup–civil war trap is rooted in the Hobbesian problem of how to share power in the absence of an absolute authority that can enforce its distribution.[16] In such an environment, the threat of violence is necessary to guarantee one's share of power.[17] The crux of the problem, however, is that force can be used for both defensive and offensive purposes[18]—to uphold powersharing or to destroy it by appropriating others' share of power. With rivals unable to credibly commit not to use force to lock in a larger share of power, each side must anticipate such a possibility, which can lead to the type of security dilemma and violent fallout seen between Salva Kiir and Riek Machar.

In the pages that follow, I demonstrate that this strategic dynamic helps to account for patterns of political instability, ethnopolitical exclusion, and large-scale political violence in postcolonial Africa as well as other weak, ethnically divided states, such as Syria and Iraq. In doing so, I offer a coherent explanation of one of the fundamental puzzles of civil war onset: what constrains rulers from making the concessions necessary to prevent the outbreak of large-scale political violence.[19] With their rivals unable to credibly commit not to exploit privileged access to the central government to usurp power in a coup, rulers, desperate to protect their sovereign rule, often reject powersharing and take their chance on a vague, distant, and long-term threat of a rebellion versus the clear and present danger of the coup d'état today. Heretofore, the politics of civil war, by which bargaining over power ends in instability and large-scale political violence, has surprisingly represented one of the key gaps in extant scholarship.

---

[16] Thomas Hobbes, *Leviathan* (Harmondsworth: Penguin, 1986). This Hobbesian problem has been at the center of a number of seminal works in political science, especially in international relations. Robert Jervis, "Cooperation under the Security Dilemma," *World Politics*, 30 (2) (1978): 167–214. James D. Fearon, "Rationalist Explanations for War," *International Organization*, 49 (3) (1995): 379–414. Robert Powell, "War as a Commitment Problem," *International Organization*, 60 (1) (2006): 169–203.

[17] Milan W. Svolik, *The Politics of Authoritarian Rule* (Cambridge: Cambridge University Press, 2012).

[18] Jervis, "Cooperation under the Security Dilemma."

[19] James D. Fearon, "Governance and Civil War Onset," Background Paper for *World Development Report 2011* (2010), Washington, DC: World Bank.

I.2 CIVIL WAR IN WEAK STATES: EXISTING APPROACHES, UNANSWERED QUESTIONS

Large-scale armed conflict between the central government and a locally supported rebel force, like the civil war that erupted in South Sudan at the end of 2013, has been at the heart of Africa's postcolonial development crisis. Since 1956, when Sudan became the first sub-Saharan African country to gain its independence, more than one-third of the world's civil wars have been in Africa, directly affecting one out of every two countries in the region, with many experiencing multiple civil wars.[20] The average civil war in Africa has lasted more than eight years, killing thousands,[21] displacing tens of thousands, reducing economic growth, stifling democracy, and spreading conflict into neighboring countries.[22] These conditions often trap countries in a cycle of violence that is difficult to break.[23] (See Map 1.2.)

Over the past ten to fifteen years, a large and impressive body of social-science scholarship has wrestled with understanding the phenomenon of large-scale political violence across Africa and other developing countries. This research program initially had a strong focus on the economic factors that drive citizens to join together, take up weapons, and challenge the state's monopoly of violence. Collier and Hoeffler, neatly synthesizing existing scholarship, framed the debate as between *greed* (citizens rebel when the opportunity costs to rebellion are low and they expect it to be lucrative) or *grievance* (citizens rebel in response to perceived injustices and discrimination by the regime).[24] However, in subsequent research by

---

[20] The civil war data is from Jim Fearon and David Laitin's updated civil war dataset.

[21] According to the Battle Deaths Dataset from the International Peace Research Institute in Oslo, there have been about 1,750,000 battlefield deaths due to civil wars in Africa between 1956 and 2005. Bethany Lacina and Nils Petter Gleditsch, "Monitoring Trends in Global Combat: A New Dataset of Battle Deaths," *European Journal of Population/ Revue Européenne de Démographie*, 21 (2) (2005): 145–166. This does not include war-related deaths due to disease, malnutrition, and other indirect causes, which would increase the figure into the tens of millions.

[22] Christopher Clapham, *Africa and the International System: The Politics of State Survival* (Cambridge: Cambridge University Press, 1996). Idean Salehyan, *Rebels without Borders: Transnational Insurgencies in World Politics* (Ithaca, NY: Cornell University Press, 2009).

[23] Paul Collier, V. L. Elliott, Håvard Hegre, Anke Hoeffler, Marta Reynal-Querol, and Nicholas Sambanis, *Breaking the Conflict Trap: Civil War and Development Policy* (Washington, DC: World Bank 2003).

[24] Paul Collier and Anke Hoeffler, "Greed and Grievance in Civil War," *Oxford Economic Papers*, 56 (4) (2004): 563–595. They particularly draw on the work of Herschell I. Grossman, "A General Equilibrium Model of Insurrections," *The American Economic Review*, 81 (4) (1991): 912–921. Jack Hirshleifer, "Theorizing about Conflict," in Keith

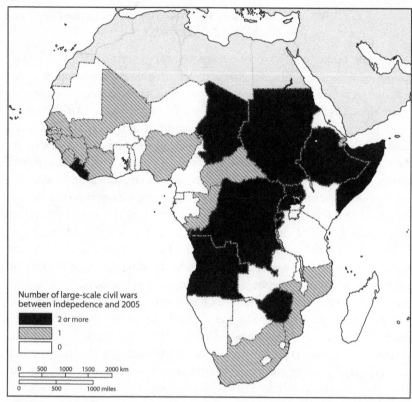

MAP I.2 Civil Wars by Country in Sub-Saharan Africa, Independence to 2005

Fearon and Laitin[25] and in Collier and Hoeffler's reappraisal of their own work,[26] the focus shifted away from the economic to the political. For one, both grievances and opportunities for rebellion are largely determined by the state's ability and willingness to protect and provide for its citizens. Moreover, the ability of citizens to form a rebel organization that can effectively challenge the state hinges on the capacity of the central government to police and control its territory.[27] This theoretical reinterpretation led to the *weak state paradigm of civil war.*

Hartley and Sandler Todd, eds., *Handbook of Defense Economics* (Amsterdam: Elsevier, 1995), pp. 165–189.

[25] Fearon and Laitin, "Ethnicity, Insurgency, and Civil War."

[26] Paul Collier, Anke Hoeffler, and Dominic Rohner, "Beyond Greed and Grievance: Feasibility and Civil War," *Oxford Economic Papers*, 61 (1) (2009): 1–27.

[27] Fearon and Laitin, "Ethnicity, Insurgency, and Civil War." Collier et al., "Beyond Greed and Grievance." For a good summary, see Fearon, "Governance and Civil War Onset."

The weak state paradigm places state capacity at the center of the analysis of civil war. Fearon and Laitin, in their seminal article, posit that the steady rise in civil war in the post-World War II period can be attributed to the wave of decolonization that occurred in the three decades between 1945 and 1975, which "gave birth to a large number of financially, bureaucratically, and militarily weak states."[28] The weak state–civil war nexus has proven particularly vicious because civil war further weakens state capacity, leading to a self-sustaining cycle of conflict.[29] Even more, internal conflicts rarely abide by international territorial boundaries and regularly spill over into weak neighboring states, contributing to conflict contagion.[30]

The weak state theory of civil war is a useful framework for understanding the global variation of large-scale political violence since the end of World War II, such as why the DRC has experienced multiple civil wars and peace has prevailed, in, say, Belgium, despite the instability of its polity. It also helps to inform the case of Sudan, which is central to this book. One cannot account for the outbreak of the civil war in Darfur in 2003 or the earlier wars between the government of Sudan and various rebel groups from South Sudan without an understanding of the weakness of the Sudanese state and its inability to penetrate and control the periphery (as well as the external sanctuary and support provided to Sudanese rebels by neighboring states, such as Ethiopia, Uganda, Eritrea, and Chad).

One of the key limitations of the weak state paradigm, however, is that in assuming that "where rebellion is materially feasible it will occur,"[31] it tends to rely too heavily on a deterministic logic to account for a highly dynamic and variable phenomenon.[32] For example, while the lack of a monopoly on legitimate violence and the state's feeble bureaucratic and

---

[28] Fearon and Laitin, "Ethnicity, Insurgency, and Civil War," p. 88.

[29] Collier et al., *Breaking the Conflict Trap*.

[30] Idean Salehyan, and Kristian Skrede Gleditsch, "Refugees and the Spread of Civil War," *International Organization*, 60 (April 2006): 335–366. Kristian Skrede Gleditsch, "Transnational Dimensions of Civil War," *Journal of Peace Research*, 44 (3) (2007): 293–309. Salehyan, *Rebels without Borders*.

[31] Collier et al., "Beyond Greed and Grievance."

[32] Stathis N. Kalyvas, *The Logic of Violence in Civil War* (Cambridge: Cambridge University Press, 2006). Jeremy M. Weinstein, *Inside Rebellion: The Politics of Insurgent Violence* (Cambridge: Cambridge University Press, 2007). Sidney Tarrow, "Inside Insurgencies: Politics and Violence in an Age of Civil War," *Perspectives on Politics*, 5 (3) (2007): 587–600.

administrative capacity renders weak states significantly more vulnerable to outbreaks of civil war than their more developed counterparts,[33] war in weak states is not inevitable nor a permanent condition. As mentioned above, despite all African countries beset by similar underlying structural conditions, only half have experienced civil war. The rest have remained peaceful throughout the post-independence period.

The weak state paradigm also poorly accounts for temporal variation within countries. The susceptibility of African states to civil war has differed across time as well as space. For example, in Sudan's Darfur, the government of Omar al-Bashir was able to effectively defeat an armed rebellion in the region in the early 1990s, but a decade later, facing a second rebellion, it failed to contain the insurgency, leading to a devastating civil war.

The primacy of the weak state paradigm has prompted the microcomparative turn in the civil war research program,[34] in which scholars have sought to shed light on the dynamic processes that explain *how* underlying structural conditions breed explosive large-scale political violence.[35] This scholarship has gone a long way toward filling the gap in our understanding of the microlevel processes that drive conflict escalation, especially the phenomenon of rebel formation.[36] But while microcomparative scholarship is better equipped to account for the specific dynamics that drive civil war, such as rebel recruitment, territorial control, and counterinsurgency, in many ways it tends to lose sight of the forest for the trees and suffers the same lacuna as the weak state theory of civil war. None offers a complete and coherent explanation of civil war onset—that is, how bargaining over state power ends in large-scale political violence and why, if the central government lacks the capabilities to effectively

---

[33] Max Weber, *Economy and Society*, 3 vols. (New York: Bedminster Press, 1968). Fearon and Laitin, "Ethnicity, Insurgency, and Civil War." Cullen S. Hendrix, "Measuring State Capacity: Theoretical and Empirical Implications for the Study of Civil Conflict," *Journal of Peace Research*, 47 (3) (2010): 273–285.

[34] For an excellent overview of the major lacunae in cross-national civil war research, see Tarrow, "Inside Insurgencies." See also Stathis N. Kalyvas, "Promises and Pitfalls of an Emerging Research Program: The Microdynamics of Civil War," in Ian Shapiro, Stathis N. Kalyvas, and Tarek Masoud, eds., *Order, Conflict, and Violence* (Cambridge: Cambridge University Press, 2008); and Christopher Blattman and Edward Miguel, "Civil War," *Journal of Economic Literature*, 48 (1) (2010): 3–57.

[35] Kalyvas, *The Logic of Violence in Civil War*. A number of important microcomparative studies preceded Kalyvas, including Elisabeth Jean Wood, *Insurgent Collective Action and Civil War in El Salvador* (Cambridge: Cambridge University Press, 2003).

[36] See, for example, Weinstein, *Inside Rebellion*. Macartan Humphreys and Jeremy M. Weinstein, "Who Fights? The Determinants of Participation in Civil War," *American Journal of Political Science*, 52 (2) (2008): 436–455.

defeat potential rebels, it does not strike a bargain with them to avoid a costly conflict.[37]

This book aims to fill this major gap in the civil war research program and offer a novel political theory of civil war onset. In doing so, it stresses the importance of a meso-level approach to the study of civil war that takes seriously the informal institutions on which political authority rests in weak states. It thus fits squarely in the informal institutional turn in comparative politics.[38]

1.3 THE INSTITUTIONAL BASIS OF PEACE IN WEAK STATES

One of the major gaps in existing civil war research is the failure to model the mediating effect that political institutions have on the risk of large-scale political violence. Several early macro-level studies identified political instability and incoherent political institutions (such as anocracy—or intermediate political regimes that are neither fully democratic or autocratic) as potentially important determinants of civil war. The conceptualization of these variables, however, privileged democratization or autocratization[39]—that is, contestation between the elite and citizens over the rules of the game.[40] In weak states, however, politics revolves not so much over the rules of the game[41] as over the distribution of power and wealth between competing networks of "violence specialists."[42]

---

[37] See Fearon's review of the civil war literature and his earlier theoretical article on the logic of war. Fearon, "Governance and Civil War Onset," p. 41. Fearon, "Rationalist Explanations for War."

[38] Gretchen Helmke, and Steven Levitsky, "Informal Institutions and Comparative Politics: A Research Agenda," *Perspectives on Politics*, 2 (4) (2004), p. 726.

[39] For the original studies linking instability and civil war, see Håvard Hegre, Tanja Ellingsen, Scott Gates, and Nils Petter Gleditsch, "Toward a Democratic Civil Peace? Democracy, Political Change, and Civil War, 1816–1992," *American Political Science Review*, 95 (1) (2001): 33–48. Fearon and Laitin, "Ethnicity, Insurgency, and Civil War." Håvard Hegre and Nicholas Sambanis, "Sensitivity Analysis of Empirical Results on Civil War Onset," *Journal of Conflict Resolution*, 50 (4) (2006): 508–535. For one of the few recent articles that revisit the instability thesis, Kristian Skrede Gleditsch and Andrea Ruggeri, "Political Opportunity Structures, Democracy, and Civil War," *Journal of Peace Research*, 47 (3) (2010): 299–310. Vreeland notes the measurement problems that also plague this literature. James Raymond Vreeland, "The Effect of Political Regime on Civil War: Unpacking Anocracy," *Journal of Conflict Resolution*, 52 (3) (2008): 401–425.

[40] Daron Acemoglu and James A. Robinson, *Economic Origins of Dictatorship and Democracy* (Cambridge: Cambridge University Press, 2006).

[41] This, of course, has changed quite significantly since the end of the Cold War. Analyzing the relationship between democratization and the coup–civil war trap represents an important avenue for future research.

[42] Throughout this book I rely quite heavily on North, Wallis and Weingast's concept of "natural states" as it encapsulates the essence of politics in postcolonial Africa quite well.

Thus, the key ordering institution in weak states is what North et al. refer to as the "dominant coalition" and, before them, the eminent Africanists Bayart, Rothchild, and Reno conceived of as "elite accommodation," "hegemonial exchange," and the "shadow state," respectively.[43] This political institution rests on a series of informal bargains that violence specialists make, in which they agree to refrain from violence and work together to share exclusive access to the central government and the rents that come from controlling the state. "The creation of rents through limiting access provides the glue that holds the coalition together" as it encourages elites to cooperate to prevent others from usurping state power and discourages infighting that ultimately reduces the rents they can extract from state power.[44]

How does elite cooperation, however, translate into societal peace, especially given that most of society is excluded from the rents generated by the state? The key to societal peace (or the central government's ability to effectively prevent or contain armed uprisings from those outside the dominant coalition) hinges on the fact that regime "elites sit at the top of, but are also embedded in, patron-client networks that extend down into the rest of society."[45] As violence specialists are only as powerful as supporters they can mobilize,[46] it is in their interests to keep these networks intact by providing patronage and security to members as well as reinforcing their shared social ties, through cultural practices[47] or

They conceive of natural states as limited access orders in which the government is not representative of the governed but controlled by a small number of violence specialists (the "dominant coalition") who convert political power into economic power, which "limits violence and makes sustained social interaction possible on a larger scale." North et al., *Violence and Social Orders*, p. 13. Violence specialists is the term that North et al. use (and, before them, Bates et al.) to describe the dominant political players in weak or stateless societies, in which powerful individuals, not the state, control violence. Robert Bates, Avner Greif, and Smita Singh, "Organizing Violence," *Journal of Conflict Resolution*, 46 (5) (2002): 599–628.

43 North et al., *Violence and Social Orders*. Jean-François Bayart, *The State in Africa: The Politics of the Belly* (New York: Longman, 1993). Donald Rothchild, "Hegemonial Exchange: An Alternative Model for Managing Conflict in Middle Africa," in Dennis L. Thomson, and Dov Ronen, eds., *Ethnicity, Politics and Development* (Boulder, Col.: Lynne Rienner, 1986), pp. 65–104. William Reno, *Warlord Politics and African States* (Boulder, Col.: Lynne Rienner, 1998).

44 North et al., *Violence and Social Orders*.

45 North et al., *Violence and Social Orders*.

46 Naomi Chazan, Peter Lewis, Robert A. Mortimer, Donald Rothchild, and Stephen John Stedman, *Politics and Society in Contemporary Africa*, 3rd edn (Boulder, Col.: Lynne Rienner, 1999), p. 113. See also North et al., *Violence and Social Orders*.

47 Abner Cohen, *Two-Dimensional Man: An Essay on the Anthropology of Power and Symbolism in Complex Society* (Berkeley, Calif.: University of California Press, 1974).

even the use of violence and fear.[48] These patron-client networks, in turn, act as the mechanisms by which the central government monitors society, mobilizes local support, and effectively represses or accommodates potential dissidents.[49] In the case of the emergence of an armed rebellion, these extensive brokerage networks are critical for the regime's ability to produce what I refer to as *cooperative counterinsurgency*, in which the central government and local communities overcome geographic distance, information asymmetries, and mistrust to cooperate in isolating and defeating the insurgents and avoiding costly large-scale political violence that may challenge the power structure.

In postcolonial Africa, these patron-client networks have often been organized along ethnic lines,[50] or based on shared descent-based social identities.[51] A legacy of the slave trade,[52] colonialism's use of tribalism to organize and control the indigenous majority,[53] and ethnicity's sociological attributes of dense, durable social connections and strong norms of reciprocity,[54] ethnicity has tended to crowd out other potential institutional sources of collective mobilization, such as class, party, nation or

Paul Brass, *Ethnicity and Nationalism: Theory and Comparison* (Newbury Park, Calif.: Sage Publications, 1991).

[48] James D. Fearon, and David D. Laitin, "Violence and the Social Construction of Ethnic Identities," *International Organization*, 54 (4) (2000): 845–877. Gerard Padró i Miquel, "The Control of Politicians in Divided Societies: The Politics of Fear," *The Review of Economic Studies*, 74 (4 (2007): 1259–1274.

[49] Richard Snyder, "Paths Out of Sultanistic Regimes: Combining Structural and Voluntarist Perspectives," in H. E. Chehabi and Juan J. Linz, eds., *Sultanistic Regimes* (Baltimore, Md.: Johns Hopkins University, 1998), pp. 49–81. Kalyvas, *The Logic of Violence in Civil War*. Jason Lyall, "Are Coethnics More Effective Counterinsurgents? Evidence from the Second Chechen War," *American Political Science Review*, 104 (1) (2010): 1–20.

[50] Robert H. Bates, "Modernization, Ethnic Competition, and the Rationality of Politics in Contemporary Africa," in Donald Rothchild and Victor A. Olorunsola, eds., *State versus Ethnic Claims: African Policy Dilemmas* (Boulder, Col.: Westview Press, 1983), pp. 152–171. Bayart, *The State in Africa*. Daniel N. Posner, *Institutions and Ethnic Politics in Africa* (Cambridge: Cambridge University Press, 2005).

[51] James D. Fearon, "Ethnic and Cultural Diversity by Country," *Journal of Economic Growth*, 8 (2) (2003): 195–222.

[52] Nathan Nunn, "The Long-Term Effects of Africa's Slave Trades," *Quarterly Journal of Economics*, 123 (1) (2008): 139–176.

[53] Mahmood Mamdani, *Citizen and Subject: Contemporary Africa and the Legacy of Late Colonialism* (Princeton, NJ: Princeton University Press, 1996). Posner, *Institutions and Ethnic Politics in Africa*.

[54] James D. Fearon and David D. Laitin, "Explaining Interethnic Cooperation," *American Political Science Review*, 90 (4) (1996): 715–735. See James Habyarimana, Macartan Humphreys, Daniel N. Posner, and Jeremy M. Weinstein, *Coethnicity: Diversity and the Dilemmas of Collective Action* (New York: Russell Sage Foundation, 2009), especially pp. 6–13. North et al., *Violence and Social Orders*.

ideology.[55] The consequence has been that, in Azam's pithy phrase, the postcolonial African state became "a means by which to federate the different ethnic groups via a coalition of their elites."[56]

Overall, then, this institutional framework suggests that one of the most important sources of peace in Africa's weak states is *ethnic powersharing*, in which ruling Big Men strike alliances with those embedded in rival ethnic groups. In fact, though largely overlooked by the civil war literature, this has been a core claim put forth by a number of Africanist scholars for some time, especially the body of work of Donald Rothchild.[57] Writing with Michael Foley in the late 1980s, Rothchild posited that "under soft state conditions" (i.e. given the weakness of formal state structures and institutions), "African ruling elites have in fact responded rather similarly to the overriding need to include ethnoregional intermediaries in the ruling coalition" by building ethnically inclusive political regimes "that made inter-ethnic conflict more manageable."[58] A large qualitative scholarship has demonstrated the deadly consequences of the breakdown of ethnic powersharing.[59]

[55] In conceiving of the role that ethnicity plays in African politics, I adopt a constructivist interpretation of ethnicity. See further discussion of this point and a review of existing scholarship on this subject in Section 2.5.2.

[56] Jean-Paul Azam, "The Redistributive State and Conflicts in Africa," *Journal of Peace Research*, 38 (4 (2001), p. 438.

[57] Donald Rothchild, "State-Ethnic Relations in Middle Africa," in Gwendolen Margaret Carter and Patrick O'Meara, eds., *African Independence: The First Twenty-Five Years* (Bloomington, Ind.: Indiana University Press 1985), pp. 71–96. Rothchild, "Hegemonial Exchange"; Donald Rothchild and Michael W. Foley, "African States and the Politics of Inclusive Coalitions," in Donald Rothchild and Naomi Chazan, eds., *The Precarious Balance: State and Society in Africa* (Boulder, Col.: Westview Press, 1988), pp. 149–171. Donald Rothchild, "Ethnic Bargaining and State Breakdown in Africa," *Nationalism and Ethnic Politics*, 1 (1) (1995): 54–72; Donald Rothchild, *Managing Ethnic Conflict in Africa: Pressures and Incentives for Cooperation* (Washington, DC: Brookings Institution Press, 1997). See also Azam, "The Redistributive State."

[58] Rothchild and Foley, "African States."

[59] See René Lemarchand, *Burundi: Ethnic Conflict and Genocide* (Cambridge: Cambridge University Press, 1996). Gérard Prunier, *The Rwanda Crisis: History of a Genocide* (New York: Columbia University Press, 1995). Francis Deng, *War of Visions: Conflict of Identities in the Sudan* (Washington, DC: Brookings Institution, 1995). J. Millard Burr and Robert O. Collins, *Africa's Thirty Years War: Libya, Chad, and the Sudan, 1963–1993* (Boulder, Col.: Westview Press, 1999). Samuel Decalo, "Regionalism, Political Decay, and Civil Strife in Chad," *Journal of Modern African Studies*, 18 (1) (1980): 23–56. Samuel Decalo, "Chad: The Roots of Centre-Periphery Strife," *African Affairs*, 79 (317) (1980): 491–509. Stephen Ellis, *The Mask of Anarchy: The Destruction of Liberia and the Religious Dimension of an African Civil War* (New York: New York University Press, 1999). A. B. K. Kasozi, Nakanyike Musisi, and James Mukooza Sejjengo, *The Social Origins of Violence in Uganda, 1964–1985* (Montreal: McGill-Queen's University Press, 1994). Julie Flint and Alexander de Waal, *Darfur: A New History of a Long War*

Recently, the ethnic powersharing hypothesis has been systematically tested in the groundbreaking work of Andreas Wimmer, Lars-Erik Cederman, and their collaborators. A major innovation made by Wimmer and Cederman was mobilizing a team of experts to create the EPR dataset that measures the distribution of state power across politically relevant ethnic groups since the end of World War II. They find that, controlling for underlying structural conditions, ethnic powersharing—or the inclusion of members of politically relevant ethnic groups in the central government—significantly reduces the risk of armed conflict.[60] In contrast to earlier research that tended to dismiss the importance of political grievances as a cause of armed rebellion, Wimmer and Cederman, building on the earlier work of Frances Stewart,[61] have argued precisely the opposite: "groups that lack representation and are marginalized in the distribution of state resources, government jobs, and public goods" have stronger motives to take up arms and violently challenge the central government.[62]

The research of Wimmer, Cederman, and others has importantly and significantly reshaped the study of civil war. One of their most important contributions is to bring politics, or the "struggles over state power,"[63] back into the study of civil war onset. A second important contribution is to demonstrate exactly how politics matters: rulers can prevent the outbreak of armed conflict by sharing state power with ethnic rivals.

There are several important gaps left by the work of Wimmer and Cederman, however. First, they almost exclusively focus on the grievance mechanism as the key source of armed rebellion.[64] Underappreciated is

(New York: Zed Books 2008). Gérard Prunier, *Darfur: The Ambiguous Genocide* (Ithaca, NY: Cornell University Press, 2005). Gérard Prunier, *From Genocide to Continental War: The "Congolese" Conflict and the Crisis of Contemporary Africa* (London: Hurst & Co., 2009). Filip Reyntjens, *The Great African War: Congo and Regional Geopolitics, 1996–2006* (Cambridge: Cambridge University Press, 2009). Christopher S. Clapham, ed., *African Guerrillas* (Bloomington, Ind.: Indiana University Press, 1998).

60 Andreas Wimmer, Lars-Erik Cederman, and Brian Min, "Ethnic Politics and Armed Conflict: A Configurational Analysis of a New Global Dataset," *American Sociological Review*, 74 (1) (2009): 316–337. Lars-Erik Cederman, Andreas Wimmer, and Brian Min, "Why Do Ethnic Groups Rebel? New Data and Analysis," *World Politics*, 62 (1) (2010): 87–119.

61 Stewart, *Horizontal Inequalities and Conflict.*

62 Cederman et al., "Why Do Ethnic Groups Rebel?," p. 106.

63 Wimmer et al., "Ethnic Politics and Armed Conflict," p. 334.

64 See also Lars-Erik Cederman, Nils B. Weidmann, and Kristian Skrede Gleditsch, "Horizontal Inequalities and Ethnonationalist Civil War: A Global Comparison," *American Political Science Review*, 105 (3) (2011): 478–495. And Cederman et al., *Inequality, Grievances, and Civil War.*

how ethnopolitical exclusion also creates opportunities for armed rebellion by emasculating the regime's political networks and significantly weakening its societal control. This book fills the gap by demonstrating how a regime's ethnopolitical network shapes its ability to elicit local support and effectively stamp out armed rebellion via cooperative counterinsurgency. Second, they fail to offer a coherent explanation of the logic of ethnopolitical exclusion—why would a given ruler exclude a politically relevant ethnic group at the cost of risking civil war? As several review articles have noted, this represents a broader weakness of the existing civil war literature.[65] Very few studies have offered a complete theory of civil war onset that accounts for costly bargaining failure.[66] This book also aims to fill this gap in the literature, explaining the strategic causes of war and peace in postcolonial Africa.

1.4 CENTRAL ARGUMENT: ETHNIC POWERSHARING, STRATEGIC UNCERTAINTY, AND THE COUP–CIVIL WAR TRAP IN AFRICA

In Africa's weak states, striking alliances with Big Men embedded in rival ethnic groups is critical for the ruler's ability to mobilize support and collect information outside of his own ethnic group, which in turn enables him to secure societal peace and thwart opportunities for armed rebellion.[67] In many ways, postcolonial rulers are adopting the same

---

[65] Fearon, "Governance and Civil War Onset." Blattman and Miguel, "Civil War."

[66] One notable exception is Barbara Walter's study of territorial conflicts, in which self-determination movements demand greater territorial autonomy or independence from the state. In such conflicts, the bargain that would prevent escalation to civil war is the government acceding to the self-determination movement's demands for territorial control. Walter posits that a leader's willingness to bargain is a function of the number of potential future challengers the regime may face. Leaders facing a higher number of potential challengers are more likely to reject bargaining with a given group, even at the cost of civil war, in a bid to build a reputation for resolve and deter other groups from demanding self-determination. Barbara F. Walter, *Reputation and Civil War: Why Separatist Conflicts Are So Violent* (Cambridge: Cambridge University Press, 2009). Walter fills an important gap in the civil war literature, offering a coherent theory of bargaining failure that leads to separatist conflicts. But of course many conflicts do not revolve around territorial control. This is one of the striking features of civil war in sub-Saharan Africa, the focus of this book. Despite the weakness and the artificiality of the state, which one might assume not only makes separation easier but in greater demand, secessionist conflicts have been rare relative to other regions of the world. Instead, conflict in postcolonial Africa has resolved around competition for state power. Pierre Englebert and Rebecca Hummel, "Let's Stick Together: Understanding Africa's Secessionist Deficit," *African Affairs*, 104 (416) (2005): 399–427.

[67] The book's central argument builds on Philip Roessler, "The Enemy Within: Personal Rule, Coups, and Civil War in Africa," *World Politics*, 63 (2) (2011): 300–346.

institutional machinery their colonial predecessors used to overcome the cultural and geographic barriers to extend control over a diverse and dispersed society.[68] Yet, with the end of colonialism and the withdrawal of the metropole's hegemonic control, the political game was fundamentally different. Independence led to the opening of the political center and increased groups' demands for self-rule "to avoid trading an old colonialism for a new one."[69] Ethnic elites rejected indirect rule as an insufficient form of political representation and demanded privileged access to the highest levels of the central government to effectively guarantee their security and a fair share of state spoils. Consequently, the postcolonial multiethnic state diverged fundamentally from its "Apartheid" predecessor.[70]

Independence, however, not only increased the price of ethnic accommodation, in which ethnic rivals demanded a share of real power, it also increased the risks. By accommodating ethnic strongmen into the central government, rulers lowered the costs their rivals faced to seizing power in a coup d'état—in which a small group of actors could displace, or even kill, the ruler through a surprise attack from *within* the regime and effect a sudden and permanent shift in the distribution of power.[71] The regional organization of African states, the Organization of African Unity (OAU), unwittingly increased incentives for coups and other irregular seizures of power through its de-facto "capital city rule," which, in effect, recognized as the legitimate sovereign any group that controlled the capital city, no matter how they came to power and how much control they had outside the capital.[72] Given the incredible rents and resources that come from being recognized as the legitimate "gatekeeper" of a state relative to being a mere power-holder,[73] the capital city rule increased the stakes for

[68] Crawford Young, "The African Colonial State and its Political Legacy," in Donald Rothchild and Naomi Chazan, eds., *The Precarious Balance: State and Society in Africa* (Boulder, Col.: Westview Press, 1988). Bruce Berman, "Ethnicity, Patronage and the African State: The Politics of Uncivil Nationalism," *African Affairs*, 97 (388) (1998): 305–341.

[69] Donald L. Horowitz, *Ethnic Groups in Conflict* (Berkeley, Calif.: University of California Press, 1985), pp. 188–189.

[70] Mamdani, *Citizen and Subject*. For systematic evidence on the postcolonial government as an ethnic federation, see Patrick François, Ilia Rainer, and Francesco Trebbi, "How Is Power Shared in Africa?," *Econometrica*, 83 (2) (2015): 465–503. Leonardo R. Arriola and Martha C. Johnson, "Ethnic Politics and Women's Empowerment in Africa: Ministerial Appointments to Executive Cabinets," *American Journal of Political Science*, 58 (2) (2013): 495–510.

[71] Luttwak, *Coup d'État*.

[72] Jeffrey Herbst, *States and Power in Africa: Comparative Lessons in Authority and Control* (Princeton, NJ: Princeton University Press, 2000), p. 110.

[73] Frederick Cooper, *Africa since 1940: The Past of the Present* (Cambridge: Cambridge University Press, 2002).

capturing and maintaining sovereign power—that is, gaining domestic and international recognition as the legal ruler of the central government. According to McGowan, between 1956 and 2001 there were 188 total coup attempts in sub-Saharan African countries, of which eighty successfully led to a new internationally recognized head of state.[74]

The strategic consequence of the emergence of the coup d'état and its international acceptance was to confront rulers with a commitment problem,[75] in which they could not be sure that their rivals were supporting them only to better position themselves to take power in the future.[76] This commitment problem is a key source of bargaining failure and conflict in weak states, namely because it prevents rulers from fully committing to peaceful powersharing. Reluctant to strengthen their rivals, rulers undersupply how much power they share. Fundamentally mistrustful, they pursue defensive safeguards, such as stacking the military and security organs with coethnics and other loyalists, in a bid to neutralize their rivals' coup-making capabilities.[77] But rather than stabilizing their regimes, such policies increase the insecurity and mistrust of rivals and undermine confidence in the ruler's commitment to share "real" power. This increases the motivation for rivals to seize sovereign power for themselves.

In this highly uncertain environment, ethnopolitical exclusion—the systematic political elimination of rival ethnic Big Men and their followers from the central government—thus becomes a way for the ruler to credibly eliminate this coup threat from the targeted group and increase the costs rivals face to capture state power. Excluded from the regime, rivals can no longer draw on the infrastructure, salaries, matériel, and manpower provided by the state in their bid to forcibly seize power and instead have to build their own army that is capable of overthrowing the whole coercive apparatus, not just part of it. The downside of such a strategy, however, is that, given its weak mechanisms of control over rival ethnic groups, the ruling group often lacks the capacity to effectively counter the rebellion, except through the use of indiscriminate violence, which can provoke large-scale political violence.

Overall, this argument fundamentally challenges how we conceive of civil war. The outbreak of large-scale political violence is not an inevitable

---

[74] McGowan, "African Military Coups d'État."

[75] Fearon, "Rationalist Explanations for War." Powell, "War as a Commitment Problem."

[76] On the effects of this strategic uncertainty on the policy-making of African rulers, see Robert H. Jackson and Carl G. Rosberg, *Personal Rule in Black Africa* (Berkeley, Calif.: University of California Press, 1982).

[77] Herbert M. Howe, *Ambiguous Order: Military Forces in African States* (Boulder, Col.: Lynne Rienner, 2001).

byproduct of structural weakness but a strategic choice that rulers make in a highly uncertain environment. Civil wars are the manifestation of the political strategies rulers choose to coup-proof their regimes from rival networks of violence specialists and consolidate their hold on sovereign power. Heretofore, the civil war literature has failed to account for the precise mechanisms linking coups and civil wars other than to posit that both are common in weak, low-income states.[78]

* * *

The corollary of this argument, however, is that, as civil wars become as strategically costly as coups (in the sense that ethnic rivals represent a clear and present threat to the ruler's hold on power whether they are *included* or *excluded* from state power), then the strategic choice becomes less clear-cut: both inclusion and exclusion pose significant risks. This points to an endogenous solution to the problem of powersharing. As a given rival's civil war capabilities or *threat capabilities*—that is, its mobilizational potential to credibly threaten to reclaim state power if it was to be excluded from the central government—increase, the strategic benefits of exclusion decrease. For example, though ethnic dominance enables the ruling group to monopolize power and rents that come from controlling the state, if pursuing such benefits provokes a costly civil war that necessitates an expensive counterinsurgency campaign, especially one with no guarantee of halting a rival's bid to capture state power, then the benefits of exclusion dissipate and may no longer outweigh the costs.

We would expect, however, the ruler's commitment to powersharing to be a function not only of the opposition's threat capabilities but also of his own group's societal power. Unless the opposition faces the same constraints as the ruling group, such that it too would face a strategically costly civil war if it tried to monopolize power in a coup, there is little preventing it from exploiting access to the central government to appropriate the ruling group's share of power. Thus, for powersharing to be self-enforcing, such that neither group has incentives to exclude the other, the costs of reneging on powersharing must constrain not just the incumbent but constrain *in expectation* any actor who may seize power in the future. Only when both sides see little strategic benefit to choosing exclusion will neither group try to permanently exclude the other and will strong rivals reluctantly accept powersharing.

---

[78] Collier, *The Bottom Billion.*

In contrast, when the ruling group and the rival group have asymmetrical threat capabilities, powersharing is less stable. Weak groups know that if they are excluded from government the chances of them reclaiming power are low, so they have strong incentives to prevent their exclusion by excluding others from power, especially if those other groups also have weak threat capabilities. For strong groups bargaining with weak groups, the benefits of exclusion are quite high as it effectively nullifies the strategic threat from the rival group and locks in control of all the rents from holding office. Thus, in increasing the incentives of ethnic exclusion, low or uneven force capabilities increase strategic uncertainty and undermine stable powersharing.

It is important to note that the presence of mutually strong civil war capabilities does not *resolve* (initially at least) the commitment problem at the heart of the coup–civil war trap. Without agreed-upon rules or institutions regulating the distribution and transfer of sovereign power, elites embedded in each group are still vying to control the executive (and gain the international recognition and rents that come with it) and anticipate their rivals have the same intentions. This can lead to political instability and can actually increase coup risk. Under such conditions, however, rival groups may prefer to share power and reluctantly trade executive authority via coups, that do not significantly alter the relative distribution of power, than accept the high mutual costs associated with a war for exclusive control of the state. This helps account for why we actually see evidence of a coup–civil war trap in postcolonial Africa rather than just the civil war trap: in some countries, rulers commit to ethnic powersharing in spite of the increased coup risk.

1.5 THEORETICAL EXPECTATIONS

Following from the central argument, this book derives and tests five broad claims:

1. **Political networks hypothesis:** Ethnic powersharing is a key source of societal peace in postcolonial Africa as it not only addresses groups' demands for access to scarce state resources but also expands the regime's political network, increasing its societal penetration and reducing opportunities for armed rebellion.

2. **Coup–civil war trap:** Ethnic powersharing, however, confronts rulers with a coup–civil war trade-off. Sharing power strengthens the regime's societal control but at the cost of increasing rivals' coup-making capabilities.

3. **Coup-proofing theory of civil war:** Ethnopolitical exclusion mitigates coup risk but at the cost of increasing the risk of civil war.

4. **Co-conspirator civil wars:** One common type of coup-proofing civil wars is between co-conspirators. Interethnic alliances increase a set of groups' capabilities to capture power but then confront the co-conspirators with a severe commitment problem after victory that often ends with regime factionalization and civil war.

5. **Threat-capabilities theory of powersharing:** When both the ruling group and a given ethnic rival possess strong civil war capabilities, such that each has the mobilizational potential to credibly threaten the central government if it were to be excluded from power, then durable, albeit fluid, powersharing should emerge as the high costs of exclusion compel both sides to share power with the other, even at the cost of greater coup risk.

1.6 RESEARCH DESIGN AND KEY FINDINGS

To build and test these five claims, the book adopts a nested research design that combines intensive case-study analysis based on rigorous and extensive qualitative research[79] with large-N quantitative analysis.[80] Figure 1.1 summarizes the research design and illustrates the movement between small-N and large-N analysis.

1.6.1 Preliminary Small-N Analysis: Darfur as a Theory-Building Case

Rather than beginning with a preliminary large-N analysis, I started with an exploratory small-N analysis of the causes of civil war in Sudan, especially in the Darfur region, based on more than eighteen months of fieldwork in-country and in neighboring countries. The Darfur case study is intended as a "heuristic"[81] or a "hypothesis-generating"[82] case study—in

---

[79] On an elaboration of the qualitative methods used, see Appendix I.

[80] Evan S. Lieberman, "Nested Analysis as a Mixed-Method Strategy for Comparative Research," *American Political Science Review*, 99 (3) (2005): 435–452.

[81] Harry Eckstein, "Case Study and Theory in Political Science," in Nelson W. Polsby and Fred I. Greenstein, eds., *Handbook of Political Science* (Reading, Mass.: Addison-Wesley, 1975), pp. 79–138. On the benefits of heuristic cases, see also Alexander L. George and Andrew Bennett, *Case Studies and Theory Development in the Social Sciences* (Cambridge, Mass.: MIT Press, 2005).

[82] Arend Lijphart, "Comparative Politics and the Comparative Method," *American Political Science Review*, 65 (3) (1971): 682–693.

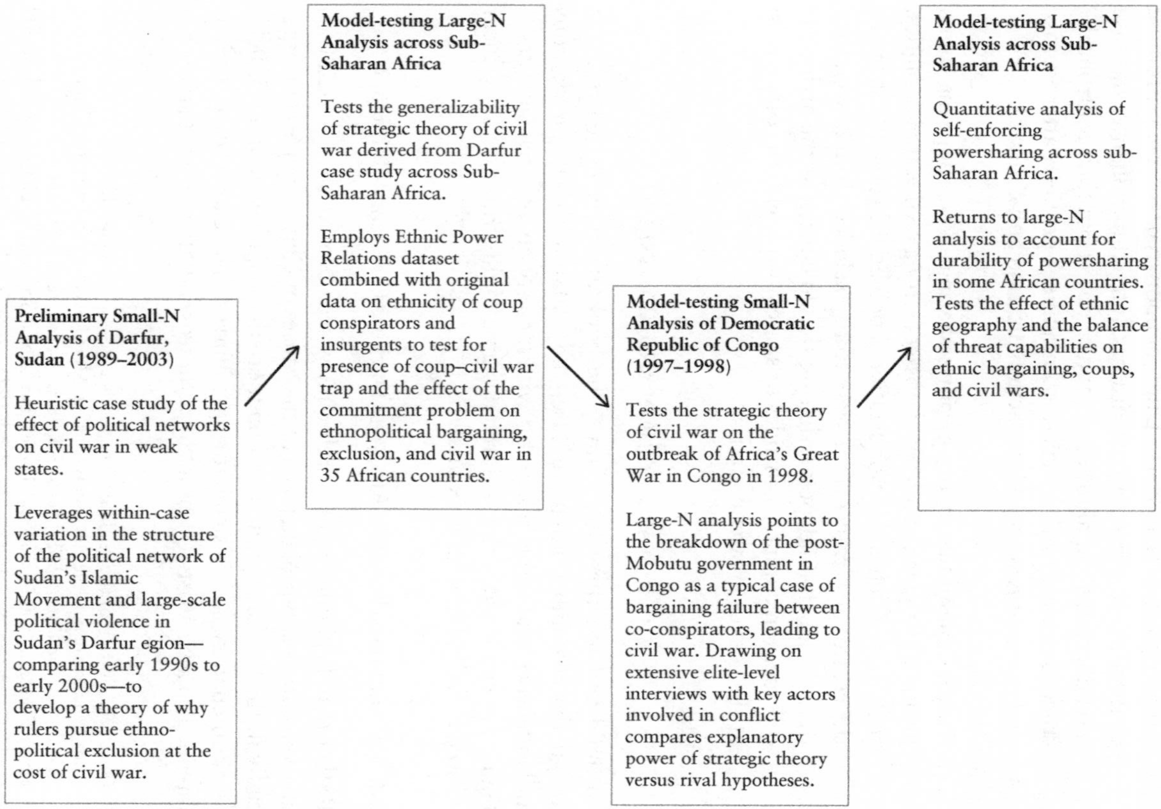

Preliminary Small-N Analysis of Darfur, Sudan (1989–2003)

Heuristic case study of the effect of political networks on civil war in weak states.

Leverages within-case variation in the structure of the political network of Sudan's Islamic Movement and large-scale political violence in Sudan's Darfur region—comparing early 1990s to early 2000s—to develop a theory of why rulers pursue ethno-political exclusion at the cost of civil war.

Model-testing Large-N Analysis across Sub-Saharan Africa

Tests the generalizability of strategic theory of civil war derived from Darfur case study across Sub-Saharan Africa.

Employs Ethnic Power Relations dataset combined with original data on ethnicity of coup conspirators and insurgents to test for presence of coup–civil war trap and the effect of the commitment problem on ethnopolitical bargaining, exclusion, and civil war in 35 African countries.

Model-testing Small-N Analysis of Democratic Republic of Congo (1997–1998)

Tests the strategic theory of civil war on the outbreak of Africa's Great War in Congo in 1998.

Large-N analysis points to the breakdown of the post-Mobutu government in Congo as a typical case of bargaining failure between co-conspirators, leading to civil war. Drawing on extensive elite-level interviews with key actors involved in conflict compares explanatory power of strategic theory versus rival hypotheses.

Model-testing Large-N Analysis across Sub-Saharan Africa

Quantitative analysis of self-enforcing powersharing across sub-Saharan Africa.

Returns to large-N analysis to account for durability of powersharing in some African countries. Tests the effect of ethnic geography and the balance of threat capabilities on ethnic bargaining, coups, and civil wars.

FIGURE 1.1 Nested Research Design

which, through intensive and iterative qualitative research, I sought to better understand the mediating effect political networks have on civil war in weak states. In doing so, I leveraged *within-case* temporal varia-tion[83] in the structure of the government's political networks and the outbreak of large-scale political violence in Darfur—comparing the early 1990s, when Sudan's Islamic Movement had a well-developed political network in Darfur and averted civil war, to the early 2000s when the network was dismantled and civil war erupted. This within-case varia-tion is useful in theory development as it has allowed me to hold constant the structural factors conventionally advanced as the cause of civil war in weak states (e.g., rough terrain, weak state structures, geographically concentrated ethnic groups, war-affected neighboring regions and states, and a large population) and formulate new hypotheses that focus on the dynamic nature of elite bargaining and political networks.

The case study is organized in three parts. Part I addresses why, despite the presence of the aforementioned structural conditions that are hypothesized to facilitate armed rebellion and hinder counterinsur-gency success, the central government in Khartoum was able to effec-tively defeat an armed rebellion in Darfur in the early 1990s. My field research pointed to the importance of the extensive political network of the National Islamic Front (NIF) in Darfur, especially among non-Arab ethnic groups, that helped to produce *cooperative counterinsurgency* in which the government and local communities cooperated to maintain societal peace and prevent an armed rebellion from taking root. Trusted Darfurian brokers within the regime's political network proved integral to helping the government and local communities overcome mistrust and information asymmetries that could have driven the government to resort to indiscriminate violence and local communities to support the rebels in exchange for protection.

Part II seeks to explain why, if the regime's Islamist network in Darfur was so consequential to keeping societal peace in the region, did Sudan's president, Omar al-Bashir choose to effectively dismantle it in 2000. My field research suggested that the split in the Islamic Movement and the dis-mantling of the Islamist network in Darfur was part of the strategy Bashir chose to coup-proof his regime from Hassan al-Turabi, the revered sheikh of the Islamic Movement and the person who engineered Bashir's rise to power. Having collaborated to seize control of the Sudanese state in 1989,

---

[83] On within-case qualitative research, see John Gerring, *Case Study Research: Principles and Practices* (Cambridge: Cambridge University Press, 2007).

Bashir and Turabi agreed on an informal distribution of power. Bashir, as an army officer leading the coup, would serve as the titular head of state, and Turabi, as secretary general of the Islamic Movement, would rule from behind the scenes. This two-headed system of governance proved unsustainable and gave way to a power struggle as both sides calculated the other was scheming to seize absolute power. As the power struggle escalated and key elites within the regime chose sides, the commitment problem intensified, and the security dilemma it engendered escalated. As Turabi orchestrated a constitutional coup to usurp power from Bashir at the end of 1999, the president struck first, mobilizing support within the military and security to dissolve the national assembly and eliminate Turabi and his loyalists from the regime. Though Turabi and Bashir were both from northern Sudan, the regime split developed an important ethnoregional dimension, as Turabi was perceived to be mobilizing "black Darfurians" against the Bashir faction. It was through this lens that Bashir targeted Darfurian Islamists to be purged from the regime.

Part III, then, explores why Bashir's coup-proofing strategy led to civil war in Darfur. I identify three mechanisms by which ethnopolitical exclusion increased the government's vulnerability to armed rebellion in Darfur. First, consistent with the argument put forth by Cederman, Wimmer, and their collaborators, it increased economic and political grievances among Darfurians, who perceived Bashir's purge as an attempt to retain power by those from northern Sudan and marginalize those from the periphery, especially Darfur. These grievances were articulated in the famous *Black Book*, a scathing and systematic critique of political inequality in Sudan penned by Darfurian dissidents and published after the split in the Islamic Movement. Second, it increased opportunities for rebellion. Bashir's restructuring of the regime's political network in Darfur emasculated its control and support from non-Arab groups in Darfur. This undermined the regime's ability to produce cooperative counterinsurgency and instead led to a heavy reliance on indiscriminate violence. Third, the shadow of Turabi loomed over early political negotiations. Unwilling to give Turabi and his supporters an opportunity to come back to power, Bashir rejected a negotiated solution and opted instead for a costly but peripheral civil war.

Overall, employing Darfur as a heuristic case study affirmed support for the political networks hypothesis but also motivated a novel strategic theory of ethnopolitical exclusion and civil war. While Sudan is an extreme example of a weak, ethnically divided state, it does not diverge in kind from other African states, in which political authority fundamentally hinges on informal bargains between elites embedded in different ethnic groups. Thus, following the nested-analysis approach and building from the Sudan case study, I then sought to test the generalizability of the book's key theoretical claims employing a large-N analysis across sub-Saharan Africa.

1.6.2 Model-Testing Large-N Analysis, Part I: Ethnic Powersharing, Coups, and Civil War in Africa

The small-N analysis of Sudan points to the importance of incorporating ethnopolitical networks into the study of civil war and modeling the strategic problems that arise from ethnic powersharing. To test the applicability of the coup–civil war trap beyond Sudan, I employ the EPR dataset developed by Wimmer et al. as well as an original dataset on the ethnicity of armed rebels and coup conspirators between independence and 2005 in sub-Saharan Africa (see Appendix 3). I use the EPR data on the distribution of power across a country's politically relevant ethnic groups as a measure of the structure of a given regime's ethnopolitical networks and the relative density of its networks across different groups. I then analyze the effect of a country's ethnopolitical configuration on the likelihood of coups and civil war.

The evidence strongly supports the hypotheses generated through the qualitative analysis of civil war in Darfur. First, Africa's weak states and strong societies problem does appear to confront rulers with a coup–civil war trap. Ethnopolitical groups incorporated in the central government are less likely to rebel but more likely to usurp power in a coup d'état. Ethnic exclusion neutralizes the coup threat from the targeted group but at the price of an increased risk of civil war. Second, counterintuitively, but consistent with a strategic theory of ethnopolitical exclusion and the breakdown of the Islamic Movement in Sudan, rulers are significantly more likely to purge the very allies that helped them come to power than other groups, and this ethnopolitical exclusion often triggers large-scale political violence. What is striking is the degree to which the breakdown of these regimes follows the causal pathway specified by the theory. Unable to agree upon the distribution of power, trust between co-conspirators frays, leading to an internal security dilemma that both sides seek to resolve by eliminating the other from power, ending in civil war. "Mini case analyses"[84] of co-conspirator civil wars in Liberia and Chad in the late 1980s offer additional support for the claim that the

---

[84] Lieberman, "Nested Analysis."

breakdown of elite powersharing has significant consequences for war and peace in post-liberation states.

1.6.3 Model-Testing Small-N Analysis: A Novel Interpretation of Africa's Great War

Building on the large-N analysis, I then move back to small-N analysis to conduct an additional test of the model and to employ process tracing to evaluate the explanatory power of the strategic theory of civil war vis-à-vis rival explanations,[85] such as conflict over natural resources or instrumental theories of conflict with incomplete information. Unlike the Sudan case, the case study of Africa's Great War—the devastating regionalized civil war that broke out in the DRC in August 1998—was only selected after the book's central theoretical claims were developed and tested quantitatively. In fact, it was the large-N analysis that first led me to conceive of Africa's Great War as a "typical case"[86] of a coup-proofing civil war between co-conspirators.[87] Most of the existing qualitative literature on Africa's Great War has tended to downplay the importance of internal strategic factors in lieu of external factors or resource competition. The fact that civil war in DRC is overdetermined (it has almost all of the factors that are predicted to cause civil war) makes it a tough case for the theory. As any number of factors could cause large-scale political violence, the outcome of interest isn't whether a civil war happened but whether it happened through the strategic process I theorize causes civil war in weak states. Extensive elite interviews with the Congolese and Rwandan protagonists involved in the overthrow of Mobutu Sese Seko and subsequently in Africa's Great War revealed that not only did the strategic alliance between Laurent-Désiré Kabila and his Rwandan comrades break down due to the strategic uncertainty that arises from powersharing in the shadow of the coup d'état but that it was the worsening internal strategic environment that drove Kabila to suddenly expel the Rwandan Patriotic Front (RPF) at the end of July 1998 in a desperate

---

[85] George and Bennett, *Case Studies and Theory Development.* Surprisingly, as Lyall notes, civil war scholars have made remarkably little use of this important methodological tool for theory testing. Jason Lyall, "Process Tracing, Causal Inference, and Civil War," in Andrew Bennett and Jeffrey T. Checkel, eds., *Process Tracing: From Metaphor to Analytic Tool* (Cambridge: Cambridge University Press, 2015), pp. 186–208.

[86] Gerring, *Case Study Research,* Chapter 5.

[87] See introduction to Chapter 9 for a description of how the quantitative data from the Ethnic Power Relations (EPR) applies to the DRC in 1997–1998.

bid to preempt a coup d'état, though at the cost of triggering the deadliest conflict since World War II.

1.6.4 Model-Testing Large-N Analysis, Part II: Ethnic Geography, Threat Capabilities, and Self-Enforcing Powersharing in Africa

This book marshals a nested research design to develop and test a strategic theory of ethnopolitical exclusion and civil war in postcolonial Africa. Not only does the book's theoretical framework account for two of Africa's deadliest civil wars—the Darfur conflict and Africa's Great War—but it informs a number of other episodes of large-scale political violence, including the Biafran War in Nigeria; Burundi's descent into a bloody ethnocracy; Uganda's decades of violence; Chad's cycle of civil wars; Liberia's civil war and state collapse; the Rwandan genocide; and, tragically, as the beginning of this book described, we can add South Sudan's post-independence civil war to the list. Up until now, no one has employed a rigorous comparative methodology to study these conflicts.

Strikingly, some states in Africa have been able to avoid the exclusion–conflict cycle despite similar underlying structural and institutional conditions (including the political salience of ethnicity, the spatial concentration and disparateness of ethnic groups, weak and neopatrimonial political institutions, and the prevalence of politics by force). In Part IV, I seek to account for this puzzle by moving back up to large-N analysis. As explained above, I argue that ethnic powersharing is more likely to emerge when both the ruling group and a given rival possess strong threat capabilities as measured by each's size as a proportion of the population and distance to the capital. To test this hypothesis, I again use the EPR dataset and my original dataset on coups and civil war as well as geospatial information on a country's ethnic geography to measure the balance of threat capabilities. Consistent with theoretical claim no. 5, I show that at the dyadic level across sub-Saharan Africa ethnic powersharing is significantly more likely when the ruler and a rival both are embedded in relatively large groups proximate to the capital. Under such conditions, ethnic powersharing endures even as it increases coup risk. In other words, when the major axis of political competition is between several large ethnic groups located near the capital, as historically has been the case in Ghana, Benin, and Mauritania, then ethnic powersharing prevails and coup risk is substituted for civil war risk. In contrast, when the major axis of political competition is between a large and small group, or several smaller groups located far from the capital, as has been the case in Rwanda, Burundi, Sudan, the DRC, and Chad, then ethnic exclusion prevails and civil war risk is substituted for coup risk.

I.7 A LOOK AHEAD

The rest of the book is organized as follows.

Having motivated the book and summarized the central argument, in Part I I review and critique existing scholarship on civil war onset. While important advances have been made over the past fifteen years, the politics of civil war onset remains a key gap. I argue that one of the reasons scholars have not developed a political theory of civil war onset is that they have failed to incorporate informal political institutions into their civil war models. In weak states, where most civil wars have occurred, societal peace hinges on the informal alliances rulers strike with violence specialists embedded in other societal groups. The key to accounting for civil war in weak states is to explain why these informal alliances break down, leading to political exclusion of key societal groups. Building on existing literature, I explore three potential logics of costly political exclusion: *exclusion because it is possible, exclusion because it is appropriate*, and *exclusion because it is necessary*. I contend that *exclusion because it is necessary*, or *strategic exclusion*, to be one of the most powerful and pernicious sources of large-scale political violence in postcolonial Africa. Chapter 4 develops this argument and posits that civil war in Africa is a function of the strategic problems that arise from powersharing in the shadow of the coup d'état. While rulers prefer to avoid costly civil war, their willingness to share power to achieve societal peace is constrained by the uncertainty that comes from incorporating ethnic rivals into the regime.

Part II further develops the book's core theoretical claims using a theory-building case study of political violence in Darfur, Sudan. Based on extensive field research in Sudan and in-depth interviews with a range of Sudanese actors, including top government officials, military officers, rebel leaders, Islamist cadres, tribal elders, opposition politicians, journalists, civil-society activists, and academics, Part II aims to further flesh out the key hypotheses developed in Part I. Chapter 5 explores how interethnic political networks reduce the risk of civil war by thwarting opportunities for armed rebellion and increasing the government's counterinsurgency effectiveness. In doing so, Chapter 5 develops the idea of cooperative counterinsurgency and shows how ethnic brokers or societal intermediaries are integral for the government to

strike the cooperative bargains with local communities that are necessary to prevent armed rebellion from taking root in a region and provoking civil war. Chapter 6 then analyzes why, if interethnic political
networks are so important for keeping societal peace, they nonetheless
break down and leave the government vulnerable to large-scale political
violence. Chapter 6 suggests that in the Sudan case, President Omar al-
Bashir calculated that dismantling the Islamic Movement and purging
Darfurian Islamists from the government was *strategically necessary* to
neutralize the coup threat posed by his former mentor and sheikh of
the Islamic Movement, Hassan al-Turabi. Chapter 7 completes Part II
by then exploring the consequences of Bashir's exclusive political strategy and the mechanisms by which ethnopolitical exclusion increases
civil war risk: intensifying political and economic grievances; increasing
opportunities for armed rebellion and reduction of the government's
counterinsurgency effectiveness; and increasing mistrust between the
ruler and his ethnic rivals.

Part III then tests the generalizability of the book's central argument beyond the Sudan case. Chapter 8 employs the EPR dataset and
an original dataset on the ethnicity of coup conspirators and major
insurgencies in Africa to test whether in fact we see evidence of a coup–
civil war trap in postcolonial Africa rooted in the commitment problem and the inefficient strategies of ethnic exclusion that it produces.
Chapter 9 tests the coup-proofing theory of civil war on one of the
most important cases of conflict in postcolonial Africa—Africa's Great
War. Extensive, original evidence is brought to bear to support the
coup-proofing theory of civil war—Kabila expelled the Rwandans to
eliminate their first-strike capabilities and increase the costs they faced
to overthrowing him.

Part IV explores the puzzle of durable powersharing and ethnic peace.
It thinks about the flip side of the coup–civil war trap: why do some
rulers embrace ethnic powersharing and accept coup risk over civil war
risk? What do we learn from these cases about the sources of credible
powersharing in weak states? It explores the relationship between ethnic
geography, threat capabilities, and durable powersharing. Not only does
this analysis help to account for the sources of powersharing, but it also
speaks to the broader puzzle of Africa's two equilibriums—why some
countries have been stuck in a violent, ethnically exclusive order and others in a peaceful, ethnically inclusive order. Heretofore, no one has been
able to account for these divergent historical trajectories. The final chapter, Chapter 11, summarizes the key contributions the book makes to

scholarship on political authority, coups, civil war, and ethnic politics. It also assesses whether the book's central argument applies to weak states outside of Africa. Evidence from current events in Syria and Iraq suggest the promise the theory has in representing a more general framework of order and violence in weak states.

PART I

PUZZLE AND THEORY

2

A Meso-level Approach to the Study of Civil War

2.1 INTRODUCTION

Civil war—large-scale political violence between a government and a domestic armed opposition—has been a key source of economic underdevelopment over the past fifty years. Collier et al. pithily describe civil war as "development in reverse," in which "society diverts some of its resources from productive activities to destruction."[1] The economic and social costs of large-scale political violence for war-affected countries and their neighbors can be quite high—ranging from economic decline to the narrowing and hardening of social boundaries to refugee spillovers to potentially genocide—and have been extensively documented in previous scholarship.[2] Beyond analyzing the consequences of civil war, scholars

---

[1] Collier et al., *Breaking the Conflict Trap.*
[2] Collier et al., *Breaking the Conflict Trap.* James C. Murdoch and Todd Sandler, "Economic Growth, Civil Wars, and Spatial Spillovers," *Journal of Conflict Resolution,* 46 (1) (2002): 91–110. Seonjou Kang and James Meernik, "Civil War Destruction and the Prospects for Economic Growth," *Journal of Politics,* 67 (1) (2005): 88–109. Patricia Justino, "War and Poverty" in *The Oxford Handbook of the Economics of Peace and Conflict,* ed. Michelle R. Garfinkel and Stergios Skaperdas (Oxford: Oxford University Press, 2012), pp. 676–705; Elisabeth Jean Wood, "The Social Processes of Civil War: The Wartime Transformation of Social Networks," *Annual Review of Political Science,* 11 (1) (2008): 539–561. Salehyan and Gleditsch, "Refugees and the Spread of Civil War." Barbara Harff, "No Lessons Learned from the Holocaust? Assessing Risks of Genocide and Political Mass Murder since 1955," *American Political Science Review,* 97 (1) (2003): 57–73. Benjamin Valentino, Paul Huth, and Dylan Balch-Lindsay, "'Draining the Sea': Mass Killing and Guerrilla Warfare," *International Organization,* 58 (2) (2004): 375–407. Hazem Adam Ghobarah, Paul Huth, and Bruce Russett, "Civil Wars Kill and Maim People . . . Long after the Shooting Stops," *American Political Science Review,* 97 (2) (2003): 189–202. Fearon and Laitin, "Violence and the Social Construction of Ethnic Identities." Collier, *The Bottom Billion.* Benjamin Crost, Joseph Felter, and Patrick

have sought to better understand why and how conflict breaks out with the hope that such knowledge will help to prevent future ones. Toward this end, a large and robust civil war research program has emerged over the past twenty years.[3]

The civil war research program has made important advances in our understanding of the macro- and microlevel causes of civil war. The macro-level scholarship has been dominated by the *weak state paradigm*—that civil war is largely a function of structurally weak states that lack the capabilities to effectively prevent or contain armed rebellions.[4] This literature links the increase in civil war since World War II to the emergence of weak, extractive states from European colonialism.[5] According to Fearon and Laitin, "These states have been at risk for civil violence for the whole period, almost entirely in the form of insurgency, or rural guerrilla warfare."[6] In contrast, microcomparative scholarship has tended to eschew the structural determinism of the weak state paradigm and instead has focused on individual agency, asking not why a country experiences civil war but "who fights"[7] and why. This has generated important new insights and debates on individual-level predictors of violence.[8] A key finding, which complements the weak state paradigm,

Johnston, "Aid under Fire: Development Projects and Civil Conflict," *The American Economic Review*, 104 (6) (2014): 1833–1856.

[3] For extensive surveys and literature reviews of the civil war research program, see Nicholas Sambanis, "A Review of Recent Advances and Future Directions in the Quantitative Literature on Civil War," *Defence and Peace Economics*, 13 (3) (2002): 215–243. Collier et al., *Breaking the Conflict Trap*. Nicholas Sambanis, "What Is Civil War?," *Journal of Conflict Resolution*, 48 (6) (2004): 814–858. Tarrow, "Inside Insurgencies." Stathis N. Kalyvas, "Civil Wars," in Carles Boix, and Susan C. Stokes, eds., *The Oxford Handbook of Comparative Politics* (Oxford: Oxford University Press, 2008), pp. 416–434. Blattman and Miguel, "Civil War." Fearon, "Governance and Civil War Onset." Adrian Florea, "Where Do We Go from Here? Conceptual, Theoretical, and Methodological Gaps in the Large-N Civil War Research Program1," *International Studies Review*, 14 (1) (2012): 78–98.

[4] Fearon and Laitin, "Ethnicity, Insurgency, and Civil War." Collier et al., "Beyond Greed and Grievance." Ann Hironaka, *Neverending Wars: The International Community, Weak States, and the Perpetuation of Civil War* (Cambridge, Mass.: Harvard University Press, 2005). Idean Salehyan, "Transnational Rebels: Neighboring States as Sanctuary for Rebel Groups," *World Politics*, 59 (2) (2007): 217–242. Gleditsch and Ruggeri, "Political Opportunity Structures."

[5] Hironaka, *Neverending Wars*.

[6] Fearon and Laitin, "Ethnicity, Insurgency, and Civil War," p. 88.

[7] Humphreys and Weinstein, "Who Fights?"

[8] Kalyvas, "Promises and Pitfalls."

is that insecurity is often a key factor that drives individuals to join a rebellion.[9]

Taken together, the macro- and microlevel scholarship offer complementary but distinct perspectives on conflict escalation or the production of greater levels of violence leading to full-scale civil war. Both offer insights into the conditions and processes that allow armed rebellion to outpace government countermobilization. The lacunae of these approaches, however, is they often fail to account for the political dynamics driving the outbreak of civil war, especially how bargaining over the distribution of power ends in large-scale political violence.

To address this gap, we need to shift our focus in the study of civil war from the macro or micro to the meso—the institutions connecting political regimes and society.[10] In this chapter, I develop a meso-level approach to the study of civil war. The central premise is that the risk of large-scale political violence is mediated by the informal political alliances and networks that represent the superstructure of weak states. As I show quite extensively, these networks are often dominated by national political and military elites vying for control of the central government. These elites are not suspended above society, however, and thus do not only operate at the macro-level. (See Figure 2.1 below.) Quite the contrary, their power comes from their embeddedness in society and their ability to mobilize societal support. Incorporating these meso-level ethnopolitical networks into models of civil war is necessary to elucidate how and why elite politics has such profound consequences on societal control and the production of local violence. Without understanding these meso-level dynamics, the pathway from high politics to civil war remains a black box.

The rest of the chapter is organized as follows. First, I critique the macro- and microlevel approaches to civil war for overlooking the importance of political bargaining. I then unpack the institutional bases of weak states and develop the *political networks hypothesis*—that, independent

---

[9] Humphreys and Weinstein, "Who Fights?" See also Stathis N. Kalyvas, and Matthew Adam Kocher, "How 'Free' Is Free Riding in Civil Wars? Violence, Insurgency, and the Collective Action Problem," *World Politics*, 59 (2) (2007): 177–216. For an important earlier work on the effect of insecurity on rebellion, see T. David Mason, and Dale A. Krane, "The Political Economy of Death Squads: Toward a Theory of the Impact of State-Sanctioned Terror," *International Studies Quarterly*, 33 (2) (1989): 175–198.

[10] Kalyvas, *The Logic of Violence in Civil War*.

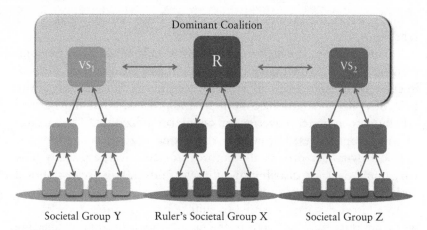

Societal Group Y   Ruler's Societal Group X   Societal Group Z

R=Ruler
VS=Violence Specialist

FIGURE 2.1 Schematic of Personal Rule in Weak States

of underlying structural factors, civil war is a function of the density of the ruler's political network across key societal groups. Next, I draw on a rich literature in African politics, which has been largely marginal to the civil war literature but which takes seriously a meso-level approach to the study of conflict. The last section summarizes the importance of a meso-level approach to civil war and asks why, if interethnic alliances are so integral to societal peace in postcolonial Africa, do they sometimes break down.

2.2 THE WEAK STATE PARADIGM OF CIVIL WAR

Civil war is a form of violent conflict within a state between the central government and one or more armed local groups over the distribution of power, resources, territory, or other goods. It is distinguished from other types of conflicts based on the *scale* of the violence (it reaches a minimum threshold of at least 1,000 battlefield deaths) and its *scope*—a minimal proportion (100 battlefield deaths in the first year) must be produced by the armed opposition.[11]

[11] Sambanis, "What Is Civil War?"

TEXTBOX 2.I A NOTE ON COUPS, REBELLIONS, AND
CIVIL WAR

This book is fundamentally interested in accounting for the phenomena of coups, rebellions, and civil wars across postcolonial Africa. It is thus important to be clear about the differences between the three outcomes. I conceive of coups and rebellions, or insurgencies, as analogues; both represent anti-regime techniques that dissidents use to force a redistribution of power. They can be distinguished, however, by their organizational basis. Coup conspirators leverage partial control of the state (and the resources and matériel that come with access to the state) in their bid to capture political power. In Luttwak's pithy phrasing, a coup "consists of the infiltration of a small, but critical, segment of the state apparatus, which is then used to displace the government from its control of the remainder."[a] In contrast, rebels or insurgents lack such access and have to build a private military organization to challenge the central government and its military.

This organizational distinction helps to account for why coups are often much more likely to displace rulers from power than rebellions. Partial control of the state, especially the most strategic points of the regime (such as, the military), lowers the mobilizational costs that dissidents must overcome to overthrow the ruler. In contrast, for those outside of the regime, the burden of mobilization to capture power is much greater; unable to rely on partial control of the state, these dissidents must build, finance, and equip their own private army that can effectively displace the entire government.

This distinction helps to account for other stylized differences between coups and insurgencies. The use of the state apparatus against the ruler also makes it difficult to sustain an open, prolonged coup conspiracy; as soon as the ruler detects one is using the state against him, he will seek to deny conspirators such access. Consequently, coups d'état, as the French phrase suggests, tend to be a sudden strike against the state executed by a small group, usually from within the military. In contrast, rebellions, which do not benefit from institutional bases of power, necessitate the building of a private military organization capable of effectively challenging the state and its military apparatus; consequently, insurgencies entail sustained and more large-scale mobilization, which is difficult to conceal and requires control of territory and societal support.

In contrast to coups and rebellions, civil war represents a form of relatively balanced large-scale violent conflict between the central government and an armed opposition, in which the violence must reach a minimal threshold of 1,000 battlefield deaths with a minimal proportion produced by the armed opposition. While civil war may result from both coup attempts and rebellions, they are more often a function of the latter, given the organizational differences between the two. As coups arise from those with "institutional bases of power within the political system,"[b] they play out following an "all-or-nothing tipping dynamic."[c] As Fearon explains, leaders of would-be coups hope that a rapid, surprise strike from within the government will immediately produce "wholesale defections within the regime (especially the military)" and immediately bring down the government. Thus, "either the coup leaders succeed or they are crushed when the hoped-for tip fails to develop."[d] If they succeed, the redistribution of power often happens very quickly with little bloodshed. If they fail, there tends to be more bloodshed, but it rarely crosses the civil war threshold *unless* the coup-plotters can effectively switch their technology of resistance from the coup to the rebellion (i.e. they can form a private army that exists outside of the government). Because of the strong relationship between rebellion and civil war and because in this book I am primarily interested in large-scale rebellion, I tend to use the terms "rebellion" and "civil war" interchangeably throughout the book and conceive of the trade-off rulers face as between coups and civil war.

[a] Luttwak, *Coup d'État: A Practical Handbook.*
[b] Huntington, Political Order in Changing Societies, p. 218.
[c] James D. Fearon, "Why Do Some Civil Wars Last So Much Longer than Others?," Journal of Peace Research, 41 (3), p. 289.
[d] Fearon, "Why Do Some Civil Wars Last So Much Longer than Others?," p. 289.

Macro-level research on civil war has been dominated by a focus on the factors that increase the feasibility of or opportunity for armed rebellion[12]—that is, the capability and willingness of opposition forces to *effectively challenge the state's monopoly on violence, form and sustain*

[12] This research stream has tended to dismiss the role that grievances, such as political exclusion, lack of freedom, or inequality, play in motivating dissidents to oppose the central government. Though, as I discuss in Section 4.2.5, the grievances approach to civil

a private army, and inflict substantial costs on the central government.[13] The theoretical premise of the *feasibility framework* is that countries in which conditions favor the formation of insurgency and hinder the government's counterinsurgency capabilities are more likely to experience civil war onset than those in which the balance of capabilities favor the state over the opposition.

A number of factors are posited to tilt the balance of capabilities in favor of insurgents over the regime and increase the likelihood of the outbreak of large-scale political violence. One of the most important is hypothesized to be the structural strength of the state as measured by GDP per capita.[14] Low-income states are plagued by low bureaucratic and administrative capacity, which undermines the government's ability to effectively police and control its territory and prevent armed challengers to the regime.[15] Making matters worse, when an armed challenge does materialize, the lack of bureaucratic capacity often results in a heavy-handed and indiscriminate military response that drives civilians to join and support the rebels, increasing the mobilizational potential of the opposition and the likelihood of conflict escalation.[16]

Beyond state capacity, other factors are hypothesized to increase the feasibility of insurgency vis-à-vis regime counterinsurgency, including:

war has experienced a resurgence with the publication of the Ethnic Power Relations (EPR) dataset and the scholarship of Wimmer and Cederman and before that the work by Frances Stewart and her collaborators on "horizontal inequalities" and Ted Robert Gurr and his research team on "minorities at risk."

[13] This is the approach that Fearon and Laitin adopted in their seminal article and that Collier and Hoeffler eventually ended up embracing. Fearon and Laitin, "Ethnicity, Insurgency, and Civil War." For a useful summary, see Fearon, "Governance and Civil War Onset." It is very similar to the general political opportunity structure model at the heart of the contentious politics literature. See Doug McAdam, *Political Process and the Development of Black Insurgency, 1930–1970* (Chicago, Ill.: University of Chicago Press, 1982). Sidney G. Tarrow, *Power in Movement: Social Movements, Collective Action, and Politics* (Cambridge: Cambridge University Press, 1994). Charles Tilly, *From Mobilization to Revolution* (Reading, Mass.: Addison-Wesley, 1978). Mark Irving Lichbach, *The Rebel's Dilemma* (Ann Arbor, Mich.: University of Michigan Press, 1995). For a recent application of the political opportunity structure model to civil war onset, see Gleditsch and Ruggeri, "Political Opportunity Structures."

[14] Fearon and Laitin, "Ethnicity, Insurgency, and Civil War."

[15] Hironaka, *Neverending Wars.* Using factor analysis, Hendrix confirms that the key dimension of stateness is bureaucratic or administrative capacity, given its importance in collecting and managing information, which is integral to the effective application of repression and accommodation. Hendrix, "Measuring State Capacity."

[16] Fearon and Laitin, "Ethnicity, Insurgency, and Civil War." See also Mason and Krane, "The Political Economy of Death Squads." Jeff Goodwin, *No Other Way Out: States and Revolutionary Movements, 1945–1991* (Cambridge: Cambridge University Press, 2001).

Population size: The larger the population, the higher monitoring costs the government faces in policing its citizens.[17]

Rough terrain: Mountainous areas of the country offer protection for potential rebels from government forces, enabling the rebels to set up training camps and military bases, increasing the costs of counterinsurgency.[18]

Regime instability: Military coups or irregular changes of leadership may lead to disarray within the central government and weaken its countermobilizational capabilities.[19]

Ethnic geography: Geographically concentrated ethnic groups can leverage dense social networks that reduce the costs of communication and cooperation, increasing the group's mobilizational capabilities while making it more costly for the government to monitor these groups.[20]

Foreign sanctuary: Rebel bases in neighboring countries boost rebel capacity because the state, constrained by international sovereignty, faces higher costs to monitoring the rebels and attacking them abroad.[21]

Economic crises: A decline in the economy lowers the opportunity cost for potential dissidents to join the rebellion while hurting the government's tax base and making it more difficult to retain the loyalty of pro-regime forces.[22]

---

[17] Fearon and Laitin, "Ethnicity, Insurgency, and Civil War." Hegre and Sambanis confirm the correlation between civil war and population but also note that this relationship could be definitional as civil war onset is distinguished from other conflicts based on a high threshold of deaths, implying that civil wars are more likely to occur in populous countries. Hegre and Sambanis, "Sensitivity Analysis of Empirical Results," pp. 514–515.

[18] Fearon and Laitin, "Ethnicity, Insurgency, and Civil War." Hendrix argues that rough terrain may also weaken state capacity. Cullen S. Hendrix, "Head for the Hills? Rough Terrain, State Capacity, and Civil War Onset," *Civil Wars*, 13 (4) (2011): 345–370.

[19] Fearon and Laitin, "Ethnicity, Insurgency, and Civil War." Hegre and Sambanis, "Sensitivity Analysis of Empirical Results." Gleditsch and Ruggeri, "Political Opportunity Structures." Daron Acemoglu, Davide Ticchi, and Andrea Vindigni, "Persistence of Civil Wars." Cambridge, Mass.: National Bureau of Economic Research, 2009.

[20] Toft, The Geography of Ethnic Violence. James D. Fearon and David D. Laitin, "Sons of the Soil, Migrants, and Civil War," *World Development*, 39 (2) (2011): 199–211. Nils B. Weidmann, "Geography as Motivation and Opportunity: Group Concentration and Ethnic Conflict," *Journal of Conflict Resolution*, 53 (4) (2009): 526–543.

[21] Salehyan, "Transnational Rebels." Salehyan, *Rebels without Borders*.

[22] Collier et al., "Beyond Greed and Grievance." Edward Miguel, Shanker Satyanath, and Ernest Sergenti, "Economic Shocks and Civil Conflict: An Instrumental Variables Approach," *Journal of Political Economy*, 112 (4) (2004): 725–753. But note that micro-level studies of armed rebellion find conflicting support for the link between income and rebel participation. Humphreys and Weinstein, "Who Fights?" Eli Berman, Michael

Overall, the feasibility framework, which I summarize as the *weak state model of civil war* given the overriding importance state capacity plays, is highly useful for understanding the global variation of large-scale political violence, such as why the DRC has experienced multiple civil wars and peace has prevailed in, say, Belgium. It also helps to inform individual cases, such as Sudan, which is central to this book. As I explain in Chapter 5, many of these structural factors are present in the Sudan case and are an important part of the story in explaining how armed groups have been able to effectively challenge the central government.

2.3 THE MICROCOMPARATIVE TURN IN THE STUDY OF CIVIL WAR AND ITS LIMITATIONS

The key limitation of the weak state model of civil war, however, is it relies heavily on a structural framework to account for a highly dynamic process. While underlying structural conditions can predict which countries are more vulnerable to civil war than others, they do not tell us *how* we get the outbreak of large-scale political violence. As Tarrow notes, none of these macro-level structural studies gets "inside the mechanisms or processes of civil war insurgencies."[23] Instead, the processes of insurgency, and, just as importantly counterinsurgency, are taken as given.[24] But, following from Mancur Olson and others, there is nothing inevitable about collective action, especially when the benefits of individual participation are low and the costs are high.[25] Drawing on Olson's insights, a number of scholars have sought to take agency seriously and shed light on the black box of conflict escalation. The pivotal work that launched the microcomparative turn in the study of civil war was Stathis Kalyvas's

---

Callen, Joseph H. Felter, and Jacob N. Shapiro, "Do Working Men Rebel? Insurgency and Unemployment in Afghanistan, Iraq, and the Philippines," *Journal of Conflict Resolution*, 55 (4) (2011): 496–528. Graeme Blair, Christine Fair, Neil Malhotra, and Jacob N. Shapiro, "Poverty and Support for Militant Politics: Evidence from Pakistan," *American Journal of Political Science*, 57 (1) (2013): 30–48.

[23] Tarrow, "Inside Insurgencies," p. 589.

[24] This is one of the key points Kalyvas and Weinstein make in their microlevel studies. Kalyvas, *The Logic of Violence in Civil War*. Weinstein, *Inside Rebellion*.

[25] Mancur Olson, *The Logic of Collective Action: Public Goods and the Theory of Groups* (Cambridge, Mass.: Harvard University Press, 1965). Though, for a dissenting view, see Kalyvas and Kocher, "How 'Free' Is Free Riding?" The central critique Kalyvas and Kocher make is that in the midst of civil war, when an individual faces the prospect of indiscriminate violence from a government, the costs of not joining a rebellion may be equal or even greater than joining—that is, one may have a better chance of survival joining a rebellion than staying on the sidelines. When the costs of nonparticipation are

The Logic of Violence in Civil War, which uses local-level conflict data from the Argolid region of Greece during its civil war in the 1940s to test his theory of selective violence.[26] Since Kalyvas's work, there has been an explosion of microcomparative research on civil war, including, but by no means limited to:

- the study of rebel organization and violence against civilians;[27]
- the consequences of violence exposure for rebel combatants;[28]
- the link between rebel mobilization and ethnic geography;[29]
- rebel recruitment;[30]
- subnational poverty and rebellion;[31]
- participation in mass violence;[32] and
- local conflict over land, resources, and political power.[33]

The microcomparative scholarship has made significant strides in advancing our understanding of the key dynamics and mechanisms that fuel civil war. But key gaps remain. Despite Kalyvas's call for a meso-theory of civil war that focuses on what he calls "alliance," in which "agency [is] located in *both* center and periphery rather than only in either one,"[34] most microcomparative research has tended to focus almost exclusively on non-state actors in the periphery. Few studies have focused on the informal political networks that connect the center with

---

so high, there really is no collective action puzzle. While this may hold in the midst of mass indiscriminate violence—usually after the war has begun—their argument is less relevant in the transition period when counterinsurgency violence is not pervasive and individuals face high individual costs to taking up weapons. For a theoretical discussion of this period, see Lichbach, *The Rebel's Dilemma*.

[26] Kalyvas, *The Logic of Violence in Civil War*. A number of important microcomparative studies preceded Kalyvas, including: Wood, *Insurgent Collective Action*.

[27] Weinstein, *Inside Rebellion*.

[28] Christopher Blattman, "From Violence to Voting: War and Political Participation in Uganda," *American Political Science Review*, 103 (2) (2009): 231–247.

[29] Weidmann, "Geography as Motivation."

[30] Humphreys and Weinstein, "Who Fights?"

[31] Håvard Hegre, Gudrun Østby, and Clionadh Raleigh, "Poverty and Civil War Events: A Disaggregated Study of Liberia," *Journal of Conflict Resolution*, 53 (4) (2009): 598–623. Halvard Buhaug, Kristian Skrede Gleditsch, Helge Holtermann, Gudrun Østby, and Andreas Forø Tollefsen, "It's the Local Economy, Stupid! Geographic Wealth Dispersion and Conflict Outbreak Location," *Journal of Conflict Resolution*, 55 (5) (2011): 814–840.

[32] Scott Straus, *The Order of Genocide: Race, Power, and War in Rwanda* (Ithaca, NY: Cornell University Press, 2006).

[33] Séverine Autesserre, *The Trouble with the Congo: Local Violence and the Failure of International Peacebuilding* (Cambridge: Cambridge University Press, 2010).

[34] Kalyvas, *The Logic of Violence in Civil War*, p. 386.

the periphery—the dominant mode of political control in weak states. Such networks have important mediating effects on the risk of conflict escalation but have been largely neglected in macro-level studies of civil war, potentially a key source of omitted variable bias.[35]

Beyond filling the gap that is left by extant macro- and microlevel scholarship and offering a more accurate explanation of conflict escalation, the other advantage of a meso-level analysis is it lends itself to a bargaining approach to civil war. Extant macro- and microlevel scholarship tends to focus primarily on *conflict escalation*—the production of greater levels of violence. The problem with theories that only address conflict escalation, as Fearon acknowledges in a critical review of the civil war literature is "they are incomplete and not coherent as explanations for civil war."

Simply noting that some factor makes rebellion more likely to succeed or be self-sustaining does not explain why it would occur. If this factor—such as a weak central state, or lots of unemployed youth, or rough terrain, etc.—makes would-be or actual rebel groups stronger relative to the central government, then why doesn't this just change the terms of implicit or explicit deal that the government offers to avoid a costly conflict?[36]

In other words, why, if the government lacks the capabilities to effectively defeat potential rebels, does it not make the necessary concessions to prevent the rebellion in the first place and avoid costly large-scale political violence?[37] An integrated theory of civil war needs to account for both bargaining failure and conflict escalation—that is, how political bargaining over the distribution of power and wealth ends in large-scale violence.[38]

---

[35] This chapter makes the case for the importance of incorporating the study of informal institutions into the study of civil war. While formal institutions are not irrelevant in weak states, by ignoring the dominant role of informal ones, we risk, as Helmke and Levitsky argue, "missing much of what drives political behavior and [hindering our] efforts to explain important political phenomena." Helmke and Levitsky, "Informal Institutions," p. 726.

[36] Fearon, "Governance and Civil War Onset," p. 41.

[37] At the heart of the bargaining puzzle is the idea that "war is costly and risky, so rational [actors] should have incentives to locate negotiated settlements that all would prefer to the gamble of war." Fearon, "Rationalist Explanations for War," p. 380.

[38] In contrast to civil war onset, a rich bargaining literature has emerged to study conflict duration and settlement, in which formal negotiations are a key part of the process. See Barbara F. Walter, *Committing to Peace: The Successful Settlement of Civil Wars* (Princeton, NJ: Princeton University Press, 2002). James D. Fearon, "Why Do Some Civil Wars Last So Much Longer than Others?" *Journal of Peace Research*, 41 (3) (2004): 275–301. David E. Cunningham, *Barriers to Peace in Civil War* (Cambridge: Cambridge University Press, 2011).

In this book, I aim to advance a meso-level theory of civil war that accounts for both bargaining failure and conflict escalation. I start by explaining the institutional bases of societal control in weak states and the mediating effect these institutions have on conflict escalation. In the next chapter, I then explore various theories of why the political bargains underpinning societal peace break down, leading to ethnopolitical exclusion and civil war.

2.4 THE INSTITUTIONAL BASIS OF PEACE IN WEAK STATES: THE POLITICAL NETWORKS HYPOTHESIS

In modeling the institutional basis of weak states, I build on the *personal rule framework* that has been at the heart of the African politics literature over the past several decades[39] and that has been usefully and elegantly generalized by North et al. in their influential work, *Violence and Social Orders*.[40] Weak states are a subset of what North et al. call "natural states," in which the state lacks a monopoly of violence and social organizations tend to be simple structures dominated by personal relationships. In such an environment, politics is dominated by competing networks of "violence specialists," those who are able to mobilize the use of force to protect themselves and their followers from rival networks.

---

[39] Important works include: Guenther Roth, "Personal Rulership, Patrimonialism, and Empire-Building in the New States," *World Politics*, 20 (2) (1968): 194–206. René Lemarchand, "Political Clientelism and Ethnicity in Tropical Africa: Competing Solidarities in Nation-Building," *American Political Science Review*, 66 (1) (1972): 68–90. J. F. Médard, "The Underdeveloped State in Tropical Africa: Political Clientelism or Neo-patrimonialism," in Christopher S. Clapham, ed., *Private Patronage and Public Power: Political Clientelism in the Modern State* (New York: St. Martin's Press, 1982), pp. 162–192. Christopher S. Clapham, "Clientelism and the State," in Christopher S. Clapham, ed., *Private Patronage and Public Power: Political Clientelism in the Modern State* (New York: St. Martin's Press, 1982), pp. 1–35. Richard Sandbrook and Judith Barker, *The Politics of Africa's Economic Stagnation* (Cambridge: Cambridge University Press, 1985). Catherine Boone, *Merchant Capital and the Roots of State Power in Senegal, 1930–1985* (Cambridge: Cambridge University Press, 1992). Bayart, *The State in Africa*. Michael Bratton, and Nicolas van de Walle, *Democratic Experiments in Africa: Regime Transitions in Comparative Perspective* (Cambridge: Cambridge University Press, 1997). Berman, "Ethnicity, Patronage and the African State." David K. Leonard, and Scott Straus, *Africa's Stalled Development: International Causes and Cures* (Boulder, Col.: Lynne Rienner, 2003).

[40] While in many ways North, Wallis and Weingast's framework of what they call "natural states" versus "open access orders" is a repackaging of key Weberian concepts about personal versus impersonal organizations and the import of traditional versus rational-legal

Order arises in natural states through the institution of what North et al. refer to as the "dominant coalition" and that Africanist scholars have labeled as "elite accommodation,"[41] "hegemonial exchange,"[42] and the "shadow state,"[43] in which violence specialists cooperate to control the state and share the rents and privileges that come with state power. As these privileges are limited to only those within the dominant coalition, it encourages elites to work together to keep the system in place and prevent others from usurping power. It also discourages infighting because elites know that violence will reduce the rents they can extract from the state.[44]

To maintain control outside of the narrow dominant coalition, elites rely on the patron-client networks in which they are socially embedded and which are a key part of their power base,[45] as illustrated in Figure 2.1. These vertical networks are held together by a basic transaction in which the patron, leveraging his privileged position within the dominant coalition, provides protection and patronage to societal clients in exchange for personal loyalty and political support.[46] Shared social identities, especially those characterized by dense and durable social connections and strong norms of reciprocity, further help to cement ties between patrons and clients.[47]

In the absence of strong formal institutions, regimes in weak states rely on patron-client networks to carry out the basic tasks of the state, such as extracting local information, collecting taxes, distributing state resources, and applying repression. "From the standpoint of the state elite," Rothchild notes, "what is attractive about a hegemonial system is its usefulness in extending central control over the country."[48] One

authority (especially given that it is a transition of social organizations based on personal relations to impersonal ones that distinguish the two orders), what makes their work innovative is that they build an argument that accounts for this transition, proposing that impersonality arises out of the types of organizations that society is able to support. Just as importantly, and especially relevant for this book, they do not take social order—the management of violence—as given but explain the political institutions that uphold peace. North et al., *Violence and Social Orders*.

[41] Bayart, *The State in Africa*.

[42] Rothchild, "Hegemonial Exchange."

[43] Reno, *Warlord Politics and African States*.

[44] North et al., *Violence and Social Orders*, p. 30.

[45] North et al., *Violence and Social Orders*, p. 30. As Chazan et al. note, "In negotiations at the center, the patron/intermediary's influence and bargaining power is dependent in no small part on that person's ability to maintain stable, informal ties with clients at the periphery." Chazan et al., *Politics and Society in Contemporary Africa*, p. 113.

[46] Chazan et al., *Politics and Society in Contemporary Africa*, p. 113.

[47] Fearon and Laitin, "Explaining Interethnic Cooperation." Habyarimana et al., *Coethnicity*, especially pp. 6–13. North et al., *Violence and Social Orders*.

[48] Rothchild, "Hegemonial Exchange," p. 84.

implication that follows is that we would expect the structure of the dominant coalition's patron–client networks—that is, the degree to which they penetrate all key societal groups—to have important consequences for the regime's ability to effectively and judiciously employ a combination of repression and accommodation to manage dissent.[49] As Richard Snyder notes, "When the dictator's patronage network is inclusive, penetrating deeply into society, political space for opposition groups is narrow because these vertical patron–client linkages both co-opt elites and extend the reach of the state's surveillance and control."[50] This leads Snyder to put forth what I label the *political networks hypothesis of civil war*: the more inclusive the regime's patronage network, the lower the risk of armed rebellion.[51] This can be illustrated via Figure 2.1. Given the weakness of formal institutions, the ruler (R) faces high costs to penetrating and cultivating support from society. Thus, alliances with different violence specialists embedded in rival societal groups are vital to extending the regime's reach and control. Without these alliances, the ruler's ability to prevent armed rebellion from members of societal group Y or societal group Z is severely compromised.

The political networks hypothesis has been largely overlooked within the civil war literature. As I mentioned, this represents a potential source of omitted variable bias. For example, though mountainous terrain, ethnic enclaves, large population, and a sparse state presence may increase the risk of conflict escalation, the regime may be able to overcome these unfavorable structural conditions if it can develop strong political ties with power brokers from the area that aid the regime with local information and leverage. One observable implication that follows is the greater the density of the dominant coalitions' patron–client networks in a given area the lower the risk of armed conflict. In the next section, I further flesh out the political networks hypothesis drawing on a rich Africanist scholarship.

2.5 PERSONAL RULE, ETHNOPOLITICAL NETWORKS, AND SOCIETAL PEACE IN AFRICA

The personal rule framework has been most widely applied in the study of postcolonial Africa.[52] Personal rule, in which political authority derives

---

[49] This is a central point Rothchild makes. "Hegemonial Exchange."

[50] Snyder, "Paths Out of Sultanistic Regimes," pp. 55–56.

[51] Snyder, "Paths Out of Sultanistic Regimes," pp. 55–56.

[52] Lemarchand, "Political Clientelism and Ethnicity." Jackson and Rosberg, *Personal Rule in Black Africa*. Leonard and Straus, *Africa's Stalled Development*. A renewed interest in authoritarian regimes, building from the work of Juan Linz and Barbara Geddes, has

not from rational–legal institutions but from a series of informal alliances rulers forge with other violence specialists, has arisen as the solution to the challenge postcolonial rulers have faced of maintaining control of their ethnically divided and geographically dispersed societies in the absence of strong political institutions or unifying national ideologies.[53] Africa's "strong societies and weak states" problem[54] derives from a long historical process of state formation under unfavorable geographic and demographic conditions compounded by the external effects of the slave trade and European colonialism.[55] Inheriting weak and ethnically divided states, most African rulers after independence eschewed the high costs of state-building and instead adopted the institutional solution employed by their colonial predecessors: *clientelism.*[56] Exploiting their statist economies (another legacy of colonialism), rulers leveraged their discretionary control of state resources to forge alliances with other power brokers and their network of followers, without which the regime would be unable to secure societal peace and territorial control.[57]

For example, one of the earliest and most important conflicts in post-independence Africa was the attempted secession of Katanga in Congo led by Moise Tshombe, leader of the Confédération des Associations Tribales du Katanga (CONAKAT). As the government of Congo only defeated Katanga's attempted secession and preserved the unity of the country with extensive military support from the United Nations, its leaders faced the challenge when the war was over of how to cultivate political support from a region far from the capital whose population was hostile to the state. Leveraging Tshombe's political networks and popularity, Congo's president, Joseph Kasavubu, brought in the former

generated a new generation of comparative research on personal regimes. H. E. Chehabi, and Juan J. Linz, "A Theory of Sultanism 1: A Type of Nondemocratic Rule," in H. E. Chehabi and Juan J. Linz, eds., *Sultanistic Regimes* (Baltimore, Md.: Johns Hopkins University Press, 1998), pp. 3–25. Barbara Geddes, *Paradigms and Sand Castles: Theory Building and Research Design in Comparative Politics* (Ann Arbor, Mich.: University of Michigan Press, 2003). Axel Hadenius and Jan Teorell, "Pathways from Authoritarianism," *Journal of Democracy*, 18 (1) (2007): 143–157. Svolik, *The Politics of Authoritarian Rule.* Jessica L. Weeks, "Strongmen and Straw Men: Authoritarian Regimes and the Initiation of International Conflict," *American Political Science Review*, 106 (2) (2012): 326–347.

53 Lemarchand, "Political Clientelism and Ethnicity."
54 Joel S. Migdal, *Strong Societies and Weak States: State-Society Relations and State Capabilities in the Third World* (Princeton, NJ: Princeton University Press, 1988).
55 Herbst, *States and Power in Africa.* Nunn, "The Long-Term Effects of Africa's Slave Trades." Mamdani, *Citizen and Subject.*
56 Berman, "Ethnicity, Patronage and the African State."
57 Rothchild, "Hegemonial Exchange." Boone, *Merchant Capital.*

secessionist leader from exile in then Northern Rhodesia (Zambia) and made him prime minister in 1964.[58]

2.5.1 The Coethnic Peace

The political networks hypothesis suggests that civil war risk in postcolonial Africa is a direct function of the structure and density of the ruler's political network. An empirical regularity consistent with this is what I call the *coethnic peace* that has largely prevailed in postcolonial Africa: African rulers have almost never faced large-scale insurgencies from their coethnics. (But, consistent with the coup–civil war trade-off, intraethnic coups have been much more prevalent; see Section 8.3.) According to data I collected on the ethnicity of major armed rebellions in post-independence Africa, I could only identify one case in which coethnics of the head of state were a significant source of anti-regime insurgents: the Zaghawa in Chad in 2005. (See Appendix 3 for a list of all rebellions in postcolonial Africa by ethnicity of insurgents.) The coethnic peace may be endogenous to subnational variation in state capacity, particularly if the ruler's ethnic group "inherited" the state at independence (and benefited from skewed state development during the colonial period). However, what is striking is that it holds even for rulers and groups who were historically marginalized and come from the poorest and weakest states, wherein we would expect the central government's bureaucratic and administrative capacity to be extremely low. Instead, I posit that the near absence of intraethnic rebellions is a direct function of the strength of the ruler's political networks with his own coethnics. To understand this association, it is important to explain why ethnicity tends to serve as the social basis of political networks in Africa.

2.5.2 The Ethnic Bases of Political Networks in Africa

In conceiving of the role that ethnicity plays in African politics, I adopt a constructivist interpretation of ethnicity. I do not assume that ethnic identities are fixed or represent one's only or most important identity.[59] One has a number of different social identities, all of which could serve

---

[58] Georges Nzongola-Ntalaja, *The Congo from Leopold to Kabila: A People's History* (London Zed Books, 2002).

[59] Kanchan Chandra, "Cumulative Findings in the Study of Ethnic Politics," *APSA-CP Newsletter*, 12 (1) (2001): 7–25. Kanchan Chandra, "Introduction," in Kanchan Chandra, ed., *Constructivist Theories of Ethnic Politics* (Oxford: Oxford University Press, 2012), pp. 1–47.

as the bases of political networks. For example, as Bayart writes, political networks could just as easily originate from "having grown up in the same village or the same area of town, by sharing a dormitory in a boarding school or a military academy, and by philosophizing all night long in the halls of residence of British or French universities."[60] Yet, as Bayart also notes, ethnicity is frequently "the channel through which competition for the acquisition of wealth, power or status is expressed" in Africa.[61]

Ethnicity's political salience in Africa is a function of a combination of sociological and institutional factors. Sociologically, ethnicity's attributes of common descent, including dense social connections (e.g., two cousins are more likely to have more social connections in common than two friends or strangers) and shared norms that are passed down from generation to generation, lower the costs of collective action for coethnics and can serve to bolster the strength of a violence specialist's political network. Let me explain.

In natural states, elites are only as powerful as their network of supporters. In competition over economic rents, those networks that wield the greatest power will capture the highest share of state resources.[62] Thus, key to the patron's success is the loyalty of his lieutenants and network unity—the degree to which the patron can mobilize his clients to protect or expand their share of power.[63] As Chazan et al. note, ethnic Big Men "must strive to maintain a loyal following within their ethnic constituencies if they are to be able to negotiate effectively at the top with other ethnic and state leaders."[64] Maintaining loyalty, however, is by no means guaranteed. The patron is well aware that "the rewards (rents) for being at the top of the patronage system are typically far higher than those for the patron's lieutenants,"[65] and his lieutenants are ambitious. Moreover, there is the risk that in this "political marketplace" the patron will be outbid or outmaneuvered by a rival and his lieutenants will defect, fracturing the network and undermining his power.[66] (A powerful example of this, discussed in Chapter 6, is within Sudan's Islamic

---

[60] Jean-François Bayart, *The State in Africa: The Politics of the Belly*, 2nd edn (Cambridge: Polity, 2009), p. 157.

[61] Bayart, *The State in Africa*, 2nd edn, p. 55.

[62] North et al., *Violence and Social Orders*.

[63] In a system in which violence is dispersed, military specialists are key to the success of the network but other specialists are as well, such as businessmen, traders, religious authorities and tribal chiefs, who can help mobilize resources for the use of the network.

[64] Chazan et al., *Politics and Society in Contemporary Africa*, p. 113.

[65] North et al., *Violence and Social Orders*, p. 36.

[66] Alex de Waal, "Dollarised," *London Review of Books*, 32 (12) (2010): 2. Chazan et al., *Politics and Society in Contemporary Africa*.

Movement. Hassan al-Turabi's downfall is largely a function of his key disciples, led by Ali Osman Taha, defecting to swing their support to a rival violence specialist, Omar al-Bashir.)

Network unity is thus vital to succeed in the game of politics, especially when it plays out in the shadow of violence and one's tolerance for the risk of exploitation is very low.[67] Maintaining the loyalty and dependability of network members is costly, however. It requires a steady supply of patronage, use of coercion both to protect and sanction followers, and a system of monitoring. Shared ethnic ties offer violence specialists a non-material resource that they can exploit to maintain network cohesion. Ethnicity's dense social networks allow for "lost-cost access to information"[68] about individuals through what Habyarimana et al. refer to as the technology mechanisms of periodicity (more frequent interactions) and reachability (better able to track each other down).[69] These mechanisms reduce monitoring costs.[70] Another channel by which ethnicity facilitates cooperation is through norms of reciprocity that are upheld through social sanctioning (i.e. if one betrays or cheats another member of the group, they will be shunned or otherwise punished by other members of the group).[71] Further lowering the costs of monitoring is the spatial concentration of ethnic groups.

Thus, from a sociological perspective, the salience of ethnicity is a function of how its attributes facilitate cooperation in a political environment in which the risk of exploitation is high and formal organizations are weak.[72] Yet other social identities with similar attributes, such as religion or ideology, could perform similarly, if not quite as effectively. Why has ethnic identity served as a primary basis of political organization and coordination in many African states? A number of scholars point to the incentive structures that arose from colonial institutions that exploited indigenous authority structures—the "customary"—to facilitate and reduce the costs of foreign domination.[73] More precisely, Posner demonstrates that it was the institutions of native authorities, in

[67] Andrew H. Kydd, *Trust and Mistrust in International Relations* (Princeton, NJ: Princeton University Press, 2005), p. 9.
[68] Fearon and Laitin, "Explaining Interethnic Cooperation," p. 718.
[69] See Table 1.1 in Habyarimana et al., *Coethnicity*, p. 7.
[70] Fearon and Laitin, "Explaining Interethnic Cooperation."
[71] Habyarimana et al., *Coethnicity*, p. 7.
[72] On how ethnicity, especially dense social networks and shared norms, foster cooperation, see Habyarimana et al., *Coethnicity*.
[73] Mamdani, *Citizen and Subject*.

which tribal leaders were granted discretionary control of a number of important resources (e.g., loans from the treasury, allocation of land, levies and fees, criminal punishments, licenses) "that generated the impetus for rural Africans to embrace and invest in their identification with their tribal groups."[74] Thus, upon independence, ethnic institutions were much stronger than other coordinating mechanisms, such as political parties, and became the basis of political competition, crowding out other institutions.[75] Ethnicity's efficiency as a vehicle for political mobilization (due to its dense social networks and norms of reciprocity) ensured that it remained the institutional backbone of politics in postcolonial Africa, though consistent with the constructivist view it is not inevitable that ethnicity will always serve as the basis of trust and cooperation.[76]

2.5.3 Dense Political Networks and Societal Control

The sociological foundations of ethnic networks help to account for the coethnic peace in Africa. If rulers rely on coethnics because shared ethnicity facilitates monitoring and reciprocity,[77] we would expect rulers to have better societal control and support among their coethnics than other societal groups. Kasara provides compelling evidence to support this claim. She finds that African rulers tend to impose higher taxes on agricultural crops grown in their home areas than those located in other parts of the country. She attributes this to the tighter political control rulers have in their ethnic homelands, as they are "better able to select and monitor influential local allies at home than they are abroad."[78] This makes it more difficult for the farmers to evade the long arm of the regime when it comes to paying high taxes and, as I argue in this book, in launching an antigovernment insurgency.

Patron–client networks, while highly unequal, are not completely exploitative, however. They also include a strong degree of reciprocity in which patrons provide patronage and protection and clients offer political support in the form of taxes, votes, or violent mobilization. Rothchild

---

[74] Posner, *Institutions and Ethnic Politics in Africa*.
[75] Horowitz, *Ethnic Groups in Conflict*. Bates, "Modernization, Ethnic Competition."
[76] James Habyarimana, Macartan Humphreys, Daniel N. Posner, and Jeremy M. Weinstein, "Is Ethnic Conflict Inevitable? Parting Ways over Nationalism and Separatism," *Foreign Affairs*, 87 (4) (2008): 138.
[77] Habyarimana et al., *Coethnicity*.
[78] Kimuli Kasara, "Tax Me If You Can: Ethnic Geography, Democracy, and the Taxation of Agriculture in Africa," *American Political Science Review*, 101 (1) (2007): 159–172.

refers to this as a "two-directional flow of demands and responses."[79] Without such internal responsiveness, clientelism risks breaking down.[80] Moreover, social norms also operate on rulers who feel intense social pressure to advantage their coethnics.[81]

Thus, while coethnics of the ruler may endure higher taxes and tighter political control, they also receive more benefits. A number of studies have leveraged advances in geospatial methods to systematically demonstrate the distributional effects of coethnicity. In Kenya, coethnics of the president have benefited from better roads.[82] Hodler and Raschky find that a ruler's home sub-region tends to have higher levels of electrification (measured from night-time lights picked up by satellites) than other parts of the country. Importantly, this ethnoregional favoritism is by no means an African phenomenon, but they do show that ethnic ties to the ruler tend to matter more in countries with weak political institutions and with poorly educated citizens. One telling example Hodler and Raschky draw upon is from Zaire in which Mobutu Sese Seko's reign in power can be tracked by the electrification of Gbadolite, the former president's hometown. Even up until the last days of Mobutu's time in office, when the country was bankrupted and the state's formal institutions virtually collapsed, the lights still shone bright in Mobutu's hometown. Within two years of Mobutu's loss of power, however, the lights in Gbadolite were noticeably dimmer. Within ten years, they were practically undetectable.[83]

Franck and Rainer show that coethnics also tend to benefit from better health and education services and have significantly lower levels of infant mortality and higher levels of primary school attendance, completion, and literacy.[84] What is striking about their results is that the effect of coethnic favoritism is not diluted by distance from the capital. "If anything," Franck

---

[79] Rothchild, "Hegemonial Exchange," p. 86.

[80] Christopher Clapham, "The Politics of Failure: Clientelism, Political Instability, and National Integration in Liberia and Sierra Leone," in Christopher Clapham, ed., *Private Patronage and Public Power: Political Clientelism in the Modern State* (New York: St. Martin's Press, 1982), pp. 76–92.

[81] Michela Wrong, *It's Our Turn to Eat: The Story of a Kenyan Whistle-Blower* (New York: Harper, 2009).

[82] Robin Burgess, Remi Jedwab, Edward Miguel, Ameet Morjaria, and Gerard Padró i Miquel, "The Value of Democracy: Evidence from Road Building in Kenya," *American Economic Review*, 105 (6) (2015): 1817–1851.

[83] Roland Hodler and Paul A. Raschky, "Regional Favoritism," *The Quarterly Journal of Economics*, 129 (2) (2014): 995–1033.

[84] Raphaël Franck and Ilia Rainer, "Does the Leader's Ethnicity Matter? Ethnic Favoritism, Education, and Health in Sub-Saharan Africa," *American Political Science Review*, 106 (2) (2012): 294–325.

and Rainer note, "larger distance between the capital and the ethnic groups in power is associated with *greater* ability of the leaders to improve the rates of primary school completion of their ethnic groups."[85] This finding supports the importance of a meso-level approach. Unfavorable structural conditions can be overcome via the informal institutional networks rulers build to penetrate society and distribute resources.

2.5.4 The Interethnic Peace?

While dense networks, strong norms of reciprocity, and spatial clustering among coethnics facilitate *intra-group* cooperation, the problem is they potentially serve as barriers to *inter-group* cooperation. Excluded from rival ethnic groups' dense social ties, rulers are not able to directly leverage the technology mechanisms of shared language, reachability, and periodicity and thus face much higher monitoring costs of non-coethnics.[86] This makes it more difficult not only to collect taxes and produce public goods,[87] but also to effectively accommodate and repress potential dissidents.[88] Mistrust due to the lack of norms of reciprocity may also make non-coethnics reluctant to share information or cooperate with the ruler, especially if they perceive it will harm members of their own group.[89]

To overcome these barriers and extend their authority beyond their own ethnic groups thus requires alliances with powerful elites embedded in different ethnic networks. As already noted, in turning to ethnic clientelism to govern their states, African rulers essentially embraced the institutional solution perfected by their European colonizers.[90] But during colonialism ethnic clientelism often took the form of indirect rule in which European administrators monopolized the central government

---

[85] Franck and Rainer, "Does the Leader's Ethnicity Matter?"
[86] Habyarimana et al., *Coethnicity*. Fearon and Laitin, "Explaining Interethnic Cooperation."
[87] William Easterly and Ross Levine, "Africa's Growth Tragedy: Policies and Ethnic Divisions," *Quarterly Journal of Economics*, 112 (4) (1997): 1203–1250. Edward Miguel, "Tribe or Nation? Nation Building and Public Goods in Kenya versus Tanzania," *World Politics*, 56 (3) (2004): 328–362. James Habyarimana, Macartan Humphreys, Daniel N. Posner, and Jeremy M. Weinstein, "Why Does Ethnic Diversity Undermine Public Goods Provision?" *American Political Science Review*, 101 (4) (2007): 709–725.
[88] Lyall, "Are Coethnics More Effective Counterinsurgents?"
[89] Nathan Nunn, and Leonard Wantchekon. "The Slave Trade and the Origins of Mistrust in Africa," *The American Economic Review*, 101 (7) (2011): 3221–3252.
[90] Crawford Young, *The African Colonial State in Comparative Perspective* (New Haven, Conn.: Yale University Press, 1994). William Reno, *Corruption and State Politics in Sierra*

and only delegated local control and authority to indigenous intermediaries.[91] After independence and the opening up of the political center,
ethnic elites and their supporters rejected indirect rule as an insufficient
form of political representation; instead they demanded privileged access
to the highest levels of the central government. Thus, in order to win the
support of power brokers embedded in different ethnic networks, rulers
had to incorporate them into the dominant coalition to assure them of
their "access to a share of the public resources controlled by the state."[92]
By giving rivals a stake in their regimes, rulers seek to gain allies and
reduce the relative benefits their rivals gain from trying to capture state
power on their own.

A number of Africanist scholars have attributed this system of ethnic
powersharing as a key source of peace in Africa's weak states. Donald
Rothchild has been one of the strongest proponents of this thesis.[93] He
cites the examples of Jomo Kenyatta of Kenya and Félix Houphouët-
Boigny of Côte d'Ivoire as African rulers who were "careful to consolidate their rule through practices of ethnic inclusion and hegemonic
exchange."[94] Azam advances a similar hypothesis drawing on similar cases; he argues that interethnic networks offer a vehicle to credibly redistribute resources to different ethnic groups, whereas violent
insurgency is likely "when the elite from one or several ethnic groups
is excluded from sharing the state bounty."[95] He too cites the regime
of Houphouët-Boigny as a paradigmatic example of societal peace
achieved through ethnic federation.[96] (Whereas, tragically, one could
cite the post-Houphouët-Boigny regimes as examples of the violent consequences when ethnic powersharing breaks down.[97]) Finally, Englebert
and Ron attribute the end of the 1997 civil war in Congo-Brazzaville
to the "patrimonial peace" Denis Sassou-Nguesso secured by co-opting

---

Leone (Cambridge: Cambridge University Press, 1995). Berman, "Ethnicity, Patronage
and the African State."

[91] Mamdani, *Citizen and Subject.* Chazan et al., *Politics and Society in Contemporary Africa.*

[92] Chazan et al., *Politics and Society in Contemporary Africa,* p. 113. See also Rothchild,
"Hegemonial Exchange."

[93] Rothchild, "State-Ethnic Relations in Middle Africa." Rothchild, "Hegemonial
Exchange." Rothchild and Foley, "African States." Rothchild, "Ethnic Bargaining and
State Breakdown in Africa." Rothchild, *Managing Ethnic Conflict in Africa.* See also
Azam, "The Redistributive State."

[94] Chazan et al., *Politics and Society in Contemporary Africa,* p. 116.

[95] North et al., *Violence and Social Orders,* p. 36.

[96] Azam, "The Redistributive State," p. 439.

[97] Arnim Langer, "Horizontal Inequalities and Violent Group Mobilization in Côte
d'Ivoire," *Oxford Development Studies,* 33 (1) (2005): 25–45.

elites from various ethnoregional militias into the government and public sector.[98]

The contributions of this qualitative literature on the pacifying effects of elite accommodation was largely marginal to the civil war research program as the latter experienced a resurgence in the early 2000s with the publication of seminal articles by Collier and Hoeffler and Fearon and Laitin. This has changed quite significantly since the late 2000s, however. Elevating ethnic politics and powersharing to the center of the study of civil war has been the introduction of the EPR dataset built by Wimmer et al. that I discuss extensively in Chapter 8.[99] Employing expert analysis of 100 scholars of ethnic politics to assess the distribution of central state power across different ethnic groups for countries in which ethnicity is (or was) politically salient since World War II,[100] the EPR dataset has allowed for some of the first systematic evidence to test Rothchild's thesis of hegemonial exchange. One of the seminal contributions made by Wimmer et al. was to show that, controlling for underlying structural factors, civil war is more likely in states that exclude politically relevant groups from the central government. They put forth a grievance-based argument, suggesting that excluded groups, who resent their loss of prestige and material benefits, seek to reverse their loss of power through armed violence.[101] But the robust association between ethnopolitical exclusion and civil war is also consistent with the political networks hypothesis raised in this chapter: the exclusion of politically relevant ethnic groups from the central government weakens the density of the regime's political networks with these groups and increases the feasibility of rebellion by the excluded group, while weakening the government's counterinsurgency capabilities.

Figure 2.2 illustrates schematically how ethnopolitical exclusion weakens the government's societal control and increases the risk of armed rebellion. With VS_2 removed from the dominant coalition, the ruler not only risks losing the support of his former ruling partner but also faces

---

[98] Pierre Englebert, and James Ron, "Primary Commodities and War: Congo-Brazzaville's Ambivalent Resource Curse," *Comparative Politics*, 37 (1) (2004): 61–81.

[99] Wimmer et al., "Ethnic Politics and Armed Conflict." Cederman et al., "Why Do Ethnic Groups Rebel?" Since then two different versions of the EPR dataset have been developed: EPR 3.0, maintained by Wimmer, and EPR-ETH, maintained by Cederman.

[100] It only covers countries and time periods within countries "in which political objectives, alliances or disputes" are "framed in ethnic terms," thus "avoiding an ethnic lens for countries not characterized by ethnic politics, such as Tanzania and Korea." Wimmer et al., "Ethnic Politics and Armed Conflict," p. 325.

[101] Cederman et al., "Why Do Ethnic Groups Rebel?"

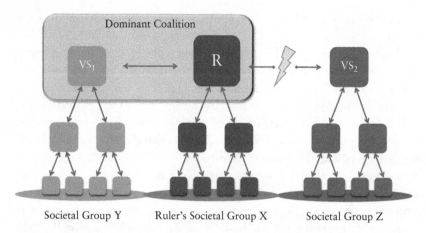

Societal Group Y   Ruler's Societal Group X   Societal Group Z

R=Ruler
VS=Violence Specialist

FIGURE 2.2 Schematic of Ethnopolitical Exclusion in Weak States

much higher costs of extracting information and cultivating support from societal group Z, increasing the risk of armed rebellion and hindering the government's capacity to effectively counter any rebellion that arises.

2.5.5 Interethnic Political Networks and Counterinsurgency Effectiveness

This meso-level argument that the structure of a regime's ethnopolitical networks affects civil war risk aligns well with several important microlevel studies on counterinsurgency. Drawing on the work of Kalyvas and Habyarimana et al., Lyall hypothesizes that interethnic alliances are crucial for the efficacy of counterinsurgency because they enable the regime to tap into local ethnic networks and thus help "attenuate the 'identification problem'[102] that all counterinsurgents confront, namely how to identify the insurgents who hide among the broader civilian population."[103] Coethnics' "reachability"[104] advantage facilitates cooperation from the local population as "they can muster a more credible deterrent threat because they can more precisely calibrate their coercion (or rewards) to specific individuals."[105]

---

[102] Kalyvas, *The Logic of Violence in Civil War*, pp. 89–91.
[103] Lyall, "Are Coethnics More Effective Counterinsurgents?" p. 15.
[104] Habyarimana et al., *Coethnicity*.
[105] Lyall, "Are Coethnics More Effective Counterinsurgents?" p. 16.

One implication of Lyall's analysis and consistent with Kalyvas's theory of selective violence[106] is that regimes that lack strong interethnic political networks, and that thus face major informational problems in identifying insurgents and their supporters, should tend to fall back on indiscriminate violence to contain armed mobilization by excluded ethnopolitical groups. There is no shortage of such examples from the government of Sudan's campaigns of mass killing in South Sudan, the Nuba Mountains, and Darfur, to Hissène Habré's collective targeting of the Zaghawa in eastern Chad, to the Rwandan genocide. Stephen Ellis also demonstrates that Liberia under the rule of Samuel Doe serves as a paradigmatic case. Ellis argues that Doe was the "first Liberian head of state since the conquest of the hinterland who excluded certain social groups entirely from political society, most notably the Gio and Mano of Nimba County."[107] Consequently, when an armed insurgency erupted in Nimba County in late 1989 from these very groups, the government received almost no local support and found it impossible to "distinguish . . . guerrillas among a generally hostile population."[108] Instead, according to Bill Berkeley, Doe's troops, almost entirely from the president's own ethnic group, the Krahn, "[killed] with abandon, raping, looting and burning villages, driving tens of thousands of Gios and Manos into the bush."[109]

---

[106] Drawing on extensive evidence from across a number of different civil wars, Kalyvas posits that counterinsurgency effectiveness is a function of the government's ability to produce selective violence—that is, to individually, rather than collectively, target dissidents. As Kalyvas argues, and Mason and Krane before him, selective violence is an effective countermobilization strategy because in meting out sanctioning based on active dissidence it creates an incentive structure for individuals to refrain from rebelling and to cooperate with the state. On the other hand, indiscriminate violence has the opposite effect: collective targeting drives individuals to support the rebels "because nonelites can no longer assure themselves of immunity from repression by simply remaining inert." Mason and Krane, "The Political Economy of Death Squads," p. 176. Facing a high risk of state repression whether they join the rebellion or not, civilians are more likely to support the rebels in exchange for protection from indiscriminate violence by the state. The production of selective violence is "heavily dependent on the quality of information available—one cannot discriminate without the information to discriminate—which itself is heavily dependent on the nature of the sovereignty exercised. Information requires collaboration." Kalyvas, *The Logic of Violence in Civil War*, p. 145.

[107] Ellis, *The Mask of Anarchy*, p. 65.

[108] Ellis, *The Mask of Anarchy*, p. 78.

[109] Bill Berkeley, *The Graves Are Not Yet Full: Race, Tribe and Power in the Heart of Africa* (New York: Basic Books, 2003), p. 48.

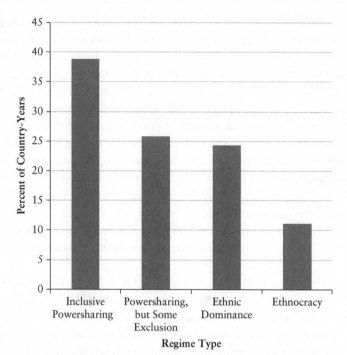

FIGURE 2.3 Modal Regime Types in Postcolonial Africa, Independence to 2005

2.6 CONCLUSION

A meso-level approach to civil war in weak states emphasizes the mediating effects interethnic political networks have on the regime's societal control and ability to effectively prevent and contain armed rebellions. If this is true, we should see evidence that rulers in ethnically divided weak states turn to ethnic powersharing to reduce the risk of large-scale political violence, as Rothchild and others note has occurred in postcolonial Africa.

As illustrated in Figure 2.3, the modal regime type in postcolonial Africa is what I conceive of as ethnic powersharing, in which no politically relevant ethnic group is excluded from the central government. (See Appendix 2 for description of different regime types.) François, Rainer, and Trebbi provide additional evidence to support this claim. They code the ethnicity of the cabinet ministers in fifteen African countries and illustrate the degree to which the ethnic composition of cabinets reflects the distribution of ethnic groups in the country.[110] As they summarize,

---

[110] François et al., "How Is Power Shared in Africa?"

"The data reject strongly the view of African autocracies as being run as 'one man shows' by a single leader and his ethnic group . . . and display instead a positive and highly statistically significant degree of proportionality to group size, suggesting a substantial degree of political bargaining occurring within these polities."[111]

The puzzle that arises from the political networks hypothesis, however, is if ethnic powersharing is so critical for societal peace and the prevention of large-scale political violence in Africa, why do rulers choose strategies of ethnic exclusion? As seen in Figure 2.3, despite the prevalence of ethnic powersharing, ethnocracies and ethnically exclusive regimes still exist. Why, if it increases the risk of civil war? In the next chapter I address this question with the goal of better understanding the logic of ethnopolitical exclusion.

---

[111] François et al., "How Is Power Shared in Africa?," pp. 18–19.

3

Theories of Ethnopolitical Exclusion

3.1 INTRODUCTION

In Africa's weak states, societal peace is contingent upon the alliances that rulers strike with power brokers embedded in different ethnic groups. Interethnic networks are critical for the regime's ability to overcome the barriers it faces to mobilizing support and collecting information from outside of its own ethnic group. If such interethnic alliances are instrumental to extending the control of the regime and keeping peace, what accounts for the phenomenon of ethnopolitical exclusion, in which rulers intentionally bar or refuse to appoint members of a given ethnic group to positions of political power at the risk of not only alienating them but also forfeiting the regime's control over them? This chapter surveys different theoretical frameworks that may help to account for this puzzle. As summarized in Table 3.1, it distinguishes between three different logics of ethnopolitical exclusion: exclusion because it is possible, appropriate, or necessary.[1]

Exclusion because it is possible, or what I also refer to as *instrumental exclusion,* conceives of rulers as wealth- and power-maximizers who, in a bid to keep economic rents and political power concentrated in their hands, build the smallest winning coalition necessary (i.e. forge the fewest interethnic alliances they have to) to maintain societal peace. Put another way, rulers exclude as much as they can get away with. Political violence breaks

---

[1] The categories "Exclusion because it is necessary" and "Exclusion because it is possible" are drawn from Julian Wucherpfennig, Philipp Hunizker, and Lars-Erik Cederman, "Who Inherits the State? Colonial Rule and Post-Colonial Conflict," Paper presented at Annual Meeting of the American Political Science Association, New Orleans, 2012. An updated version of their paper was published as: Julian Wucherpfennig, Philipp Hunziker, and Lars-Erik Cederman, "Who Inherits the State? Colonial Rule and Postcolonial Conflict," *American Journal of Political Science,* (60)(4) 2016: 882–898.

TABLE 3.1 *Logics of Ethnopolitical Exclusion*

Exclusion because it is possible (instrumental exclusion)	Exclusion because it is appropriate (ethnonational exclusion)	Exclusion because it is necessary (strategic exclusion)
Exclusion is a tool to maximize control of rents and political power.	Exclusion is a means to credibly signal the ruler is committed to taking care of his own.	Exclusion is a tool to insulate the ruler's hold on power and coup-proof his regime.
Conflict arises when rulers miscalculate how much exclusion they can get away with.	Conflict arises when rival ethnonationalist groups reject the dominant group's political legitimacy.	Conflict arises when rivals, blocked from the central government, resort to armed rebellion to try to capture state power.

out when the ruler miscalculates the mobilization capabilities of a given group and the costs of excluding its members from the central government.

Exclusion because it is appropriate, or *ethnonational exclusion*, focuses on how cultural beliefs and ideologies structure political alliances. Rulers are conceived to be not only power- and wealth-maximizers but also ethnonationalists. Thus, they choose political strategies that they feel are most culturally appropriate or legitimate, which may affect one's acceptance of the costs of violence (e.g., violent conflict is justified as the necessary price to pay for self-rule).

Exclusion because it is necessary, or *strategic exclusion*, focuses on the strategic underpinnings of ethnopolitical exclusion. Rulers seek to forge interethnic alliances to secure peace, but not if it threatens to undo their hold on power. Powersharing poses two key strategic threats to the ruler's political survival. The first is that, in parceling out the state to other ethnic groups, the ruler potentially alienates his own supporters, who worry that powersharing will eat into their share of rents and power. The second fear is that sharing power with members of other ethnic groups will lower the costs they face to capturing sovereign power for themselves. This fear that powersharing will result in a sudden shift in the distribution of power in favor of ethnic rivals exacerbates the anxiety of the ruler's coethnics and intensifies the first strategic problem. According to this strategic framework, ethnopolitical exclusion is a strategy to mitigate coup risk and preserve the ruler's (and his coethnics') hold on power.

Each of these theoretical frameworks helps to account for patterns of ethnopolitical exclusion in sub-Saharan Africa after independence. But, compared to economic and cultural theories, I argue the strategic logic is a more powerful driver of *ethnopolitical exclusion that leads to large-scale political violence* for two key reasons.

First, in contrast to instrumental exclusion, strategic exclusion is generally not self-correcting. In instrumentalist models, the outbreak of violence reflects the ruler has miscalculated the level of exclusion he can get away with and is predicted to adjust his strategy accordingly to avoid a costly conflict. In strategic models, the outbreak of violence has the opposite effect. Rather than disconfirming the logic of exclusion, it reinforces the ruler's prevailing assessment that the rival group is intent on seizing power at any cost and it is too risky to grant them access to the central government. The ruler doubles down on exclusion, calculating it is preferable to face his rivals from outside his government than from within,[2] and the war continues.

The limitation of ethnonational theories of political exclusion is that they tend to discount the powerful nationalist pressures that rulers in the post-independence period have felt. Rulers in post-independence Africa have faced the challenge of being both the ethnic "Big Man"—the equivalent of the tribal chief who sits atop of but is also embedded in a social group[3]—and the "father of the nation," who represents all of the country's ethnic groups.[4] These dual pressures manifest themselves in the form of a two-level game in which the ruler is simultaneously bargaining with his coethnics and members of rival ethnic groups. Cultural theories contend that rulers are unable to manage this two-level game because nationalist and ethnonationalist bases of legitimacy are contradictory. Ethnic inclusion weakens the ruler's credentials as an ethnonationalist and vice versa. While competing cultural pressures are important, it is difficult to isolate their effects from the severe strategic constraints rulers are under from their coethnics and their coethnics' strategic concerns about rival ethnic groups. It is because this cultural pressure is backed up by the credible threat of a coup d'état that makes this two-level game so pernicious for African rulers. The upshot of this is that those ethnocracies that have emerged in postcolonial Africa, such as in Burundi, Rwanda, and Sudan,

---

[2] In Chapter 10, I posit the exception to this is when both the ruling group and the opposition group possess strong threat capabilities. This only prevails, however, in 34 percent of all dyads.

[3] Utas, *African Conflicts and Informal Power*.

[4] Michael G. Schatzberg, *Political Legitimacy in Middle Africa: Father, Family, Food* (Bloomington, Ind.: Indiana University Press, 2001).

are as much a function of the ruler's policies to manage strategic threats as they are rooted in an ideology of ethnonationalism.

In the rest of this chapter, I explore these different theoretical frameworks and their relevance in accounting for ethnopolitical exclusion in postcolonial Africa. First, however, I clearly define the concept of ethnopolitical exclusion.

3.2 WHAT IS ETHNOPOLITICAL EXCLUSION?

Political exclusion entails the barring or intentional non-appointment of representatives of a subset of the population from the central government. Exclusion is a universal feature of politics, occurring in both autocracies and democracies. For example, in the US political system, there is almost perfect exclusion of members of the political opposition from the president's cabinet, leading to the incumbent party's monopoly on executive policy-making.[5] Yet exclusion in the United States and other democracies does not have the same destabilizing effects as in weak, authoritarian regimes because of key institutional, legal, and economic safeguards that protect the excluded groups and the strength of the state's formal institutional capacity, which ensures that social peace is not threatened by political competition and change.

In democracies, regular elections ensure that the opposition has a free and fair opportunity to reverse the exclusion. Moreover, checks and balances prevent the incumbent party from exploiting its political dominance to adopt policies that would violate the constitutional rights of the excluded groups. Just as importantly, the state bureaucracy, which is responsible for carrying out basic functions of the state, such as the provision of key public goods, is apolitical and is required to treat all citizens as equal before the law. Consequently, one's access to basic public goods, such as rule of law, security or education, does not change after an alternation of power.[6] Finally, even though one may be excluded politically from the central government, inclusive economic institutions, such as open markets and secure property rights, ensure that a person's political affiliation does not infringe upon their economic opportunities.[7]

---

[5] Robert Farley, "Three Cabinet Appointees from Opposing Party is Unmatched," Politifact. com, February 10, 2009. Available at www.politifact.com/truth-o-meter/statements/2009/feb/10/barack-obama/Three-Republicans-Cabinet-Most (accessed August 22, 2016).

[6] Bruce Bueno de Mesquita, James D. Morrow, Randolph M. Siverson, and Alastair Smith, *The Logic of Political Survival* (Cambridge, Mass.: MIT Press, 2003).

[7] Daron Acemoglu and James A. Robinson, *Why Nations Fail: The Origins of Power, Prosperity and Poverty* (New York: Crown Publishers, 2012).

In weak, authoritarian regimes, such as those that have dominated African states since independence, the situation is very different. The same protections and rights are not offered to excluded groups.[8] Members of the opposition are often denied basic human liberties: right to life, freedom from torture, freedom of speech, and freedom of movement. Public goods tend to be severely underprovided, and those services that are offered are selectively allocated to pro-regime groups. For example, Human Rights Watch documented how in Ethiopia in 2010, the ruling Ethiopian People's Revolutionary Democratic Front (EPRDF) systematically withheld services such as agricultural inputs, micro-credit, and job opportunities from those in the political opposition.[9] With formal opportunities to reverse their exclusion nonexistent or severely compromised, members of the opposition face the daunting prospects of perpetual political marginalization and limited economic opportunities given the lack of inclusive economic institutions. To the excluded groups, the use of force is seen as one of the few ways to capture a share of power and protect their members' basic rights.

As discussed at length in Chapter 2, the problem for regimes in weak states is that exclusion is a two-way street. While it makes life miserable for the opposition, thus encouraging its members to defect to the ruling party and weakening their mobilizational capabilities if they choose to resist, it also increases the costs of political control of excluded groups. Denied access to basic political rights and economic resources, members of the excluded group are less likely to voluntarily pay taxes, provide information, or otherwise offer their political support to the central government. Moreover, exclusion weakens the ruler's political and personal ties with powerful elites embedded in these groups who could help to mobilize the group's members to support the central government. When these groups are geographically concentrated, exclusion also weakens the regime's territorial control. Overall, then, political exclusion in weak states can be doubly destabilizing: it often provokes resistance to the regime while compromising the regime's capabilities to effectively control this resistance.

Given the ethnic bases of politics in Africa, in this book I focus on ethnopolitical exclusion—the intentional non-appointment of members of a given ethnic group from positions of "real political power" (i.e. those who

---

[8] A survey of Human Rights Watch's reporting since its founding in 1978 makes this point very powerfully. For example, see its reports: *Behind the Red Line: Political Repression in Sudan* (New York: Human Rights Watch, 1996); *Bashing Dissent: Escalating Violence and State Repression in Zimbabwe* (New York: Human Rights Watch, 2007); *"One Hundred Ways of Putting Pressure": Violations of Freedom of Expression and Association in Ethiopia* (New York: Human Rights Watch, 2010).

[9] Human Rights Watch, *"One Hundred Ways of Putting Pressure."*

control key levers of state power, such as the military, security, and the flow of economic rents). I focus on these positions of "real political power" because in weak states power does not emanate from legal or constitutional authority but from an individual's ability to mobilize resources and the use of force.[10] Because control of rents and use of coercion are integral for violence specialists to be able to offer patronage and protection to their followers and keep their political networks intact, elites excluded from real political power and only offered nominal positions within the government will not be able to build as large political networks. Again, this marginalization is a double-edged sword for the ruler; it weakens his rival's mobilization capabilities but at the cost of weakening the regime's control of the societal group from which the rival comes.

Let us now turn to different theories that account for why rulers would exclude members of rival ethnic groups from their regimes.

TEXTBOX 3.1 A NOTE ON ETHNIC "GROUPS" AS
THE UNIT OF ANALYSIS

Throughout this chapter and book, I use the label "ethnic groups" as stylistic shorthand *for individuals who identify as and are identified as members of the same ethnic group.* This label also represents substantive shorthand for the dynamic process of collective mobilization among individuals with shared ethnic descent. (Thus, for example, ethnic bargaining presumes that members of a given group are able to collectively organize among themselves in order to bargain with members of another ethnic group over scarce resources.) There is nothing given about this collective mobilization. Nor does it imply that members of groups always have common preferences or that group boundaries are fixed.[a] Nonetheless, following from a large literature in political science, including, most recently, the insightful work of Habyarimana et al., there are strong theoretical and empirical grounds to privilege the importance of collective mobilization along ethnic lines in countries in which ethnicity is politically salient, given ethnicity's dense and durable social connections and strong norms of reciprocity relative to other social identities and institutions in many African countries.[b]

[a] Chandra, "Cumulative Findings in the Study of Ethnic Politics." Kanchan Chandra, "What Is Ethnic Identity and Does It Matter?," Annual Review of Political Science, 9 (1) (2006): 397–424.
[b] Posner, *Institutions and Ethnic Politics in Africa.* James Habyarimana, Macartan Humphreys, Daniel N. Posner, and Jeremy M. Weinstein, "Coethnicity and Trust," in Karen S. Cook, Margaret Levi, and Russell Hardin, eds., *Whom Can We Trust? How Groups, Networks, and Institutions Make Trust Possible* (New York: Russell Sage Foundation, 2009), pp. 42–64.

---

[10] Reno, *Warlord Politics and African States.*

3.3 INSTRUMENTAL THEORIES OF ETHNOPOLITICAL EXCLUSION

3.3.1 The Limitations of Basic Economic Models of Ethnic Rule

One obvious starting point in thinking through the sources of ethnopolitical exclusion is the economic logic of such a strategy. As explained in Chapter 2, order in weak states arises from the manipulation of the economy to generate rents that are then only shared among members of the dominant coalition.[11] Because rents are private goods, such that one's consumption reduces the amount others can consume, members of the ruling coalition have an incentive to maintain a small dominant coalition to maximize not only their wealth but also their power (since the more wealth in the ruler's hands, the more dependent society is upon him for resources).[12]

Building from this basic insight, scholars have constructed a simple instrumental model of ethnic rule: rulers favor their coethnics because their ethnic groups serve as a "form of a minimum winning coalition, large enough to secure benefits in the competition for spoils but also small enough to maximize the per capita value of these benefits."[13] Ethnicity is superior to potential other sources of mobilization, such as ideology or political party, because its ascriptive quality, in which one's ethnicity cannot be easily chosen or changed by individuals, makes it hard for those outside the winning coalition to "switch" their identity to gain access to state spoils.[14] As Caselli and Coleman write, "Ethnicity provides a technology for group membership and exclusion which is used to avoid indiscriminate access to the spoils of conflict. Without such a technology groups become porous and the spoils of conflict are dissipated."[15]

It is without a doubt that competition over scarce state resources has been a key source of ethnopolitical exclusion in postcolonial Africa. From the Apartheid government in South Africa to the Arabist regimes in Sudan to the Hutu and Tutsi ethnocracies in Rwanda and Burundi,

---

[11] Acemoglu and Robinson, *Why Nations Fail*. North et al., *Violence and Social Orders*.
[12] Bueno de Mesquita et al., *The Logic of Political Survival*.
[13] Bates, "Modernization, Ethnic Competition."
[14] James D. Fearon, "Why Ethnic Politics and 'Pork' Tend to Go Together," in *mimeo* (Stanford University, 1999). See also Francesco Caselli and Wilbur John Coleman, "On the Theory of Ethnic Conflict," *Journal of the European Economic Association*, 11 (s1) (2013): 161–192.
[15] Caselli and Coleman, "On the Theory of Ethnic Conflict," p. 188.

respectively, each was sustained by members of the ruling elite who feared that political reform and ethnic inclusion would eat into their monopoly control of the spoils of the state. Lest we think that such dynamics are anachronistic in contemporary Africa, Michela Wrong's exposé of tribal rule in Kenya as a means to maximize rents for the ruling group strongly suggests otherwise.[16] Members of the so-called "Kikuyu mafia" parlayed their dominance of the shadow state under Mwai Kibaki in order to personally enrich themselves through the Anglo-Leasing procurement scandal. By keeping the shadow state exclusive to those groups from Central Province, they prevented other groups from diluting the spoils that came with controlling the State House.[17]

The limitation of simple instrumental models, however, is that they fail to take into account the costs of ethnopolitical exclusion. While rulers seek to maximize spoils, they prefer to do so "without precipitating a reaction (such as violent protest or rebellion) from the ethnic group that would be even more costly to suppress."[18] If exclusion provokes large-scale violence, such a strategy may actually make the regime worse off, in terms of the amount of rents available to the ruling coalition, because of the costs they now have to divert to putting down armed rebellion.[19] As the elites realize this (either prospectively or retrospectively), they should sue for peace, and ethnic inclusion will be maintained or restored. Again, the Kenya case is illustrative here: within weeks of the violence breaking out after the disputed 2007 election, a powersharing agreement was signed between Mwai Kibaki and his opponent, Raila Odinga.

3.3.2 A Dynamic Economic Model of Ethnic Rule

This suggests a more dynamic instrumental model of ethnic rule that takes into account "the logic of anticipated responses" is necessary.[20] A dynamic instrumental model still predicts that rulers will seek to build minimum winning coalitions and exploit ethnic exclusion to maximize rents but will do so more strategically. In Fearon's felicitous phrase, rulers "calibrate the

---

[16] Wrong, *It's Our Turn to Eat*.

[17] Wrong, *It's Our Turn to Eat*.

[18] Rupen Cetinyan, "Ethnic Bargaining in the Shadow of Third-Party Intervention," *International Organization*, 56 (3) (2002), p. 649.

[19] Fearon, "Rationalist Explanations for War." North et al., *Violence and Social Orders*. For an alternative view, see David Keen, *Useful Enemies: When Waging Wars Is More Important Than Winning Them* (New Haven, Conn.: Yale University Press, 2012).

[20] Cetinyan, "Ethnic Bargaining," p. 649.

level of exclusion to what they can get away with."[21] Thus, in contrast to the basic instrumental model which predicts all African regimes will be ethnocracies (a gross contradiction of the empirical record), it expects rulers will build minimum winning coalitions across politically relevant ethnic groups[22] and will still use exclusion depending on the cost of repressing an armed challenge from a given group.

A key implication that follows from a dynamic instrumental model is that rulers should include groups proportionate to their mobilizational capabilities. As Cetinyan argues,

Stronger groups—stronger either because of their independent means or because of those made available through the aid of an outside supporter—should demand, and get, more [from the central government]. Groups whose violent mobilization would prove more disruptive and be more costly to subdue should choose demands for treatment that reflect their relative strength. Commensurate with their superior ability to mobilize, the concessions they receive should be greater than those of their weaker counterparts.[23]

Consistent with this point, Cetinyan shows that ethnopolitical groups with coethnics that control the neighboring state (and thus would have access to powerful external supporters) are less likely to suffer political discrimination.[24] Whereas François et al. find that, in a sample of fifteen African countries, rulers tend to allocate cabinet positions proportionally to population shares across ethnic groups.[25] (Though it is important to note their sample excludes some of Africa's most ethnically dominant regimes.)[26]

Another empirical pattern consistent with the "exclude if you can get away with it" thesis is the fair amount of path dependency between a group's initial access to the central government at independence, which is heavily shaped by colonial policies, and subsequent exclusion from the

---

[21] Fearon, "Governance and Civil War Onset," cited in Wucherpfennig et al., "Who Inherits the State?"
[22] François et al., "How Is Power Shared in Africa?"
[23] Cetinyan, "Ethnic Bargaining," p. 657.
[24] Cetinyan, "Ethnic Bargaining," p. 657.
[25] François et al., "How Is Power Shared in Africa?"
[26] Their data excludes six of Africa's most ethnically dominant regimes according to the EPR dataset: Angola, Burundi, Ethiopia, Rwanda, Sudan, and South Africa. Overall, of the non-island sub-Saharan African countries excluded from their sample, more than 40 percent are ruled by ethnically dominant regimes between independence and 2005 (in which a group is coded by EPR as "monopoly" or "dominant") compared to less than 25 percent of those country-years included in their sample.

central government.[27] According to data from the EPR 1.0 dataset, of the 128 ethnoregional groups to experience some exclusion after independence through 2005, forty-seven of these groups (36 percent) were excluded at the time of independence. Because, as Horowitz and other scholars have noted, a group's access to the central government at independence is largely a function of differential rates of modernization (i.e. access to education, exposure to formal markets, employment in colonial bureaucracy, and urbanization), we would expect those groups excluded at independence to be weaker (i.e. to have lower mobilizational capabilities) than included groups. Subsequent rulers then exploited these groups' weakness to continue to exclude them from the regime.

3.3.3 Endogenizing Mobilizational Capabilities: Exclusion as a Means to Weaken Rival Groups' Capabilities

Rulers know, however, that a given group's mobilizational capabilities are dynamic and that they are particularly sensitive to a group's access to resources. Since the state is the most important source of wealth in weak states, a group's capabilities are to a degree endogenous to access to the central government. Recognizing this, rulers may use exclusion as a means to weaken rival groups' mobilizational capabilities in order to reduce the share of power it will have to offer the group (or a key faction of the group) in the future. In other words, rulers exclude not merely to hoard wealth but as part of a dynamic process to expand their power and exert control over rival groups.[28]

This helps to account for the high levels of volatility seen within Africa's ruling coalitions, in which rulers are constantly co-opting rivals into the regime to win their support but then dismissing them when the ruler calculates they may be getting too powerful.[29] Mobutu Sese Seko, president of former Zaire (now the DRC) from 1965 until 1997, was a master at this "revolving door of politics." As Sandbrook writes:

---

[27] Wucherpfennig et al. convincingly show that in sub-Saharan Africa different approaches to political control between the French and British help to account for variation in access to governments at independence. The British use of indirect rule, which "granted traditional rulers in the periphery substantial autonomy," the authors argue, strengthened the bargaining power of rural elites and led to their systematic incorporation in inaugural governments. In contrast in the absence of indirect rule in French colonies, peripheral groups found it difficult to overcome their political marginalization resulting from remoteness to the center of power. Wucherpfennig et al. "Who Inherits the State?"

[28] I thank Will Reno for raising this insightful point.

[29] Jackson and Rosberg, *Personal Rule in Black Africa*.

No potential challenger is permitted to gain a power base. Mobutu's officials know that their jobs depend solely on the president's discretion. Frequently, he fires cabinet ministers often without explanation. He appoints loyal army officers and other faithfuls as provincial governors, but only to provinces outside their home areas. And he constantly reshuffles and purges his governors and high army command. Everyone is kept off balance. Everyone must vie for his patronage. Mobutu holds all the cards and the game is his.[30]

Mobutu was able to play the game of "revolving door politics" so effectively because of the degree to which he monopolized state resources, and it was only through him that other power brokers could gain access to wealth.[31]

3.3.4 Exclusion with Imperfect Information: A Stylized Model of Civil War against Instrumental Rulers

To review, instrumental models of ethnopolitical exclusion view exclusion as a consequence of the dynamic process of powersharing in weak states in which rulers seek to manipulate access to the state to weaken their rivals' capabilities as they "calibrate" the minimal share of power they have to concede to avoid costly conflict. On its own, however, the instrumental framework cannot get us to civil war. While it captures the essence of political competition in weak states and the volatility and violence inherent to this process, it offers no predictions about whether the ruler is able to build a minimally inclusive regime that would prevent civil war. To predict the outcome of this bargaining process, additional theoretical mechanisms are necessary. One key mechanism is the role that imperfect information plays as the ruler and rival violence specialists bargain over power. Without complete information about the rival's resolve and capabilities, it is difficult for the ruler to calculate the minimal level of powersharing necessary and may lead the ruler to miscalibrate how much exclusion they can get away with because, for example, they may underestimate the rival's mobilizational capabilities and their own ability to counter them.

Rulers of weak states face two potential sources of incomplete information. One is inherent to the bargaining process and arises from the

---

[30] Sandbrook and Barker, *The Politics of Africa's Economic Stagnation*, p. 92. cited in Alex Thomson, *An Introduction to African Politics* (London and New York: Routledge, 2011), p. 120.

[31] For a generalized model of how kleptocrats exploit their monopoly of wealth to divide and conquer the opposition, see Daron Acemoglu, Thierry Verdier, and James A. Robinson, "Kleptocracy and Divide-and-Rule: A Model of Personal Rule," *Journal of the European Economic Association*, 2 (2–3) (2004): 162–192.

asymmetry of information that bargaining partners have—neither knows the other side's true capabilities and the true price one is willing to accept in bargaining. This information asymmetry creates incentives for parties to misrepresent their capabilities to win greater concessions. Because both sides recognize that the other has an incentive to exaggerate their capabilities, they each tend to dismiss the price the other side offers at face value.[32] As they go in circles over the veracity of each other's claims relative to their capabilities, violence may be the only way to credibly determine the real balance of capabilities and for a deal to be reached.

Compounding information asymmetries are the challenges rulers of weak states face in collecting information. As discussed in Chapter 2, rulers of weak states have to rely on their patron–client networks to monitor for threats to their regimes. The problem, however, is those areas where the regime is most in need of information, such as ethnic enclaves excluded from the central government, is where the regime has the least penetration and fewest brokers. To compensate, the ruler may rely on nearby regional contacts or coethnics and other "foreign" agents deployed to monitor the excluded group. However, these outside brokers often are not embedded in the ethnic networks of the excluded group and possess little genuine information about the group's capabilities and demands. Moreover, as these agents tend to come from rival groups, it is not always in their interest to accurately convey information to the central government, particularly if it means it will lead the central government to accommodate the excluded group and reduce the spoils for those already in the regime.

A stylized example may help to illustrate how instrumental exclusion with imperfect information leads to civil war in weak states. A ruler is bargaining with a rival violence specialist over the distribution of power and economic rents. The ruler prefers to buy the rival's loyalty and support for the smallest share of rents he can, while the rival seeks to maximize his share. As they negotiate, the ruler has to calculate the costs of losing the support of this violence specialist and his ethnic network. Private information, however, makes it difficult for the ruler to accurately gauge the rival's mobilizational capabilities because he knows the rival has an incentive to exaggerate his capabilities to maximize his share of rents. Unable to reach an agreement, the rival and his network are barred from the dominant coalition. Bargaining failure poses costs for both the ruler and the rival. The rival loses access to an important source of resources that he needs in order to keep his network intact. The ruler

[32] Fearon, "Rationalist Explanations for War."

loses a key source of local information and support from the societal group where the violence specialist is embedded. Both sides threaten to use violence to inflict costs on the other and shift the balance of capabilities in their favor. The ruler calculates that, barred from the regime, his rival will lose support among his network and a new power broker will emerge from the societal group that he can buy at a cheaper price. But the ruler may underestimate the violence specialist's local support and ability to mobilize an armed rebellion, leading to conflict escalation. The ruler responds with greater levels of repression to put down the rebellion, but, without patron–client networks penetrating the societal group he lacks the local information necessary to produce selective violence, and repression tends to be indiscriminate, leading to full-scale civil war. These civil wars should be self-correcting, however, as the violent conflict reveals the true capabilities of the rival violence specialist, and the ruler and rival are able to agree upon the share of rents the rival should receive.[33]

3.4 CULTURAL THEORIES OF ETHNOPOLITICAL EXCLUSION

The "exclusion where it is possible" model captures a key dynamic of African politics as rulers seek to maximize rents and power while avoiding costly political violence. This requires an incredible amount of skill as rules have to simultaneously negotiate with a number of different power brokers and try to accurately gauge their mobilizational potential. De Waal refers to this as "retail patronage politics," in which a ruler has to "weigh up the price, in money, of a particular individual's loyalty and make him an offer" while calculating how that price will fluctuate in the future.[34] A ruler's longevity hinges on his ability to read this "political marketplace" (no easy task given the information problems he faces) and to "his readiness to ensure that just enough is paid."[35]

The limitation of this instrumental framework, however, is that it accounts poorly for why rulers fail to offer the minimum concessions necessary to secure peace in the face of large-scale political violence, especially once a given rival's true capabilities have been revealed. For example, what accounts for the persistence of violent postcolonial ethnocracies

---

[33] These wars may continue, however, due to factors exogenous to the model, such as the credibility of the concessions the ruler makes to the rival to secure peace. See Walter, *Committing to Peace*. Fearon, "Why Do Some Civil Wars Last So Much Longer than Others?"
[34] De Waal, "Dollarised."
[35] De Waal, "Dollarised."

in, say, Sudan, Rwanda, Burundi, or South Africa? Why do some rulers exclude along ethnic lines in spite of the expectation that this will provoke an armed conflict?

A rival logic of ethnopolitical exclusion in weak states focuses on the cultural bases of political rule. It views rulers not only as power or wealth maximizers but as ethnonationalists, who choose a political strategy that they feel is most culturally appropriate or legitimate. Andreas Wimmer makes this culturalist argument both in his groundbreaking articles with Lars-Erik Cederman and Brian Min,[36] and in his book, *Waves of War*.[37] Wimmer attributes exclusion to the rise and spread of the modern nation-state in low-income countries and the influence of "ethnonational principles of political legitimacy—that is, the state is ruled in the name of an ethnically defined people and rulers should therefore care for 'their own people.'"[38] According to this framework, political competition revolves around who has the right to govern the state. Once one group is ascendant, such as the Afrikaners in South Africa, they then seek to maintain their hold on power and benefit "one's own" at the exclusion of other groups because it is "right" and "just."

Wimmer's culturalist model informs a number of important cases in sub-Saharan Africa, including Sudan. Since independence, Sudan's central government has been dominated by a riverain Arab elite who "embraced an Arab nationalism based on a genealogy that stretched into the Islamic Arab past."[39] This deep-rooted Arabic–Islamic ideology has profoundly shaped the regime's political policies, especially in the way it has engaged the country's non-Arab and non-Muslim populations. As Francis Deng extensively argues, the dominant Arabic–Islamic ideology legitimated exclusionary practices against non-Arabs and non-Muslims as well as justifying the use of violence to put down resistance to their exclusive rule.[40] One prominent example of this is the reframing of the war in the South and Nuba Mountains into a *jihad*, in which pro-government fighters were "elevated to the rank of *mujahideen* (fighters for

---

[36] Wimmer et al., "Ethnic Politics and Armed Conflict." Cederman et al., "Why Do Ethnic Groups Rebel?"
[37] Wimmer, *Waves of War*.
[38] Wimmer et al., "Ethnic Politics and Armed Conflict," p. 321.
[39] Amir H. Idris, "Beyond 'African' and 'Arab' in Sudan," in Francis Mading Deng, ed., *New Sudan in the Making? Essays on a Nation in Painful Search of Itself* (Trenton, NJ: Red Sea Press, 2010), p. 199.
[40] Deng, *War of Visions*.

Allah's cause)" and those who died on the battlefield were "decreed as *Shuhada* (martyrs)."[41]

Ethnonational ideologies have similarly shaped regime policies in other ethnically exclusive regimes such as Rwanda and South Africa, but, on the whole, ethnocracies in Africa have been the exception rather than the rule. Many African rulers have recognized that basing their rule on ethnonationalism is unfeasible in their multicultural states and instead have sought publicly to present themselves as the "father of the nation," representing all of the country's people rather than only their own ethnic group.[42] To back up this claim, rulers such as Leopold Senghor in Senegal, Félix Houphouët-Boigny of Côte d'Ivoire, and Julius Nyerere of Tanzania built inclusive regimes representing most of the country's politically relevant ethnic groups.

This is not to suggest, however, that African rulers have been immune to the very ethnonational pressures Wimmer describes. But it is to argue that more often than not this social and political pressure from coethnics is conveyed privately, given public expectations of national integration. Consequently, most postcolonial rulers in Africa find themselves playing a two-level game. (See Figure 3.1 below.) On one hand, they are seeking publicly to serve all of the country's people and derive legitimacy as the father of the nation. At the same time, the ruler is privately bargaining with members of his own ethnic group, with whom he has strong social and political ties.[43] The Kibaki government in Kenya is illustrative. According to Wrong,

In naming his cabinet, Kibaki had presented himself as a leader of national unity, careful to distribute all but the key ministries across the ethnic spectrum. But in his hour of need, like any sick man, he reached for what was familiar and safe, and that meant sticking with the tribe. The popular press, noticing the trend, soon coined a phrase for this circle, the real power behind the throne. "The Mount Kenya Mafia," it called them, a reference to the mountain that dominates Central Province.[44]

---

[41] Mansour Khalid, *War and Peace in Sudan: A Tale of Two Countries* (London and New York: Routledge, 2003), p. xxviii. For a critical examination of the Islamist government's call for jihad in Nuba Mountains, see Alex de Waal and A. H. Abdel Salam, "Islamism, State Power and *Jihad* in Sudan," in Alex de Waal (ed.), *Islamism and Its Enemies in the Horn of Africa* (Bloomington, Ind.: Indiana University Press, 2004), pp. 71–113.

[42] Schatzberg, *Political Legitimacy in Middle Africa*.

[43] As Habyarimana et al. show, internalized norms of reciprocity within ethnic groups can have powerful effects on individuals to discriminate in favor of their coethnics. Habyarimana et al., *Coethnicity*.

[44] Wrong, *It's Our Turn to Eat*, p. 73.

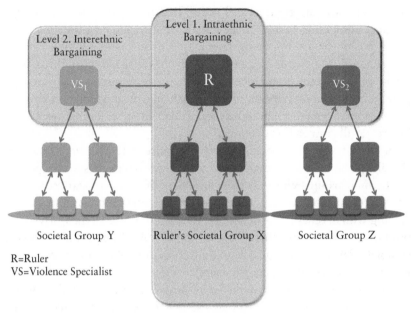

FIGURE 3.1 Ethnic Politics as a Two-Level Game

What emerges out of this two-level game are not ethnocracies but rulers seeking to forge ethnically balanced regimes—accommodating their own coethnics who demand privileged positions within the regime while also striking alliances with power brokers embedded in other ethnic groups. The key puzzle then is why are rulers unable to maintain this ethnic balance. I argue that social pressure alone is insufficient to account for why this ethnic balance breaks down leading to large-scale political violence.[45] A much more powerful force comes from the strategic constraints African rulers face, which I turn to next.

3.5 STRATEGIC THEORIES OF ETHNOPOLITICAL EXCLUSION

3.5.1 Ethnic Bargaining as a Two-Level Game

Why do rulers exclude ethnic rivals from power if it leads to costly conflict? Cultural theories suggest because rulers are convinced of the

---

[45] Wimmer et al. concede this point that their model fails to account for the "logic of [the] escalation process" by which ethnic powersharing ends in civil war. "Ethnic Politics and Armed Conflict," p. 321.

appropriateness of ethnic rule. I argue that nationalist ideologies represent a competing source of legitimacy in Africa's post-independence states, pushing rulers to pursue more ethnically inclusive regimes. I model this dynamic as a two-level game,[46] in which, consistent with theories of ethnic outbidding,[47] rulers face the challenge of retaining in-group support and warding off hardline challengers, while forging and maintaining alliances with violence specialists embedded in other ethnic networks. Figure 3.1 illustrates this dynamic.

In the two-level game illustrated in Figure 3.1, on one dimension (Level 2), the ruler is bargaining with violence specialists embedded in rival ethnic groups who seek their fair share of access to state resources and representation in the government. At the same time, the ruler is bargaining with his coethnics (Level 1), who want to preserve their privileged position and maximize their share of spoils.[48] As discussed above, with complete information about the mobilization capabilities of the rival ethnic group we would expect the ruler to offer the minimal concessions necessary to avoid costly conflict. The problem, however, is that, given the self-limiting nature of weak states, any concessions the ruler makes to the rival group inevitably dilute the spoils of his coethnics. Even if the ruler prefers to build an inclusive regime, his coethnics, eager to protect their share of spoils, may reject powersharing and threaten to dispose the ruler if he brings rival ethnic power brokers into the dominant coalition. Given their privileged position, power, and proximity to the ruler, his coethnics' threat of a coup d'état is credible, and the ruler's hands are tied.[49] In this scenario, the ruler prefers to build an inclusive regime, but strategic constraints from his coethnics prevent such a policy, leading to ethnic exclusion and possibly civil war. This game produces an ethnonationalist policy, but rulers are responding to a logic of consequences not the logic of appropriateness that Wimmer emphasizes.

---

[46] Robert D. Putnam, "Diplomacy and Domestic Politics: The Logic of Two-Level Games," *International Organization*, 42 (3) (1988): 427–460.

[47] Alvin Rabushka and Kenneth A. Shepsle, *Politics in Plural Societies: A Theory of Democratic Instability* (Columbus, Ohio: Merrill, 1972); Joseph Rothschild, *Ethnopolitics: A Conceptual Framework* (New York: Columbia University Press, 1981); Horowitz, *Ethnic Groups in Conflict*.

[48] Stephen M. Saideman, "Is Pandora's Box Half Empty or Half Full? The Limited Virulence of Secessionism and the Domestic Sources of Disintegration" in David A. Lake and Donald Rothchild, eds., *The International Spread of Ethnic Conflict* (Princeton, NJ: Princeton University Press, 1998), pp. 127–150.

[49] This is a key tenet of the selectorate theory: Don't divert money from your winning coalition to those outside or you won't be in power for long. Bruce Bueno de Mesquita and

3.5.2 Burundi and Rwanda: Exemplars of Ethnic Politics as a Two-Level Game

Burundi and Rwanda in the early 1990s illustrate this dynamic. After decades of exclusive Tutsi rule and episodic outbreaks of mass violence against Hutus—including massacres in 1988 that killed an estimated 20,000 people—in the late 1980s, Burundi's president, Pierre Buyoya, pursued a more accommodative political strategy.[50] In the face of acute international pressure following the 1988 massacres,[51] and as it became increasingly clear "that a strategy of rule based solely on oppression could not continue indefinitely,"[52] Buyoya built a more ethnically balanced cabinet and promised a series of political reforms. Despite facing pressure from within the military, including several abortive coups, Buyoya pushed forward; multiparty presidential and parliamentary elections were held in 1993.

In the landmark elections, Buyoya and his National Unity and Progress party (L'Union pour le Progrès National; UPRONA) were defeated at the polls by the Hutu-supported Front pour la Démocratie au Burundi (FRODEBU) and its presidential candidate, Melchior Ndadaye. Buyoya accepted the results, making way for the first Hutu-led government since the country's independence. But in the months after the election, the Tutsi-dominated military, apprehensive about the transition and its consequences for their privileged position, struck twice: first in a July coup attempt and then again in October. Though both coup attempts technically failed, in the second coup the mutinous soldiers assassinated Ndadaye and effectively derailed the political transition.[53] The putsch preserved the military's political dominance and quashed the new ethnic equilibrium that the elections brought, but at the cost of precipitating a new round of bloodletting and a civil war that would not end until 2006.

While Tutsi military elites sabotaged ethnic accommodation in Burundi in 1993, in Rwanda it was a powerful group of Hutu political extremists, known as the *akazu*, who served as the key spoilers.[54] This group,

---

Alastair Smith, *The Dictator's Handbook: Why Bad Behavior Is Almost Always Good Politics* (New York: PublicAffairs, 2011).

[50] For a political history of this critical period in which the Hutu–Tutsi, intra-Tutsi, and intra-Hutu dynamics are all explored up through the 1993 elections, see Lemarchand, *Burundi*.

[51] Lemarchand, *Burundi*.

[52] Peter Uvin, "Ethnicity and Power in Burundi and Rwanda: Different Paths to Mass Violence," *Comparative Politics*, 31 (3) (1999): 252–271, at p. 266.

[53] Lemarchand, *Burundi*.

[54] Prunier, *The Rwanda Crisis*.

which had strong ties to Rwanda's president, Juvénal Habyarimana, and his wife Agathe, was motivated by an ethnonationalist ideology of Hutu power that viewed Tutsi as a *"race* alien to Rwanda, and not an indigenous *ethnic group."*[55] Its members vehemently opposed the August 1993 powersharing accords in Arusha that Habyarimana signed with the Rwandan Patriotic Front (RPF), a predominantly Tutsi rebel movement that invaded Rwanda from Uganda in October 1990. To thwart the implementation of the Arusha Accords, and "preserve the gains" made since the 1959 revolution when power was taken from the Tutsi,[56] the *akazu,* led by Colonel Théoneste Bagosora, seized de-facto control of the government after the death of Habyarimana in a plane crash on April 6, 1994.[57] The Hutu extremists immediately murdered the moderate Hutu prime minister, who should have taken over the reigns of the government. As Mamdani notes, "the death of the president and the killing of the prime minister removed precisely those leaders who had publicly championed an agenda for 'ethnic reconciliation' between Hutu and Tutsi."[58]

Overall, the cases of Burundi and Rwanda in the early 1990s are powerful examples of the difficulties rulers face in managing the two-level game of ethnic politics. The cost of striking a deal with ethnic rivals (Level 2) was that it provoked an internal rebellion from within their own ethnic groups (Level 1), leading the ruler's ethnic group to reclaim its monopoly on power but at the cost of civil war with their ethnic rivals. This path to ethnopolitical exclusion and civil war is essentially equivalent to the instrumental theory of exclusion laid out in Section 3.3 but in which the ruler's coethnics are calling the shots and not the ruler. (See the Mount Kenya Mafia pulling the strings of the Kibaki government.[59]) But this path to civil war raises the same puzzle we grappled with in Section 3.3. If the hardliners are rational, we would expect them to take into consideration the very high costs of ethnopolitical exclusion. In the Rwanda case, of course, the breakdown of the Arusha Accords triggered the genocide, but it also reignited the war that the RPF was able to quickly win, taking

---

[55] Emphasis in original. Mahmood Mamdani, *When Victims Become Killers: Colonialism, Nativism, and the Genocide in Rwanda* (Princeton, NJ: Princeton University Press, 2001), p. 190.

[56] Alison Des Forges, *"Leave None to Tell the Story": Genocide in Rwanda* (New York: Human Rights Watch, 1999), p. 99.

[57] Prunier, *The Rwanda Crisis.*

[58] Mamdani, *When Victims Become Killers,* p. 215.

[59] It is always a fascinating question as to whether the rulers are simply pawns of the hardliners in their shadow state or are leading and directing the hardliners. (According to Wrong, this is a question that John Githongo grappled with as he sought to get to the bottom of the Anglo-Leasing scandal.) By nature of their position as head of state, they

power by force. Why would the Hutu extremists risk it all to destroy the Arusha Accords? At this point we could return to two key mechanisms already discussed: imperfect information and ethnonationalist ideology. According to the former, the Hutu extremists underestimated the costs of the breakdown of the Arusha Accords, whereas the latter mechanism suggests their extreme ethnonationalist ideology blinded them to the cost of the genocide.[60] There is no doubt that the Hutu power ideology was a key factor in why the conflict would become a genocide.[61] But to explain why the Arusha Accords broke down (and why democratization broke down in Burundi), we have to understand how another powerful mechanism affects ethnic bargaining in Africa's weak states: the logic of the commitment problem, in which rival ethnic groups are unable to credibly commit not to exploit their share of power to capture absolute power in the future.

3.5.3 Ethnic Bargaining and the Commitment Problem

Ultimately, what Hutu and Tutsi hardliners in Rwanda and Burundi sought was to maintain their monopoly of power. They feared power-sharing or democratization not simply because it diluted their power but because it opened the door for their rivals to monopolize power for themselves. In Burundi, the Tutsi-dominated military feared Ndadaye would harness the executive authority he gained through democratic elections to entrench Hutu control and disband the army, leaving Tutsi powerless and defenseless.[62] In Rwanda, the *akazu* feared that the Arusha Accords, which granted the RPF control of 50 percent of the officer corps, the ministry of interior, and the right of return of refugees who fled after the 1959 revolution, would open the door for the rebels to seize power and reinstitute Tutsi hegemony.[63] As Straus notes, it was the fear that "the RPF was abrogating its stated commitments and secretly readying for battle" (compounded by events in Burundi that convinced some hardliners that

---

are supposed to be a moderate and inclusive leader and publicly seek to convey as much. This probably accounts for why, from Habyarimana in Rwanda to Bashir in Sudan, the ruler is seen as more moderate than his shadow state even when that may not be the case. On Githongo and Kenya, see Wrong, *It's Our Turn to Eat.*

[60] On the role ideology plays in genocide, see Scott Straus, "'Destroy Them to Save Us': Theories of Genocide and the Logics of Political Violence," *Terrorism and Political Violence*, 24 (4) (2012): 544–560.

[61] Prunier, *The Rwanda Crisis.* Des Forges, *"Leave None to Tell the Story."* Mamdani, *When Victims Become Killers.* Straus, *The Order of Genocide.*

[62] Uvin, "Ethnicity and Power."

[63] Bruce D. Jones, *Peacemaking in Rwanda: The Dynamics of Failure* (Boulder, Col.: Lynne Rienner, 2001). Mamdani, *When Victims Become Killers.*

Tutsis "would never share power") that led the hardliners to prepare "to defend themselves and defeat the RPF once and for all, *if war resumed*."[64]

The lack of credible commitments by the RPF not to exploit the Arusha Accords to usurp power increased the Hutu hardliners' fears that accommodation would open the door to a large, rapid, and irreversible shift in the distribution of power.[65] In other words, ethnic powersharing, which lowers the costs and barriers for rivals to execute such a shift and to appropriate absolute power via a coup d'état or other type of internal challenge, gives rise to a commitment problem—that is, it increases uncertainty that any agreement to share power today will not be upheld in the future.[66]

Ethnic-based politics intensifies the commitment problem in two key ways. First, the weakness of the ruler's political networks in other ethnic groups reduces his monitoring and sanctioning capabilities and thus increases his uncertainty about the threat posed by his rivals. Second, the ethnic nature of politics, in which it is expected that the ruler will favor his own coethnics over others, implies that any shift in the distribution of power will not only have negative repercussions for the ruler himself but also his coethnics as they have few assurances the new ruler will continue to favor them. In fact, they expect the opposite; they may be the target of persecution and repression. This fear expands the circle of those who have a stake in any shift in the distribution of power and accounts for how elite conflict can have such significant societal consequences. The potential catastrophic costs if any rival group is able to convert a share of power into absolute power also explains why the ruler's coethnics are willing to support costly policies of ethnic exclusion.[67]

According to this model of ethnopolitical exclusion, rulers exclude or limit rivals from the central government as a way to circumscribe rivals' capabilities to take power in a coup d'état and resolve the commitment problem that arises from sharing power. One implication of this logic is

---

[64] Emphasis in original. Straus, *The Order of Genocide*, pp. 43–44.

[65] Powell proffers that this mechanism is at the root of all commitment problems. Powell, "War as a Commitment Problem."

[66] Fearon, "Rationalist Explanations for War." Powell, "War as a Commitment Problem." Acemoglu and Robinson, *Economic Origins*.

[67] In Burundi and Rwanda, history casts a dark shadow over political bargaining, as events in the past color how parties read their rivals' motivations and intentions in the present. In Rwanda, members of the Akazu emphasized that they had to "preserve the gains" made since the 1959 "social revolution" or else the RPF would "restore the dictatorship of the extremists of the Tutsi minority," as one pamphlet published in 1991 described it. Des Forges, *"Leave None to Tell the Story,"* p. 64. Thus, the history of the Tutsi monarchy and fears that Tutsi politicians would try to restore it contributed to the commitment problem the ruling Hutu elite believed they faced in their strategic interactions with the RPF.

that rulers are more likely to target those groups who pose the greatest coup risk to their regime. Moreover, unlike instrumental exclusion caused by information problems, strategic exclusion is not self-correcting, even if it leads to large-scale political violence. The outbreak of an armed rebellion merely reinforces the ruler's view that their rival cannot be trusted and is intent on using any means to seize absolute power. In the next chapter, I further develop the intuition that ethnopolitical exclusion is a strategic response to the commitment problem that arises from power-sharing in the shadow of the coup d'état.

3.6 CONCLUSION: THE PRIMACY OF STRATEGIC MODELS OF ETHNOPOLITICAL EXCLUSION

A meso-level approach to civil war emphasizes the importance that political networks play in mediating conflict risk in weak states. The puzzle is why rulers fail to maintain inclusive regimes if ethnopolitical alliances play such an integral role in keeping the peace. In this chapter, I have reviewed three distinct theoretical frameworks that account for the phenomenon of ethnopolitical exclusion. I have argued that the most pernicious cause of ethnopolitical exclusion is not greed or ideologies of ethnonationalism but the strategic uncertainty that haunts rulers of Africa's weak states as they seek to share power but lack guarantees their rivals will not exploit access to the central government to seize power for themselves. Building on this claim, in the next chapter I explain how the commitment problem that underpins strategic uncertainty in weak states represents a coherent and complete theory of civil war onset.

4

The Strategic Logic of War in Africa

4.1 INTRODUCTION

A salient feature of many civil wars in postcolonial Africa is that they are often structured along ethnoregional lines. The rebels predominantly recruit and mobilize from ethnic groups that are socially, and often geographically, distinct from the ethnic groups that dominate the central government.[1] Though these conflicts are organized along ethnic lines, it does not imply that they are fundamentally about ethnicity—that is, individuals are motivated to fight to advance the interests of their ethnic group vis-à-vis other groups (though the status of the ethnic group to which one belongs is not unimportant either).[2] Instead, these conflicts are fundamentally over the distribution of political power and securing the benefits that come with controlling the central government in weak states. Ethnicity is important in as much as it represents the vehicle (or more aptly, the networks) that rival groups of violence specialists mobilize as they compete for power.

The puzzle is why rival networks of violence specialists are unable to agree to parcel out the state and share power as a way to prevent costly large-scale political violence. This is especially puzzling in the civil wars in Darfur, Chad, Liberia, the DRC, Guinea-Bissau, Burundi, Côte d'Ivoire, Uganda, and Zimbabwe because the key protagonists

---

[1] See Appendix 3 for a list of armed rebellions and the ethnic groups from which they draw significant support.
[2] Sambanis and Shayo are right to suggest that academics have gone too far in categorically rejecting any role for group status and one's interest in seeing the group to which they belong do well. Nicholas Sambanis and Moses Shayo, "Social Identification and Ethnic Conflict," *American Political Science Review*, 107 (2) (2013): 294–325.

of the war were allies before they were belligerents. What accounts for the breakdown of powersharing, given the high costs of such an outcome?

As I argue in Chapter 3, ethnopolitical exclusion is a regular feature of the politics of low-income, weak states. Though rulers seek to build large, representative governments to legitimize their rule, severe budget constraints make it hard to sustain them. Exclusion becomes a necessity, and rulers have to become skilled at divide and rule and leveraging the politics of the revolving door—constantly cycling elites from different parts of the country in and out of the regime in a bid to give them just enough so they don't rebel but not too much that they are making them too powerful or squandering precious patronage. Rulers regularly miscalculate how much exclusion they can get away with and find themselves facing rebellions they do not anticipate. This is an important pathway to conflict in many weak states.

In other cases, however, civil war seems to be caused by a fundamentally different type of exclusion. There is nothing judicious about the exclusion that triggered the Biafran War or Africa's Great War in the DRC or the Liberian civil war. In these cases, the level of exclusion is not a miscalculation but a deliberate policy. The central argument of this book is that such extreme policies of ethnopolitical exclusion are not driven by ancient hatreds or greed or lust for power but a strategy intended to consolidate power, coup-proof their regimes, and increase the costs their rivals face to capturing sovereign power. Underpinning this deliberate exclusion is the commitment problem that I argue represents a particularly pernicious source of alliance breakdown in Africa's weak states. In this chapter, I specify precisely how the commitment problem derails ethnic powersharing and leads to civil war. In doing so, I argue that the preventive and preemptive war models developed by international relations scholars serve as useful frameworks in accounting for the breakdown of elite bargaining in Africa's weak states.

4.2 BUILDING BLOCKS OF A STRATEGIC THEORY OF CIVIL WAR

4.2.1 Coups, Strategic Uncertainty, and the Capital City Rule

The essence of the commitment problem that plagues ethnic powersharing is the ruler's fear that granting their rivals access to the central government will set in motion or open the door to an eventual large, rapid, and irreversible shift in the distribution of power,[3] in which the ruler and his network will be displaced from power by a rival ethnic network, which in turn will cause a material decline in the group's access to scarce economic rents and leave it vulnerable to the predations of the state.[4]

This *strategic uncertainty* represents one of the fundamental differences between colonial and postcolonial rule in Africa. During colonialism, the metropole served as an external guarantor of the stability of the central government. But, with the loss of their colonies, European powers no longer offered a blanket security guarantee.[5] It is worth quoting Jackson and Rosberg at length on this point:

Colonial rule in Africa had basically been bureaucratic rule. Colonial governments were run for the most part by administrative officials appointed by the imperial European authority to whom they were ultimately responsible. Not only the regular administrative staff, but also the colonial governor and other senior officials were appointees of the European authority. They were *officeholders* whose authority and powers were specified and delegated to them by the imperial authority (in the case of British colonies, for example, by the Colonial Office, the Cabinet, and ultimately the British sovereign) ... African independence necessarily meant a fundamental change and reorientation of political authority. A new African ruler would not be occupying an office whose authority and power were delegated by a higher authority ... Contemporary African rulers have no higher authorities to draw upon when legitimacy wanes and power is required ... As a consequence, it is possible for African rulers to fall from power in a way that colonial governors never could—that is, by their own miscalculations or because of a political situation that overwhelms them. Colonial governors could only fall from imperial favor and be removed from office or (more likely) be transferred

---

[3] Powell, "War as a Commitment Problem."

[4] In this book I focus primarily on interethnic bargaining. Bargaining within ethnic groups also confronts elites with a commitment problem, but, as explained in Chapter 3 (see Section 3.5), we would expect strategic uncertainty between ethnic groups to supersede intraethnic bargaining problems, considering the costs of losing power would be shared by members of the ruling group if their ethnic rival was to seize the state and usher in a major redistribution of power. As the ruling group concentrates power in its own hands, however, and the immediate strategic threat posed by ethnic rivals dissipates, the commitment problem between coethnics should intensify, often playing out along subgroup divisions based on geography or social differences (e.g., different clans). This suggests a fractal nature of political bargaining over state power between elites embedded in different networks of trust. The empirical evidence bears this out. intraethnic instability is more likely when the ruling group dominates the central government and does not share power with ethnic rivals. Interestingly this breakdown of intraethnic cooperation is more likely to lead to coups than civil war.

[5] Of course, the former colonial powers did not retreat completely. The British and especially the French would sometimes intervene in former colonies to prop up allied regimes.

elsewhere. When colonialism was at last brought to an end, it was the colonial *system* that was "defeated" and not the governors and their staffs.[6]

The problem was not decolonization, Jackson and Rosberg go on to emphasize, but that the colonial governments left behind such weak formal institutions that were incapable of facilitating peaceful political competition. Even before the European powers fully withdrew from Africa, violent contestation for control of the state, often along ethnic lines, arose. In 1959, a social revolution in Rwanda completely overturned the power structure.[7] The Rwandan Tutsi went from being the top social, political, and economic class to a persecuted and politically excluded minority, with many fleeing to neighboring countries.[8] Other violent regime changes soon followed. In Togo in 1963, a unit of colonial army veterans from the Kabré ethnic group assassinated Togo's independence leader and inaugural president, Sylvanus Olympio, setting in motion a significant reversal of the ethnic distribution of power within the Togo government as northerners usurped power from the southern Ewe.[9]

As Jeffrey Herbst explains, and it is worth quoting him extensively as well, the 1963 putsch in Togo and the response by the OAU would set a dangerous precedent for the rest of the continent.

There was significant sentiment to condemn the [Togo] coup because African leaders were obviously afraid that the same fate might be visited upon them. However, after a brief period of ostracism, Togo was allowed to reenter normal diplomatic relations with other African countries and to sign the Charter of the Organization of African Unity. While the OAU Charter does (article III, paragraph 5) offer "unreserved condemnation, in all its forms of political assassination," leaders were not willing to make judgments about the legitimacy of governments. As Boutros-Ghali noted, there was no attempt similar to the Central American effort (the so-called Tobar Doctrine) to not recognize governments that had come to power via forceful means. Instead the OAU established a decision-making rule that preserved African borders and prevented any kind of external competition while requiring only minimal levels of effective domestic sovereignty. To do so, the OAU said, in effect, *that if an African government is in control of the capital city, then it has the legitimate right to the full protection offered by the modern understanding of sovereignty.* Thus, Olympio's killers were recognized as the legitimate government of Togo because they controlled Lomé, not because

[6] Emphasis in original. Jackson and Rosberg, *Personal Rule in Black Africa*, pp. 15–17.
[7] Prunier, *The Rwanda Crisis*, p. 50. Mamdani, *When Victims Become Killers*.
[8] Prunier, *The Rwanda Crisis*.
[9] Horowitz, *Ethnic Groups in Conflict*, p. 482. Samuel Decalo, *Coups and Army Rule in Africa: Motivations and Constraints*, 2nd edn (New Haven, Conn.: Yale University Press, 1990), pp. 213–214.

they were perceived by the Togolese as legitimate or because they physically controlled the territory of the country.[10]

The technology of the coup d'état and the OAU's de-facto "capital city rule,"[11] which, in effect, recognized as the legitimate sovereign any group that controlled the capital city, no matter how they came to power and how much control they had outside the capital, would have profound consequences on the postcolonial political game. It increased incentives for violence specialists to not only gain access to the dominant coalition but also to capture the position of head of state, from which they would gain international prestige and access to external rents denied to rivals.[12] By 1970, there would be thirty-five coup attempts across sub-Saharan Africa, of which nearly 70 percent were successful.[13] Not only could coups lead to a change in the ruler, they could also, as seen in Togo, have profound consequences for the distribution of power across different ethnic groups. As illustrated in Figure 4.1, coups would be the modal source of *ethnic transfers of power*[14] in postcolonial Africa, accounting for nearly 60 percent of such changes. By 2001, African states would experience some 188 coups,[15] though the success rate dropped to 40 percent as rulers became better skilled at coup-proofing.

Equally rife would be purges[16]—the removal of regime insiders perceived to be disloyal or excessively independent—as rulers sought to preempt or prevent threats to their hold on power.[17] For example, in Togo, after the 1963 coup, Gnassingbé Eyadéma's rise to head of the army

---

[10] Emphasis added. Herbst, *States and Power in Africa*, p. 110.

[11] Herbst, *States and Power in Africa*, p. 110.

[12] Cooper describes African states as gatekeeper states that "sit astride the interface between a territory and the rest of the world, collecting and distributing resources that derived from the gate itself: customs revenue and foreign aid; permits to do business in the territory; entry and exit visas; and permission to move currency in and out." Cooper, *Africa since 1940*, p. 157.

[13] McGowan, "African Military Coups d'État."

[14] I consider an ethnic transfer power to have occurred when the ethnic groups or coalitions categorized as "senior partner," "dominant" or "monopoly" by the EPR dataset are replaced by another ethnic group or coalition. See Appendix 3 for complete list of ruling group changes.

[15] McGowan, "African Military Coups d'État."

[16] I conceive of purges and coups as analogous technologies in that both entail a faction within the dominant coalition exploiting their partial control of the state to effectively capture the remainder. They differ in that coups are executed by nonincumbents and purges are a tool of incumbents.

[17] Jackson and Rosberg, *Personal Rule in Black Africa*, pp. 52–58.

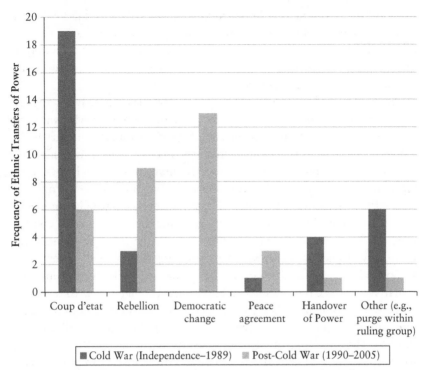

FIGURE 4.1 Sources of Ethnic Transfers of Power in Africa, Independence to 2005

(1965) and then president (1967) was only possible after he purged and imprisoned his chief rival, Emmanuel Bodjolle.[18]

4.2.2 Preventive and Preemptive War as a Model for Elite Politics in Africa

One of the paradoxes of Africa's unique postcolonial institutional structure is that whereas strong sovereignty institutions helped mitigate external conflict between new states with arbitrary borders, it undermined domestic order as rivals competed for sovereign power. As Herbst notes, this institutional structure flipped traditional political science models of domestic and international politics on their heads: "the politics between countries was extremely well-ordered (as opposed to the Hobbesian

[18] Both Eyadéma and Bodjolle were members of the military veterans who challenged Olympio, but it was Eyadéma who ended up actually executing the assault. Samuel Decalo, *Historical Dictionary of Togo* (Metuchen, NJ: Scarecrow Press, 1987).

model of international relations) while domestic politics did not evidence many signs of stability."[19] One implication of this paradox is that, as other scholars have argued, we would expect models of bargaining in anarchy—central to the study of international relations—to be highly relevant to domestic politics in Africa.

Starting with Posen, a number of scholars have effectively applied international relations theories of war to internal conflict.[20] Motivated by a surge of ethnic conflicts after the end of the Cold War, the primary focus has been on the security dilemmas that arise in environments of "emerging anarchy"[21] when the state has failed or is failing and can no longer regulate communal conflict.[22] Yet, as Hobbes demonstrates so powerfully, the state itself is an anarchic system; order is endogenous to whether individuals resolve the problem of violence.[23] Thus, any theory of internal conflict needs to begin with political order[24]—that is, the strategic interactions between violence specialists who are competing for political power.

Both violence specialists in a weak state and states in the international system face the same basic Hobbesian problem: how to maintain a peaceful "covenant" when rivals, operating in a state without an absolute authority, must use the threat of force to uphold the distribution of power.[25] The problem to arise from such an environment is that the use of force is necessary to defend one's share of power, but it can also be used to appropriate others' power. The inability of rival sides not to use their force capabilities to lock in a larger share of power is the essence of the commitment problem that arises from anarchy. While violence is costly and destroys resources that could be shared between them,[26] short-term economic costs are not sufficient to induce powersharing when the use of

---

[19] Herbst, *States and Power in Africa*, p. 109.

[20] Barry R. Posen, "The Security Dilemma and Ethnic Conflict," *Survival: Global Politics and Strategy*, 35 (1) (1993): 27–47.

[21] Posen, "The Security Dilemma and Ethnic Conflict."

[22] James D. Fearon, "Ethnic War as a Commitment Problem." Paper presented at the 1994 Annual Meeting of the American Political Science Association, New York, August 30–September 2, 1995. Russell Hardin, *One for All: The Logic of Group Conflict* (Princeton, NJ: Princeton University Press, 1995). David A. Lake and Donald Rothchild, "Containing Fear: The Origins and Management of Ethnic Conflict," *International Security*, 21 (2) (1996): 41–75. Erik Melander, "The Geography of Fear: Regional Ethnic Diversity, the Security Dilemma and Ethnic War," *European Journal of International Relations*, 15 (1) (2009): 95–124.

[23] Hobbes, *Leviathan*.

[24] North et al., *Violence and Social Orders*.

[25] North et al., *Violence and Social Orders*. Svolik, *The Politics of Authoritarian Rule*.

[26] Fearon, "Rationalist Explanations for War." North et al., *Violence and Social Orders*.

force by any faction can also "permanently alter the strategic balance of power"[27] and bring about "long-term, compounding rewards."[28] Fearon uses the analogy of a duel between gunslingers to illustrate this severe type of commitment problem in which the use of force can "permanently eliminate" the other, thus negating "strategies of conditional cooperation such as tit-for-tat."[29]

Fearon notes, however, that his gunslingers analogy represents an "extreme case," with limited relevance to explaining war between states,[30] which is a point of general consensus among international-relations scholars.[31] The basic limitation of a Hobbesian framework to the study of international relations, as Jervis first notes, is that "states are not as vulnerable as men are in a state of nature."[32] Advances in military technology have strengthened the "hard shell" of the state,[33] reducing the offensive advantages of a first strike[34] and extending the "shadow of the future," which allows for repeated interactions and the establishment of cooperative institutions, such as sovereignty.[35]

But if Fearon's analogy poorly translates to interstate relations, it has a striking literal resemblance to the strategic interactions that dominate politics in weak states, in which physical annihilation is a very real possibility. For example, take the case of the Derg, the Marxist revolutionary organization that ousted Ethiopia's long-serving emperor, Haile Selassie,

---

[27] Blattman and Miguel, "Civil War." See also Powell, "War as a Commitment Problem." Fearon, "Rationalist Explanations for War," p. 402.

[28] Michelle R. Garfinkel and Stergios Skaperdas, "Conflict without Misperceptions or Incomplete Information: How the Future Matters," *The Journal of Conflict Resolution*, 44 (6) (2000): 793–807.

[29] Fearon, "Rationalist Explanations for War," p. 402.

[30] Fearon, "Rationalist Explanations for War," p. 403.

[31] As Reiter shows, preemptive wars "almost never happen" between states. Dan Reiter, "Exploding the Powder Keg Myth: Preemptive Wars Almost Never Happen," *International Security*, 20 (2) (1995): 5–34. Schweller categorically states that extreme security dilemmas between states are "historically very rare and should not be generalized." Randall L. Schweller, "The Logic and Illogic of the Security Dilemma and Contemporary Realism: A Response to Wagner's Critique," *International Theory*, 2 (2) (2010): 288–305, at p. 294.

[32] Jervis, "Cooperation under the Security Dilemma," p. 172.

[33] John H. Herz, "Rise and Demise of the Territorial State," *World Politics*, 9 (4) (1957): 473–493.

[34] The development of nuclear weapons threatened to obliterate conventional defensive capabilities and disrupt the offense–defense balance. This balance was restored, however, with the development of secure second-strike capabilities. Robert Jervis, *The Meaning of the Nuclear Revolution: Statecraft and the Prospect of Armageddon* (Ithaca, NY: Cornell University Press, 1989).

[35] Jervis, "Cooperation under the Security Dilemma."

in 1974. After coming to power, the military junta would be wracked by a series of political power struggles that were resolved with the gun. In the space of three years, four leading members of the new government were physically liquidated as Mengistu Haile Mariam maneuvered to capture sovereign power.[36] In one notorious incident, a literal shoot-out erupted between rival Derg factions during a meeting of the Standing Committee on February 3, 1977, at its Grand Palace headquarters, leading to the death of eight Derg members, including its chairman, Teferi Banti.[37]

Short of being killed, the other fear that motivates political elites is that they will be politically eliminated from the regime in a coup d'état or purge, in which their rivals stealthily convert partial control of the state into absolute control.[38] Political elimination not only denies individuals access to the privileges that come from being at the center of power (e.g., control of the military, economic rents, international recognition) but is also a blow to one's "Big Man" status. It is this possibility of being physically or politically eliminated in a surprise attack that distinguishes elite politics in weak states from international politics. The theoretical upshot is that violence specialists face a much more severe commitment problem than states do in the international system. Given the low mobilization costs necessary to seize power via a coup (organizing a small group of conspirators in the military) vis-à-vis the material benefits (sovereign power), rulers cannot take for granted the loyalty of those around them. Instead, they have to prepare for the worst. Thus, they try to strengthen their defensive capabilities by stacking the military and security organs with coethnics and other loyalists,[39] ensuring they control the stream of economic rents and forging alliances with international supporters who

---

[36] General Aman Andom, the head of state installed in power after the overthrow of Selassie, was executed on November 24, 1974. Andom's successor, Teferi Banti, would meet the same fate when he was killed in a shoot-out at the Derg's headquarters in February 1977. Atnafu Abate and Sisay Habte, the second and third most influential members of the Derg behind Mengistu were also physically eliminated on November 13, 1977 and July 13, 1976, respectively. Andargachew Tiruneh, *The Ethiopian Revolution, 1974–1987: A Transformation from an Aristocratic to a Totalitarian Autocracy* (Cambridge: Cambridge University Press, 1993).

[37] Marina Ottaway and David Ottaway, *Ethiopia: Empire in Revolution* (New York: Africana, 1978). Others suggest that Benti and the other Derg members were summarily executed. Martin Meredith, *The Fate of Africa: A History of Fifty Years of Independence* (New York: Public Affairs, 2005).

[38] Luttwak, *Coup d'État*.

[39] Howe, *Ambiguous Order*. See also Cynthia H. Enloe, *Ethnic Soldiers: State Security in Divided Societies* (Athens, Ga.: University of Georgia Press, 1980).

can back them in case of an internal conflict. But the problem of such policies, of course, is, in Jervis's famous conceptualization, that they are indistinguishable from offensive moves—that is, these policies protect the ruler but also increase his capabilities for attack (in this case, to purge or eliminate other power-holders from the regime)[40] and decrease the security of others in the regime. Fearing the ruler is planning to purge or kill them, rivals countermobilize and prepare to launch a preemptive strike to halt the ruler's power grab.

Beyond the Ethiopia example, another paradigmatic case of elite bargaining descending into an internal security dilemma is seen in Uganda in the late 1960s. After independence from the United Kingdom in 1962, Uganda had been a parliamentary democracy, but the constitutional order broke down in 1966 when the prime minister, Milton Obote, backed by the military, executed an *autogolpe* and installed himself as executive president with immense powers. After the self-coup, Obote promoted Idi Amin, his key ally in the military, as top commander of the Ugandan Army.[41] Power in Uganda became concentrated in the hands of Obote and his right-hand man, Amin. Both elites sought to maintain and expand their patron–client networks within the regime. Obote had already created the General Service Unit, a secret police unit led by one of his relatives, and cultivated support among Langi and Acholi contingents in the army.[42] As commander of the army, Amin began to recruit individuals from his home area in the West Nile District, especially from the Lugbara, Madi, Kakwa, and Nubian tribes (mainly Sudanic-speakers) to balance against the predominance of soldiers ethnically closer to Obote, namely from the Acholi and Langi tribes. By one estimate, between 1968 and 1969 there was a 74 percent increase in Sudanic-speakers in the Uganda Army.[43] Further increasing uncertainty was the murder, in late January 1970, of Amin's deputy and potential successor, Brigadier Pierino Okoya.[44] In short, Obote and Amin's efforts to strengthen their support within the military had the consequence of decreasing the security of the other side. Locked in the security dilemma, eliminating the other side from power was deemed the only credible way out.

[40] Jervis, "Cooperation under the Security Dilemma."
[41] Idi Amin led the military assault on the first president of Uganda, Mutesa II, that propelled Obote to power.
[42] Kenneth Ingham, *Obote: A Political Biography* (London and New York: Routledge, 1994).
[43] Amii Omara-Otunnu, *Politics and the Military in Uganda, 1890–1985* (Basingstoke: Macmillan, 1987), p. 87.
[44] Kasozi et al., *The Social Origins of Violence in Uganda*, pp. 102–103.

4.2.3 Decapitating the Snake: The Strategic Logic of
Purges and Coups

In preemptive war models, war becomes a way to resolve the severe commitment problem by permanently altering the strategic balance of power and eliminating the rival state.[45] Coups and purges are intended to serve the same purpose in elite bargaining in weak states: to destroy a rival's first-strike capabilities by eliminating its partial control of the regime. As Zimbabwe's Robert Mugabe said in 1982 about his rival Joshua Nkomo and his supporters within the government, they "are like a cobra in a house. The only way to deal effectively with a snake is to strike and destroy its head."[46] In Uganda in the early 1970s, as the security dilemma intensified between Obote and Amin, the latter launched a coup to preempt what he perceived was his imminent arrest and to protect his privileged position within the regime.[47]

Purged from the dominant coalition and the government, the targeted factions face much higher costs to winning back power as these violence specialists can no longer exploit their privileged control of the state's coercive apparatus to execute a coup d'état. As Horowitz notes, "Once an ethnocratic regime is in power, opposition [from rival groups] is not likely to make its will felt through further coups."[48] Instead, the purged networks have to switch their technology of resistance to an armed rebellion if they wish to take back power. The challenge for the purged groups—and the ruler knows this—is that armed rebellions require much higher mobilizational costs than coups.[49] Bereft of access to the state itself, dissidents can no longer draw on the salaries, matériel, and manpower provided by the state in their bid to forcibly seize power (except that which they take with them when they are displaced) and instead have to build their own army that is capable of overthrowing the whole coercive apparatus, not just part of it. Moreover, purged groups no longer benefit from proximity to the key levers of power but often have to fight their way to power from a societal or foreign base, which may require

---

[45] Blattman and Miguel, "Civil War," p. 13.

[46] Joseph Lelyveld, "Mugabe Government Confiscates Property Owned by Nkomo Party," *New York Times*, February 17, 1982.

[47] Jan Jelmert Jorgensen, *Uganda: A Modern History* (London: Croom Helm, 1981).

[48] Horowitz, *Ethnic Groups in Conflict*, p. 499.

[49] On the different strategies of violence that coup-plotters and insurgents employ, see Fearon, "Why Do Some Civil Wars Last So Much Longer than Others?" On the "radically different" resources required for coups versus insurgencies, see Paul Collier and Anke Hoeffler, "Grand Extortion: Coup Risk and the Military as a Protection Racket" (University of Oxford, 2006).

covering a considerable distance (on the importance this distance has on the outcome of political bargaining, see Chapter 10). Thus, the purged dissidents face the challenge not only of building a private army but also of sustaining it over an extended period of time and avoiding factionalization, which is a chronic problem for armed groups.[50]

4.2.4 The Mechanics of Ethnopolitical Exclusion

Powersharing in weak states confronts rulers with a severe commitment problem as they have no guarantees that rival power-holders will not exploit their partial control of the state to usurp sovereign power. Purging rivals effectively neutralizes their first-strike capabilities and increases the costs they face to reclaiming power via an armed insurgency. Exclusion is not costless for the regime, however. As explained in Chapter 2, rulers in Africa's weak states depend on striking alliances with violence specialists embedded in different ethnic networks to maintain societal control. To mitigate the costs of alliance breakdown, rulers face the challenge of *selective exclusion*: purging rival violence specialists while co-opting their ethnic networks to ensure they do not forfeit societal and territorial control.[51] But what frequently happens is the opposite: as elite accommodation breaks down, rulers resort to systematic purges along ethnic lines, targeting not only their rivals but also their rivals' coethnics.

For example, Idi Amin's preemptive coup against Obote did not just target the president but involved a witch hunt against other Langi and Acholi in the regime, as Decalo explains:

Extermination squads composed largely of Nilotic and Sudanic personnel systematically purged each army camp of suspected Obote loyalist officers and soldiers. Langi and Acholi officers were sequestered and individually murdered both before and after the attempted 1972 pro-Obote invasion from Tanzania . . . The immense gaps in the army's hierarchy and rank and file caused by the liquidation

---

[50] David E. Cunningham, "Veto Players and Civil War Duration," *American Journal of Political Science*, 50 (4) (2006): 875–892. Michael Findley and Peter J. Rudloff, "Combatant Fragmentation and the Dynamics of Civil War," *British Journal of Political Science*, 74 (1) (2012): 1–41.

[51] Given the geographic concentration of many ethnic groups in Africa, when exclusion falls along ethnic lines it not only compromises societal leverage, it also forfeits control of terrain, which provides the insurgents with invaluable space from where they can organize and launch military operations. As Weidmann notes, building on Toft, geographically concentrated ethnic groups should have denser political, economic, and social networks that they can tap into to overcome the collective action problems that inhibit rebellion. Weidmann, "Geography as Motivation." Toft, *The Geography of Ethnic Violence*.

of Langi and Acholi members opened the door for massive recruitment and promotion of personnel personally loyal to Amin from Uganda's Nubians, Southern Sudanese, Nilotics, and Zairien refugees ... Since less than one-third of the original army remained intact, in a sense the entire army—Amin's major power prop, though he had constant difficulties in controlling it—was rebuilt from the ground up as a force committed to the hegemony of one region, the far north, and loyal to one individual, Amin.[52]

The parallels with Burundi are striking. In Burundi in 1965, after a coup attempt by a group of Hutu army and gendarmerie officers, the ruling Tutsi elite went to great lengths to eliminate Hutu from the government, thus destroying the ethnic balance that existed within the regime in the first years after independence and turning Burundi into what Horowitz calls an "ethnocracy."[53] As Lemarchand explains:

The mutineers took a huge gamble and lost—but the losses involved far more than the extermination of thousands of Hutu after the aborted coup. Also lost was an opportunity for the Hutu leadership to share in the exercise of power. After the extensive purges of the army and gendarmerie and the physical elimination of every Hutu leader of any standing, power became the exclusive monopoly of Tutsi elements.[54]

A similar sequence of events occurs in Liberia after infighting between the president, Samuel Doe, and his best friend and co-conspirator, Thomas Quiwonkpa. (Doe and Quiwonkpa collaborated to seize power in a coup in 1980.) In the wake of a failed bid by Quiwonkpa to forcibly overthrow Doe, state security services purged Quiwonkpa's Gio kinsmen and the linguistically related Mano from the armed forces and indiscriminately massacred civilians from these ethnic groups.[55] In the months and years after the coup attempt, Doe restructured his regime, filling the gap left by the exclusion of clients from the Gio and Mano with his Krahn coethnics and the Mandingo, who, as "outsiders," were seen as nonthreatening and more "trustworthy."[56] Meanwhile, the Gio were almost completely excluded from the government "since they were suspected of disloyalty

[52] Decalo, *Coups and Army Rule in Africa*, pp. 165–166.

[53] Horowitz, *Ethnic Groups in Conflict*.

[54] Lemarchand, *Burundi*, p. 71.

[55] Berkeley, *The Graves Are Not Yet Full*.

[56] As Ellis notes, after the violent falling out with Thomas Quiwonkpa (an ethnic Gio), Samuel Doe strengthened his political ties with the ethnic Mandingo, who are generally seen as "foreigners" by other Liberians because of their historical roots in the Sahel. In fact, "in the aftermath of the Quiwonkpa coup attempt, Doe explicitly recognized the Mandingo as a Liberian ethnic group," given their presence in Nimba County and other parts of the north and west of the country. Ellis, *The Mask of Anarchy*, pp. 60–61.

to President Doe."[57] A similar fate was met by the Malinké in Guinea after the 1985 coup by Traoré; the Zaghawa in Chad after the 1989 coup by Djamous and Déby; and the Yakoma in the Central African Republic (CAR) after a coup attempt in 2001 by soldiers loyal to former president, André Kolingba.

Given the large political and social costs of ethnopolitical exclusion, why aren't rulers able to purge more selectively? Or, from the perspective of ethnic followers, why aren't they able to reach some type of agreement with the ruler to avoid the high costs of ethnopolitical exclusion?

The breakdown of the regime along ethnic lines is a consequence of how elite competition for power hardens the ethnic organization of politics and reduces the interethnic trust and cooperation that is necessary for the ruler and their rivals' coethnics to reach a deal. As explained in Chapter 2, rulers use the institution of shared ethnicity, with its dense informational networks and strong norms of reciprocity, as a mechanism to reduce uncertainty and facilitate cooperation in an environment in which formal institutions are weak and the risks of violent exploitation are real.[58] Consistent with these mechanisms, rulers, such as Mobutu Sese Seko in former Zaire,[59] relied on not only coethnics but especially family members and those from their hometown in which social connections are particularly dense and norms of reciprocity should be especially strong.

The problem, however, is that because of ethnicity's visibility, in which it "can be ascertained through superficial data sources" (such as name, place of birth, and physical features) and its stickiness, in which ethnic attributes cannot be easily changed,[60] seeing the ruler stack key strategic positions with coethnics combined with a general understanding of ethnic solidarity leads those outside the ruler's ethnic group to conclude that they will only obtain marginal positions within the ruler's political network. Instead, they have greater faith in their own ethnic patrons, who they feel they can monitor and hold to account via shared ethnic

---

[57] Ellis, *The Mask of Anarchy*, p. 66.

[58] Habyarimana et al., *Coethnicity*.

[59] According to Michela Wrong, "Mobutu's Equateur tribesmen were considered natural warriors, and they had long enjoyed disproportionate representation in the army. But Mobutu took the principle to a new extreme, packing the upper echelons of the security forces with his ethnic kin . . . In public he preached Zairean nationhood, but Mobutu trusted only his own tribe with his safety. Within the Ngbandi, members of Mobutu's family did the best, and general's stars were bestowed on cousins and brothers-in-law." Michela Wrong, "The Emperor Mobutu," *Transition*, 81/82 (2000): 92–112.

[60] Kanchan Chandra, "What Is Ethnic Identity and Does It Matter?" *Annual Review of Political Science*, 9 (1) (2006): 397–424.

networks. Thus, if a conflict emerges between their patron and the ruler, individuals are more likely to side with their patron for fear that their group's loss of power will deny them not only access to state resources but also protection from state violence, which is the ultimate benefit that violence specialists offer to their clients.[61] The outcome of this "politics of fear"[62] is that it hardens ethnic divisions (in the sense that expectations of reciprocity are very high within but not between ethnic groups). This increases the costs rulers face of striking a bargain with their rivals' coethnics in two fundamental ways. For one, this leads the ruler to calculate that most members of a given ethnic group will be loyal to their coethnics and are thus too dangerous to keep them within the system lest they continue to support their leaders' bid to capture sovereign power (and potentially launch a coup on their behalf or help them in some other material way, such as passing along key information and resources that the purged elites can use in their armed rebellion).[63] Second, even if rulers are willing to strike a deal with members of the perceived "enemy group," their risk aversion will lead them to discount the positions of power they offer, increasing the likelihood such nominal overtures are rejected by members of the targeted group.[64]

Additionally it is important to note that the purged elites have an incentive to exploit the "politics of fear" (i.e. we need to stick together to defend ourselves against the predation of the regime) to keep their network intact and prevent their clients from defecting to the regime, which would undermine the purged elites' power and bargaining leverage.

4.2.5 From Ethnopolitical Exclusion to Civil War

The argument advanced so far posits that uncertainty leads rulers to employ ethnopolitical exclusion as a solution to the commitment problem. But given the strong societies, weak states institutional dichotomy in

---

[61] North et al., *Violence and Social Orders.*

[62] Padró i Miquel, "The Control of Politicians."

[63] While the ruler knows that their rivals may have different levels of support and loyalty within their ethnic group, establishing this is costly, however. Moreover, the time-sensitive nature of purging disloyalists from the regime prevents the ruler and his supporters from properly vetting individuals within the regime and erring on the side of a more comprehensive or indiscriminate exclusive strategy. This is discussed further in the context of Sudan. See Section 6.3.1 Ethnicity as a Source of Attribute Substitution.

[64] Members of the targeted group may be inclined to take the positions due to a desperate material situation or because of political rivalry with the power brokers who have been purged from the regime. But they will be under heavy social pressure from their coethnics

Africa, we would expect this strategy merely substitutes civil war risk for coup risk. There are three key channels by which ethnopolitical exclusion increases the risk of armed rebellion.

1. First, following from Wimmer et al.,[65] it *intensifies political and economic grievances* as members of excluded groups not only feel that are they being denied their fair share of economic rents but often resent their suffering and persecution at the hands of the government's repressive apparatus. Taking up weapons thus represents both a vehicle to reclaim power and a means to protect members of the group from the tyranny of the regime.

2. Second, the group's exclusion from the central government *increases opportunities for armed rebellion and reduces the government's counterinsurgency effectiveness*. For one, it increases the pool of dissidents opposed to the regime. But without access to local information and support, the government lacks the capabilities to selectively accommodate and repress these dissidents.[66] Bereft of local leverage and information, the regime is unable to produce selective violence and instead often resorts to indiscriminate counterinsurgency tactics.[67] Though over the long run indiscriminate violence may slow the rebellion and prevent it from posing a threat to the capital, in the short term it often inflames the conflict as it drives individuals and communities to support the rebels[68] and triggers full-scale civil war.

3. Third, the exclusion–mobilization cycle *further deepens mistrust between the ruler and his ethnic rivals*, which worsens the commitment problem that motivated the ruler to choose exclusion in the first place. This prevents both sides from reaching a negotiated solution that would end the war.

not "to sell out." The more marginal position offered by the regime, the lower the likelihood they will be willing to incur these high social costs.

[65] Wimmer et al., "Ethnic Politics and Armed Conflict." Cederman et al., "Why Do Ethnic Groups Rebel?"

[66] To compensate for the loss of societal power brokers from the purged network, the ruling elite often turn to other groups from the same region or deploy their own coethnics, as Samuel Doe did with the Mandingo in Nimba County in the 1980s. But often these "foreign" or regional intermediaries are a poor substitute for intraethnic brokers. Even if they have familiarity with the local terrain, their inability to penetrate the rivals' ethnic networks makes it difficult for them to acquire accurate information about dissident activities carried out by members of the excluded group. On the efficacy of tapping into ethnic networks for counterinsurgency operations, see Lyall, "Are Coethnics More Effective Counterinsurgents?"

[67] Kalyvas, *The Logic of Violence in Civil War.*

[68] Goodwin, *No Other Way Out.*

4.3 SUMMARY AND HYPOTHESES

The coup-proofing theory of civil war posits that civil war in Africa is a function of the strategic problems that arise from powersharing in the shadow of the coup d'état. While rulers prefer to avoid costly civil war, their willingness to share power to achieve societal peace is constrained by the uncertainty that comes from incorporating ethnic rivals into the regime: they may exploit their access to the central government to execute a future coup d'état and usurp sovereign power.

Though in the previous sections I have focused on how the commitment problem that arises from powersharing is analogous to preemptive war, it can lead to both preventive and preemptive exclusion. In the latter, as discussed above, the rival is perceived to present an immediate and imminent threat, and the incumbent strikes first to destroy that threat. In the former, the ruler calculates that powersharing may not lead to an immediate threat but will set in motion a gradual shift in the distribution of power that will strengthen his rival's capabilities to one day seize power in a coup and, in anticipation of this possibility, refuses to share real power.[69] In both cases, barring or purging rival networks of violence specialists from central state power helps to resolve or mitigate the commitment problem that comes with powersharing, but at the cost of increasing the risk of civil war. But this is a risk rulers are often willing to accept as they calculate it is necessary to protect their hold on power and increase the costs their rivals face to capture the central government. In short, civil war is the price rulers are willing to pay to coup-proof their regimes from rival networks of violence specialists and consolidate their hold on sovereign power.

The coup-proofing theory of civil war generates several broad postulates and testable implications that I test in the next two parts of the book.

1. **Political networks hypothesis:** Ethnic powersharing is necessary for societal peace as it facilitates the regime's political control outside the ruler's ethnic group and reduces opportunities for armed rebellion.

    H1: Ethnic powersharing reduces civil war risk.

2. **Coup–civil war trap:** Ethnic powersharing, however, confronts rulers with a coup–civil war trade-off. Sharing power strengthens the

---

[69] We would expect the type of exclusionary strategy the ruler pursues, whether preventive or preemptive, to have important implications on the time between exclusion and the outbreak of conflict. Preemptive exclusion is more likely to be followed by immediate risk of large-scale political violence.

regime's societal control but at the cost of increasing rivals' coup-making capabilities.

H2: Ethnic powersharing increases coup risk.

3. **Coup-proofing theory of civil war:** Given the higher mobilizational costs necessary to seize power in an armed rebellion than a coup and the premium placed on sovereign power, rulers often hedge their bets on civil war and employ ethnopolitical exclusion as a coup-proofing strategy.

H3: Ethnopolitical exclusion substitutes civil war risk for coup risk for members from the targeted ethnic group.

4. **Coup-making capabilities as a predictor of ethnopolitical exclusion and co-conspirator civil wars:** One of the key observable implications that distinguishes the strategic logic of ethnopolitical exclusion from economic or cultural explanations is that we should see rulers targeting those groups with the greatest coup-making capabilities for ethnopolitical exclusion. I argue that this dynamic helps to account for one of the surprising phenomena seen in postcolonial Africa: co-conspirator civil wars. Interethnic alliances increase the groups' capabilities to capture power but then confront the co-conspirators with a severe commitment problem after victory that often ends with regime factionalization and civil war.

H4: Rulers are significantly more likely to target groups with strong coup-making capabilities for exclusion, including the very allies that helped them come to power—their *co-conspirators*—than other less threatening groups.

4.4 EMPIRICAL STRATEGY

To explore and test these hypotheses, I employ a mixed-methods research design and report the results consistent with how the research was carried out. (See Figure 1.1 in Chapter 1.) I begin in Part II with an in-depth case study of variation in large-scale political violence in Darfur, Sudan, which serves as a theory-building case. Figure 4.2 illustrates the structure of the extended theory-building case study and how it elucidates the book's central theoretical argument developed in Part II.

Consistent with H1, Chapter 5 presents qualitative evidence from Darfur that illustrates how the Sudan government's interethnic political network helped the regime to effectively defeat an armed rebellion it faced in the region in the early 1990s. The qualitative evidence offers new

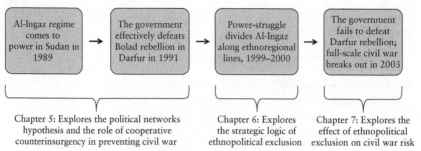

FIGURE 4.2 Sudan's Al-Ingaz Regime and Civil War in Darfur: An Extended Theory-Building Case Study

insights into how interethnic political networks strengthen the regimes' counterinsurgency capabilities by facilitating cooperation between the government and local communities. But consistent with H2 and the idea of the coup–civil war trap, while the alliance between Islamists from riverain Sudan and Darfur, Sudan, was necessary to keep societal peace, it also increased the capabilities of those from Darfur of seizing power in a coup d'état. This fear became particularly acute as a power struggle played out between Omar al-Bashir, the president of Sudan, and Hassan al-Turabi, the leader of the Islamic Movement, as described in Chapter 6. In line with H3, in the face of what he perceived as a growing threat from Turabi and his allies from western Sudan, Bashir purged them from the regime, substituting civil war risk for coup risk. Chapter 7 explores how these regime divisions contributed to civil war in Darfur through the three channels identified above: grievances, opportunity structure, and sustained bargaining failure.

In Chapter 8, I go beyond the Darfur case to test hypotheses H1–H4 using the EPR dataset. With data on groups' access to the central government and original data on the ethnicity of coup conspirators and insurgents, we can systematically test the idea of the coup–civil war trap as well as to ascertain whether we see evidence of both preventive and preemptive exclusion leading to civil war. Chapter 9 then uses process tracing to test the strategic theory of civil war on the case of Africa's Great War.

PART II

THEORY-BUILDING CASE STUDY

5

Political Networks, Brokerage, and Cooperative Counterinsurgency

Civil War Averted in Darfur

5.1 INTRODUCTION

Sudan represents a paradigmatic weak state.[1] Since the creation of the modern Sudanese state in the early 1820s, after Muhammad Ali Pasha, governor of Egypt for the Ottoman Empire, conquered and annexed the territory, the central government in Khartoum has faced the challenge of broadcasting authority outside the Nile River heartland, where the capital, Khartoum, sits. One needs to merely follow the roads leading out of Khartoum to appreciate the limited reach of the state.[2] As illustrated in Map 5.1, what is striking is that the tarmacked roads going west and south out from the center abruptly end in En Nahud, North Kordofan, and Renk, Upper Nile (indicated by the Xs on Map 5.1), becoming unpaved roads before reaching the densely populated areas further into South Sudan and beyond Kordofan to Darfur. (In contrast, the primary roads from Khartoum north to Egypt, northeast to Port Sudan, and east to Kassala are completely paved.)

With such limited infrastructure in the periphery, it should be of no surprise that the Sudanese state is incredibly centralized. In 2001, state governments only generated 2 percent of total public revenue. (In other words, the federal government collected 98 percent of all taxes.)[3] With

---

[1] Chapters 5–7 analyze Sudan before it split into two countries in 2011.

[2] According to the United Nations Conference on Trade and Development, in 1999 Sudan had the lowest density of roads of all least-developed countries in the world. United Nations Conference on Trade and Development, *Statistical Profiles of the Least Developed Countries* (New York: United Nations, 2005). Available at www.unctad.org/en/docs/ldcmisc20053_en.pdf (accessed August 22, 2016).

[3] This reflects not only a lack of capacity but also restrictions put in place by the federal government to limit the states' authority to collect taxes.

MAP 5.1 Political Topography of Sudan (2001)

limited local capacity, states have been heavily dependent on intergovernmental transfers from Khartoum.[4] Again, the states in Darfur and South
Sudan fare poorly compared to other parts of the country. Per-capita

[4] World Bank, *Sudan: Stabilization and Reconstruction*, vol. I (Washington, DC: World
Bank, 2003), p. 81.

revenue in Darfur is almost a third of the average for all northern Sudan states.[5]

The structural weakness of the Sudanese state and the pernicious center–periphery divide have been constant themes in Sudanese history and go a long way toward accounting for the country's conflict-ridden history—from the Mahdist Revolution (the Islamo-nationalist revolution that expelled the Turco-Egyptian regime in the early 1880s) to the near constant warfare in South Sudan.[6] It is no less important in understanding the outbreak of the Darfur civil war in 2003.

In many ways, the outbreak of the 2003 Darfur conflict reads like a stylized description of civil war onset in a weak state: A small group of dissidents from the Fur and Zaghawa ethnic groups, aggrieved by local insecurity and their region's political and economic marginalization, took up weapons, first in self-defense against rival local militias and then against the Sudanese government. Operating in rural Darfur, far from Khartoum, the capital and center of power, and exploiting the region's mountainous terrain around Jebel Marra and the weakness of Sudanese state institutions in Darfur, the rebels, who at first called themselves the Darfur Liberation Front (DLF), overwhelmed the government's isolated and poorly defended police and army outposts. The government tried to hit back, marshaling the few military battalions it had stationed in the region (most remained stationed in South and East Sudan) as well as pro-government militias from local Arab tribes. But the atrocity-laden counterattack failed to arrest the rebellion as much as it drove local communities to join and support the insurgents. As the insurgency spread and opened new bases outside of Jebel Marra in North Darfur, it struck an alliance with the SPLA based in South Sudan, who began to transfer substantial material support (some originating from Eritrea) to the Darfurian rebels' bases in Dar Zaghawa. Cross-border support from the Chadian army also strengthened the rebels' capabilities, facilitating their spectacular surprise attack on El Fasher, the capital of North Darfur, in April 2003. Humiliated and panicked, the government of Sudan, fearing the insurgency would spread to the interior of the country, unleashed a

---

[5] Per-capita revenue in the three Darfurian states in 1998 was 687 Sudanese dinars versus 1822 Sudanese dinars for all states in northern Sudan. If Khartoum State and Red Sea State, the two states with the most economic activity are excluded, Darfur's revenue per capita is still only half of the northern states average (1,374 Sudanese dinars). Calculated based on data from World Bank, *Sudan: Stabilization and Reconstruction*, vol. II: *Statistical Appendices* (Washington, DC: World Bank, 2003).

[6] Robert O. Collins, *A History of Modern Sudan* (Cambridge: Cambridge University Press, 2008), p. 14.

massive and indiscriminate counterattack, executed by a combination of the Sudanese Armed Forces (SAF) and the notorious *janjawiid* militias. The counterinsurgency eventually slowed the rebellion, forcing a military stalemate, but at a devastating cost to the region's civilian population.

As illustrated in Table 5.1, the core variables often associated with the weak state paradigm (see Section 2.2) perform quite well in accounting for conflict escalation in Darfur. The Darfurian rebels took advantage of weak state institutions, a large population, the geographic concentration of their ethnic groups, mountainous terrain, external support from Eritrea (via the SPLA), and transnational kinship ties in Chad to launch a formidable insurgency that won a string of some forty military victories in 2002 and 2003. Only through massive indiscriminate violence and displacement was the Sudan government able to contain the rebellion.

The Darfur case, however, also reveals the inherent limitations of the weak state paradigm—namely, that it is too static to account for the dynamic process of civil war. While the factors described in Table 5.1 increase the latent risk of civil war in Darfur, they poorly account for temporal variation in large-scale political violence in the region, such as why full-scale civil war broke out in 2003 but not before. In fact, in the early 1990s, with the presence of the same structural conditions, the government of Sudan was able to effectively defeat an armed rebellion it faced in Darfur without committing mass atrocities and avoiding civil war. That is the key puzzle that this chapter addresses: How, given that structural conditions overdetermine conflict in Sudan, especially in Darfur, was the government of Sudan able to effectively defeat a rebellion it faced in the region in the early 1990s?

In-depth interviews with a number of key actors involved in the conflict provide evidence to support the political networks hypothesis. The Islamic Movement's strong network among Darfurians, especially those from non-Arab groups, enhanced its societal control and counterinsurgency capabilities. In addition to improving the regime's access to local information, its extensive political network facilitated the regime's ability to elicit cooperation from local communities that ensured they refrained from helping the insurgents—what I label the "brokerage mechanism." Overall, Chapter 5 illuminates how an extensive political network facilitates *cooperative counterinsurgency*.

The rest of the chapter is as follows: I begin by providing a historical background to Sudan and its violent conflicts. I then describe the origins and rise to power of Sudan's Islamic Movement before turning my attention to the Islamic Movement's network in Darfur. Next I explain the impact of

TABLE 5.1 *Structural Determinants of War in Darfur, Sudan*

Determinants of civil war	Mechanisms and relevance to Darfur case
Weak state institutions	Darfur is poorly served by both state infrastructure (e.g., there are no tarmacked roads connecting the region to the capital Khartoum) and state institutions (such as the state bureaucracy and police force). Weak state capacity undermines the government's ability to effectively accommodate and repress potential opposition (Fearon and Laitin 2003; Hendrix 2010).
Population size	Relative to other regions in northern Sudan, such as the East or North, Darfur has a large population, estimated to be 6 million people pre-conflict, or 25 percent of the population of northern Sudan. More populous territories are hypothesized to experience more conflict because of greater monitoring costs for the government (Fearon and Laitin 2003; Hegre and Sambanis 2006).
Ethnic geography	Ethnic groups in Darfur are organized territorially, which is hypothesized to increase civil war risk by facilitating opposition coordination and increasing the monitoring costs for the government (Weidmann 2009).
Mountainous terrain	In the middle of Darfur stands Jebel Marra (Marra Mountain) (alt. 10,000 feet), which roughly covers an area of 55 miles by 40 miles. Rugged terrain is hypothesized to increase civil war risk by providing sanctuary for rebellions, which increases feasibility (Fearon and Laitin 2003).

(continued)

TABLE 5.1   *Continued*

Determinants of civil war	Mechanisms and relevance to Darfur case
External support	Darfur is surrounded by conflict-affected and weak states, the most important being Chad and the region (and now the state) of South Sudan. Conflict-affected neighbors are hypothesized to increase civil war risk as a critical source of sanctuary and matériel for potential rebels (Salehyan 2007, 2009).
Transnational kinship ties	A number of ethnic groups straddle the Sudan–Chad border, such as the Zaghawa, which is hypothesized to serve as another source of resources and support for potential rebels (Gleditsch 2007; Cederman, Girardin, and Gleditsch 2009).

the Islamic Movement's seizure of power on the politics of Darfur. The last three parts of the chapter analyze the emergence of an armed movement in Darfur led by Daud Bolad; how the government effectively leveraged its network in Darfur to countermobilize against Bolad; and what we learn from this episode about *how* interethnic political networks facilitate cooperative counterinsurgency.

5.2 HISTORICAL BACKGROUND

5.2.1 Social Structure

Sudan, formerly Africa's largest country before South Sudan gained independence on July 9, 2011, sits in the northeastern quadrant of the states. (See Map 5.1.) As one country, it was contiguous with nine other states Egypt to the north; Eritrea and Ethiopia to the east; Kenya, Uganda, and the DRC to the south; and Central African Republic, Chad, and Libya to the west. Port Sudan, the country's major port on the Red Sea, is only 150 kilometers from Saudi Arabia. The capital, Khartoum, sits at the confluence of the Blue and White Nile Rivers, which originate from Ethiopia and Uganda respectively. From Khartoum northward the Nile flows as a single river. The Nile River Valley, the area from north of Khartoum to Dongola in northern

Sudan, is home to the country's historical ruling elite, *awlad al-bahr* ("sons of the river"). Characteristic of the political topography of other African states,[7] power radiates from this region, diminishing as it extends into the hinterland, such as the western region of Darfur, which was the last region to be incorporated into the country in 1916, or to the South, which was separated from the North by the British colonial administration.

Demographically, the country is one of the most diverse in Africa. According to the EPR, politics has revolved around thirteen politically relevant ethnic constellations, with Arabs from the Nile River Valley, in particular the Ja'aliyin, Shaigiya, and Danagla, dominating the central government. Regional, religious, and cultural identities are also important. Four broad cultural-religious social groups exist in Sudan and are seen by some Sudanese as reflecting a certain social hierarchy. Distinct from the dominant political and economic class comprised of the Muslim Arabs from the Nile River Valley (including the Ja'aliyin, Shaigiya, and Danagla) are other Muslim Arabs (such as the Misseriya, Rizeigat, and Hamar), whose homelands are outside of the Nile River Valley and many of whom maintain a nomadic lifestyle. Non-Arab (African) Muslims, including the Fur and Zaghawa from Darfur and Nuba from the border of North and South Sudan, represent another social grouping, who, according to Idris, despite being Muslims, are stigmatized by their "slave status or origins"[8] and "have never been fully accepted into society and have not been treated by the Arabized and Islamized state as citizens with social and political rights."[9] The final grouping includes the non-Muslim, non-Arab (African) peoples from southern Sudan, which includes the Dinka, Nuer, and Shilluk among others. As both non-Arabs and non-Muslims, southern Sudanese often faced both societal and governmental discrimination and persecution.[10] The emergence of the SPLM in the

---

[7] Herbst, *States and Power in Africa*.

[8] Parts of Sudan, especially South Sudan, were long the target of slave raids, which has had a lasting impact on societal relations within the country. In fact, according to Deng, "the Turko-Egyptian conquest in 1820–1821 was fundamentally motivated by the desire to recruit Blacks as slave soldiers for the Egyptian army." Francis Mading Deng, "The Legacy of Slavery," in Francis Mading Deng, ed., *New Sudan in the Making? Essays on a Nation in Painful Search of Itself* (Trenton, NJ: Red Sea Press, 2010), p. 102. The persistence of the slave trade into the 1800s reinforced the notion among some northern Muslims that they are of a "superior Arab identity asserting descent from either the Prophet Muhammad or other distinguished Arabian ancestors . . . and the peoples of Southern Sudan, the Upper Blue Nile and the Nuba Mountains as 'enslaveable' non-Arabs." Idris, "Beyond 'African' and 'Arab' in Sudan," p. 198.

[9] Idris, "Beyond 'African' and 'Arab' in Sudan."

[10] Deng, *War of Visions*. Jok Madut Jok, *War and Slavery in Sudan* (Philadelphia, Pa.: University of Pennsylvania Press, 2001).

1980s and its calls for a secular and pluralist Sudan as an antidote to the northern assimilationist model strengthened a distinctive non-Arab identity for many peoples.[11]

5.2.2 More War than Peace: An Overview of Sudan's History since Independence

The modern Sudanese state has its origin in the nineteenth century when a Turco-Egyptian invasion sought to occupy the territory as an extension of the Egyptian province of the Ottoman Empire. The primary institutional legacy of the Turkiyah (as this period of colonization was known) was the introduction of a centralized administration located in Khartoum that incorporated the disparate kingdoms, ethnic groups, and stateless societies indigenous to the territory into a single political entity based on clientelism and repression.[12]

In the 1880s, a nationalist uprising, originating in western Sudan, spread throughout the country, taking the form of an Islamic revolution. The uprising, known as the *Mahdiyya*, was led by Muhammad Ahmad Ibn Abdallah, who proclaimed himself the "Mahdi," meaning "the guided one," and sought to replace the corrupt and oppressive Turco-Egyptian administration rule with an Islamic state.[13] After the fall of Khartoum in January 1885, the Mahdists consolidated their control of the country, establishing an Islamic state. The liberation of Sudan was short-lived, however. In 1896, the British, fearful of French and Italian encroachment in the region, and on the prized Nile River, launched a massive expeditionary force to defeat the Mahdists and colonize Sudan. By the end of 1898, the British had destroyed the Mahdist army.

To establish and maintain political control, the British also relied on clientelism and repression. From Khartoum, where economic activities were overseen and the colony managed, the colonial administrators worked with northern Arab elites, particularly the leaders of the two dominant Sufi religious sects: the Ansar and the Khatmiyya. These constituencies benefited from educational and vocational opportunities offered by the colonial state[14] and would eventually lead the nationalist movements that

---

[11] Ann Mosely Lesch, *The Sudan: Contested National Identities* (Bloomington, Ind.: Indiana University Press, 1998), p. 15.

[12] Peter Woodward, *Sudan, 1898–1989: The Unstable State* (Boulder, Col.: Lynne Rienner, 1990).

[13] For a thorough history of the Mahdi revolution, see P. M. Holt, The *Mahdist State in the Sudan, 1881–1898* (Oxford: Clarendon Press, 1958).

[14] Nowhere was this more apparent than in Sudanese enrollment for Gordon Memorial College in Khartoum (the predecessor of the modern-day University of Khartoum), the

mobilized for independence.[15] In the rural areas, the British ruled through its policies of indirect rule, a British colonial policy invented by Lord Lugard and applied first to Nigeria and subsequently to other British colonies, in which the colonial government empowered tribal chiefs (real or constructed) to govern indigenous populations. These policies led to the tribalization and marginalization of the rural areas, while resources and political power became concentrated in Khartoum.

Rather than rule the country as one entity, however, the British increasingly separated parts of the hinterland, especially the non-Muslim South, from the rest of the country. In 1922, the Closed District Ordinances was passed which required individuals to obtain permits from the colonial administration to travel to the South and parts of Darfur. In 1930, the British administration formalized a Southern Policy to rule the two regions separately. By isolating the South, the objective, according to Harold MacMichael, the British civil secretary in Sudan in the 1930s, was "to build up a series of self-contained racial and tribal units with structure and organization based, to whatever extent the requirements of equity and good government permit, upon indigenous customs, traditional usage and beliefs."[16] Thus the British encouraged the spread of Christianity and the establishment of English as the lingua franca at the expense of political and economic modernization, which was ongoing in the North. This colonial legacy of disproportionate development translated into northern political and economic domination of the newly independent Sudanese state.

After the end of World War II, with nationalism on the rise throughout Africa and other colonies, the British, under pressure from northern politicians and the Egyptians (who were keen on reducing the number of states along the Nile River), unified the two regions and established a single legislative assembly to represent the entire country.[17] As the British made further preparations to withdraw, southern Sudanese found themselves more and more politically marginalized. During the Sudanization of the country's civil service, only six southerners were appointed to some 800 positions,

British-run school for indigenous Sudanese that sought "to train loyal servants of the Sudan government." "The great majority of students were drawn from the northern riverain provinces: in 1929, some 311 of 510 were from Khartoum and Blue Nile Provinces, while Kassala accounted for only ten, the Red Sea Province for one, and Darfur and the entire Southern Sudan were unrepresented." M. W. Daly, *Empire on the Nile: The Anglo-Egyptian Sudan, 1898–1934* (Cambridge: Cambridge University Press, 1986), p. 385.

[15] Heather J. Sharkey, *Living with Colonialism: Nationalism and Culture in the Anglo-Egyptian Sudan* (Berkeley, Calif.: University of California Press, 2003).

[16] Robert O. Collins, *Shadows in the Grass: Britain in the Southern Sudan, 1918–1956* (New Haven, Conn.: Yale University Press, 1983), p. 173.

[17] Lesch, *The Sudan*, p. 34.

while only three southerners participated in the forty-six-member national constitutional commission, which rejected their calls for a federal constitution.[18] Ultimately, for those from South Sudan, independence was seen to be merely a change of colonial masters, "with the northerners taking over from the British and defining the nation in accordance with the symbols of their Arab-Islamic identity."[19] With southern protests of neocolonialism falling on deaf ears, an army mutiny in 1955 among southerners in the town of Torit in South Sudan was a precursor for decades of southern armed resistance in a bid to force the northern-dominated post-independence governments to address their political grievances.

At independence on January 1, 1956, Sudan's government, led by the National Unionist Party (NUP), failed to address the southerners' discontent and was unable to establish a permanent constitution that could unite the fragile and fractured country. Less than six months after independence, the NUP government lost a no-confidence vote and was replaced by a coalition between the Umma Party and the People's Democratic Party. Faced with economic crisis and nationwide strikes in 1958, the new government handed over power to the army. The army junta, led by Major General Ibrahim Abboud, accelerated a program of Arabization and Islamization in the south, escalating the growing conflict, which would become a full-scale civil war in 1963.

The southern rebels, known as Anyanya,[20] at first drew largely from Equatoria Province, from where one of their leaders, Joseph Lagu, came. (Lagu, one of only two southerners admitted to the Sudan Military College in 1958, defected from the army in 1963 and was present at the founding of the rebellion.)[21] With very weak political networks in South Sudan, the central government in Khartoum struggled to contain Anyanya, despite the rebellion in 1964 numbering not more than "5,000 insurgents scattered in fragmented units under no single command."[22] Divisions among the rebels would plague their military effort over the next five years. In 1969, however, Lagu, benefiting from external support from Israel,[23] was able to consolidate control of the Anyanya and

[18] Lesch, *The Sudan*, p. 34.
[19] Deng, *War of Visions*, p. 102.
[20] Anyanya is a variant of the word for snake poison in the language of the Madi, a tribal group whose traditional homeland lies south of Juba and straddles the Sudan and Uganda border and from where some of the first leaders of the rebellion came, including Joseph Lagu.
[21] Collins, *A History of Modern Sudan*, p. 104.
[22] Collins, *A History of Modern Sudan*, p. 80.
[23] Israel began supporting the southern rebellion after the Six-Day War in 1967 and intensified its support after Jaafar al-Nimeiri's seizure of power in Khartoum in May 1969;

the rebellion, reorganized as the Southern Sudan Liberation Movement/ Front, demonstrated a greater capacity to inflict more significant costs on the government forces.[24]

With the war intensifying, political change in Khartoum opened the door for peace talks. In 1969, Jaafar Nimeiri, a military officer from northern Sudan, seized power in a coup d'état. A follower of Nasser and his pan-Arab socialist ideology, Nimeiri came to power backed by officers in the Sudanese Communist Party (SCP). The influence of the SCP pushed Nimeiri to take a more accommodative stance toward the South, and, on June 9, 1969, merely sixteen days after coming to power, his government announced the Declaration of Regional Autonomy that recognized the historical and cultural differences between North and South Sudan and offered the South regional autonomy within a unified Sudan to address southern grievances.[25] In July 1971, Nimeiri was nearly deposed from power in a coup d'état by Communist-backed military officers. The coup attempt did not derail the momentum for peace, however. In March 1972, a historic peace accord was signed between the government of Sudan and the Southern Sudan Liberation Movement. The Addis Ababa Agreement, as it was known, included a number of far-reaching provisions; it offered South Sudan regional autonomy governed by a High Executive Council and People's Regional Assembly, representation in the central government, the incorporation of the rebel forces in the army, and freedom of religion as well as English as the principal language for the southern region. Most importantly, it stipulated that the provisions of the agreement could not be amended without a three-quarters vote in the national assembly and a two-thirds vote in a referendum in South Sudan. Signing the peace deal shored up Nimeiri's fragile domestic position and improved his reputation among Western countries, including with the United States, which, after the crackdown on the SCP, supplanted the Soviet Union as Sudan's new major foreign patron.

By the late 1970s, however, Nimeiri's political calculus had changed. The Addis Ababa Agreement had brought domestic and international acclaim, but it did not underwrite political stability in the North. Between 1976 and

the Israelis viewed Nimeiri as a radical pan-Arabist in the vein of Nasser and sought to balance against him. Tim Niblock, *Class and Power in Sudan: The Dynamics of Sudanese Politics, 1898–1985* (Albany, NY: State University of New York Press, 1987), pp. 273–274.

[24] Douglas H. Johnson, *The Root Causes of Sudan's Civil Wars: Peace or Truce* (Oxford: James Currey 2011), p. 37.

[25] Robert S. Kramer, Richard Andrew Lobban, and Carolyn Fluehr-Lobban, *Historical Dictionary of the Sudan* (Lanham, Md.: Scarecrow Press, 2013), p. 325.

1978, Nimeiri faced four forcible attempts on his hold on power from the northern opposition, including two coup attempts and two armed incursions from Libya. The armed incursions were led by prominent northern opposition forces, the Umma Party and the Islamic Movement. In an attempt to strengthen his regime and support base in the North, Nimeiri pursued a policy of "national reconciliation" in which he struck an alliance with his former adversaries. Hassan al-Turabi, the leader of the Islamic Movement and Sorbonne-trained lawyer, would become attorney general.

The National Reconciliation swung the pendulum of political influence back in favor of northern political forces. This did not bode well for the South. The political shift coincided with Nimeiri's personal and political embrace of Islamism. Under the influence of a small group of religious clerics, Nimeiri implemented *sharia* (Islamic) law in September 1983.[26] The adoption of Islamic law was strongly opposed in the South, both on religious grounds and as a violation of the spirit of the Addis Ababa Agreement, which stipulated southern autonomy on cultural and religious policies. The September Laws were one of many policies the Nimeiri government adopted in the early 1980s that amounted to a complete abrogation of the Addis Ababa Agreement. Other violations of the peace accord included unilateral division of the South into three regions and repudiation of the South's economic independence; appropriation of oil income generated by oil exploration in the South (that should have gone to the southern government); Nimeiri's interference in the southern High Executive Council (including the arbitrary dissolution of the body and the southern regional assembly in 1980 and 1981); and attempts to redraw the north–south border in a bid to transfer oil-rich and agricultural-rich areas to the North.[27]

It was amid a general deterioration of trust in the central government that in January 1983 a group of soldiers from the 105th battalion in Bor, southern Sudan, refused orders to be transferred to northern Sudan. The mutineers viewed the transfer of southern soldiers to the north as an attempt by Nimeiri to further weaken the South. Dr. John Garang, a

---

[26] Many believe Turabi, as attorney general, orchestrated the implementation of the September 1983 laws, but, while he did endorse them, it was more the work of a small group of Sufi clerics who were close to Nimeiri.

[27] The seminal sources on the breakdown of the Addis Ababa Agreement include Mansour Khalid, *Nimeiri and the Revolution of Dis-May* (Boston, Mass.: KPI, 1985). Abel Alier, *Southern Sudan: Too Many Agreements Dishonoured* (London: Ithaca Press Reading, 1992). Lesch, *The Sudan*. For a useful summary, see David H. Shinn, "Addis Ababa Agreement: Was It Destined to Fail and Are There Lessons for the Current Sudan Peace Process?" *Annales d'Ethiopie*, 20 (2004): 239–259.

lecturer at the Sudan Military College and former rebel during the first war, was sent to mediate with the mutineers. Garang, sympathetic to the grievances of the mutineers and having lost all faith in Nimeiri, joined the defecting soldiers.[28] When the army moved against the intransigent unit, the Bor soldiers fled to Ethiopia, taking their vehicles and weapons with them. They also inspired a series of other desertions, mutinies, and revolts in the South throughout the year.[29] The mutinous groups found sanctuary in Ethiopia, where they united to form the SPLA. War had once again erupted in the South.[30]

The "Second Sudanese Civil War" varied from the first civil war in several important ways. First, the locus of the initial rebellion was among the Dinka and Nuer communities rather than Equatorians. Second, Garang, who would become the chairman of the SPLA, sought to nationalize the conflict. He rejected the prevailing discourse that framed the war as a "southern problem" and secession as a solution to the political roots of the conflict. Instead, Garang called for the creation of a "New Sudan"—a secular, democratic, multicultural, multiracial, and federal government that would correct the ethnic, racial, political, religious, and regional fault lines that have divided the Sudanese people. To quote Garang:

The SPLA is determined to fight for a democratic and new Sudan where social justice, freedom and human dignity for all flourish. We fight for a new democratic Sudan in which the nationality question is correctly solved. We fight for a Sudan in which the problem of uneven development is solved such that all the regions of the country, especially the most neglected areas, receive a fair and accelerated socioeconomic development. We fight for a Sudan free from racism; a Sudan in which power is vested in the masses, exercised by them and in their interests; a Sudan in which there is no monopoly of power by any group whether ethnic, religious or regional. We are committed to the liberation of the Sudan; and to us liberation is a continuous process involving not only political and economic liberation, but also liberation of the mind so that the Sudanese are proud of their identity, their heritage, history, values and their historic struggle. We are committed to wrest power from the minority clique in Khartoum and give it to the masses. *Finally, I would like to reiterate that the SPLA/SPLM is a genuine Sudanese Movement that is not interested in concessions for the south, but a*

[28] Some suggest that Garang was party to the conspiracy before the mutiny began. Jok, *War and Slavery in Sudan.*

[29] Douglas Johnson and Gérard Prunier, "The Foundation and Expansion of the Sudan People's Liberation Army," in M. W. Daly and Ahmad Alawad Sikainga, eds., *Civil War in the Sudan* (London: British Academic Press 1993), pp. 124–125.

[30] Important variation existed within the South as to which communities sided with the rebels and which sided with the government at the outset of the conflict. For the local fault lines of the conflict and details on intra-southern violence in the 1980s, see Johnson, *The Root Causes of Sudan's Civil Wars.*

movement that is open to all people of the Sudan to join and participate in the building of the new and democratic Sudan.[31]

Garang argued that only the complete transformation of the state could solve its various ills. In calling for a New Sudan, Garang sought to take the war to the North and recruit allies from northern communities, such as in Nuba Mountains, eastern Sudan, Darfur, and even among Arabs, who had been disadvantaged by the country's structure of power.

This represents the third key difference with the first Sudanese civil war: the rebels made important inroads into northern Sudan, especially the Nuba Mountains and southern Blue Nile. As Douglas Johnson notes, "the way was often prepared for the [SPLA] by [the government's use of] Arab militias . . . who vicitimised the non-Muslim (and even some Muslim) black populations of those areas, and thus produced ready sympathizers for the SPLA."[32] One of the most important militia forces was the *murahaliin*, which primarily came from the Misseriya and Reizigat Baggara groups living just north of the north–south border. With strong political links with the Umma Party, given the number of Ansaris among the Baggara, Khartoum's reliance on the *murahaliin* as a proxy force increased significantly when Sadiq al-Mahdi of the Umma Party became prime minister in 1986 after the downfall of the Nimeiri regime in an intifadha and military coup.[33] Facing drought and loss of land to mechanized farming, the Baggara who joined the *murahaliin* were enticed by opportunities to claim new fertile land, loot villages, and enslave southerners.[34] The use of the *murahaliin* would have devastating consequences for the local civilian population, however, as the force became integral to the scorched-earth counterinsurgency campaign employed by the government.[35]

---

[31] John Garang, *John Garang Speaks*, edited by Mansour Khalid (London: KPI Limited, 1987), p. 36.

[32] Johnson, *The Root Causes of Sudan's Civil Wars*, pp. 83–84.

[33] This was due to the preexisting links between the Umma Party and the Baggara as the latter were generally members of the Ansar sect and supporters of the Umma Party. Johnson, *The Root Causes of Sudan's Civil Wars*, p. 82.

[34] Johnson, *The Root Causes of Sudan's Civil Wars*.

[35] Alex de Waal, "Some Comments on Militias in Contemporary Sudan," in M. W. Daly and Ahmad Alawad Sikainga, eds., *Civil War in the Sudan* (London: British Academic Press, 1993). For a personal account of the human-rights abuses committed by the murahaleen, see Dave Eggers, *What Is the What? The Autobiography of Valentino Achak Deng: A Novel* (New York: Random House, 2006).

5.2.3 Sudan's Arab–African Divide and the Contours of Civil War

One key implication of Khartoum's devastatingly effective use of Arab militias is that, as Garang and the SPLA pushed north, they failed to bridge the country's Arab–African ethnopolitical cleavage.[36] During the first war, this cultural cleavage was not as salient as the regional divide between the North and South. But, as the war spilled over into the North, the Arab–African divide would become the dominant master cleavage. As Francis Deng explains:

> Unlike its secessionist predecessors, the Sudan People's Liberation Movement and Army (SPLM/A) recast the objective of the war as the liberation of the whole country and the creation of a New Sudan, in which there would be no discrimination on the grounds of race, ethnicity, religion, culture or gender. This recasting of the war objectives appealed to the non-Arab regions of the North, which began to see themselves as Africans and became more conscious of their own marginalization by the Arab-dominated center.[37]

The Arab–African divide presents a political puzzle, however. In terms of marginalization, Arab groups outside of the Nile River Valley are more similar in terms of their material conditions to non-Arab groups in the periphery than riverain Arabs. (In other words, a Baggara from southern Kordofan is likely to have similar socioeconomic status to a Nuba from southern Kordofan than to a Shaigiya or Ja'aliyin from northern Sudan.) Yet, since the war was nationalized in the 1980s, almost all of Sudan's rebel movements have come predominantly from "African groups," such as the Dinka, Nuer, Nuba, Ingessana, Zaghawa, Fur, Masalit, and Beja. In contrast, members of "Arab groups" have tended to stay on the sidelines or have predominantly fought in pro-government militias.[38] This pattern of violence has been poorly explained in the existing literature. Journalists tend to simply take it as a given, implying that ethnic and cultural differences are too strong to be overcome. Academics, on the other hand, tend to elide over a discussion of why the Arab–African divide seems so important. Instead, they favor materialist accounts of rebellion. For example, Douglas Johnson implies that land dispossession accounts for patterns of rebellion in northern Sudan.[39] Yet, he also suggests that land dispossession

---

[36] Mamdani provides a useful history of how British colonial policies contributed to this ethnopolitical divide. Mahmood Mamdani, *Saviors and Survivors: Darfur, Politics, and the War on Terror* (New York: Doubleday, 2009).

[37] Francis Deng, "Sudan at the Crossroads," in Francis Mading Deng, ed., *New Sudan in the Making? Essays on a Nation in Painful Search of Itself* (Trenton, NJ: Red Sea Press, 2010)

[38] See Johnson, *The Root Causes of Sudan's Civil Wars.*

[39] Johnson, *The Root Causes of Sudan's Civil Wars.*

contributed to the formation of the *murahaliin*. Thus, land dispossession may have contributed to armed mobilization, but it fails to distinguish why individuals may fight with or against the central government.

Consistent with a meso-level approach to civil war, one would expect the conflict dynamics to be mediated by extant political and economic networks between central elites and various peripheral groups. For example, as explained above, as the SPLA pushed north, the government of Sadiq al-Mahdi supported the *murahaliin* militias from the Misseriya and Reizigat Baggara groups to counter the SPLA. Strong political and religious networks tied Sadiq al-Mahdi's Umma Party to these groups as they shared Ansari religious affiliation. Personal ties cemented these networks. Babo Nimir, the paramount chief of the Misseriya, one of the most influential Baggara tribes, married into the Mahdi family.[40] Moreover, the military general responsible for organizing the *murahaliin*, Fadallah Burma Nasir, was also a Misseriya.[41] Nasir would be appointed state minister of defense in 1987 by Sadiq al-Mahdi and would remain a high-ranking member of the Umma Party.

Yet, the Ansari and Khatmiyya networks that served as the backbone of Sudan's two dominant political parties, while extremely weak in South Sudan, penetrated both "Arab" and "African" ethnic groups in northern Sudan. Mansour Khalid suggests these networks account for why civil war had been avoided in Darfur for most of Sudan's postcolonial history as it raged in South Sudan since the early 1960s:

Why then have the people of Darfur, together with other politically or economically disadvantaged areas in Sudan's geographic north, continued to suffer their affliction in silence, while southerners, without ceasing, persevered in their struggle against what they perceived to be political marginalization and economic neglect? Sectarian affiliation, especially in the case of Darfur, had something to do with it. In reality, affiliation to the two major Islamic sects (Ansar and Khatmiyya) was so staunch in Kordofan and Darfur, in the west, as it was in the Red Sea and Kassala in eastern Sudan, that those regions became the main bastions of support for the two sectarian-based political parties (Umma and National Unionist). The two parties ruled the Sudan during successive multiparty regimes and throughout their rule sought to maintain the political status quo and ensure acquiescence to it by their supporters in those regions.[42]

[40] Richard Cockett, *Sudan: Darfur and the Failure of an African State* (New Haven, Conn.: Yale University Press, 2010).

[41] Prunier, *Darfur*.

[42] Mansour Khalid, "Darfur: A Problem within a Wider Problem," in Salah M. Hassan and Carina E. Ray, eds., *Darfur and the Crisis of Governance in Sudan: A Critical Reader* (Ithaca, NY: Cornell University Press, 2009), p. 37.

If, as Khalid suggests, cross-cutting political networks helped central governments in Khartoum avoid large-scale political violence in Darfur throughout the post-independence period, why does large-scale violence break out in 2003? To answer this question, it is critical to understand how the political networks connecting the center and Darfur change over time. One of the most significant developments was the overthrow of the government of Sadiq al-Mahdi in a coup d'état in 1989 by the NIF. The NIF sought to systematically dismantle the Ansari and Khatmiyya networks to weaken the political support of the sectarian parties. The NIF had its own cross-cutting Islamist network, which its members simply referred to as the *tanzim* (or organization, in Arabic), that penetrated the periphery, especially Darfur, which it sought to leverage to establish societal control. The *tanzim* could not match the depth of the patron–client networks of the traditional political parties with their roots in the Sufi sects which have been active in Sudan for 150–200 years, but it nonetheless represented a formidable political network that penetrated every major town in northern Sudan. In the next several sections I describe the rise of the *tanzim* and analyze its consequences for the NIF's control in Darfur.

5.3 THE ORIGIN AND ORGANIZATION OF SUDAN'S ISLAMIC MOVEMENT

As successive Sudanese governments, both civilian and military, failed to establish a stable central government and bring peace to southern Sudan in the 1960s and 1970s, an Islamic Movement was growing in strength and cultivating a national following. Calling for the establishment of an Islamic order to save the country from sectarianism, conflict, and corruption, more and more Sudanese embraced the movement as an alternative to the traditional political parties. Through patient organization, a savvy tactical alliance with Nimeiri in the late 1970s, shrewd investments in Islamic banks in the 1970s, recruitment in the army and establishment of an elaborate and self-sufficient security apparatus in the 1970s and 1980s, by the late 1980s the Islamists were in a position to seize control of the state. In this section, I review the rise of Sudan's Islamic Movement or National Islamic Front.

5.3.1 The Rise of the National Islamic Front

The roots of the NIF extend back to the 1940s when Sudanese students studying in Egypt at Al-Azhar University embraced the Islamist teachings of Hassan al-Banna and interacted with members of Banna's Muslim Brotherhood.[43] Upon returning to Sudan, these students disseminated the ideology of the Muslim Brotherhood and found a receptive following, particularly among rural students from the west, who were excluded from the dominant riverain political class,[44] which was preparing to assume control of the Sudanese state at independence.[45] In 1954, the Sudanese Muslim Brotherhood (al-Ikhwan) was formed, but it remained autonomous from the Muslim Brotherhood in Egypt. In its early years, the Ikhwan, limited by its size[46] and the dominance of the traditional political parties,[47] served as a pressure group for the adoption of an Islamic order based on an Islamic constitution.

The Sudanese Ikhwan suffered a blow when, in 1959, its leader, al-Rashid al-Tahir, was arrested and sentenced to five years in prison for conspiring to overthrow the military government. Al-Tahir's involvement in a coup attempt with communist elements (the archrival of the Islamists) caused dissension within the Islamic organization. With its leader in jail and the movement divided, the Ikhwan's activities and influence waned over the next few years.

In 1964, the Ikhwan experienced a resurgence with the return of Dr. Hassan al-Turabi to Sudan. Turabi had been active in the Islamic Movement since his days as a student at the University of Khartoum in the early 1950s, in which he was a member of the executive committee of the Islamic Liberation Movement, a precursor organization to the Muslim Brotherhood. He then left for Europe to study for an MA at the University of London (1957) and a Ph.D. in law at the Sorbonne in Paris (1964). Abroad, Turabi became heavily engaged in global Islamic issues (he co-founded and became secretary general of the Islamic Society for the Support of the Algerian Cause), while following closely the development

---

[43] The history of the Islamic Movement in Sudan is drawn from Abdelwahab El-Affendi's authoritative account, *Turabi's Revolution: Islam and Power in Sudan* (London: Grey Seal, 1991).

[44] Interview with Ali al-Haj, Bad Godesberg, Germany, January 18, 2007.

[45] Peter Woodward, "Sudan: Islamic Radicals in Power," in John L. Esposito, ed., *Political Islam: Revolution, Radicalism, or Reform?* (Boulder, Col.: Lynne Rienner, 1997), pp. 95–114, at p. 98.

[46] According to El-Affendi, "Ikhwan was itself a far from well-organized group at the time, and in no position to set up and control a nationwide organization. Its members were mostly students or recent graduates, the oldest being in their mid-twenties, while their numbers did not exceed a few score." *Turabi's Revolution*, p. 57.

[47] The dominant political parties of the day, the Umma Party and the National Unionist Party, each derived support from the two principal Sufi sects and dwarfed the Muslim Brotherhood at independence.

of the Islamic Movement at home. Turabi returned to Sudan in 1964 and accepted a position in the Faculty of Law at the University of Khartoum. He became an outspoken critic of the Abboud regime and encouraged the student protests that coalesced in October 1964 and that would lead to Abboud's fall from power.

In 1964, Turabi was elected secretary general of the Islamic Charter Front (ICF), a political coalition of the Muslim Brotherhood and smaller Sufi groups. Hoping to expand the Islamic organization beyond its elitist core, Turabi sought to draw support from all walks of Sudanese society and to create a self-sufficient movement that did not have to rely on other parties and entities to implement its Islamic program. He also steered the movement in a more political direction. This provoked a conflict with the old guard close to the Egyptian Ikhwan, who resisted expansion and felt the movement should remain underground and focus on social and educational activities.[48] Turabi prevailed, however, and purged the old guard, replacing them with young, modern, and devout Islamists—a move that would not only strengthen Turabi's control of the Islamic Movement but would strengthen his reputation as one who would not brook dissent to his rule. Having eliminated the old guard, in the 1970s Turabi rebuilt the Ikhwan, and the *tanzim* was born.

The 1970s would prove a critical period for the Islamic Movement with the coming to power of the secular and socialist military officer, Jaffar Nimeiri, in a coup d'état. With the new government initially supported by its archrival, the Sudanese Communist Party, the Ikhwan fiercely resisted the Nimeiri regime, first through demonstrations organized by its supporters in the universities and then, in alliance with other opposition political parties, as part of the National Front that was conducting operations out of neighboring Libya. The military pressure from Libya, including the spectacular and bloody invasion in 1976,[49] forced Nimeiri to adopt a more accommodative posture to the opposition.

A year later, Nimeiri initiated the National Reconciliation in which he offered the northern opposition groups amnesty if they joined the ruling Sudan Socialist Union and promised to support his regime. Though, as Turabi admitted, "participation in the Socialist Union was against all our instincts," he recognized that it provided an invaluable opportunity for the

---

[48] Interview with Ali al-Haj, Germany, January 18, 2007.
[49] The forces involved in the 1976 invasion included the Umma Party, Islamic Movement, and other regional groups. Up to one year prior to the operation, the dissidents were infiltrating Khartoum and caching weapons in preparation for the attack. The attack failed, however, leading to as many as 3,000 deaths. El-Affendi, *Turabi's Revolution*, p.109.

Islamic organization in its goal to further penetrate society and develop as a national movement.[50] The Islamists seized on it and, under the guise of the National Reconciliation, began to infiltrate critical government institutions such as the military and security. Moreover, the movement began to build up and strengthen its own internal security apparatus and intelligence network.[51] The Ikhwan also took advantage of the introduction of Islamic banking in the Sudan in 1978, which favored Islamists in its employment and loan policies and was initially avoided by the traditional business class.[52] These developments transformed the Islamic organization into what Abudallahi Gallab has described as a "corporation," with Turabi serving as its chief executive officer.[53] It was during this time, in a series of shura council meetings, that Turabi decided, in consultation with his disciples, that "they should work to take power."[54]

In April 1985, Nimeiri was overthrown by the army after several days of violent nationwide strikes against rising food and petrol prices. A Transitional Military Council assumed control of the government, and multiparty parliamentary elections were held in 1986. With the reintroduction of multiparty politics, the Ikhwan launched a political party, the National Islamic Front, to participate in the elections. Having developed into a national movement, the NIF increased its vote share from 5 to 21 percent of the vote between the 1965 and 1986 elections,[55] though most of its gains were made in the graduate constituencies.[56] In the rural areas it still lagged far behind the traditional political parties, the Umma and the DUP (the Democratic Unionist Party, the successor to the NUP). Nonetheless, the NIF was now clearly a national political player, and by 1988 it was back in government as a coalition partner. Turabi served as attorney general and then foreign minister. But the NIF's participation in

---

[50] Mohamed E. Hamdi, *The Making of an Islamic Political Leader: Conversations with Hasan al-Turabi* (Boulder, Col.: Westview Press, 1998), p. 21.

[51] Interview with Ali al-Haj, January 18, 2007. Interview with Abdallah Hassan Ahmed, one of the leaders of the Islamic Movement at time of 1989 coup, Khartoum, January 25, 2007.

[52] El-Affendi, *Turabi's Revolution*, p. 116.

[53] Abdullahi A. Gallab, *The First Islamist Republic: Development and Disintegration of Islamism in the Sudan* (Burlington, Vt.: Ashgate, 2008).

[54] Interview with Abdallah Hassan Ahmed, January 25, 2007.

[55] Atta El-Battahani, "Multi-Party Elections and the Predicament of Northern Hegemony in Sudan," in Michael Cowen and Liisa Laakso, eds., *Multi-party Elections in Africa* (Oxford: James Currey, 2002), p. 266.

[56] In graduate constituencies in which voting was limited to those who had at a minimum completed secondary school, the NIF won almost 40 percent of the vote and ended up winning twenty-three of the twenty-eight special seats. El-Battahani, "Multi-party Elections," pp. 263–264.

the central government would be short-lived as Prime Minister Sadiq al-Mahdi faced severe discontent from officers in the military.

The military, facing a deteriorating situation in southern Sudan in the war against the SPLA, grew frustrated with Sadiq al-Mahdi and his continued reliance and support for the *murahaliin* from Kordofan and Darfur at the expense of the official armed forces. Pressure mounted on al-Mahdi when his minister of defense, General Abd al-Majid Khalil, resigned in February 1989, calling for the prime minister to either provide the military with the resources necessary to prosecute the war or negotiate with the SPLA.[57] The minister of defense was also aggravated by the increasing influence of the NIF in the coalition government, in particular Turabi's role as deputy prime minister and foreign minister, as he felt it was hamstringing his ability to acquire military support from Egypt and Saudi Arabia.[58] A day after Khalil's resignation, an ultimatum was sent by 150 senior officers to al-Mahdi, giving him one week to reform the government, alter his foreign policy and begin peace talks with the SPLA. Under the weight of this pressure, in mid-March al-Mahdi dissolved the cabinet and built a new government with partners who endorsed negotiations with the SPLA. The NIF refused to join as the peace talks called for a suspension of *sharia*, or Islamic law, which was a central pillar of its Islamist program. The military's ultimatum, and the changes adopted by Sadiq al-Mahdi, raised clear red flags for the NIF. Moreover, the NIF became concerned as it perceived other factions within the military, including its rivals the Baathists and Communists, were plotting coups d'état.[59] The NIF feared either of these developments—a political settlement with the SPLA or their rivals taking power in a coup—would deliver a severe, if not irrevocable, blow to its survival as an organization and its plans to build an Islamic state in Sudan. Facing such an uncertain future, the NIF moved first and seized power in a coup d'état on June 30, 1989.[60]

The coup d'état ushered in the Al-Ingaz (Salvation) Revolution. The Islamic Movement orchestrated the revolution, but, to mask its influence, the coup-plotters banned the NIF along with all other political parties and jailed Turabi. The public face of the new government was the

---

[57] Lesch, *The Sudan*, p. 83.

[58] El-Affendi, *Turabi's Revolution*, p. 189.

[59] Interview with Professor Ibrahim Ahmed Omer, member of Islamic Movement's shura council at time of coup, Khartoum, January 28, 2007. Interview with Abdallah Hassan Ahmed, January 25, 2007.

[60] As one Islamist characterized it, "It was a pre-emptive coup. They thought their existence was at stake." Interview with Abel-Rahim Hamdi, London, July 3, 2009.

Revolutionary Command Council (RCC), which was composed entirely
of military officers, and a civilian council of ministers. Real power, however, rested in the Islamic Movement and its *tanzim*, which operated as a
shadow government.

5.3.2 The *Tanzim*

At the time the Islamists seized power, the *tanzim*, which was first developed in the 1970s, was at the height of its organizational potency. The
tanzim as a ruling organization diverged from the stylized model of weak
states described in Chapter 2 in several important ways. First, as illustrated
in Figure 5.1, it had a tightly integrated, hierarchical structure rather than
one in which power was dispersed among interlocking networks of factions of violence specialists (as portrayed schematically in Figure 2.2). At
the top of the hierarchy sat Hassan al-Turabi, deferentially referred to as
sheikh by his followers, as the secretary general. Administratively, he was
supported by an executive committee—the secretariat. Informally, he was
advised by a group of six Islamists whom he selected to help him prepare
for the movement's seizure of power.[61] In his decision-making, the secretary
general consulted the movement's shura council, which was comprised of
some of the most important members of the movement. Below the shura
was the general conference, which included representatives of the Islamic
Movement from throughout Sudan.[62] This structure existed nationally and
was replicated in each of the country's nine provinces. (Shortly after the
coup, Turabi formally dismantled the *tanzim* in order to build a new organizational structure whose membership would go beyond Islamists and
incorporate Sudanese society more broadly. This new organization would
become the National Congress Party (NCP). As I discuss in Chapter 6, the
dismantling of the *tanzim* would contribute to institutional uncertainty
within the regime. Despite the formal dismantling of the *tanzim*, the network of Islamists remained the backbone of the regime's political apparatus and was the principal organizational structure that connected the
Islamists at the top of the Sudanese state to the periphery.)

Access to the *tanzim* was exclusive, which facilitated cooperation
among Islamists as it strengthened their social identity and personal

---

[61] The Group of Six included Yassin Omar al-Imam, Abdullah Hassan Ahmed, Ali al-Haj
Mohamed, Ibrahim al-Sanousi, Ali Osman Mohamed Taha, and Awad Ahmed al-Jaz.
[62] Interview with Ali al-Haj, January 18, 2007. Interview with Abdallah Hassan Ahmed,
January 25, 2007.

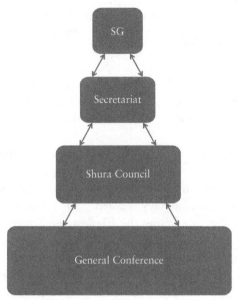

FIGURE 5.1 Organizational Structure of Sudan's Islamic Movement

bonds while generating incentives to work together to retain the benefits of membership in their own hands. Entry was only gained after one proved his or her loyalty and commitment to the Islamic Movement,[63] which one demonstrated through years of religious study, participation in social programs, political mobilization, and intensive training in security and intelligence activities in camps spread throughout the Sudan.[64] Members were recruited as early as secondary school and the *tanzim* kept meticulous records of its members.[65] The NIF then used these records to screen recipients for banking loans, educational scholarships, and government appointments, which would become the key material benefits of membership in the *tanzim*. Beyond mutual material interests, the bedrock of the *tanzim* would become the strong fraternal bonds (*asabiyyah* in Arabic) that formed among Islamists as they studied, prayed, trained

[63] According to one ranking member, "Political allegiance was paramount to the Islamic Movement not religious training." Interview with Abel-Rahim Hamdi, July 3, 2009.
[64] Interviews with various members of Sudan's Islamic Movement. See also Gabriel Warburg, *Islam, Sectarianism, and Politics in Sudan since the Mahdiyya* (Madison, Wisc.: University of Wisconsin Press, 2003), p. 207.
[65] Interview with Abdallah Hassan Ahmed, January 25, 2007.

and worked together. As many of their activities occurred underground, it intensified the intimacy of members' interactions and the levels of trust that they had to place in each other. This represented a second point of divergence from other African regimes.[66] Members' Islamists identities trumped tribal and regional ones and would serve as the basis of collective action. In fact, Islamist members were socialized to disavow what were seen as atavistic parochial identities that hindered modernization and social progress.[67]

The strength of sectarian and tribal identities presented the NIF with several problems, however. First, it ensured that its social engineering project, which sought to efface these traditional identities through the spread of Islamism, was fiercely resisted.[68] In response, after coming to power, Al-Ingaz, the new name the Islamists embraced, would turn to extreme levels of repression and state violence to try to enforce its social project, which far surpassed anything Sudanese society had experienced before, including during military rule by Abboud and Nimeiri.[69] Second, while members of the *tanzim* trusted each other, there remained a large trust gap between societal forces and the new Al-Ingaz regime. During times of crisis when the regime needed to quickly mobilize society, it fell back on ethnic mobilization, as I describe occurred in Darfur during the first rebellion (see Section 5.6). Third, as mistrust within the regime would break down and Islamist bonds would fray in the late 1990s, members would fall back on regional and ethnic ties as I describe in Chapter 6. Ironically, the Islamic Movement, which sought more than any other organization to transcend traditional societal divisions and transform Sudanese society, would, in the end, break down along ethnoregional lines, in fact the very same ones that brought down Sudan's first Islamist government—the Mahdiyya in the 1880s.

[66] As I explained in Section 2.2, political networks in Africa's weak states are often organized along ethnic lines but need not be. The NIF is a great example of a political movement in post-independence Africa in which ethnic ties did not serve as the basis of the political organization.

[67] Interview with a number of Islamists in Islamic Movement.

[68] The NIF's social planning has been summarized by one of its leading theoreticians as a "continuing revolution for the remoulding of the human being and the institutions in society in accordance with Qur'anic guidance." Cited in de Waal and Abdel Salam, "Islamism, State Power and Jihad in Sudan," 89.

[69] Abdullahi A. Gallab, *The First Islamist Republic: Development and Disintegration of Islamism in the Sudan* (Burlington, VT: Ashgate, 2008). Human Rights Watch, *Behind the Red Line: Political Repression in Sudan*.

5.4 THE *TANZIM* IN DARFUR

The strength of the *tanzim* was not uniform across Sudan and this would have important implications for the Islamists' political control after coming to power. Not surprisingly, there were limited numbers of Islamists from the predominantly Christian South Sudan and among people from the Nuba Mountains who traditionally have had stronger cultural and political ties with those from South Sudan than from Khartoum. (Also the Nuba tend to have strong regional political organizations, such as the General Union of the Nuba Mountains.) Consequently, war which was raging in South Sudan and Nuba Mountains when the Islamists came to power (see Section 5.2.2) continued and intensified as Al-Ingaz, in a bid to mobilize popular support for its new government, labeled the insurgents enemies of Islam and declared *jihad* against southerners and people from the Nuba Mountains.[70] In contrast, however, *Darfur was a region in which the tanzim "was one of the most fully developed."*[71]

5.4.1 History of the Islamic Movement in Darfur

The roots of the Islamic Movement in Darfur go back to the 1960s when Suliman Mustapha, a Zaghawa from northern Darfur, was elected to parliament as a member of the Islamic Charter Front (one of only five seats the ICF won in the 1965 election). Mustapha, one of the first Zaghawa to obtain a university degree, inspired many of his kinsmen and other Darfurians to follow his example at a time when Zaghawa communities were undergoing important socioeconomic changes as drought and desertification forced many to migrate from their tribal homeland in northwestern Darfur to southern and central Darfur.[72]

Following Mustapha's influence, a wave of Zaghawa joined the Islamic Movement, abandoning their traditional affiliations with the Umma Party. Over time the Zaghawa became one of the most active groups in the NIF. The Zaghawa gained such prominence in the Islamic Movement, including in the *tanzim*, the security, and the Popular Defense Forces, that communal rivals of the Zaghawa in North Darfur tended to equate the NIF with the Zaghawa and would despise the governorship of al-Tayib

[70] de Waal and Abdel Salam, "Islamism, State Power and Jihad in Sudan."
[71] El-Affendi, *Turabi's Revolution*, p. 141.
[72] Fouad Ibrahim, "The Zaghawa and the Midob of North Darfur – a Comparison of Migration Behaviour," *GeoJournal* 46, no. 2 (1998): pp. 135–140. A number of Islamists from the Zaghawa I interviewed mentioned how influential Mustapha was.

Ibrahim Muhammad Khair (discussed below) between 1991 and 1993 for his close relationship with members from the tribe.[73] Reflecting on the role of the Zaghawa in Al-Ingaz after the coup d'état, a member of the northern Rizeigat tribe asserted, "The police were Zaghawa. The judges, Zaghawa. The military, Zaghawa. When Arabs went to complain, they would ignore them . . . The Arabs felt unrepresented."[74]

The Darfurian presence in the Islamic Movement went far beyond just the Zaghawa. One of Turabi's closest advisers and a member of his inner cabinet was Dr. Ali al-Haj, a Borno from South Darfur. Other top party leaders hailed from Darfur. Like the Zaghawa, these Darfurians embraced the Islamic Movement for offering them "a route to overcoming their marginalization [and] becoming full, emancipated citizens of Sudan."[75]

The central recruiting grounds for the movement were intermediate or secondary schools, where Islamist teachers were able to influence impressionable young people. The teachers often also chaired Qur'an associations, which would meet after school and serve as a front for the Islamic Movement. Intrigued by the secrecy of the organization and the opportunity to travel to other parts of the Sudan, such as Kassala or Shendi, to interact with other members of the *tanzim*, many Darfurians joined.[76] After secondary school, these young devotees would then meet again at the University of Khartoum where they participated in the movement's underground cells that dominated the university and battled against the state's security forces. These students would go on to become key members of the Islamic *tanzim* in Darfur and benefited from the Islamists' decision to join the Nimeiri government when they could obtain government jobs and experience. (Daoud Bolad's biography exemplifies this recruitment process: see Section 5.6.)

According to some of Turabi's disciples, the NIF's strong following in Darfur also reflected a calculated political strategy by their sheikh. According to Ghazi Salahuddin Atabani, "Hassan al Turabi had a prescient vision of Darfur . . . He learned from history. The Mahdi [the

---

[73] When I was in Sudan in 2005 and 2006 trying to track down al-Tayib Ibrahim Muhammad Khair for an interview, I inquired about his whereabouts from some of the elites from northern Rizeigat in Khartoum who had developed a close relationship with the government for their role in mobilizing the Abbala tribal militias against the SLA in 2003. They revealingly said, "Why do you ask us? Why don't you inquire among his friends the Zaghawa?"

[74] Interview with medical doctor from Darfur working in Khartoum, February 19, 2006.

[75] Alex de Waal, "Darfur Policy Forum: After the Genocide Determination, What's Next?" Available at https://www.ushmm.org/confront-genocide/speakers-and-events/all-speakers-and-events/darfur-policy-forum-after-the-genocide-determination-whats-next (accessed October 4, 2016).

[76] Interview with Zaghawa Islamist in Khartoum, March 20, 2006.

Islamo-nationalist revolutionary leader in the 1880s who liberated Sudan from the Turco-Egyptian colonial regime] had faced the elite of northern Sudan who rejected and ridiculed Mahdism. So he turned to the west and stormed the Nile from Kordofan and Darfur."[77]

One challenge to Turabi's "western political strategy," however, was the political heavyweight in the region, the Umma Party, founded in 1945 with the support and patronage of the son of the Mahdi, Abd al-Rahman al-Mahdi. Drawing on the religious organization that the Mahdi founded (the Ansar), the Umma Party was able to build a strong political machine in western Sudan. The battle for Darfur would come to a head in the 1986 elections. The NIF felt it could exploit the organizational gains it made under Nimeiri and steal some seats from the Umma Party in Darfur. Despite investing a considerable amount of resources in its Darfur campaign, the NIF was soundly defeated in the geographical constituencies. Relying on its well-oiled Ansar network and foreign support from Egypt and Libya, the Umma Party pumped money, sugar, and other patronage to the tribal leaders and other clients in order to mobilize voters.[78] The Umma Party won thirty-four out of thirty-nine seats in the region. The NIF did well among the educated elites, however, capturing all of the graduate constituencies in Darfur.

After being routed in the 1986 election in Darfur by the Umma Party, the NIF was determined to destroy the Ansar's political networks in the region. Thus, as the *tanzim* in Darfur remained dominated by educated (non-Arab) Islamists, the NIF recognized that, unless it was able to woo the tribal leaders and other rural Darfurian elites to its side, it would never achieve political dominance in the region.[79] It also decided that if the old guard refused to cooperate, it would have to cultivate the support of new elites to rival the traditional notables. Thus, after coming to power, the NIF instituted policies, such as redrawing administrative boundaries in Darfur in a bid to undermine the traditional authority of the large tribes in the region that tended to support the Umma Party and mobilize the support of new clients from smaller tribes and those who recently immigrated to Sudan.[80] Both non-Arab tribes (such as the Fur and Masalit) and Arab tribes (including the Baggara Rizeigat and Misseriya) fell victim to

---

[77] Quoted in Flint and de Waal, *Darfur: A New History of a Long War*, p. 19.
[78] Interview with Ali al-Haj, January 18, 2007. Interview with Amin Mahmoud, a NIF candidate for election in 1986, Khartoum, March 7, 2006.
[79] Interview with Abdel Rahim Hamdi, London, July 3, 2009.
[80] Interview with Fur tribal leaders who bore the brunt of this policy, Nyala, South Darfur, December 6, 2005.

the NIF's strategy of divide and rule (*farriq tasud* in Arabic)—what one Darfurian politician described as the "worst legacy of Turabi."[81]

5.5 AL-INGAZ AND THE PACIFICATION OF DARFUR

5.5.1 The Fur–Arab Conflict in the Late 1980s

In the late 1980s when the NIF came to power, the region of Darfur was smoldering from a devastating communal conflict. The violence in Darfur stemmed from a conflict that pitted one of the largest ethnic groups in Darfur, the Fur, who traditionally are sedentary farmers, against nomads from a coalition of different Arab groups. The conflict revolved around competition for natural resources between farmers and nomads but was exacerbated by an extreme Arabist ideological movement that was spreading across the Sahel at the time, pushed by the government of Muammar Gaddafi of Libya, and the free flow of arms due to a proxy war between Chad and Libya.[82]

By 1988, a full-scale civil war was raging in Darfur between a coalition of twenty-seven Arab tribes and the Fur militias. Some of the hardest hit communities were Fur villages in Wadi Salih, in southwest Darfur, a rich agricultural region. According to an investigation by the Sudanese Relief and Rehabilitation Commission in January 1989, in the last few months of 1988 some fifty-seven villages had been burned, 378 people killed, 108 people wounded and 42,000 driven from their homes during the previous few months.[83] Racial ideologies served to intensify the violence as both sides accused the other of genocidal intentions.[84] As the war spiraled out of control, the Sudanese government should have intervened, but it too was paralyzed by ethnic divisions. The central government of Sadiq

---

[81] Interview with Yusuf Takana, former minister of international development, Khartoum, July 25, 2005.

[82] Sharif Harir, "'Arab Belt' versus 'African Belt': Ethno-Political Conflict in Dar Fur and the Regional Cultural Factors," in Sharif Harir and Terje Tvedt, eds., *Short-Cut to Decay: The Case of the Sudan* (Uppsala: Nordiska Afrikainstitutet, 1994), pp. 144–185. Prunier, *Darfur*.

[83] Africa Watch, *The Forgotten War in Darfur Flares Again* (London: Africa Watch, 1990), p. 5.

[84] These perceptions were revealed at the reconciliation conference in which the Fur delegation asserted that "[t]he dirty war that has been imposed upon us [i.e. the Fur], began as an economic war but soon it assumed a genocidal course aiming at driving us out of our ancestral land in order to achieve certain political goals," while the Arab delegation retorted that "let us not be in doubt about who began this war: it is the Fur who in their quest to extend the so-called 'African belt' . . . wanted to remove all the Arabs from this soil." Harir, "'Arab Belt' versus 'African Belt,'" pp. 146–147.

al-Mahdi was accused of supporting the Arab coalition and the regional Darfur government of being sympathetic to the Fur. In May 1989, one of the bloodiest battles of the conflict occurred when a 3,000-strong Arab militia force attacked near Kass, south of Jebel Marra.[85] Despite suffering extensive casualties,[86] the Fur, strengthened by weapons from Hissène Habré, Chad's president, and new military techniques (e.g., trenches were dug around susceptible villages to thwart the effectiveness of the Arab militia raids[87]), repulsed the attack. After the pitched battle near Kass, the Arabs learned that the Fur could not be easily defeated, and the former opted for negotiations.[88] By the time a reconciliation conference opened in El Fasher in May 1989, hundreds of villages had been burned, tens of thousands of livestock had been lost, and over 3,000 Darfurians had been killed, with the Fur suffering more than 80 percent of the deaths.[89]

5.5.2 Promises of Peace, but More Violence

Shortly after taking power, the Islamists declared that one of their key priorities was to bring peace and reconciliation to the warring groups in Darfur. But in the first eighteen months after the coup, violence continued in the region despite the signing of a reconciliation agreement by the warring tribes within the first days of the NIF seizing power. The outbreak of a civil war in Chad in the second half of 1989 and the spillover of the conflict into Darfur undermined the reconciliation agreement reached in July 1989. As Harir describes it, "eight months after the peace agreement was signed, the Fur 'militia forces' and the Arab 'knights' were engulfed in a full-scale civil war in which Fur villages were burned and Arab camps were shelled daily."[90] With foreign forces remaining in Darfur, the Arab and Fur militias refused to disarm. Al-Ingaz was accused of perpetrating the conflict by backing the Arab tribes, in a similar manner to the Sadiq al-Mahdi government.[91] Arrests of opposition leaders, including

---

[85] Africa Watch, *The Forgotten War in Darfur Flares Again*, pp. 5–6.

[86] According to Africa Watch, the government admitted 460 casualties, with some estimates as high as 1,500. *The Forgotten War in Darfur Flares Again*.

[87] Prunier, *Darfur*, p. 69.

[88] Prunier, *Darfur*, p. 69.

[89] This information comes from Harir who gathered it from the proceedings of the tribal reconciliation conference held in El Fasher throughout May, June and July of 1989, which reflects official police records. Harir, "'Arab Belt' Versus 'African Belt.'" Prunier suggests a figure three times as high. Prunier, *Darfur*, p. 65.

[90] Harir, "'Arab Belt' Versus 'African Belt,'" p. 178.

[91] In a memorandum written in May 1991, Zaghawa tribal leaders also accused the government of "plans to put political power in the hands of Arab ethnic groups in Dar Fur."

prominent Fur, after the coup in its sweeping crackdown of potential sources of opposition to the new Islamist regime contributed further to this perception.

In 1990 and 1991, however, the central government moved to reduce the violence in Darfur. First, it signaled to the Chadian rebels operating in Darfur that they could no longer use the region as a staging ground for their rebellion.[92] (Shortly thereafter, the Chadian rebels, led by Idriss Déby, launched a blitzkrieg attack on the Chadian government and successfully overthrew the regime of Hissène Habré on December 2, 1990.) Second, President Bashir appointed a new governor in Darfur who oversaw an aggressive disarmament campaign in line with the Arab–Fur reconciliation agreement. These two events would help to bring an element of stability the region had not experienced in years.

5.5.3 A New Governor Disarms Darfur

Déby's victory in Chad helped to reduce some of the violence in Darfur, but the region remained insecure due to an abundance of weapons, continued armed robbery, and the recurrence of ethnic conflict, despite the Arab–Fur reconciliation agreement signed in July 1989. Some Darfurians, particularly from the Fur tribe, held accountable the first governor appointed by Al-Ingaz, Abul Ghassim Mohammed Ibrahim, a military officer from the Shaigiya tribe in northern Sudan, for failing to restore stability to the province. They felt "he was supporting the Arab militias," actively recruiting Arab immigrants from Chad into the regime's popular committees and granting them other privileges, such as allowing them to stay on Fur lands.[93] (Other Sudanese, Darfurians, and non-Darfurians, insist this was more of a systematic policy originating from Turabi himself as part of his effort to spread Islamism throughout the region. Critics felt Turabi saw Arabs as more reliable vanguards in the spread of Islamism

---

Quoted in "Sudan Government Fails to Insure Stability and Peace in Darfur," Sudan Human Rights Organization Press Release, March 1, 2003. See also Africa Watch, *The Forgotten War in Darfur Flares Again*; A. Agaw Jok Nhial, Nur Tawir Kafi, and Eltigani Seisi, "Human Rights Abuses in Sudan," *Review of African Political Economy*, 20 (58) (1993): 110–118. For an alternative view of this period, see James Morton, "Conflict in Darfur: A Different Perspective" (HTPSE, June 2004). Available at www.jfmorton.co.uk/pdfs/ConfDar.pdf (accessed August 22, 2016).

[92] Interview with Darfurian Islamists, Khartoum, January 23, 2007.
[93] Interview with Darfurian Islamists, Khartoum, January 23, 2007.

than non-Arabs.[94] Contradicting this claim is, as I have described, it was non-Arab Islamists who dominated the *tanzim* in Darfur.)

Importantly, however, the Islamist network in Darfur and the interactions between the central government and Darfurian intermediaries ensured the top decision-makers in Al-Ingaz learned of the local grievances with the governor. One particular meeting, held in Khartoum in May 1991 between President Bashir, the governor of Darfur, Abul Ghassim, and a group of Darfurian leaders to discuss how the Ingaz government could support the region, proved to be a key turning point.[95] At the meeting, Abul Ghassim and his allies presented a rosy picture of the situation in Darfur and described to Bashir how the Ingaz government was succeeding in bringing peace to the region. These dubious statements infuriated the Fur present at the meeting. Salaheddin Mohammed al-Fadul, one of the Fur tribal leaders and importantly also an Islamist since his student days,[96] stood up and declared, "This man is not telling the truth about the conditions on the ground" and went on to describe to Bashir how armed robbery was continuing, especially in Fur areas, and the lack of implementation of the Fur–Arab reconciliation agreement.[97] According to those present, this exchange undercut Bashir's confidence in Abul Ghassim. Not long after the meeting, Bashir replaced him as governor with another northern military official, Dr. al-Tayib Ibrahim Muhammad Khair, known as al-Tayib "Sikha," who was also a high-ranking Islamist and member of the RCC.

While there is no conclusive evidence to confirm that Abul Ghassim was replaced because of this meeting,[98] the Fur who attended believed this to be the case. According to Fur interviewed, the new governor, al-Tayib "Sikha" was "an acceptable choice"[99] and a "very serious and a fair

---

94 As one Darfurian intellectual observed: "When [the NIF] came to power, it came to give the Arabs the upper-hand. The machinery it used to do this was political Islam . . . the Fur are the first group that established an Islamic state in Sudan and helped spread it in West Africa, but the NIF felt it cannot trust them in spreading its civilization project. Instead they depended on Arabs who are less religious but more loyal." Personal interview, Khartoum, July 19, 2005.

95 Interview with Amin Mahmoud, a Fur Islamist from Zalingei, Khartoum, January 23, 2007.

96 Fadul would become the magdum of the Fur in south Darfur in 2006. See Jérôme Tubiana, Victor Tanner, and Musa Adam Abdul-Jalil, "Traditional Authorities' Peacemaking Role in Darfur," *Peaceworks*, 83, United States Institute of Peace, 2012.

97 Interview with Salaheddin Mohammed al-Fadul, Khartoum, January 30, 2007. Confirmed by Dr. Idriss Yusef, personal interview, Khartoum, January 28, 2007.

98 Some also suggest that Déby did not have good relations with Abul Ghassim, and, after ousting Habré, Déby asked Bashir to replace Abul Ghassim as governor of Darfur.

99 Interview with Amin Mahmoud, a Fur Islamist from Zalingei, Khartoum, January 23, 2007.

man."[100] Al-Tayib "Sikha" impressed the Fur by beginning to learn the Fur language and showing respect for Fur culture and the Sultanate.[101]

At the time al-Tayib "Sikha" became governor, the government was trying to disarm the Darfur region. In April 1991, the minister of interior, General Faisal Ali Abu-Salih, toured Darfur and announced all "unauthorized weapons" were to be collected. After his appointment in August 1991, al-Tayib "Sikha" was tasked with accelerating the disarmament process. Over the next several months the government would collect tens of thousands of weapons. According to Fur members of the *tanzim*, al-Tayib "Sikha" personally "would visit the tribes, calling on people to put down their weapons at a time when violence prevented the Fur from moving outside their villages."[102] The government was seen as implementing policies to protect the Fur.

Throughout this period, Al-Ingaz employed members of the *tanzim*, civilian ministers, and the army to try to reduce the number of weapons in the region. As one Zaghawa minister in Darfur described it, he traveled throughout North Darfur and collected thousands of weapons in exchange for the promise of compensation (which never came).[103] The army was also employed in the disarmament campaign but tended to act in a heavy-handed fashion, leading to several massacres.[104]

By November 1991, Darfurian government officials were celebrating the "demilitarization of the region" and seeing some gains in reducing tribal conflict. In hindsight, non-Arab Darfurians would look back and complain that the weapons-collection program disproportionately targeted them, but not the Arab nomads,[105] who were allowed to keep their weapons on the grounds that their vocation as nomads required having weapons to protect

---

[100] Interview with Fur Islamist from Kass, Khartoum, January 27, 2007.
[101] Interview with Salaheddin Mohammed al-Fadul, January 30, 2007.
[102] Interview with Fur Islamist from Kass, Khartoum, January 27, 2007.
[103] Interview with Ali Shammar, member of Islamic Movement and state minister in early 1990s, Khartoum, November 13, 2005.
[104] The most notable massacre was in Al-Wadha, South Darfur, in early 1991 by a Sudanese general, Samir Mustapha Khalil. This led some Zaghawa to perceive that Al-Ingaz government was intent on persecuting them. Interview with retired non-Islamist Zaghawa military officer, N'djamena, August 6, 2009.
[105] In November 1991, the *Sudan Democratic Gazette*, a newsletter published in London by Bona Malwal, a southerner, commented, the African tribes "are being officially described as armed robbers. This description has provided a justification for the campaign to forcibly disarm the African tribes whilst ignoring the weaponry in the hands of the Arab tribal militias," whose arms are not considered illegal "because they were originally supplied by Khartoum" (p. 6).

their animals.[106] Nonetheless, by October 1991, the level of violence in Darfur was the lowest it had been in years.

5.6 A DISAFFECTED ISLAMIST AND THE COALESCENCE OF A DISSIDENT GROUP

In 1989 and 1990, as Darfur once again erupted in ethnic violence (and before the disarmament program was initiated), an exiled group of Fur was in the planning stages of forming an armed insurgency with the goal of entering Darfur to both protect and mobilize the Fur against the Arab militias that continued to operate in spite of the reconciliation agreement. The exiled group was led by Daoud Yahya Bolad, an Islamist from the Fur tribe who gained prominence within the Islamic Movement as a university student and who would go on to be one of the NIF leaders in Darfur.

Bolad was born near Nyala in southern Darfur in 1952. He grew up in a family belonging to the Mahdist Ansar sect, which politically supported the Umma Party. In primary school, he learned Arabic by studying the Qur'an, and in intermediate school he was recruited into the Muslim Brotherhood by one of his schoolteachers.[107] Bolad joined the Islamic Movement at a time when the organization was growing into a national movement and fighting an ideological battle with the SCP for the support of the country's educated elite and a political battle against the regime of Jaafar Nimeiri who came to power in a coup d'état in 1969 initially supported by the SCP.

In 1971, Bolad entered the University of Khartoum to study engineering and impressed his brothers in the Muslim Brotherhood with his activism and devotion to the Islamist cause.[108] That same year he was jailed and tortured by police for his political activities.[109] After his release from jail, he remained active with the Islamic Movement, and in 1975 he became the first non-riverain northerner to be president of the Khartoum University Student Union (KUSU), an extremely influential position among the Islamists, whose support base rested with the students and

---

[106] Interview with Ali Shammar, Khartoum, November 13, 2005.

[107] Harir, "'Arab Belt' Versus 'African Belt,'" pp. 297–299.

[108] Many northern Islamists I met in Khartoum often remember Bolad as a friend and devoted brother in the movement. When I ask them why he left the movement and took up arms, they often shake their heads, not understanding what led him "astray." Personal interviews. Khartoum, 2005–2006.

[109] Prunier, *Darfur*, p. 73.

among the political class in general, which often led to "an accelerated track to national political leadership."[110]

At a time when the Islamists were forced underground, the KUSU played an integral role in their political program. As Harir explains:

KUSU, *de facto*, was the executive body of the Islamic Movement above the ground. On a more general level, it coordinated, activated and led the widely spread national opposition against Nimeiri's regime. Hence, the chairman of the Khartoum University Students' Union mediated between the interned leadership of the Islamic Movement and the Brotherhood on the one hand and the leadership of the national opposition abroad and its cells on the other—but more importantly carried out street actions such as rioting, demonstrations and general protest activities between 1971 and 1978 . . . On another level, the chairman of KUSU worked closely with Turabi, Ali Osman Taha and the presently prominent leaders of the Khartoum regime. Besides ideological affinities, which are basic, the chairman also developed personal and friendly relations with prominent personalities in the Islamic Movement in a manner befitting a top leader.[111]

Bolad excelled as KUSU president. Moreover, his impressive oratory skills, tough character, and knowledge of the Qur'an earned him the deep respect from his brothers in the movement. After university, Bolad returned to Nyala where he served as the NIF's secretary general of South Darfur[112] and also started a carpentry and iron business financed by an Islamic bank.[113] He ran for parliament in the South Nyala constituency in the 1986 election but lost, and some in the NIF blamed him for the party's poor showing in the region.[114]

After the 1986 election, as the Fur–Arab conflict erupted, Bolad became increasingly concerned by the communal violence, especially as some of his Fur relatives were killed in the fighting.[115] He voiced his concerns within the Islamic Movement, but to no avail.[116] When Turabi entered the cabinet in 1988 and "silenced all criticism of the . . . mayhem in Darfur,"[117] Bolad became critical of the Islamist leader and accused

[110] Julie Flint and Alexander de Waal, *Darfur: A Short History of a Long War* (London: Zed Books, 2005), pp. 20–21.

[111] Sharif Harir, "Racism under Islamic Disguise," in Hanne Veber et al., *Never Drink from the Same Cup: Proceedings of the Conference on Indigenous Peoples in Africa* (Copenhagen: IWGIA and the Centre for Development Research, 1993), at p. 300.

[112] Interview with Amin Mahmoud, Khartoum, January 23, 2007.

[113] Harir, "Racism under Islamic Disguise," p. 301.

[114] Interview with Ali Shammar, Khartoum, Sudan, March 29, 2006.

[115] Interview with Ahmed Ibrahim Diraige, Fur, former governor of Dafur in 1980s and leader of Sudan Federal Democratic Alliance, London, March 2006.

[116] Correspondence with former member of *tanzim* from Darfur, April 17, 2006.

[117] Prunier, *Darfur*, p. 73.

him of complicity in the violence.[118] Bolad increasingly questioned the movement's claim to equality. In a letter to a friend, Bolad revealed his frustration: "even when I go to the mosque to pray, even there, in the presence of God, for them I am still a slave [*abd*] and they will assign me a place related to my race."[119]

Exacerbating Bolad's growing disenchantment with the Islamic Movement was a bitter power struggle over leadership of the *tanzim* in western Sudan with Ali al-Haj. As a senior member of the Islamic Movement, Bolad expected to be leader of the NIF in Darfur, but Turabi selected Ali al-Haj.[120] As the power struggle mounted, Bolad was accused of corruption and funneling funds from the NIF to support the Fur.[121]

After the coup d'état, however, Bolad increased his activities on behalf of the NIF, perhaps in the hope of receiving a high-level position in the new government. He traveled throughout Darfur, holding meetings and calling for citizens to support the new regime. He was also working toward Fur–Arab reconciliation, collecting blood money among the Fur to pay the Arabs and calling on Arabs to put down their weapons.[122] As jobs were handed out to Islamists after the coup, Bolad was appointed as an engineer in a power station in Khartoum, a very lowly position for a former leader of the KUSU. Meanwhile, the violence resumed in Darfur, and Bolad left the country for Egypt.

In November 1989, Bolad convened a meeting in Cairo with other Fur elites, including Ahmed Diraige, the former governor of Darfur and leader of the Darfur Development Front.[123] At the top of their agenda was what to do about the persistent and devastating violence against the Fur by the Arab militias, even in spite of the reconciliation agreement. It was at this meeting that they decided to create a movement with both a political and a military wing that would serve to protect the Fur.[124] They recognized that they needed financial and military support and identified Hissène Habré of Chad, who had been supplying weapons to the Fur militia in the 1980s and who had been secretly assisting the SPLM through

---

[118] Interview with Ahmed Ibrahim Diraige, London, March 2006.

[119] Quoted in Prunier, *Darfur*, p. 73.

[120] Interview with Ahmed Ibrahim Diraige, March 2006. Interviews with Darfurian Islamists, 2005–2006.

[121] Correspondence with former member of *tanzim* from Darfur, April 17, 2006. Interview with Abdallah Hassan Ahmed, January 25, 2007.

[122] Interview with Fur Islamist from Kass, Khartoum, January 27, 2007.

[123] Interview with Ahmed Ibrahim Diraige, March 2006.

[124] Interview with SLA member whose father was present at the meeting, Asmara, Eritrea, February 26, 2005.

Ethiopia,[125] as a suitable patron. They were hoping Habré would allow them to build training camps in Chad from where they could launch an invasion into Darfur.[126]

After the Cairo meeting, they met again in Addis Ababa, Ethiopia, from where Bolad, along with Diraige and several other Fur, went to N'djamena to try to solicit support from Habré. Yet when they met Habré in 1990 he was preoccupied with the growing insurgency led by Déby coming from Dar Zaghawa. Focused predominantly on defending eastern Chad from Déby's forces, Habré was not in a position to help the Fur movement. The group flew back to Addis Ababa and tried to figure out its next move.[127]

While waiting in Addis, two fateful events changed the course of the dissident activities. First, Déby, supported by the NIF, overthrew Habré, ending any hopes they had of launching an insurgency from Chad into Darfur. Second, they met representatives of the SPLM, which had been working out of Ethiopia since the rebel movement was founded in 1983. In Addis they met Mansour Khalid, Yassir Arman, and other members of the SPLM who were eager to introduce the Fur group to Dr. John Garang, the leader of the SPLM/A, who was in Meridi, western Equatoria, commanding military operations.[128] After trekking for more than a month from Ethiopia to Equatoria, they met a receptive Garang. Garang convinced Bolad's group to think beyond its parochial concern about the Fur and to work to change the whole political system and embrace his vision of a New Sudan. The group decided to join the SPLM/A and open a new front in Garang's war against the central government in Darfur, following the model of the Nuba Mountains.[129]

5.7 INSURGENCY VERSUS COUNTERINSURGENCY IN DARFUR, 1991–1992

Over the next three months, the group of Fur (fifteen in total) remained in the SPLA bases in southern Sudan where they received military training. Garang assigned Commander Abdel Aziz al-Hilu, who was from the Nuba Mountains but whose father was from the Masalit, a tribal group

---

[125] Interview with Yassir Arman of the SPLA, Khartoum, March 29, 2006.
[126] Interview with Ahmed Ibrahim Diraige, March 2006.
[127] Interview with SLA member whose father fought with Bolad, Asmara, Eritrea, February 26, 2005.
[128] Interview with Yassir Arman of the SPLA, March 29, 2006.
[129] Interview with Ahmed Ibrahim Diraige, March 2006.

based in West Darfur, to lead the Bolad contingent. The group of Fur was to be accompanied by 1,000, predominantly Dinka, soldiers. The goal was to reach Jebel Marra, establish a military base, and launch attacks throughout Darfur with the support of antigovernment militias and other Fur, who Bolad expected to rise up and support the insurgents. Bolad had sent several agents to the Jebel Marra region to mobilize local support.

In July 1991, the contingent of SPLM members led by Bolad and al-Hilu made their move from the South into Darfur. They trekked by foot through western Bahr al-Ghazal into southwestern Darfur in an area with few paved roads and rugged terrain. Shortly after they left for Darfur, the SPLA was rocked by a major split between Garang and several of his disaffected rebel commanders that would lead to a protracted and devastating war between rival rebel factions over the next decade.[130] Despite the disruption and weakened logistical support, Bolad and al-Hilu went forward with the operation. To try to avoid Arab tribal homelands, they crossed as close to Central African Republic as possible. (See Map 5.2.)

After three months of trekking through western Bahr al-Ghazal and then along the CAR and Sudan border into southern Darfur, the expeditionary force was first spotted in early November in Radom National Park by a wildlife park ranger.[131] Catching the government by surprise, the SAF quickly mobilized a battalion from al-Geneina in western Darfur with the aim of cutting off the rebels as they moved westward along the border. As the SPLA force moved west, its first military engagement was not with the SAF but the Fursan, a militia from the Beni Halba, a cattle-herding (Baggara) Arab tribe whose homeland is in southwestern Darfur (around the district of what today is called Edd al Fursan). In this early battle, Bolad lost a notebook containing precise details of the planned operation, which was recovered by pro-government forces, proving to be a huge intelligence coup for the government.[132] Moving westward, the first military engagement with the SAF battalion from Geneina occurred

[130] This coup was orchestrated by Riek Machar and several other high-ranking SPLA leaders who differed with Garang over the control of the rebel movement and its political strategy. In Salva Kiir's speech on December 16, 2013, mentioned in Section 1.1, this is the 1991 event he is referring to.

[131] Information from this section comes from a confidential lessons-learned document written by the Sudanese Armed Forces. "Darfur Lions Military Operation," Sudanese Armed Forces, undated. Interviews with Darfurian Islamists knowledgeable of the episode also proved very useful, including Khalil Ibrahim, the late leader of the Justice Equality Movement (JEM), who was one of the leaders of the *tanzim* in Darfur at the time, Asmara, Eritrea, February 24, 2005.

[132] Flint and de Waal, *Darfur: A New History of a Long War*, p. 24. Interview with Amin Mahmoud and Ali Shammar, Khartoum, January 23, 2007.

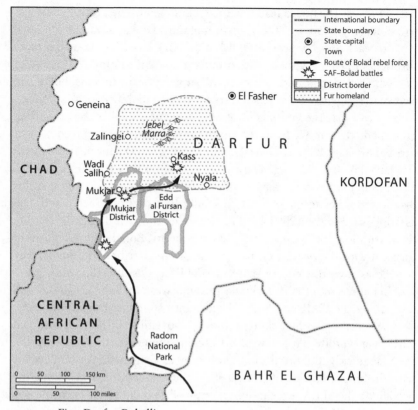

MAP 5.2 First Darfur Rebellion, 1991–1992

just inside the Mukjar District. The SPLA recorded a decisive victory, killing 166 government soldiers and putting the SAF on the defensive.

As they pushed forward to the town of Mukjar, the government mobilized two battalions of the SAF, which again the SPLA forces overwhelmed. After this victory, Bolad and his forces set up camp in Kass area on the foothills of Jebel Marra, the mountain sanctuary they set out for with the expectation that thousands of Fur recruits would join them once they secured a base there.[133]

But Bolad was unaware the government had disarmed the Fur militias only months before.[134] With the Fur militias disarmed and the insurgents lacking the capacity to protect local forces as they organized, many Fur

---

[133] Interview with Yassir Arman of the SPLA, Khartoum, March 29, 2006.
[134] According to Fur informants who met Bolad after he was captured, he admitted he did not realize the situation had changed.

hesitated to join the rebellion for fear of being vulnerable to government reprisals. In fact, one Fur in the Islamic Movement felt compelled to warn Bolad about the local sentiment: "I succeeded in sending a letter to Bolad, in which I told him the security situation had changed; it was better than when he left. We fear that the people will not join him. We asked him if it is possible to go back. If he were arrested, we are not sure if we would be able to help or not."[135]

As the SPLA made its way toward Jebel Marra, Darfur's governor, al-Tayib "Sikha," called several Fur Islamists to Nyala to discuss how to counter the rebellion. As one Fur in the *tanzim* explained,

Dr. al-Tayib "Sikha" gathered the leaders of Fur in Nyala and formed a committee. He asked us to go to Zalingei and Wadi Salih and then report back to discuss with him what to do next. In the field we were informed that the local government [under the orders of the army] arrested some of the Fur leaders . . . because they feared the Fur will support Bolad.[136]

Concerned that these arrests would worsen the conflict and drive the Fur to join the rebellion, the committee asked the people not to join the rebellion and promised to compel the government to cease the arrests.

Upon returning to Nyala, they informed al-Tayib "Sikha" that the Fur did not support Bolad, mainly because the rebellion was seen as SPLA (i.e. a "southern movement"), but if the arrests continued it would drive them into the hands of the insurgents. Trusting his brothers in the *tanzim* as credible interlocutors, al-Tayib "Sikha" instructed the Sudanese security to stop arresting the Fur. Moreover, the governor ordered the Arab militias that had looted animals from the Fur to return them in order to ensure the local communities did not support the rebels.[137]

The Fur brokers would provide one final check on government atrocities when the SAF lost track of Bolad's forces for fourteen days after the SPLA unit had been blocked from going to Jebel Marra and was dispersed in Wadi Salih by the Fursan militia, supported by the government army. In its frustration over not being able to locate Bolad, the army once again increased its harassment of Fur villages, who the military believed were harboring the rebels. Again the Fur Islamists intervened. Some interceded directly with the security forces to ensure the release of their kinsmen,[138] while others again appealed to al-Tayib "Sikha," warning of

[135] Interview with Amin Mahmoud, Khartoum, March 7, 2006.
[136] Interview with Amin Mahmoud, Khartoum, January 23, 2007.
[137] Interview with Salaheddin Mohammed al-Fadul, Khartoum, January 30, 2007.
[138] Interview with Fur Islamist from Kass, Khartoum, January 27, 2007.

the consequences if the atrocities continued. Instead of using the army to search for Bolad, they suggested that it would be more politically accept-able to use the Fur themselves. In the end, it would be a Fur who found Bolad hiding in Deleig town and turned him over to the government. After his capture, Bolad was shown on television, "in which he appeared bat-tered and exhausted but composed . . . and promised a trial for his 'trea-sonable act' . . . [but he] was too embarrassing a phenomenon to live to defend himself in a court of law."[139] Instead, the former top Islamist was executed by a security officer.

5.8 ANALYSIS AND THEORETICAL IMPLICATIONS: EXPLORING THE POLITICAL NETWORKS HYPOTHESIS

In 1991, the government of Sudan effectively defeated what I label the First Darfur Rebellion,[140] when the SPLA, backing the disaffected Islamist Daud Bolad, sought to extend their war against Khartoum into western Sudan. What accounts for how Al-Ingaz was able to defeat Bolad's force, despite such unfavorable structural conditions? Drawing on extensive interviews with Islamists in the *tanzim*, Fur tribal leaders, members of the Bolad rebellion, officials in the SPLA, and Sudanese military officers, I have presented evidence demonstrating that integral to the regime's ability to effectively put down the First Darfur Rebellion short of mass violence was the strong political network it could leverage in the region at the time. The First Darfur Rebellion thus helps to flesh out the *political networks hypothesis of civil war* developed in Section 2.4.

The case study also helps to illuminate *how* interethnic political net-works effectively reduce the risk of civil war. First, the Islamic *tanzim* helped to implement a disarmament campaign the government carried out prior to Bolad's force entering Darfur. With the Fur militias disarmed, many Fur hesitated to join the rebellion for fear of being vulnerable to government reprisals. The thousands of armed Fur that Bolad had told the SPLA would rise up and join them once they entered Darfur never materialized. With very little local support, Bolad's rebellion stalled.

---

[139] Harir, "Racism under Islamic Disguise," p. 302.

[140] This does not seem an unreasonable connotation as the leaders of the SLA and the JEM insurgencies in the early 2000s were clearly inspired by Daud Bolad and felt that they were continuing the struggle that he had started. For example, the leaders of the JEM who wrote the *Black Book* described Bolad as a martyr, while Abdel-Wahid Mohamed al-Nur, the leader of the SLA, said he was continuing the revolutionary movement begun by Bolad. Interview with Abdel-Wahid Mohamed al-Nur, Asmara, Eritrea, February 22, 2005.

Second, strong interethnic networks in Darfur helped the government to minimize indiscriminate violence that may have triggered a full-scale civil war as happened in South Sudan and the Nuba Mountains in the 1980s and that would happen in Darfur in 2002 and 2003.[141] As the SPLA entered into Darfur and engaged government forces, the governor, al-Tayib "Sikha," activated Fur Islamists in the *tanzim* to help in counter-mobilization. These trusted brokers played two crucial roles. First, consistent with Kalyvas's theory of selective violence[142] and the evidence Lyall provides from Chechnya,[143] they helped to provide the government with accurate information about the location and movement of the rebels as well as to distinguish active dissidents from the broader population. But, in addition to denouncing the rebels to the government, they also played a crucial role in ensuring the government was able to maintain its control in Darfur and facilitate cooperation between the government and local Fur communities during a time when uncertainty and mutual suspicion nearly drove the sides to choose costly, non-cooperative strategies (i.e. the government choosing to attack Fur villages for fear they were going to support the rebels, and noncombatants joining the rebellion in the face of indiscriminate violence). In the next section, I elucidate the theoretical mechanisms about how local brokers help to maintain the government's control and produce what I call *cooperative counterinsurgency*.

5.8.1 Dense Political Networks, Brokerage, and Cooperative Counterinsurgency

In Darfur in the early 1990s many local Fur communities were predisposed to oppose the Bolad rebellion. Though many probably sympathized with Bolad's political goals, they were wary of more violence in their homeland. The Arab–Fur war that ravaged their communities in the late 1980s had finally ended and peace had returned to the region. They feared that with Bolad's rebellion they would once again incur the wrath of the Arab militias and government security, and, with their

---

[141] Many of the Fur I interviewed about this period indicated that the government's counterinsurgency operations were not characterized by large-scale atrocities or a scorched-earth campaign. De Waal makes a similar assessment when he compares the government's devastating and indiscriminate counterinsurgency operations in April 2003 in Darfur to the "level-headed" response in 1991 in which "there were arrests and a crackdown, but no indiscriminate attacks on communities suspected of sympathising with the SPLA." See Justice Africa, "Prospects for Peace in Sudan: April 2003," April 28, 2003.

[142] Kalyvas, *The Logic of Violence in Civil War.*

[143] Lyall, "Are Coethnics More Effective Counterinsurgents?"

self-defense forces disarmed they would be defenseless in the face of such an onslaught. The problem they faced, however, was that while they preferred the new peaceful status quo, they worried that they would be thrust into the middle of a new war. In particular, they feared that the government would attack their villages, regardless of their material support for Bolad, but merely on suspicion. This fear and the catastrophic costs of being defenseless in the face of a government offensive could potentially push the local communities to support the rebels in an attempt to increase their capabilities to defend themselves. In short, the government's inability to credibly commit not to attack local communities may have had the unintended consequence of driving communities who were not inclined to support the rebellion to support them.

Of course, this was the very outcome the government wanted to avoid. It preferred that the local Fur communities supported the government or at least stayed neutral as Bolad's rebellion sought to gain a foothold in the region. The problem for the government, however, was they had no guarantees that the Fur would remain neutral. If the Fur reneged on their promise of neutrality, it would be very costly for the government as it would allow the rebels to gain a foothold in the area and, in this case, reach the all-important sanctuary of Jebel Marra. This uncertainty had the effect of predisposing the government to prepare to preemptively attack any village that might assist the rebels, which in turn increased the communities' fear of being attacked.

Overall, then, though local communities and the government wished to avoid large-scale violence, they faced a classic Prisoner's Dilemma strategic situation, in which neither wanted to choose peace if the other side was going to choose war. With no way of enforcing cooperation, they risked choosing non-cooperative strategies: the local communities turning to the rebels for protection; the government resorting to collective violence to prevent the rebels from gaining a foothold.

How can this commitment problem be resolved? The First Darfur Rebellion points to the brokerage role that local intermediaries who are both trusted by powerful figures in the government and the local communities can play to maintain collaboration and ensure cooperation. As trusted brokers, they can credibly communicate to both sides the other's intentions (e.g., they can convey to the government that the local communities oppose the rebellion and will support the government if it refrains from attacking them, while convincing the communities that if they stay on the sidelines the government will leave them alone). They can also help with enforcement, as seen in the Darfur case, shuttling back and forth between the two sides to ensure that each is upholding its side of the bargain, and, if not, trying to facilitate a solution that would keep the sides on a cooperative path (e.g., communicating to the government that the communities were upset by the theft of their animals by the Fursan militias). In sum, dense political networks facilitate cooperation between the government and local communities and help to avoid a descent into civil war that neither wants.

5.8.2 How Strong Political Networks Hinder Local Mobilization

Before concluding, it is important to address a rival hypothesis advanced by Sudan scholar Alex de Waal. De Waal suggests that the First Darfur Rebellion was "ill-fated" from the start because of the SPLA's tactical decision to send Bolad accompanied by a 1,000-strong Dinka force by foot into Darfur (across the land of the Baggara—the cattle-herding Arabs who live in southern Darfur and who already had been mobilized against the southern rebels) at a time when the SPLA was in disarray both due to the loss of its foreign sanctuary in Ethiopia and the coup against Garang. There is no doubt that these factors weakened the potency of the insurgency. But I would argue that Bolad's very decision to turn to the SPLA is endogenous to the Islamic Movement's control of Darfur. Bolad had to mobilize outside of Darfur due to the strength of the *tanzim* in the region. According to those working with Bolad, it was only after other mobilizational channels were blocked, either in Darfur or from Chad, that the dissidents—after a chance encounter with top SPLA officials in Addis Ababa—joined the SPLA.

For its part, the SPLA was following a model that was working in other regions of northern Sudan, including the Nuba Mountains and the Blue Nile. The aim of the incursion was not to ensconce SPLA troops in the hostile areas of northern Sudan but to form strategic alliances with other marginalized groups under distress because of local insecurity and poor governance. Often the SPLA found, once the initial links were made between the SPLA and the mobilized groups, the government did the rest of the work in provoking a full-fledged insurrection through its indiscriminate and destructive counterinsurgency operations.[144] Thus, what proved critical in averting a full-blown insurgency in Darfur was the government's ability to disarm the Fur self-defense forces and minimize

---

[144] See Alex de Waal, *Famine that Kills Darfur, Sudan* (Oxford: Oxford University Press, 2005), p. xvi.

indiscriminate violence as the Fursan and the Sudanese military attacked the SPLA. Neither of these would have been possible without the strength of the *tanzim* in Darfur in the early 1990s.

5.9 CONCLUSION: POLITICAL NETWORKS AND THE FEASIBILITY OF ARMED REBELLION

Qualitative analysis of Darfur in the early 1990s points to the importance of taking seriously the intermediary effect of political networks on conflict escalation in weak states. As explained in Chapter 2, in fragile states the ruling regime often cannot rely on strong state structures to countermobilize against dissident forces. Instead, they have to turn to political networks that connect the regime with society. An in-depth qualitative analysis of the First Darfur Rebellion not only helps to substantiate the political networks hypothesis, but it helps to illustrate *how* dense political networks help to avert civil war in weak states. In contrast to the grievance mechanism advanced by Wimmer, Cederman and others (i.e. that excluded groups have greater motivations to rebel than included groups),[145] the case study places greater emphasis on how ethnopolitical inclusion and the denser and more extensive political networks that result from such a political alliance reduce the feasibility of armed rebellion. Beyond serving as informants, these trusted local intermediaries embedded in the regime's extensive political network help to facilitate collaboration between the regime and local communities and help produce what I call cooperative counterinsurgency, in which the government commits to refraining from collective attacks on local communities, and, in turn, local communities commit to not support the rebel movement. Cooperative counterinsurgency mitigates the indiscriminate violence that drives individuals to join the rebel movement in search of protection,[146] and, just as importantly, weakens the support lines of the rebels. The upshot is that cooperative counterinsurgency leaves the rebels like fish out of water and increases the likelihood of their swift military defeat.

---

[145] Wimmer et al., "Ethnic Politics and Armed Conflict." Cederman et al., "Why Do Ethnic Groups Rebel?"

[146] Mason, "The Political Economy of Death Squads."

6

The Strategic Logic of Ethnopolitical Exclusion

The Breakdown of Sudan's Islamic Movement

6.1 INTRODUCTION

In 1992, Sudan's Al-Ingaz regime was able to effectively defeat an armed incursion into Darfur heavily backed by the SPLA. This military victory is significant because it starkly contrasts with the outcome in the Nuba Mountains and southern Blue Nile in which the SPLA's military incursions provoked full-scale civil war. It is also significant because a decade later the Sudanese government would be unable to effectively defeat an armed rebellion in Darfur. Why was the government able to defeat the First Darfur Rebellion but not the Second? I argue that one of the most important reasons is that the *tanzim*—the network of Islamists that represented the backbone of Al-Ingaz that came to power in 1989— factionalized along ethnoregional lines in 2000, leading many Islamists from western Sudan, especially those from non-Arab groups in Darfur, to be effectively purged from the regime. The loss of these Darfurian Islamists, including some of the very same individuals who helped to prevent the First Darfur Rebellion from escalating to a full-scale civil war, significantly constrained the government's ability to execute a cooperative counterinsurgency campaign in Darfur and increased the feasibility of armed rebellion, resulting in the 2003 civil war.

If regime factionalization would be so costly, why was Sudan's president, Omar al-Bashir, unable to make the concessions necessary to keep the regime intact? This chapter addresses that question. In doing so, it treats this case as an incidence of ethnopolitical exclusion and seeks to explore if the hypotheses described in Chapter 3 account for this outcome. Figure 6.1 offers a simple rendering of the factionalization of the NIF in 2000. As I discuss at length throughout this chapter, the split between Hassan al-Turabi

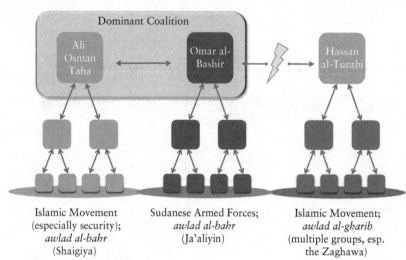

FIGURE 6.1 The Factionalization of Sudan's Islamic Movement, 1998–2000

and his former protégés, Ali Osman Taha and Omar al-Bashir, was fundamentally a political conflict between these different power brokers. As trust dissipated among Islamists and this conflict intensified, members of the regime coalesced into different factions. These factions revolved around common political interests but were also cemented by personal ties and broader social identities, including region and ethnicity, which structured how individuals understood the conflict. As illustrated in Figure 6.1, by the late 1990s the regime's top political elites tended to draw support from different societal groups. Bashir and Taha's networks drew largely from *awlad al-bahr* ("sons of the river"), the area along the Nile River Valley from where Sudan's traditional ruling class comes. In contrast, though Turabi did not come from Darfur (despite propaganda suggesting otherwise), Turabi's network was much stronger among *awlad al-gharib* ("sons of the west"), especially non-Arabs from Darfur.

Consistent with the theoretical discussion of the various logics of ethnopolitical exclusion in Chapter 3, one could tell three different stories about why the power struggle between the Turabi faction and the Bashir faction led the regime to split along ethnoregional lines.

1. **Instrumental exclusion:** Riverain Arab Islamists exploited the power struggle between Bashir and Turabi to purge those from western Sudan from the regime to increase their share of the rents derived from the state just as Sudanese oil production was coming on line. But riverain Islamists underestimated the costs of such a

purge in Darfur. They recognized losing Darfur Islamists, especially those from the Zaghawa tribe would be costly, but they assumed they could overcome the loss of these intermediaries by turning to other Darfurians, especially local elites from Arab tribes (who would go on to become the leaders of the so-called *janjawiid*). Moreover, they were confident that as long as they had a strong alliance with Idriss Déby of Chad (a Zaghawa himself), the Zaghawa dissidents would not be able to use Chad as a launching pad for a rebellion and their mobilizational capabilities would be limited.

2. **Ethnonational exclusion:** As conflict intensified within the Islamic Movement in the late 1990s, riverain Arab ethnonationalists feared that Turabi was intent on bringing the *zurga* (a racial epithet used to refer to those of African descent)[1] to power. In the eyes of the ethnonationalists, this represented a threat to the Arab foundations of the Sudanese state, and ethnopolitical exclusion was integral to preserving the Arabness of the state. Bashir, as a Ja'aliyin, who trace their lineage to the tribe of Prophet Muhammad, was the right man to preserve the Arabic integrity of the state.

3. **Strategic exclusion:** Omar al-Bashir and Ali Osman Taha moved against Turabi and those perceived to be Turabi loyalists because they were convinced that their former sheikh was maneuvering to eliminate them from power and would stop at nothing until he achieved absolute power. Exclusion was necessary to preempt this future shift in power. To neutralize Turabi's capabilities of capturing power, however, required not just politically eliminating their sheikh but also his network of followers inside the regime who represented a threat to their hold on power. As Turabi's political network was seen to be particularly strong among the Zaghawa and other non-Arab Darfurians, the Bashir faction calculated it was too risky to keep Islamists from these groups within the regime (not because of where they were from but because of their perceived strong political ties with Turabi). Purging Turabi's network was intended to increase the costs their sheikh faced to

---

[1] Zurga' is "from a root-word meaning 'blue,' a word that signifies blackness and is used in Sudanese Arabic to refer to non-Arabs." John Ryle, "Disaster in Darfur," *The New York Review of Books*, 51 (13) (August 12, 2004). The label became prevalent in Darfur during the Fur–Arab war in the 1980s. See Harir, "'African Belt' Versus 'African Belt.'"

reclaiming power. Unable to seize power from within, he would have to turn to an *intifadha* or an armed rebellion. This would give the Bashir faction time to countermobilize, both domestically and internationally.

In the rest of this chapter I offer a descriptive analysis of the factionalization of Al-Ingaz with an eye toward analyzing which explanation accounts for the split in the Islamic Movement along ethnoregional lines. The empirical evidence helps to flesh out the primacy of the strategic hypothesis. It is abundantly clear that the breakdown of trust within the Islamic Movement in the late 1990s, especially after the failed assassination attempt of Egypt's president, Hosni Mubarak, contributed to a power struggle within the regime and intensified the Bashir group's fear that Turabi was preparing to orchestrate a future shift in the distribution of power that would eliminate them and consolidate power in his hands. Purging Turabi and his faction was seen as the only credible way to resolve this commitment problem while increasing the costs Turabi and his allies faced to reclaiming power in the future.

There is also evidence to suggest that instrumental and ethnonationalist factors shaped how political bargaining played out within the regime. For example, some within the Islamic Movement believe that biased allocation of government positions and resources along ethnic lines sowed the seeds of the conflict. Others suggest that Bashir's mishandling of the crisis was exacerbated by information asymmetries, especially regarding the capabilities of Chad's president, Idriss Déby, to contain any potential rebellion to emerge in Darfur. Finally, it is also clear that ethnonationalist discourse and historical memory over which groups had the "right to rule" affected how the conflict was understood. But these factors alone were insufficient to lead to a fundamental break in the Islamic Movement. Instead, I argue that they ultimately contributed to regime factionalization in that they instigated and intensified the commitment problem that was at the heart of the breakdown of Al-Ingaz.

The rest of the chapter is organized into three parts. The first seeks to account for the emergence of the power struggle between Turabi and Bashir and why it could not be resolved short of the factionalization of the regime. The second part then seeks to explain why the political conflict became structured along regional and ethnic lines. The third part analyzes the strategy the Bashir faction chose to coup-proof the regime from Turabi and increase the costs Turabi and his allies faced to reclaiming political power.

6.2 THE SHEIKH VERSUS THE FIELD MARSHAL[2]

From the outset, the Al-Ingaz regime was characterized by dual centers of power.[3] Though the coup was orchestrated and executed by the Islamic Movement, the Islamists concealed their involvement for fear that the Americans and Egyptians would reject an "Islamist coup," scuttling the Al-Ingaz revolution before it began. Instead, the public face of the coup was a relatively unknown field marshal, Omar al-Bashir, and other military officers, who immediately formed the fifteen-man RCC. A key element of the deceit involved the imprisonment of Turabi and other Islamist leaders.[4] Thus, after the coup, formally the Sudanese state was controlled by the military, but real power rested with Turabi (even from prison) and the *tanzim*, which operated as a shadow government and had "supreme jurisdiction" over the state.[5] This naturally led to friction between the state and shadow state. As Professor Ibrahim Ahmed Omer, a prominent member of the movement's shura council in the 1980s and secretary general of the NCP in 2000, commented, "There was a problem

---

[2] Section 6.2, including Sub-sections 6.2.1–6.2.3, are based on multiple personal interviews with a number of the top Islamists in the Islamic Movement. Unless a quote or information is directly attributed, they are cited throughout as "Top Al-Ingaz officials." All interviews were in Khartoum unless otherwise noted: Sayeed al-Khateeb, March 22, 2005, May 29, 2005, February 8, 2006; Ghazi Salahuddin Atabani, March 22, 2005, August 10, 2010; al-Tayib Zain al-Abdin, March 26, 2005, July 30, 2005; Mohamed El-Hassan El-Fadil, March 27, 2005, July 13, 2008; Mohammed Hassan al-Amin, April 13, 2005, November 26, 2005, March 30, 2006, July 20, 2008; Mohammed al-Amin Khalifa, April 13, 2005, October 29, 2005, February 20, 2006; Qutbi al-Mahdi, August 9, 2005, February 22, 2006, January 24, 2007; Mutrif Siddiq, August 13, 2005, March 20, 2006, July 26, 2008; Majzoub al Khalifa Ahmed, Abuja, Nigeria, April 6, 2006; Ali al-Haj, January 18, 2007, November 23, 2009; Abdallah Hassan Ahmed, January 25, 2007, January 29, 2007, January 31, 2007; Ibrahim Sanousi, January 30, 2007, July 14, 2008; Ibrahim Ahmed Omer, January 27, 2007; al-Haj Adam Yusuf, July 22, 2008; Abdel Rahim Hamdi, London, July 3, 2009, Khartoum, April 26, 2010.

[3] For an excellent overview of the conflict between the formal state run by Bashir versus the shadow state run by Turabi, see Abdelwahab El-Affendi, "The Future of the Islamist Movement," *African Arguments*, April 13, 2008, accessed at http://africanarguments.org/2008/04/13/the-future-of-the-sudanese-islamist-movement (accessed October 5, 2016).

[4] All indications suggest this deception worked as the reporting at the time by US intelligence failed to identify Turabi as the ringleader of the coup. Interview, Washington, DC, 2011.

[5] El-Affendi, "The Future of the Islamist Movement." Exacerbating this institutional uncertainty was Turabi's decision to dissolve the National Islamic Front, including the leadership council, the shura, and provincial councils, shortly after the coup, in favor of creating a new and expanded organization (eventually to take the form of the National Congress) that would help the Islamists extend their control beyond the Islamic Movement. Thus, a new shura council was formed that included members of the military who carried out the coup, in addition to the top Islamists. But these new structures lacked influence, and Turabi continued to rely on the old *tanzim* to maintain his influence.

when we took power. The secretary general of the Islamic Movement was very powerful, but we also had a state on our hands."[6] This institutional dualism was supposed to be temporary, however. The plan the Islamists agreed upon was that the RCC would serve as a placeholder until the new regime consolidated power and Islamist civilians took over control. There was no precise time frame for the civilianization of the regime other than it was expected to occur after several years.

From prison, Turabi continued to direct and guide the *tanzim* and consulted with its secretariat during evening meetings, but he delegated the day-to-day operations to his deputy, Ali Osman Taha, whom Turabi had known for years and fully trusted.[7] Turabi and Taha are a study in contrasts.[8] Turabi is an iconoclast. He is bold, brash, and charismatic—and does not shy away from confrontation. Taha is reserved and cautious. Often described as a fox, Taha quietly and subtly maneuvers to stay ahead of his rivals. His power came from the efficiency and skill with which he managed the *tanzim*'s security and financial operations.[9] Moreover, as the liaison with the military leaders in the RCC, Taha cultivated connections with the military, including Bashir, that Turabi would never have.[10]

After being released from prison, Turabi left Taha in control of the RCC and the domestic portfolio, while the sheikh devoted his attention to his international Islamist agenda, including organizing the Popular Arab and Islamic Conference (PAIC), which Turabi envisaged would bring together disparate Arab and Islamic groups to create a "single pan-Islamic authority" and serve as a fundamentalist alternative to the Arab League and the Organization of the Islamic Conference.[11] Khartoum was to be the headquarters of this new international Islamist organization. The PAIC's general assembly meetings, which drew Islamist delegates from some forty-five

---

[6] Interview with Professor Ibrahim Ahmed Omer, Khartoum, January 28, 2007.

[7] According to a leading Islamist, "Turabi was fully trusting Ali Osman Taha . . . Turabi would not listen to any complaint about him." Interview with top Al-Ingaz official.

[8] Flint and de Waal compare the two: "The charismatic Turabi was the sheikh: aloof from the details, organizing the grand sweep of strategy. The introverted Ali Osman was the chief executive, scrutinizing the implementation of policy." They provide a valuable biographical background of Taha in Flint and de Waal, *Darfur: A New History of a Long War*, p. 26.

[9] According to one of his peers, "Taha spent the money the way he wanted to. There was no accountability. He was not corrupt in the Mobutu sense, but corrupt in that he spent money in unaccountable ways, like the incident in 1995." Interview with top Al-Ingaz official.

[10] Turabi was left in prison longer than originally planned, which, looking back, he claims was the beginning of the alliance between Bashir and Taha. Interview with Hassan al-Turabi, Khartoum, January 31, 2007.

[11] De Waal, "The Politics of Destabilisation in the Horn, 1989–2001," in Alex de Waal, ed., *Islamism and Its Enemies in the Horn of Africa* (Bloomington, Ind.: Indiana University Press, 2004), pp. 193–194.

states, including Algeria, Bosnia, Pakistan, and the Philippines, were held in 1991, 1993, and 1995. Osama bin Laden, who was welcomed into Sudan in 1991, is alleged to have been one of the key financiers of the PAIC.

It was on one of his many trips abroad that Turabi was attacked at the Ottawa airport, on May 26, 1992, in a chance encounter with an exiled Sudanese martial-arts expert and karate world champion who was a fierce opponent of the Islamist regime. The attack left Turabi incapacitated for several weeks as he recovered in a hospital in Ottawa. (Many Islamists thought he might die.) Hospitalized in Ottawa, Turabi was further removed from the running of the government he had brought to power. Turabi's near-death experience frightened him that he might perish before seeing his Islamist project come to fruition. Upon his release, he accelerated his plans to civilianize the government. In 1993, the RCC was dissolved, and the Islamists began to formally take over the government. For example, Taha became the minister of social affairs, "from which he sought to mobilize the public behind the ideological goals of the revolution in order to create a cohesive society conforming to the Islamist code of behavior."[12]

But this transition did not resolve the dual centers of power. Turabi continued to operate a shadow state and maintained oversight committees assigned to each minister, even among high-ranking Islamists. This created tension between Turabi and these Islamists in the government. Turabi began to step on the toes of some government officials as he tried to orchestrate state policies as leader of the Islamic Movement but without having a position in the government. Taha was one of the first ministers to dissolve Turabi's "shadow committee." In addition to the tension between the state and the *tanzim*, the dissolution of the RCC drove a wedge between Turabi and the military officers, who, as the caretakers of the government after the coup, were reaping the spoils of power.

6.2.1 The Assassination Attempt on Hosni Mubarak and the Breakdown of Trust within Sudan's Islamic Movement

Cracks within the Islamic Movement worsened in the aftermath of a failed assassination attempt against Egypt's president, Hosni Mubarak, as he arrived in Addis Ababa on June 25, 1995, for the annual OAU meeting. Sudanese security was complicit in the plot[13] as it provided the assailants from the militant group al-Gama'a al-Islamiyya with visas and even weapons via

---

[12] Lesch, *The Sudan*, p. 117.
[13] In early 1996, the government of Ethiopia submitted a report to the United Nations Security Council detailing the alleged extent of Sudanese involvement in the assassination

the Sudanese embassy in Ethiopia.[14] In the wake of the attempt, the United Nations Security Council placed economic sanctions on the Sudanese government. The Egyptians blamed Turabi for the assassination plot.

According to almost all Al-Ingaz insiders I interviewed, however, the assassination plot was "outside of Turabi's direct personal knowledge," as one leading Islamist phrased it.[15] Instead, it was a clique in Sudan's security, under the supervision of Taha[16] that was complicit in the assassination attempt.[17] Turabi was outraged when he learned of the participation of the movement's security officers[18]—not least because it revealed to him that a security cabal within the regime was operating beyond his control. As one ranking member stated, the key issue the assassination attempt raised was, "How could such an incident slip through their system? This was the problem for Turabi. He had fundamental trust in the system," and this was a clear sign it was breaking down.[19]

In the wake of the attack, Turabi and Bashir met privately (which was a rarity) and decided to break up the security clique involved. Taha, who

---

attempt. A Security Council press release summarized Ethiopia's findings: "According to Ethiopia's investigation, those involved in the assassination attempt were members of a terrorist organization called al-Gama'a-Islamia. The two main leaders were based in Khartoum. Of the nine deployed in Addis Ababa, one escaped, and three were now in the custody of Ethiopian authorities. Two had been killed during the attack, and three others were killed five days later during a shoot-out with security personnel. The terrorists in custody admit that: their leaders live in Khartoum; the plot was hatched in Khartoum; their mission to assassinate President Mubarak was given to them in Khartoum; and the weapons intended to be used in their mission were flown into Addis Ababa by Sudan Airways from Khartoum. Moreover, the passports they possess, in virtually all cases, were prepared for them in Khartoum." See "Security Council Calls on Sudan to Extradite Suspects in Attempted Assassination of Egyptian President," SC/6170 press release, January 31, 1996. Available at www.un.org/News/Press/docs/1996/19960131.sc6170. html (accessed August 22, 2016).

[14] Lawrence Wright, *The Looming Tower: Al-Qaeda and the Road to 9/11* (New York: Vintage Books, 2007), p. 214.

[15] Interview with top Al-Ingaz official.

[16] Interview with top Al-Ingaz officials. See also Galal Nassar, "The Hamza Connection," *Al-Ahram*, 725 (January 13–19, 2005).

[17] Several other sources corroborate Turabi's noninvolvement. See "Sudan: Will the Spooks Take Over?" *Mideast Mirror*, May 15, 2000; Roland Marchal, "Le Soudan d'un conflit à l'autre," *Les Études du CERI*, 107–108, September 2004; Ahmed Kamal El-Din, "Islam and Islamism in Darfur," in Alex de Waal, ed., *War in Darfur and the Search for Peace* (Cambridge, Mass.: Harvard University Press, 2007), p. 107.

[18] Contributing to the tension within Al-Ingaz's inner circle after the failed assassination bid was a fierce debate over what to do with the assassins hiding in Sudan. Turabi allegedly upbraided those who suggested killing the assassins to wash their hands of the problem. Interviews with top Al-Ingaz officials.

[19] Interview with top Al-Ingaz official.

had developed close relations with key regime security officers since the 1989 coup and was forced to admit his foreknowledge of the plot,[20] was admonished. Nafie Ali Nafie, the head of external security at the time, was demoted to secretary of agriculture. Though Bashir was the one who had Nafie transferred out of security, Nafie came to resent Turabi for his demotion.[21] "After the assassination attempt, Turabi became the enemy, and they started thinking how they can get rid of him," one Bashir loyalist in the NCP said.[22]

According to Dr. Ghazi Salahuddin, a leading Islamist and presidential adviser to Omar al-Bashir, the assassination attempt, and the shake-up it caused at the highest echelons of the Islamic Movement, would have far-reaching consequences for the unity of the regime. It not only increased mistrust between the top cadres, but it weakened the movement's fraternity or social solidarity (*asabiyyah*) that produced a sense of "shared history and a *shared future*" and served as the "main safeguard against splits."[23] The divisions generated by the failed assassination attempt led those at the top of the Islamic Movement to start questioning others' commitment to this shared future.

6.2.2 The Conflict between Bashir and Turabi

In the wake of the failed assassination attempt, Sudan faced international sanctions from the UN and the United States and increased international pressure over its links with terrorist organizations. It proved the death knell for Turabi's PAIC, and the sheikh devoted more attention to his domestic political program. After winning an uncontested seat for the national assembly in March 1996[24] and being selected speaker of the parliament, Turabi set out to revitalize his domestic Islamist program, which was failing due to the movement's heavy reliance on repression and violence to maintain control of society.[25] In a meeting in 1997 with the top leaders of the Islamic Movement, Turabi laid out his vision for Al-Ingaz's future. At the top of the agenda

---

[20] Interview with top Al-Ingaz officials. See also Nassar, "The Hamza Connection."
[21] Nassar, "The Hamza Connection."
[22] Interview with top Al-Ingaz official.
[23] Interview with Dr. Ghazi Salahuddin, Khartoum, August 13, 2010.
[24] Turabi's challenger withdrew from the electoral contest on the first day of voting out of protest over irregularities in the polls.
[25] The sheer scale and intensity of the state violence under Al-Ingaz far surpassed anything Sudanese society had experienced before, including the military rule by Abboud and Nimeiri. See Human Rights Watch, *Behind the Red Line*. African Rights, *Facing Genocide: The Nuba of Sudan* (London: African Rights, 1995).

was drafting a permanent constitution that reaffirmed Islamism and legal-
ized federalism as the formal government structure.[26] Turabi declared that
the president could no longer serve as both head of the military and head
of government; Bashir would have to resign as military chief. Moreover, the
president could expect to have his authority reduced as power was devolved
to the states. The new ruling party, the National Congress Party, which was
created in 1992 as the successor organization to the NIF, would be expanded
to include social and political associations from throughout the country.
Excluded from the party, however, would be security and military personnel,
who Turabi felt no longer had a role in politics.

Many of these key elements, including the creation of a permanent
constitution, federalism, and the transfer to civilian rule, had been agreed
to by top-ranking Islamists well before the NIF seized power.[27] Now that
they were being put into practice, however, the military and security officers who had been in controlling positions since the 1989 coup resisted
such change. Moreover, in controlling the formal apparatus of the state,
these officers had strengthened their control of coercive and patronage
resources that increased their bargaining power vis-à-vis Turabi. Thus,
Bashir and those in the military stiffly resisted Turabi's call for reforms.
"Now is the time for a new coup d'état," high-ranking military officers
intimated after the meeting.[28]

Turabi paid no attention and steamrolled ahead. With strong support in parliament and from party members, Turabi succeeded in getting
the 1998 constitution passed. Taha, playing his cards close to his chest,
publicly endorsed the new course, but Bashir grew concerned. According
to one NCP member, "Bashir looked at these changes not as political

[26] Federalism had been a core principle for Sudan's Islamic Movement since the 1960s. In
1991, it adopted a federalist system, reorganizing Sudan's nine regions into nine states.
In 1994, it divided them into twenty-six states. But the adoption of federalism did not
translate into improved governance, as a report from the Crisis Group notes: "Instead of
devolving power to the grassroots as the government proclaimed, this reformed federal
system stretched the state's meagre resources thinly over a much inflated public sector
and failed to deliver the anticipated basic social services. A major aim of the increase in
public positions, as several prominent researchers convincingly argued, was to tighten
the nationwide grip of the National Islamic Front by placing its members and co-opted
clients in position of influence." (International Crisis Group, "Darfur Rising: Sudan's
New Crisis," *Africa Report*, March 25, 2004, fn. 34.)

[27] In 1987, the NIF published a political charter that called for a federal structure to govern
Sudan and suggested "that the parliamentary system of government might be preferred, as
it is based on collegiate executive power and allows for any political convention or usage
governing regional representation or balance." The charter is reprinted in the appendix of
Gallab's book on the Islamist movement: Gallab, *The First Islamist Republic*.

[28] Interview with a top Al-Ingaz official who attended the meeting.

reforms but as a threat to his personal power."[29] This drove Bashir into an alliance with the security cabal he had tried to break up after the Mubarak assassination attempt.

A key turning point in relations between Bashir, Turabi, and Taha occurred when the vice president, Zubair Mohammed Salih, was killed in a plane crash in February 1998. A group of party elders was called upon to help select Zubair's replacement, and they recommended three potential candidates for the position of vice president: Turabi, Taha or Ali al-Haj, a Darfurian and former minister of federal affairs. Among these three candidates, Bashir would choose the new vice president. Bashir, shrewdly, said that he could not possibly serve above the great sheikh and that he would have to step down rather than have Turabi as his deputy. This prompted Turabi to withdraw from consideration and to endorse Ali al-Haj for the vice presidency. But Bashir rejected Ali al-Haj, declaring "he could not work with him," and selected Taha.[30] In turn, Turabi removed Taha as deputy secretary general of the ruling party, the NCP, appointing Ali al-Haj in his place. This decision embittered Taha, who, according to Turabi, "started to shift openly against him after becoming vice-president."[31] The battle lines were being drawn: on one side, controlling the state, was Bashir in alliance with Taha and the security cabal who had orchestrated the assassination attempt against Hosni Mubarak, and, on the other, Turabi, Ali al-Haj, and others in the resurgent NCP.

A decade after coming to power, the deep bonds of fraternity that had been the hallmark of Sudan's Islamic Movement and that supplanted regional, ethnic, and tribal ties had been broken. Open consultation within the shura council gave way to secret meetings by these rival factions, heightening suspicion and mistrust. Bashir and his allies in the security clique feared that Turabi might use his dominance of the party and his position as speaker of the national assembly to have them all replaced. After all, in the late 1960s he did not hesitate to purge the old guard Islamists who were close to the Egyptian Ikhwan and who opposed his political vision.[32] To preempt such a possibility, a group of ten members, including Nafie Ali Nafie and Mutrif Sidiq, who were sidelined after the Mubarak assassination, secretly prepared a memorandum that challenged Turabi's control of the NCP. Introduced at the NCP's shura council in December 1998, the Memorandum of Ten, as it became known, blindsided Turabi. Calling for

[29] Interview with Al-Ingaz official.
[30] Interview with NIF official.
[31] Interview with Hassan Turabi, Khartoum, January 31, 2007.
[32] Hamidi, *The Making of an Islamic Political Leader.*

the party to be reformed in order to resolve the multiple centers of power that existed, it proposed creating a new executive body, the Leadership Bureau, under the chairmanship of the president (Bashir) not the secretary general (Turabi). This change would strip Turabi of his powers of ministerial appointment and delegate them to Bashir, who now controlled both the state and the party. Incensed by what he viewed as the betrayal of his disciples, Turabi sought to strike back.

In 1999, he toured throughout the country, mobilizing support among the rank and file in the Islamic Movement and the NCP in preparation for the party's general conference in October 1999.[33] Already by September the shura of the NCP annulled the reforms proposed by the signatories of the Memorandum of Ten. The Leadership Bureau was dissolved and scheduled to be replaced by a new Leadership Authority, under the chairmanship of the secretary general.[34] A month later, in an impressive display of Turabi's grassroots support, thousands of NCP members at the general conference ratified the establishment of the Leadership Authority and, even more significantly, voted to remove almost all the signatories of the Memorandum of Ten from the shura council.[35] But the conference was also an effort to reconcile the growing divide between Bashir and Turabi. The party members cheered ecstatically when, in an attempt to show a unified leadership, Bashir and Turabi embraced each other at the opening of the conference. In a bid to reassure Bashir, as Turabi was reelected as the party's secretary general and had his powers strengthened, the conference also nominated Bashir as the NCP's nominee for the presidential election, scheduled for 2000.[36]

But, if Bashir's renomination as the NCP's candidate for the presidency was intended to reassure the anxious military man and his allies, Turabi's next move had the opposite effect. In November, Turabi tabled a series of amendments to the new constitution. The amendments struck directly at Bashir's grip on power: they proposed creating a prime minister accountable to the parliament; instituting the direct elections of governors, who

[33] "The Turabi Counterattack," *Indian Ocean Newsletter*, April 3, 1999.
[34] Critically, the Leadership Authority became "the sole leadership body charged with endorsing candidates for vice president and other top government jobs." Mohamed Ali Saeed, "Sudan's Ruling Party Restores Powers to Leader," *Agence France Presse*, September 18, 1999.
[35] One top-ranking official suggested that Turabi rigged the voting to achieve this outcome, and "that this was a turning point because Turabi signaled he was prepared to play dirty." Interview with top Al-Ingaz official.
[36] Mohamed Osman, "Ruling National Congress Holds Party Conference," *Associated Press*, October 7, 1999.

before had been appointed by the president; and authorizing parliament to be able to remove the president with a two-thirds majority vote. The proposals were tantamount to a constitutional coup.

Facing a clear loss of authority, if not the outright loss of power, Bashir, supported unconditionally by Taha and the security cabal, refused to accept this. On the fourth day of Ramadan, December 12, 1999, Bashir struck first, executing a self-coup: he dissolved the national assembly, declared a three-month state of emergency, and deployed the military to secure key strategic points in the capital.

6.2.3 Al-Qasr versus Manshiya

Bashir's autogolpe effectively thwarted Turabi's constitutional coup but did little to allay the paranoia of Bashir, Taha, Nafie, and others sitting in the presidential palace (Al-Qasr) about the threat Turabi and his allies—the Manshiya group—posed.[37] Bashir feared that, having been blocked in the national assembly, surely Turabi would make a forcible bid for power. After all, it was the sheikh who ordered the coup that brought the NIF to power in June 1989. In the 1960s, Turabi was involved in the mass demonstrations that brought down the government of Major General Ibrahim Abboud, the country's first military president. As Mutrif Sidiq described Turabi, "He is a dirty and daring man. He can use any means to come back to power."[38] Another former Turabi disciple said, "Everyone was sure that Turabi was preparing for a final showdown and was prepared to bring the temple down on everyone. According to our intelligence, he was leaving no stone unturned in his attempt to come back to power. He was bloodthirsty and would topple the regime at any cost."[39]

In the early part of 2000, the primary fear was that Turabi and his allies would attempt a coup d'état. Reports of meetings between Turabi and military officers increased the Bashir group's paranoia.[40] In May, Bashir publicly accused Turabi of inciting factions in the military, police, and security against the government.[41] According to Turabi loyalists, Bashir's paranoia was justified. After the Fourth of Ramadan decrees, a large group of military officers loyal to Turabi leaned on the sheikh to issue a

---

[37] Manshiya is the neighborhood in Khartoum where Turabi's house is located. Turabi's house was always an important place for him to hold court and became the informal HQ for his faction in their conflict with the Bashir group.

[38] Interview with Mutrif Siddiq, Khartoum, July 26, 2008.

[39] Interview with top Al-Ingaz official.

[40] Interview with top Al-Ingaz official.

[41] *Al-Ray al-Aaym* (Khartoum), May 5, 2000.

call to arms against Bashir, but Turabi refused for fear that it would lead to too much "bloodshed."[42] He seemed to favor popular mobilization, which he publicly endorsed as the solution to military dictatorships.[43] Over the next year, several anti-regime protests broke out, the most serious in the latter part of September 2000, when rioting started in Nyala, South Darfur, and spread to several other states.[44]

Turabi's assessment reflected Bashir's strength in the military and the security forces. With the support of the security cabal, Bashir could count on strong support from state security networks. Taha's backing was particularly important in this regard as his control of the NIF's finances since the 1989 coup translated into a strong patronage network that reached deep into security. Moreover, as the power struggle worsened with the sheikh in 1998 and 1999, Bashir became more directly involved in the army in a bid to shore up his support. He increased the officers' retirement allowances, doled out new vehicles, and offered them better housing. On the eve of declaring a state of emergency, Bashir reportedly purged 300 to 400 pro-Turabi officers from the army.[45]

Nonetheless, the "outcome, week by week, looked uncertain,"[46] and Bashir could take nothing for granted. While the president had backing from critical elements of the military and security, he still worried about Turabi loyalists within the regime whom their sheikh had personally recruited. These "enemies within" lowered the costs Turabi faced to reclaiming power. Depending upon where they were located within the regime, their inside position potentially granted them license to carry weapons, control of state resources, and access to privileged information, all of which enhanced Turabi's mobilization capabilities. At war with their former sheikh, Bashir and his supporters sought to eliminate any and all advantages that Turabi might have been able to exploit to retake power. Over the next year, state security carried out a systematic but methodical campaign to purge Turabi allies and sympathizers from the

---

[42] Bashir's allies concur but claim Turabi's concern about "bloodshed" was mainly motivated by the fact that it would have been spilled disproportionately by his side. Interviews with top Al-Ingaz officials.

[43] As Turabi said in an interview in May 2000, "we have grown accustomed to the Sudanese people confronting any military regime in Sudan when the latter seeks to wipe out the political forces, as was the case with [former military rulers] 'Abbud and Numayri." Cited in Bruce Maddy-Weitzman, *Middle East Contemporary Survey*, vol. XXIV: 2000 (Tel Aviv: Moshe Dayan Center for Middle Eastern and African Studies, 2003), p. 519.

[44] Maddy-Weitzman, *Middle East Contemporary Survey*.

[45] "What Does Bashir's 'Second Coup' Mean for Sudan?" *Mideast Mirror*, December 14, 1999.

[46] Flint and de Waal, *Darfur: A New History of a Long War*, p. 103.

regime.[47] A second wave of purges occurred after Turabi, in a stunning about-face, forged an alliance with his former archenemies, the SPLA.[48]

The challenge for Bashir was how to identify disloyalists, particularly when private information made it difficult to ascertain an individual's true loyalties.[49] In this regard, three factors worked in Bashir's favor. First, the intimacy of the Islamist movement helped. For decades, the Islamists studied, worked, and lived together. Often operating underground to shield their activities from state authorities, the Islamists became a tight-knit group in which members developed strong personal bonds. This familiarity made it difficult for individuals to conceal their loyalties. Second, the protracted and open nature of the power struggle within the NCP revealed which leader party members were lining up behind. Third, additional information was gleaned by permitting Turabi to form an opposition political party, the Popular National Congress, in May 2000 as the sheikh's top political supporters purged themselves from the regime.

These three factors contributed to what appeared to be a relatively clean, though hostile, breakup of the NCP at the highest levels. The bloodbath that many feared as the power struggle reached its apogee in December 1999 and continued into 2000 was avoided. But the regime split was not as contained as initially seemed. As the personal power struggle escalated between Turabi and Bashir in 1998 and 1999, it coincided with and fueled an ethnoregional conflict that had been simmering within the Islamic Movement since the mid-1990s and that was about to be blown wide open. Given the growing politicization of ethnicity before and especially after the split in the Islamic Movement, ascriptive identity would serve as a heuristic device to sort allies from enemies during this period of uncertainty, contributing to a significant restructuring of the regime's political network along ethnoregional lines.

6.3 THE ETHNOREGIONAL DIMENSION TO THE ELITE CONFLICT

One puzzle about the political conflict between Bashir and Turabi is why it occurred along ethnoregional lines with Bashir turning to Islamists from riverain Sudan to shore up his hold on power and Turabi drawing support

---

[47] International Crisis Group, *God, Oil and Country: Changing the Logic of War in Sudan* (Brussels: International Crisis Group, 2002).

[48] Flint and de Waal, *Darfur: A New History of a Long War.*

[49] Turabi sought to exacerbate this problem by instructing his followers not to publicly declare their loyalty.

from western Sudan. This is surprising because, as described in Chapter 5, the strength of Sudan's Islamic Movement was its members' social solidarity that cross-cut traditional tribal, regional, and racial divisions. Developed over decades of intimate and intensive religious, political, and social interactions and cemented by common beliefs in the principles of Islamism and the importance of implementing their Islamist project, these social ties facilitated the formation of a tight-knit and coherent organization. To individuals alienated by the country's traditional political parties, this was one of the principal attractions of the Islamic Movement: "No one asked about your tribe. They said: 'Islam is our mother and father.'"[50] In fact, cadres were instructed not to involve themselves in parochial or tribal matters as it would distract from the movement's singular objectives of implementing its Islamist project.[51] At times, this pitted Islamists against their kinsmen who expected the members of the *tanzim* to use their privileged positions to advocate on behalf of their group.[52]

After the 1989 coup and the Islamists' takeover of government, brotherhood suffered as competition for state spoils materialized. Consistent with instrumental models of ethnic politics described in Chapter 2, some Islamists perceived that ascriptive identity structured the allocation of scarce state resources. In particular, they felt that Al-Ingaz was replicating historical patterns of ethnic domination, in which northern riverain Arabs controlled a majority stake at the expense of other more populous societal groups.[53] Bolad's defection from the Islamic Movement foreshadowed this ethnoregional conflict.

One early incident that engendered such claims was the 1996 election for the secretary general of the NCP. The party congress voted overwhelmingly for a candidate from Darfur, al-Shafi' Mohammed Ahmed, but the results were overturned by Turabi, and the position was given to a northerner, Dr. Ghazi Salahuddin Atabani. According to Jibril Ibrahim, the post per se wasn't that important, "but the way that it was handled was poor and gave

---

[50] Quote by Taj al Din Bashir Nyam, a Darfurian who joined the Muslim Brothers as a student in the 1980s. Flint and de Waal, *Darfur: A New History of a Long War*, p. 19.

[51] Interview with al-Haj Adam, Khartoum, July 22, 2008.

[52] As mentioned, some Zaghawa bitterly remember a violent military operation carried out by the Sudanese Armed Forces (SAF) in Wadha, southern Darfur in 1991, presumably against banditry, but which seemed to be specifically targeting Zaghawa villages. Despite high-level representation in the *tanzim* in Darfur, Zaghawa civilians felt the Zaghawa Islamists did nothing to stop it. Interview with retired non-Islamist Zaghawa military officer, N'djamena, August 6, 2009. Interview with Ali Shammar, Khartoum, February 9, 2006.

[53] Interviews with Darfurian Islamists, Khartoum, 2005–2007. According to Jibril Ibrahim, a Darfurian member of the Islamic Movement and future leader of the JEM, "By 1995

the impression that the leaders were imposing someone on the members."[54] Darfurians, and Islamists from other peripheral parts of Sudan, protested the move and sought to prevent Dr. Ghazi's appointment, but their objections fell on deaf ears.[55] Such events motivated a group of Islamists led by a young Darfurian, Dr. Khalil Ibrahim, to begin meeting in secret to discuss the limitations of the Al-Ingaz regime and how it could be reformed.[56]

The selection of a new vice president after the death of Zubair raised further doubts about the inclusiveness of the regime. Despite Turabi's support for the candidacy of Ali al-Haj, Bashir rejected the nominee and selected Ali Osman Taha, a Shaigiya from riverain Sudan. To some non-riverain Islamists, this confirmed their suspicions that Bashir and an influential group around him were anti-westerner. In contrast, Darfurian Islamists, forgiving but not forgetting their sheikh's earlier manipulation of the selection of the secretary general, felt the party under Turabi's control was becoming "more open than the government."[57] Turabi replaced Taha as deputy secretary general with Ali al-Haj while several other Islamists from western Sudan served in prominent positions in the party. Thus, as the power struggle played out between Bashir and Turabi, many Islamists from western Sudan, and especially Darfur, felt their interests were better served if Turabi prevailed. They supported the sheikh's calls for a strong party and a weakened executive and viewed with suspicion the Memorandum of Ten, observing that most of the signatories were top Islamists from northern riverain Sudan. When Turabi rallied the party against the Memorandum of Ten and tabled the constitutional amendments that proposed weakening power of the executive vis-à-vis the assembly and the states, he received strong support from Darfurians. "It is we who called for the changes to the constitution," one Darfurian Islamist claimed. Consequently, many Darfurian Islamists were particularly aggrieved by the Fourth of Ramadan decrees: "Westerners perceived Bashir's coup was against them not Turabi. We felt the northerners were taking power."[58]

But as the Islamists from western Sudan felt Bashir and his riverain allies were conspiring against them, those around Bashir sensed the converse

---

Darfurians started murmuring that they were not adequately represented. They felt they received only marginal posts and the resources allocated to the region were very small." Personal interview, London, July 2008.

[54] Interview with Jibril Ibrahim, London, July 2008.
[55] Interviews with Darfurian Islamists; see also El-Affendi, "The Future of the Islamist Movement."
[56] Flint and de Waal, *Darfur: A Short History of a Long War.*
[57] Interview with Jibril Ibrahim, London, July 2008.
[58] Interview with Jibril Ibrahim, London, July 2008.

was true: Turabi was allying with the *gharaba* (those from western Sudan) in a plot to remove them from power. First, there was the replacement of Ali Osman Taha with Ali al-Haj as his deputy in the Islamic Movement. Then, as speaker of the assembly, Turabi was perceived to have entered into an alliance with a "black [African] power group" in parliament with the goal of changing the constitution such that Turabi's power eclipsed Bashir's.[59] This "made people in the military very nervous because of the 'black' element in the military. Blacks were 80 percent of the army and they were trying to reduce it."[60] Finally, there was Turabi's grand tour to the provinces, where he mobilized support for constitutional changes that threatened to overturn the country's traditional power structure.[61]

6.3.1 Ethnicity as a Source of Attribute Substitution

Ultimately, tribalism or regionalism did not motivate political behavior, despite how many Sudanese interpret historical events ex post. Turabi, who is a northerner (though whose identity would become a matter of much discussion as the conflict played out), did not elevate Darfurians and others from western Sudan because he cared about the status of *gharaba* vis-à-vis riverains.[62] It was the same for Bashir. Though Bashir's social identification with his tribe, the Ja'aliyin, and ethno-region (riverain Arabs) is much stronger than the more cosmopolitan Turabi (in the sense that Bashir cares about these groups' statuses and seeks to resemble other members of these groups),[63] it is wrong to suggest that Bashir selected Taha over Ali al-Haj for the vice presidency because he sought to advance the wellbeing of riverain Arabs relative to other groups.

---

[59] Interview with member of the NCP and former high-ranking cabinet member, 2009. According to Mutrif Sidiq, "When he was speaker of the parliament, it was evident he was supported by Darfurians." Personal interview, Khartoum, March 20, 2006.

[60] Interview with member of the NCP and former high-ranking cabinet member, 2009.

[61] As one Bashir ally stated, "It was Turabi who tried to exploit ethnic divisions within the movement when he started to mobilize support from the states." Personal interview, Khartoum, 2005.

[62] Though born in Kassala in eastern Sudan, Turabi comes from a famous religious family that is descended from Wad Turabi, a holy man of the Bidairiya Arabs, who resided in a village some 50 miles southeast of Khartoum. Richard Leslie Hill, *A Biographical Dictionary of the Sudan* (London: Cass, 1967). According to Abdullahi Ali Ibrahim, Turabi is not a traditionalist who is constrained by the "blind loyalties" to his lineage. Instead, Turabi "described his people as adept at forging tradition rather than submitting to its alleged imperative. He described them as 'free' and open for change." Abd Allah Ali Ibrahim, "A Theology of Modernity: Hasan Turabi and Islamic Renewal in Sudan," *Africa Today*, 46 (3) (1999): 195–222.

[63] On social identification, see Moses Shayo, "A Model of Social Identity with an Application to Political Economy: Nation, Class, and Redistribution," *American Political Science*

Instead, the patterns of behavior followed a clear political logic. Both Bashir and Turabi were seeking to maximize their power and needed allies they could trust to achieve their goal. Bashir turned to Taha because he had strong personal ties with him that stretched back from the early days after the coup. They also shared similar preferences regarding the value of a strong central government relative to the power of the regions.[64] For his part, Turabi replaced Taha as deputy in the party because Turabi thought the party should serve as a counterbalance to the state and wanted to keep the party free from the influence of the executive (which Taha had become a part of). Moreover, as Turabi realized the extent of the resistance coming from Bashir and other Islamists who favored retaining a highly centralized system, Turabi seemed to have made a crude political calculation that his best hope in displacing Bashir and his allies was to tap into historical grievances among those from Sudan's periphery who had been disadvantaged by such a system. Of course, Turabi's supporters did not only come from Darfur and western Sudan, but many did. Thus the geographical roots of political preferences in Sudan (with those from the Nile River Valley favoring a strong centralized government and those from the periphery favoring stronger state governments) go a long way toward accounting for the regional nature of the Turabi and Bashir split. A final key factor that may account for Bashir's decision to fall back on riverain Arabs, especially those from his own tribe, the Ja'aliyin, was the informational advantage that comes from shared ethnicity. (See Section 2.5.2 for an extensive discussion of this mechanism.) Thus, Bashir's reliance on Ja'aliyin and other riverain Arabs in the most strategic positions, especially as uncertainty was increasing,[65] may have been an attempt to reduce the monitoring costs of those who had the greatest potential to overthrow him in a coup.

Because of ethnicity's visibility, however, both sides could discern that the other was mobilizing members of certain ethnic groups.[66] Even though both Turabi and Bashir pursued such ties for political, geographic,

---

Review, 103 (2) (2009): 147–174. And Sambanis and Shayo, "Social Identification and Ethnic Conflict."

[64] A number of Islamists who supported federalism conveyed stories about battles they had with Taha over the distribution of power and resources to the region. Interview with Ali al-Haj, January 18, 2007. Interview with al-Haj Adam, Khartoum, July 22, 2008.

[65] As de Waal notes, "Following the 1999 split and Turabi's imprisonment, President Bashir and his lieutenant, Vice-President Ali Osman Taha, relied increasingly on their own kinsmen, security officers and Islamist cadres drawn from precisely the same Nile Valley tribes fingered in the Black Book." Alex de Waal, "Deep Down in Darfur: Nothing Is as We Are Told in Sudan's Killing Fields," *Review of African Political Economy*, 32 (106) (2005): 653–659, at p. 656.

[66] On the importance of ethnicity's visibility, see Chandra, "What Is Ethnic Identity and Does It Matter?"

and informational reasons and not for ethnic reasons per se, to the other side it also looked like and could be ethnic mobilization. Thus, even if both sides had a highly sophisticated understanding of politics, which they did, and knew the other side very well, which they did, they could be susceptible to using readily available information about ethnicity as an attribute substitute for the more intangible and potentially misrepresented information about political loyalty, especially as time pressures increased and one felt they could not afford the time it took to learn another's true political affiliation.[67] This cognitive bias would cause both sides to systematically overestimate the importance ethnicity played in political mobilization and, in doing so, reinforced the perceived ethnic nature of the conflict.

6.3.2 Rumors, Historical Memory, and the Politicization of Ethnicity

If ethnoregional differences within the Islamic Movement were perceived to be of increasing importance as the power struggle between Bashir and Turabi escalated, the uncertainty produced by the Fourth of Ramadan decrees and the split within the Islamic Movement further increased the salience of ethnicity, in the sense that more and more Islamists viewed politics through an ethnoregional lens.[68] For example, one of the first ministers to resign in protest of Bashir's palace coup was Mohamed al-Amin Khalifa, the Minister of Cabinet Affairs. The resignation shocked the Bashir faction. As a retired colonel and one of the original members of the RCC who collaborated with Bashir in the 1989 coup d'état, Khalifa was expected to fall in line on the side of the president. When he followed Turabi instead, his resignation not only infuriated but also alarmed the leaders of the Bashir group. It suggested that the president could not readily discern people's political identities, and increased fears among the Bashir faction that Turabi was trying

---

[67] On attribute substitution, see Daniel Kahneman and Shane Frederick, "Representativeness Revisited: Attribute Substitution in Intuitive Judgment," in Mie Augier and James G. March, eds., *Models of a Man: Essays in Memory of Herbert A. Simon* (Cambridge, Mass.: MIT Press, 2004). Daniel Kahneman, *Thinking, Fast and Slow* (New York: Farrar, Straus & Giroux, 2011). On ethnicity as an uncertainty reduction device, see Henry E. Hale, *The Foundations of Ethnic Politics: Separatism of States and Nations in Eurasia and the World* (Cambridge: Cambridge University Press, 2008).

[68] Alex de Waal also makes this point in various writings at the time and later writings about Darfur. See Alex de Waal, "Tragedy in Darfur," *Boston Review*, October/November 2004.

"to create a military wing."[69] Furthermore, as a Darfurian of non-Arab descent, Khalifa's resignation reinforced the perceived salience of ethnicity and the efficacy of using ethnoregional identity as a heuristic device to sort allies from enemies.

Elites on both sides further ethnicized the conflict by seeking to exploit fears of victimization at the hands of ethnic rivals to consolidate support from within their ranks.[70] Those in the Bashir camp spread the meme that Turabi was emulating the famous nineteenth-century Sudanese religious revolutionary the Mahdi, who led the anticolonial uprising that overthrew the Turco-Egyptian administration in 1885. Though a northerner, the Mahdi mobilized considerable support from western Sudan. Moreover, the Mahdi's deputy and successor, Khalifa 'Abdallahi ibn Muhammad, was from Darfur. The Mahdi comparison was intentionally inflammatory as it stirred memories of the massacres committed by Khalifa's army of *gharaba* against the Ja'aliyin, the tribe of Bashir, in Matamma in 1897.[71] The insinuation of the rumormongers was clear: If Turabi were to lead the *gharaba* to power as the Mahdi had done, what would prevent a repeat of history?

Other rumors swirled. Turabi's origins became a matter of debate. He was said not to be a "real" northerner but alleged to be from the Bargu (a non-Arab) tribe in Darfur. On the other side, Darfurian Islamists claimed that secret meetings were being held in Shendi and other parts of northern Sudan in which Nafie Ali Nafie, a Ja'aliyin and key hardliner in the Bashir faction, celebrated the coup against Turabi and declared to their coethnics that "we did it to protect you."[72]

---

[69] Interview with Mutrif Siddiq, Khartoum, March 20, 2006.

[70] Rui de Figueiredo Jr. and Barry R. Weingast, "The Rationality of Fear: Political Opportunism and Ethnic Conflict," in Barbara F. Walter and Jack Snyder, *Civil Wars, Insecurity, and Intervention* (New York: Columbia University Press, 1999).

[71] As the *Historical Dictionary of Sudan* explains, "Initially the Ja'aliyin offered broad support to the Mahdist movement in the 1880s, both out of religious conviction and the perception of economic advantage in lifting Turkish control. The Mahdi's most prominent general, 'Abd al-Rahman al-Nujumi, was one of many important Ja'ali Mahdists. However, during the reign of the Khalifa 'Abdullahi, many Ja'aliyin became disillusioned with the Khalifa's favoring of his Baqqara kinsmen. This disillusionment turned to open rebellion among the people of Matamma, across the Nile from Shendi, who in 1897 were massacred by a Mahdist army led by the Khalifa's cousin Mahmud Ahmad." Kramer et al., *Historical Dictionary of the Sudan*, p. 227.

[72] According to Jibril Ibrahim, after Bashir purged Turabi, "Taha and others went to the North and explained to their tribes 'you will lose everything to Turabi and westerners if you don't side with us'." Interview, Abuja, Nigeria, April 9, 2006.

6.3.3 *The Black Book* and the Coming Coup d'État

Sharpening the ethnoregional nature of the conflict was the publication, a few months after the Fourth of Ramadan decrees of an anonymous document, entitled *The Black Book: Imbalance of Power and Wealth in Sudan*. Written by Khalil Ibrahim and other Darfurian Islamists who objected to historical inequities in the country's distribution of power and wealth and that continued under the Al-Ingaz regime, *The Black Book* was secretly published and shrewdly distributed to have maximum impact. The main distribution points were some of Khartoum's most influential mosques during Friday sermons, but copies were also placed on the desks of Bashir and other high-ranking government officials, signaling to Sudanese security that their former brothers retained privileged access to the presidential palace.[73] The next day, copies were disseminated throughout the country's largest cities. The government's attempt to suppress the document by buying up all the copies merely created a market for its reproduction and increased intrigue.[74]

The book was explosive because it laid bare northerners' political domination at the expense of those from other regions. The heart of the document contained pages of descriptive statistics displaying the distribution of top ministerial appointments by region since independence. Despite representing only 5 percent of the population, the authors calculated that members of the northern region had, on average, filled 65 percent of ministerial positions in all governments between independence and 1999. Moreover, they accused Bashir of perpetuating the northern dominance of the government with the Fourth of Ramadan decrees and of doing little "to avoid the tribalism and regionalism as promised in earlier slogans."[75]

Despite the fact that the Al-Ingaz regime built by Turabi did not escape the authors' scorn,[76] to the Bashir group, *The Black Book* confirmed the dangerous coalescence of a threat from Turabi and Islamists from

---

[73] William Wallis, "Darfur's Darkest Chapter," *Financial Times*, August 21, 2004.

[74] Interview with Abubakar Hamid Nour, member of the JEM, coauthor of *The Black Book*, Ndjamena, Chad, August 7, 2009.

[75] Seekers of Truth and Justice, *The Black Book: Imbalance of Power and Wealth in Sudan* (Khartoum, 2002), p. 12. For a summary, see http://www.sudanjem.org/sudan-alt/english/books/blackbook_part1/book_part1.asp.htm.

[76] "The new government operated under the slogans: Civilizational Project, Islamization of life, equality and justice and the principle of citizenship. Unfortunately, these slogans soon gave way to unchallenged hegemony of the Northern Region." Seekers of Truth and Justice, *Black Book*.

western Sudan,[77] especially from non-Arab tribes in Darfur, from where the authors principally came. In the eyes of Bashir and the security clique, the document was intended to incite a revolution. As one pro-government newspaper headline warned at the time, "This book is a prelude to a coup d'état."[78] But, in the eyes of the riverains, the coup threatened not just Bashir—the North's historical domination of power and wealth in Sudan stood in the balance.

Those around Bashir saw *The Black Book* as the work of Turabi and another weapon in his arsenal to try to overthrow them.[79] Turabi made matters worse when, in his characteristic audacious and controversial style, he said he had no relation to the book but that he endorsed it, warning that any time there was domination of power by any tribe, party or organization in Sudan it could lead to violence and revolt.

6.4 ETHNIC EXCLUSION AND ETHNIC BALANCING

To the Bashir group there could be no doubt that Turabi was exploiting ethnoregional divisions to try to reclaim political power. As Mutrif Siddiq declared in an interview, "A majority of Darfurians, particularly non-Arabs, gathered with Turabi. He tried to utilize them, especially those in the army, to consolidate his position against Bashir."[80] The consequence of this ethnicized view of politics was that it colored how the Bashir group distinguished between allies and enemies during this precarious and uncertain time. As Dr. Sayeed al-Khateeb, another member of the NCP and one of the signatories of the Memorandum of Ten, admitted, there was a tendency by the government to employ a crude ethnic calculus in identifying Turabi sympathizers: "The Arab tribes will be with us, and the African tribes will be with Turabi . . . We overestimated the threat of Turabi, and underestimated what the government could do."[81]

Of the non-Arab tribes, the Bashir group was particularly wary of the Zaghawa. As mentioned in Chapter 6, the Islamists from the Zaghawa were some of the most active in Al-Ingaz, participating in security, the police and the regime's Popular Defense Forces (*Defa Shabi*). After the coup of 1989, Khalil Ibrahim, a young Zaghawa from Tina, would

---

[77] Interview with Ibrahim Ahmed Omer, Khartoum, January 28, 2007.

[78] Al-Akhbar al-Ayom, Khartoum, Sudan, May 10, 2000.

[79] One newspaper described *The Black Book* as "a time bomb that is thrown in this conflict between Palace and Manshiya." *Al-Wafaq*, April 24, 2000.

[80] Interview with Mutrif Siddiq, Khartoum, March 20, 2006.

[81] Interview with Sayeed al-Khateeb, Khartoum, May 29, 2005.

become head of the *tanzim* in Darfur, while others, including Adam Tahir Hamdoun, Yusuf Libis, Sulieman Jammous, and Jibril Ibrahim (Khalil's brother) would take up prominent roles in the national *tanzim*. In the late 1990s, however, Khalil would become disillusioned with Al-Ingaz and left Sudan in 1998 to pursue studies in Netherlands.[82] The other top Zaghawa Islamists remained, pushing for reform of the Islamic Movement and backing Turabi's constitutional amendments. After the split in the Islamic Movement, many defected from the NCP and were now seen as some of the most active anti-regime dissidents, authoring *The Black Book*, joining Turabi's Popular Congress Party, and leading protests in El Fasher in September 2000.

Even though several Zaghawa Islamists continued to support the government and remained in the NCP, according to the Bashir group's ethnic shorthand, the Zaghawa were collectively labeled as Turabi sympathizers.[83] This view was made clear to the Zaghawa shura council,[84] when, in a visit to the leaders of the organization in the early months of 2000, one of the top NCP officials asked, "Why have *all* the leaders of the Islamic front from Zaghawa gone with Turabi?"[85]

To win back the "traitors," the Bashir group at first turned to patronage and suasion. Most of the Zaghawa Islamists rejected offers of money and positions in the government, however, as mere token gestures that would not address their core concerns about the need to fundamentally redistribute power. The NCP's attempts to induce the Zaghawa shura to convince its members to break from Turabi's party also failed.[86] Bashir even turned to Idriss Déby, president of Chad (and a Zaghawa), for help. Déby, also concerned with the rift between Zaghawa Islamists and Bashir for fear it may eventually complicate his strong relations with Khartoum,[87] willingly obliged, calling one prominent pro-Turabi Zaghawa as many as five times to convince him of the error of his way.[88] On another occasion in 2000, Déby invited five prominent Zaghawa Islamists to N'djamena

---

[82] Flint and de Waal, *Darfur: A Short History of a Long War*.

[83] A Zaghawa from the National Congress, who sided with the Bashir group, reiterated this sentiment, "The first impression of the central government after the split was all Zaghawa were with Turabi." Personal interview, Khartoum, January 23, 2006.

[84] Zaghawa shura is an informal group of Zaghawa who meet to discuss matters of import for their tribe.

[85] Interview with member of the Zaghawa shura council, Khartoum, March 15, 2006.

[86] The members of the shura council rejected this proposal, explaining to the NCP officials this was not one of its functions.

[87] In retrospect, some Chadian Zaghawa see the split between Bashir and Turabi as a key turning point in the political relations between Sudan and Chad. Personal interviews, N'djamena, Chad, August 2009.

[88] Interview with Adam Tahir Hamdoun, Khartoum, March 5, 2006.

and lectured them. According to one participant in the meeting, Déby said, "I am a personal friend of Bashir. The government of Bashir has been very good to you people. You shouldn't take any position against him. I am ready to pick up the phone and call him. Whatever you want he will give it to you."[89]

As the Zaghawa Islamists resisted the government's overtures, the NCP feared the defectors would coordinate with those remaining inside to bring Turabi back to power. One extreme position was expressed by a Darfurian Arab who remained with Bashir and in the NCP: "The plot of the Zaghawa was very clear to the government and the [Bashir group] moved against them. [The Zaghawa] wanted to make Hassan al-Turabi chairman of the Republic . . . and then they would succeed him after Turabi passed away . . . After this plot had been disclosed by President Bashir, in the whole of Sudan they have been treated with suspicion, including in Darfur."[90] This tribalist invective proved effective at increasing government paranoia about the Zaghawa, and the Bashir group complemented its patronage and suasion with harsher tactics. It began to purge Zaghawa, who remained in sensitive organs, such as the army, police, and security. One governor of Darfur after the split acknowledged that "security people, such as Salah Gosh, were getting rid of Zaghawa or transferring them out of Darfur."[91] This left the Zaghawa with the impression that after the split none of their kinsmen were left in security.[92]

6.4.1 The Ascendancy of the Abbala Arabs

As the NCP "lost the best cadres in Darfur after the split,"[93] it recognized the potential costs for its societal support and control in the region. To compensate for the loss of the Zaghawa and other Darfurian Islamists, the regime sought out new Darfurian intermediaries and strengthened its ties with the Zaghawa's rival in Darfur: the Abbala (camel-herding) Arabs. In contrast to the non-Arabs in Darfur, historically the Abbala had not been active either in government or the Islamic Movement. But

[89] Interview with Jibril Ibrahim, Abuja, Nigeria, April 9, 2006.
[90] Interview with Jibril Abdullah, Khartoum, March 7, 2006.
[91] Interview with Ibrahim Suleiman, Khartoum, March 7, 2006. The security, led by Salah Gosh, was particularly aggressive in its targeting of Zaghawa. Part of the reason may have been a personal rivalry between Salah Gosh and Yusuf Libis, a fellow engineer, prominent security officer and Zaghawa who sided with Turabi.
[92] Interview with Sulieman Jammous, Furawiya, Sudan, July 2, 2005.
[93] Interview with Qutbi al-Mahdi, Khartoum, November 22, 2005.

this political inertia had hurt them as they found themselves politically marginalized in Darfur and Khartoum. One famous incident occurred in Gineik, North Darfur, in 1992, when the Zaghawa leveraged their influence in Al-Ingaz to mobilize effectively to block the government from granting the northern Rizeigat a *hakura* ("right to land").[94] But with the split in the Islamic Movement and the exit of the Zaghawa Islamists, a political opportunity presented itself, and the Abbala seized it.[95] At the time of the split, the governor of North Darfur, Abdalla Safi al-Nur,[96] was an Abbala of the Ereigat Rizeigat, who appreciated the political importance of cultivating strong relations with the central government to advance one's group's interests.[97] A general in the air force and a non-Islamist, Safi al-Nur proved to be a strong ally for the Bashir group in Darfur during this critical time. Tending to be "very harsh on Turabi supporters," especially the Zaghawa Islamists,[98] he oversaw the government's countermobilization efforts against Turabi's Popular Congress in 2000 and 2001 as the latter tried to provoke mass demonstrations in El Fasher in September 2000. Over the next few years, as the Zaghawa were transferred out of security in Darfur, Safi al-Nur "responded by putting his kinsmen into key local security posts."[99]

Safi al-Nur was part of a group of Abbala, who, after the split, became increasingly influential as the key intermediaries linking North Darfur and the Bashir group. Others included General Hussein Abdalla Jibril, an Ereigat Abbala who as a member of parliament chaired the Parliamentary

---

[94] There is disagreement between the Zaghawa and the Abbala as to what the objective of the Gineik conference was. The Abbala say it was merely to discuss provision of services to the local people. The Zaghawa saw it as an attempt by the government to grant the northern Rizeigat a hakura, if not directly, then indirectly. "The government wanted to . . . lay the foundations for the locality. We strongly rejected this idea. Any settlement in Darfur will require a rearrangement of the hakura—this is the problem." Interview with Ali Shammar, Khartoum, Sudan, March 29, 2006. One non-Darfurian working in the Ministry of Economic Planning in the early 1990s, however, saw a letter sent to his ministry by the deputy wali of Darfur, Ahmed Ibrahim al-Tahir. It asked for funds for the settlement of Arab nomads in North Darfur on grounds that in their traditional areas they are deprived of services, including water, schools, and medical facilities. Personal interview, Khartoum, March 2006.

[95] Or, as Abdalla Safi al-Nur obliquely put it, "After the separation, many others found a chance." Personal interview. Khartoum, August 1, 2009.

[96] Safi al-Nur served as governor from 1998 until 2002.

[97] According to Ibrahim Yahya, former governor of West Darfur and member of the Islamic Movement. Flint and de Waal, *Darfur: A New History of a Long War*, p. 65.

[98] Interview with Qutbi al-Mahdi, Khartoum, November 22, 2005.

[99] De Waal, "Deep Down in Darfur," p. 656. Note, however, that others offer a more positive assessment of Safi al-Nur's tenure. For example, Safi al-Nur's deputy, Sharif Mohamedein,

Security and Defense Committee and led the investigation into the "bandits" based in Jebel Marra in April 2002, and Jibril Abdalla, one of the few Abbala active in the Islamic Movement, but who sided with Bashir and was virulently anti-Zaghawa. A third influential Abbala was Sheikh Musa Hilal, the chief of the Mahamid Rizeigat.

6.4.2 Sheikh Musa Hilal Moves to Misteriha

Since the conflict between the Fur and Arabs of the late 1980s, Hilal had earned a reputation as "a troublemaker, a hothead who was 'inciting tribal hatred and conflict.' "[100] After a major clash with the Zaghawa in 1996, Hilal relocated his tribal headquarters from Aamo, the traditional base of the Mahamid near Kutum, but which was feeling the effects of years of drought and desertification, to the greener pastures of the land just south of Kebkabiya and north of Jebel Marra.[101] This would prove a critical turning point in the history of the Darfur conflict as it would lead to an increase in violence against the Fur communities in the area and cause the Fur to reorganize their militias that were disarmed in 1991.

According to a top state official in North Darfur, from his new base in Misteriha, Hilal quickly established himself as the "absolute leader" of the area—or, as another official put it, he "lorded over the Fur."[102] Feeling he was above the law, Hilal refused to pay taxes, and his kinsmen, looking for land to graze their camels, violently encroached on the farms of the neighboring Fur.

This unruliness inevitably led to a clash with local authorities in Kebkabiya, who were trying to pressure Hilal to end the raids on the farmers in the region. They sent reports to Safi al-Nur, the governor in El Fasher, describing the imperative for state action. Safi al-Nur summoned Hilal to El Fasher, questioning him about his refusal to pay taxes and the problems he was causing with the farmers. Even more, the governor invoked the memory of Hilal's father, the long-serving sheikh of the Mahamid,

a Zaghawa who remained in government after the split, suggested he did as best he could to balance the demands of different constituencies in North Darfur and was not "against the Zaghawa" as some have claimed. There was conflict with some Zaghawa politicians, especially after contentious legislative election and subsequent riots, but it was merely political. Interview with Sharif Mohamedein, Khartoum, July 28, 2008.

[100] Quote of former governor of Darfur. Flint and de Waal, *Darfur: A New History of a Long War*, p. 54.

[101] Flint and de Waal, *Darfur: A New History of a Long War*, p. 65.

[102] Interview with Ali Shammar, Khartoum, March 29, 2006.

Hilal Mohamed Abdalla.[103] According to one state official present at the meeting, Safi al-Nur said, "Your father was a very just tribal leader. But what you are doing is against your father's legacy."[104] Hilal was instructed to pay back the taxes he had avoided since moving to Misteriha.[105] The "big sheikh" ignored the order,[106] boasting to his tribesmen in Misteriha that he was supported by the vice president in Khartoum.[107] These boasts appeared credible when a high-level security committee from the central government, led by al-Tayib "Sikha," the former governor of Darfur, visited Kebkabiya in November 2000 after Hilal had been arrested by the local commissioner. Hilal protested he was acting in self-defense, and the security committee ordered his release. According to one local official from Kebkabiya, "After his release, the attacks continued again . . . The government knew that Musa Hilal had more weapons than police or army in the area" but were afraid of provoking him.[108]

After the exit of the Darfurian Islamists from the regime, the central government needed allies in Darfur, and elites of the Abbala, who have their own grievances over lack of land rights and political marginalization, gradually moved to fill the void. In a situation that was almost completely the reverse of ten years before, it was Musa Hilal, not Khalil Ibrahim, who took advantage of a close relationship with al-Tayib "Sikha" and other top elites in Khartoum.

6.5 ANALYSIS AND THEORETICAL IMPLICATIONS: EXPLORING THE STRATEGIC LOGIC OF ETHNOPOLITICAL EXCLUSION

A decade after coming to power, Sudan's Islamic Movement suffered a devastating split that tore apart the regime and factionalized its political network. Drawing on extensive interviews with members of Sudan's

---

[103] For a background of Hilal Mohamed Abdalla, see Flint and de Waal, *Darfur: A New History of a Long War.*

[104] Interview with Ali Shammar, Khartoum, March 29, 2006.

[105] Interview with Ali Shammar, Khartoum, March 29, 2006.

[106] Whereas Hilal viewed himself as a "big sheikh" in an interview with Emily Wax of the *Washington Post*, he seemed to dismiss Safi al-Nur as a "small sheikh." According to a relative of Musa Hilal, "Sheikh Musa did not respect Safi al-Nur because he came from a small tribe [Ereigat Rizeigat]." Personal interview, Khartoum, Sudan, March 28, 2006. See Emily Wax, "In Sudan 'A Big Sheikh' Roams Free," *Washington Post*, July 18, 2004.

[107] Several Darfurian Islamists commented that Musa Hilal had strong ties with the late vice president, Zubair Mohammed Saleh.

[108] Local official based in Kebkabiya in 2000 and 2001. Personal interview. Khartoum, April 2, 2006.

Islamic Movement from the Bashir faction and the Turabi faction, the case study has identified the key dynamics contributing to regime breakdown. They include:

Institutional disarray: Turabi's dismantling of the formal structures of the NIF after coming to power increased uncertainty about the rules governing decision-making and how power and resources were to be allocated. Institutional competition between those members serving in the state and those remaining in the shadow state further increased uncertainty.

Breakdown of trust: The failed assassination attempt against Hosni Mubarak increased mistrust between Turabi and a key security clique within the regime, led by Turabi's deputy, Ali Osman Taha. Many have identified this event as a key turning point due to the damage it caused to the movement's fraternity or social solidarity (*asabiyyah*). After this event, a seed of doubt crept into members' minds whether their shared history guaranteed a shared future.[109]

Political competition and fears of a large, rapid shift in the distribution of power: As trust frayed, political competition intensified. Turabi pushed through a new constitution to weaken the power of the presidency, and Bashir's allies pushed through new rules to weaken Turabi's control of the party. This political competition increased fears that each side was conspiring to initiate a radical shift in the distribution of power that would permanently eliminate the other faction from power.

Incumbent strikes preemptively to destroy rival's coup-making capabilities: Fearing Turabi was orchestrating a constitutional coup, Bashir struck first. He dissolved the national assembly, the vehicle Turabi was using to emasculate Bashir's power, and deployed the military onto the streets of Khartoum.

Ethnic exclusion as a coup-proofing strategy: Bashir's preemptive strike was intended to block Turabi's ability to execute a constitutional coup. But the Bashir group feared Turabi's next move would entail using his allies in the military and security to take the state by force. To further increase the costs Turabi faced to seizing power, the Bashir group moved to purge Turabi allies from the regime. As the conflict became structured along ethnoregional lines, the Bashir group tended to use ethnicity as a heuristic to sort loyalists from disloyalists. Of course, this does not imply that only Darfurians joined Turabi's Popular Congress Party and only riverine Arabs remained

---

[109] Interview with Dr. Ghazi Salahuddin, Khartoum, August 13, 2010.

with Bashir. Prominent Islamist riverains, such as Abdalla Hassan Ahmed, joined the Popular Congress, while Darfurians (including members of the Zaghawa) remained with the National Congress. But the tendency to use ethnicity as a source of attribute substitution (i.e. making judgments based on accessible ascriptive information versus less accessible information about one's true political loyalties) did have material consequences for Bashir's political network. Key societal groups, such as the Zaghawa from Darfur, were collectively treated with suspicion and undersupplied key positions within the regime's political and security networks.

Ethnic balancing: As the conflict intensified with Turabi, the Bashir group increasingly relied on its coethnics at the top levels of security and political power, while in Darfur it strengthened its relations with the Abbala and other Arabs who were seen as more loyal to Bashir than non-Arabs. Moreover, as historical rivals of the Zaghawa, they were seen as an effective way to balance against any threat that may emerge from Turabi and his followers in western Sudan. Whether coincidence or not, this national and local shift in the balance of power corresponded with an increase in insecurity in Darfur as Arab militias became more brazen in their encroachment of non-Arab areas around Jebel Marra, Kebkabiya, and Dar Zaghawa.

6.6 CONCLUSION

Overall, a case study of the split in the Islamic Movement in 1999 and 2000 illustrates the usefulness of the strategic model of ethnopolitical exclusion developed in Chapters 3 and 4. While instrumental and cultural factors were not irrelevant, a qualitative analysis of the breakdown of the Al-Ingaz regime highlights the central importance of the commitment problem in undermining powersharing and driving elite factions to try to forcibly eliminate the other from power. While Turabi and his protégés, Bashir and Taha, had gained much in cooperating to capture control of the Sudan state, by the late 1990s the two sides began to lose faith that the other was committed to sharing power going forward. Instead, each side began to fear that their former allies were secretly, and then openly, conspiring to bring about a future shift in the distribution of power that eliminated its rival from the regime. Given the catastrophic consequences of such an outcome—the loss of power, privilege, and protection that comes from controlling the state apparatus—both sides began to prepare for such an outcome, which locked them in an internal security dilemma.

As the conflict intensified, Bashir leveraged his incumbency advantage to thwart Turabi's constitutional coup and to purge Turabi and his perceived supporters from the regime. While this extreme measure consolidated Bashir and Taha's hold on power and increased the costs Turabi faced to reclaiming power, it also entailed costs for the Bashir group—namely, weakened societal control in Darfur and an increased risk of civil war. In the next chapter, I explore how Bashir's coup-proofing strategy and restructuring of his political network reduced the government's counterinsurgency capacity in Darfur and contributed to the outbreak of civil war.

7

Political Exclusion and Civil War

The Outbreak of the Darfur Civil War

7.1 INTRODUCTION

This chapter seeks to account for the onset of the Darfur civil war in 2003. Its central claim is that the outbreak of the Darfur civil war can be linked to the exclusionary political strategy Sudan's president, Omar al-Bashir, chose to neutralize the threat posed by his former mentor and the secretary general of the Islamic Movement, Hassan al-Turabi. Consistent with the coup–civil war trap hypothesis, Bashir's strategy to purge Turabi and his supporters from the central government substituted civil war risk for coup risk.

This chapter, thus, helps to elucidate the mechanisms by which ethnopolitical exclusion increases the risk of armed rebellion, as summarized in Table 7.1. The evidence suggests that ethnopolitical exclusion not only inflames societal grievances against the central government, as Wimmer et al. argue, but it also increases the *feasibility*, or *opportunity*, of armed rebellion through two important channels.[1] First, it increases the pool of violence specialists who oppose the central government, increasing their capabilities to mount effective resistance to the government. Second, and consistent with the political networks hypothesis of civil war developed in Chapter 2, ethnopolitical exclusion reduces the government's counter-insurgency capabilities. It not only weakens the government's ability to monitor and effectively repress dissidents but also emasculates its broker-age networks which are essential to secure support from local communi-ties and prevent an armed rebellion from taking root. Thus in Darfur we

---

[1] Wimmer et al., "Ethnic Politics and Armed Conflict." Cederman et al., "Why Do Ethnic Groups Rebel?" Cederman et al., "Horizontal Inequalities."

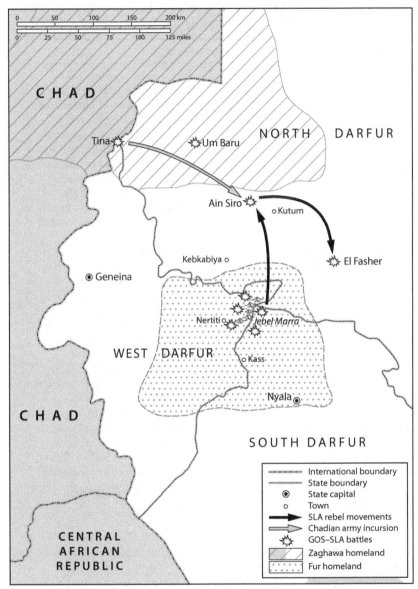

MAP 7.1 The Outbreak of the Second Darfur Rebellion, July 2002–April 2003

see that, in direct contrast to the early 1990s, when the Bashir government leveraged the *tanzim* to produce a cooperative counterinsurgency campaign against the Bolad rebellion (see Chapter 5), in the early 2000s the Bashir government's dismantling of the *tanzim* undercut such capabilities,

TABLE 7.1 *Channels by Which Ethnopolitical Exclusion Increases Civil War Risk: Evidence from Sudan*

Channel	Evidence
Grievances	Darfurian Islamists outraged by Bashir's power grab. Feelings of disempowerment are articulated in the publication of *The Black Book: Imbalance of Power and Wealth in Sudan.* Government stops its support for building the Western Salvation Road to connect Khartoum with Darfur. Politicization of ethnicity both at the top of the regime and within Darfur.
Increased opportunities for armed rebellion and counterinsurgency weakness	Darfurian Islamists defect from the regime increasing the pool of dissidents. The Islamic Movement's *tanzim* in Darfur is dismantled, reducing the number of trusted brokers from the Fur and Zaghawa ethnic groups. Government's support base in Darfur shifts to Abbala Arabs, emboldening Darfurian Arab power brokers to use violence to increase access to land.
Deepening mistrust worsens commitment problem	Post-exclusion mobilization and regime–dissident interactions reinforce threat posed by Turabi and *gharaba*, further weakening Bashir's commitment to give them real power.

forcing the regime to resort to non-cooperative counterinsurgency that ended up inflaming the rebellion and stoking full-scale civil war.

The chapter also shows how, even in the face of escalating violence, rulers remain constrained by the commitment problem that led them to pursue ethnopolitical exclusion in the first place. In the Darfur case, even as the region stood on the brink of full-scale civil war, the Bashir group rejected a negotiated solution to the armed conflict, largely out of fear that the concessions necessary to end the war would grant Turabi and his allies a political opening they could exploit to reclaim power for themselves at the expense of the Bashir group.

The rest of the chapter is organized as follows. First, I describe the origins of the two armed movements that rebel against the central government, leading to the Darfur civil war. I analyze to what degree the rebel movements were a product of the split in the Islamic Movement. While there is strong evidence to suggest that the factionalization of the Islamic Movement increased grievances in Darfur and directly contributed to one rebel movement, the JEM, a second rebel group, the Sudan Liberation Army (SLA)—initially the stronger of the two armed movements—was very much a product of local insecurity in Darfur. Second, I analyze how the breakdown of the regime's Islamist network in Darfur affected the government's counterinsurgency capabilities and its ability to secure local cooperation against the rebels. Third, I explore why, in the face of an intensifying armed rebellion, the government rejected a negotiated solution, risking full-scale civil war. The evidence suggests not only that the Bashir regime felt constrained by the shadow of Turabi but also that it made a strategic mistake by relying heavily on the support of Chad's president, Idriss Déby, to counter the Darfur rebellions. Bashir turned to Déby partially as a way to overcome the loss of support among the Sudanese Zaghawa after the split with Turabi. As a Zaghawa himself, Déby—Bashir hoped—could serve as a counterweight to the Darfur rebellion and leverage his shared ethnicity to extract information about the rebels. But this plan backfired as the Chadian military refused to obey Déby's orders to fight against the Darfurian rebels. In an original empirical finding, I describe how it was the Chadian military's collusion that proved critical to the rebels' ability to deceive the SAF and attack El Fasher in late April 2003.

7.2 THE ORIGINS OF THE SECOND DARFUR REBELLION

In less than three years after the NCP formally divided into two parties, a devastating civil war would engulf Darfur. Two rebel groups would lead the insurrection: the SLA and the JEM. The JEM was led by Khalil Ibrahim, an Islamist and the former leader of the *tanzim* in Darfur, who was one of the authors of *The Black Book*. The emergence of the JEM was a direct consequence of the split in the Islamic Movement. Though Khalil and other Darfurian Islamists started to become disillusioned with the Islamic Movement as early as the mid-1990s and began to work on *The Black Book* prior to the Fourth of Ramadan decrees, it was after the split, when many were forced out of the government and the NCP, that they started to consider armed opposition. In 2001, a group of them assembled in N'djamena to discuss the way forward and to possibly operate out of Chad into Darfur. But Déby caught wind of the meeting and tried to have Khalil arrested.[2] Khalil fled Chad and returned to Europe, where he concentrated on developing his organization's political program. Back in Europe, Ibrahim struck an alliance with Ali al-Haj, and they organized a conference in Germany in April 2003 for opponents of the government from across Sudan, forming what they called the "Union of the Marginalized Majority."[3] In its first battle with government forces in March 2003, the JEM was soundly defeated. While the JEM did much to raise political consciousness in Darfur, its forces on the ground in the early stages of the war were limited. The JEM gained strength as the conflict persisted and, in May 2008, launched the first rebel attack on Sudan's capital, Khartoum.

On the other hand, the SLA proved to be the more potent rebel force in the early phases of the conflict (2002–2005). The origins of the SLA go back to August 2001, when a group of non-Islamist dissidents from the Fur and Zaghawa formed an alliance to create a military organization that was able to stand up to the central government and, what the dissidents perceived to be Khartoum's proxy forces in Darfur: the Arab militias.

The Fur faction of the alliance was led by a lawyer and secularist, Abdel Wahid Mohamed al-Nur. Abdel Wahid had been trying to organize an opposition force since the early 1990s, when he and other Fur activists began to discuss how they could continue the revolution Bolad had started.[4] But the mobilization foundered as the Islamist network in the 1990s hindered a Darfur-based rebellion, while Idriss Déby's alliance with Khartoum blocked Fur dissidents from operating out of Chad. Similar to the Fur, there had been some Zaghawa in opposition to the central government throughout the 1990s trying to build a rebellion. Two of the most prominent Zaghawa in the opposition were Sharif Harir[5] and Adam Shogar, who were part of the Sudan Federal Democratic Alliance

[2] Interview with Jibril Ibrahim, Abuja, Nigeria, April 9, 2006.
[3] International Crisis Group, "Darfur Rising: Sudan's New Crisis," *Africa Report*, March 25, 2004.
[4] Interview with Abdel Wahid Mohamed al-Nur, Abuja, Nigeria, April 7, 2006.
[5] Harir defected from Sudan after several of his family members were killed by security forces in Darfur in 1991 as part of the disarmament campaign. See footnote 104 in Chapter 5.

(SFDA). But the NIF network again precluded penetration in Darfur, and the SFDA joined the other Sudanese dissident groups in Asmara, Eritrea.[6]

Conditions changed, however, in the aftermath of the split in the Islamic Movement. "All Darfur was boiling," reflected Minni Minnawi, a Zaghawa who returned to Darfur from Nigeria in 2001 and became the secretary general of the SLA.[7] The battle over the constitutional amendments and Fourth of Ramadan decrees and the subsequent purging of many Darfurian Islamists from the NCP seemed to substantiate the central thesis of *The Black Book*, which continued to be distributed clandestinely or via word of mouth. Darfurians increasingly viewed the central government as pro-riverain and anti-westerner.

7.2.1 The Effect of the Split in the Islamic Movement on Rebel Mobilization

The split in the NCP not only heightened Darfurians' political consciousness and intensified their political grievances as manifest in *The Black Book*, but it also contributed to an increase in the politicization of ethnicity *within* Darfur. As non-Arab Islamists exited the regime and the Abbala and other Arabs gained greater influence as brokers, Darfurians perceived that the central government was backing the latter against the former. According to one interviewee residing in Kebkabiya in 2001, who went on to join the rebels in 2003:

The separation of Arab and non-Arab tribes was not there or only minor before the split;[8] then it became more noticeable. After the separation, it was very clear: Bashir does not need us and only supports Arab tribes . . . The government did not defend non-Arab tribes. Instead they gave ammunition and weapons to Arab tribes.[9]

---

[6] In fact, in the mid-1990s, top Al-Ingaz officials sent Shogar's relatives in the *tanzim* abroad to meet Shogar and convince him to abandon the SFDA and return to Khartoum. The outreach was successful, and Shogar returned to Khartoum, where he spent the next five years or so, before once again rebelling against the central government. Interview with Zaghawa relative of Shogar and member of Islamic Movement, Khartoum, August 18, 2005.

[7] Interview with Minni Minnawi, Abuja, Nigeria, April 10, 2006.

[8] Before "if there was a person to fill a job in the government he had to be in the Islamic Movement, but then [after the split] it seemed you had to be from Ja'aliyin, Shaigiya, or Danagla." Interviews with SLA members from North Darfur, N'djamena, Chad, August 7, 2009.

[9] Interviews with SLA members from North Darfur, N'djamena, Chad, August 7, 2009.

In addition to any cues picked up from national political developments and the split in the NCP, this assessment was a reaction to the surge in violent raids that occurred in the areas of Jebel Marra and Kebkabiya between 2000 and 2002. According to a petition a group of Fur submitted to President Bashir in May 2002, between July 15, 2000 and April 28, 2002, there were more than 150 attacks on Fur villages in the area of Kebkabiya, Jebel Marra, Zalingei, and Kass.[10] A Fur elder described the feeling among their community in the face of the violence:

The Fur felt that the attacks were not ordinary; the Arabs said they would like to evacuate the Fur from their land. Because there was no response from the government, they decided to depend on themselves . . . They opened military training camps. Soldiers in the army stopped their contacts with the government. They found Fur tribal leaders receptive to their requests.[11]

A sequence of violent clashes in late 2000 and 2001 between the Zaghawa from Dar Gala and the Aulayd Zeid, an Abbala Arab tribe in the northern part of West Darfur, elicited a similar assessment by the Zaghawa, who also viewed the split in the Islamic Movement as adversely affecting members from their group. After more than fifty Zaghawa were killed in May 2001 in a clash with the Aulayd Zeid, a group of Zaghawa living in the Kornoi area assembled in existing self-defense camps to prepare for future violence.[12] During this time, Abdel Wahid Mohamed al-Nur, the leader of the Fur dissidents, established connections with the Zaghawa and suggested forging an alliance to coordinate their activities. By the end of July 2001, a group of seventeen Zaghawa was on its way to Jebel Marra to join the Fur who had established training camps in the mountains.[13]

Over the next nine months, the Zaghawa, some of whom had fought with the Chadian army and supported Déby's rise to power,[14] trained

---

[10] Polloni lists 156 attacks in an annex. Flint and de Waal indicate 181 attacks during this time. Domenico Polloni, "Darfur in Pieces," UNDP: Conflict Analysis Tools No. 6, 2005.

[11] Interview with elder from Fur royal family, El Fasher, Darfur, May 1, 2005.

[12] According to one Zaghawa tribal leader who met the rebels at this time: "I went with three vehicles to self-defense camps of Zaghawa and told them now is the time for peace as the government will deploy the police reserve. But the rebels had no trust in the government and tried to take my vehicles by force, and I went back to El Fasher." Interview with Shartay Adam Sabi, El Fasher, Sudan, December 15, 2005.

[13] Interview with Abdel Wahid Mohamed al-Nur, Asmara, Eritrea, February 22, 2005. Interview with Minni Minawi, Asmara, Eritrea, February 23, 2005. Flint and de Waal, *Darfur: A New History of a Long War*, p. 86.

[14] In 1989 and 1990, Sudanese Zaghawa hosted and supported Déby in his rebellion against the Habré regime. See Section 8.7.2. Interview with Hassan Bargu, Khartoum, March 15, 2006.

the Fur and started to secretly organize an insurgency.[15] With the militia attacks continuing, the rebels found it easy to recruit soldiers to join the movement. Moreover, local communities willingly supported the rebels. The first joint rebel operations attacks were raids against police posts or poorly defended army garrisons in early 2002 with the goal of testing the waters and obtaining weapons from the government. After an attack on an army outpost in Tur in July 2002, the rebels distributed a crude manifesto, identifying themselves as the DLF, faulting the government for siding with Arab militias against the non-Arabs, and demanding *diya* (blood money) be paid for the string of recent attacks on Zaghawa and Fur.[16]

The next six months would be a critical juncture in the history of the Darfur conflict. The DLF was still a small force and isolated in Jebel Marra. Its capacity was limited and the group's demands were parochial. Though they railed against the central government for marginalizing Darfur and called for Khartoum to finish the Western Salvation Road (see Textbox 7.1), their primary concerns focused on the local violence that plagued their communities. The Fur were demanding government protection from the increasing number of attacks by armed nomads on Jebel Marra; the Zaghawa were demanding *diya* to be paid as compensation for the Zaghawa Dar Gala killed by the Awlad Zeid in May 2001.[17]

TEXTBOX 7.1   A NOTE ON THE WESTERN
SALVATION ROAD

The Western Salvation Road would be one of the most significant casualties of the split in the Islamic Movement. In the mid-1990s, the Al-Ingaz regime proposed building a 1,200-kilometer road, the Western Salvation Road, which would finally connect Darfur with the country's capital. To help finance the road's construction, estimated at a cost of US$350 million, Al-Ingaz, led by Ali al-Haj, one of the strongest proponents of the road project, convinced Darfurians to ration sugar. As the states and Darfurians themselves covered half the cost

---

[15] "Our success depended on the secrecy of the movement. We created many camps in the mountains of Jebel Marra." Interview with Abdel Wahid Mohamed al-Nur, Asmara, Eritrea, February 22, 2005.

[16] Polloni, "Darfur in Pieces," p. 38. See also "Death in Darfur," *Africa Confidential*, November 22, 2002.

[17] According to three Zaghawa interlocutors sent by the Zaghawa shura council to meet with rebels in August 2002. Interviews with Ali Thor al-Khalla, Khartoum, August 14, 2005, February 27, 2006. Interviews with Ali Shammar, March 29, 2006, July 22, 2008, July 26, 2009. Interviews with Omda Adam Salim, March 1, 2006, March 4, 2006.

of the road, the central government would pay the other half. The road's construction was undertaken by a consortium, led by one of the country's wealthiest businessmen, al-Haj Adam Yagoub, who also happened to hail from Darfur. Yagoub invested a considerable amount of his company's money in the road's construction as the government raised the money through rationing. After four years, the rationing produced roughly $50 million, but the money disappeared, and the road construction stalled as Yagoub's consortium ran out of money. To continue construction, the consortium applied for a loan from the Islamic Development Bank in Jeddah, Saudi Arabia. In turn, the bank asked the government of Sudan to guarantee the loan, but, coming at the height of the conflict between Bashir and Turabi, Sudan's Minister of Finance, Dr. Abdel Wahab Osman, refused, saying, "the road is not a priority for us." The Western Salvation Road was left incomplete—a symbol of the region's neglect by the central government and a mobilizing point for Darfurians, who had sacrificed for its construction. Interview with member of road-construction consortium who travelled to Jeddah to apply for loan, N'djamena, Chad, August 8, 2009. Interviews with various other top Al-Ingaz officials, 2005–2010.

7.3 A CRITICAL JUNCTURE IN DARFUR: NON-COOPERATIVE COUNTERINSURGENCY

Almost exactly eleven years after Fur leaders confronted Bashir about the continued violence in Darfur and demanded greater protection for their communities (see Chapter 5), they were once again petitioning the president about attacks on Fur villages. Prior to this meeting between the Fur leaders and the president, the central government had confirmed the presence of an armed group based in Jebel Marra. In response to these developments, in May 2002 Bashir announced the creation of a committee for the "Restoration of State Authority and Security in Darfur" to be chaired by the governor of North Darfur, Ibrahim Suleiman.[18] Like it did in 1991, the central government was turning to a governor to oversee the stabilization of Darfur. As a former minister of defense and chief of staff of the army, Suleiman, a Darfurian from the non-Arab Berti tribe, had the right résumé for the job. Moreover, he appreciated the security concerns of the Fur that were driving them to take up weapons and refuge in Jebel Marra. In a press conference in Khartoum in June 2002, he stated "that

---

[18] Flint and de Waal, *Darfur: A New History of a Long War*, p. 84.

the motives for the tribal clashes in Darfur were not ethnic cleansing but the fear of the indigenous groups of the area of the Arab tribes who have settled at Kebkabiya. They fear that the Arabs would confiscate the only fertile land in the area."[19]

The problem for Ibrahim Suleiman was that, in contrast to the governorship of al-Tayib "Sikha," the organizational potency and hierarchy of the regime was in shambles. First, the *tanzim* was defunct. The governor could not activate a series of trusted brokers who could immediately be deployed to help in the countermobilization process. This forced Suleiman to create an ad-hoc brokerage network as he tried to negotiate with the dissidents encamped in Jebel Marra and cultivate support from the Fur communities living around the mountain. The problem was not finding local intermediaries willing to serve as interlocutors between the government and rebels; many Fur and Zaghawa were concerned about the violence in the region and wished to help prevent the conflict from spiraling out of control. The problem was that these ad-hoc intermediaries lacked leverage with the government, especially state security.

As explained in the analysis of the First Darfur Rebellion, one of the difficulties of producing cooperative counterinsurgency is, though local communities and the government often prefer to avoid large-scale violence, they face a classic Prisoner's Dilemma. Local communities are reluctant to withdraw their support to the rebels if the government is going to attack them regardless; the government is reluctant to reign in its military and security forces if the local communities are going to continue to support the rebels. The case evidence from Darfur in the early 1990s suggests the important brokerage role that local intermediaries, who are trusted by both sides, can play to ensure cooperation. (See Chapter 5.) Not only can they serve as credible messengers of the other side's intentions (e.g., they can convey to the government that the local communities oppose the rebellion and will support the government if it refrains from attacking them while convincing the communities that if they stay on the sidelines, the government will leave them alone), they can also help with enforcement. During the Bolad rebellion, one of the key roles that Fur brokers played was shuttling back and forth between local Fur communities and the government to ensure each side was upholding its end of the bargain and, if not, to try to facilitate a solution that would keep the sides on a cooperative path. This last point is especially important and is where the

---

[19] "Sudan: Forty-Nine Arrested Over Tribal Clashes in Western State," BBC Monitoring International Reports, June 10, 2002. (Original source: *Khartoum Monitor*, June 9, 2002).

process broke down in Darfur in 2002. The Fur and Zaghawa intermediaries that the government turned to as the rebellion began had almost
no leverage with the power brokers in the central government. Though
they would meet with some of the key security hawks in the regime (see
below), they failed to convince the government to change their tactics.
*In fact, the government would unleash indiscriminate attacks while they
were promising otherwise in meetings with Fur representatives.* This hurt
the credibility of these Fur as brokers and pushed the local communities
to support the rebels, not least because it represented a potential source
of protection from the government and *janjawiid* militias.

The second factor that undermined the organizational potency of the
regime was the emergence of overlapping networks of political control
since 1991. In contrast to al-Tayib "Sikha," who, as a leading member of
the *tanzim*, had singular control of operations in Darfur and the trust of
the central government, Suleiman did not benefit from such a position. As
the security cabal around Bashir moved to consolidate its grip on power
to insulate itself from the Turabi faction, it would emerge as the real
power behind the throne with its own networks and agents throughout
the country. Comprised predominantly of "trusted" riverain Arabs in the
security services, Ibrahim Suleiman was excluded from this shadow government. Thus, Suleiman found himself competing with agents of state
security and military intelligence who had their own ideas as to how to
resolve the conflict in Darfur. According to one non-Islamist member of
the cabinet in 2002 and 2003, "Ibrahim Suleiman was 'in charge,' but not
in charge. Operations were run from Khartoum not from El Fasher. The
government had a double command structure and eventually got rid of
one [when they fired Ibrahim Suleiman]."[20]

7.3.1 The Failure of Local Mediation Efforts

One of Ibrahim Suleiman's early initiatives was to hold several tribal
conferences to resolve the ongoing conflict around Jebel Marra and
Kebkabiya. On August 16, 2002, the first of the conferences—the Fur
Leadership Conference—was held on the foothills of Jebel Marra at the
town of Nertiti. The Fur leaders saw the meeting as an opportunity to
mediate between the government and the rebels in the mountain while
gaining security guarantees for the Fur communities who were aggrieved
by the ongoing violence committed by armed nomads. The Fur delegates

---

[20] Interview with Sudanese presidential adviser (2002–2004), Khartoum, March 31, 2006.

knew that de-escalation of the conflict hinged on their ability to coordinate action between the rebels and the government.[21] The conference's closing statement reflected the grand bargain they envisaged was necessary to stave off war: it demanded that "the state carry out its duties in a decisive and firm way to stop the repeated aggressions carried out by some Arab tribes (*janjawiid*) against the land and possessions of the Fur," while calling for the rebels to end their attacks on the police.[22] In a move intended to contribute to the de-escalation of the conflict and reassure the Fur, Suleiman had Musa Hilal arrested and even went as far as removing him as *nazir*, or tribal leader, of the Mahamid.[23] This decision did not go down well with Hilal or some of his tribesmen who felt "they arrested Sheikh Musa in a very shameful way."[24] After Hilal was arrested and sent all the way to Port Sudan, ten of the thirteen Omdas (or chiefs) of the Mahamid traveled to Khartoum to meet with Taha and Nafie, "complaining that you cannot appoint a sheikh by force."[25] As a proud tribal leader, Hilal's arrest was humiliating. Privately he began to tell security officers that the governor, Ibrahim Suleiman, was supporting the rebels.[26]

Any progress the Fur felt would come from the Nertiti Conference and Suleiman's bold move against Hilal was quickly undercut, however, by a complementary tribal conference held in September for Arabs living around Jebel Marra. Intended to discuss development programs for Arab communities and cultivate their support for a peaceful resolution to the worsening conflict, the Fur would view it as "a declaration of war"[27] by the Arabs of central Darfur backed by state security. What worried the Fur was the communiqué that called for the government to deal with the Fur militias and "liquidate" the Popular Defense Forces, which was seen as supporting the Fur.[28] When, in the weeks after the conference, there were more than twenty raids on Fur villages around Kass, the Fur concluded that the attacks were linked to the Kass conference, raising suspicions that a secret deal had been struck between Sudan's security forces and delegates from small Arab tribes around Jebel Marra. After the

[21] Interview with Fur delegate at the meeting, Khartoum, April 9, 2006.
[22] Closing statement of Leadership Conference, cited in Flint and de Waal, *Darfur: A New History of a Long War*, p. 85.
[23] Julie Flint, "Beyond 'Janjaweed': Understanding the Militias of Darfur," *Small Arms Survey*, June 2009.
[24] Interview with Abdalla Safi al-Nur, Abuja, April 7, 2006.
[25] Interview with relative of Musa Hilal, Khartoum, March 25, 2006.
[26] Interview with relative of Musa Hilal, Khartoum, March 25, 2006.
[27] Flint and de Waal, *Darfur: A New History of a Long War*, p. 86.
[28] Flint and de Waal, *Darfur: A New History of a Long War*, p. 86.

Kass "catastrophe," some of the Fur elites who hoped to contribute to a peaceful de-escalation of the conflict at the Nertiti conference lamented their inability to "convince the government to stop the attacks."[29]

Any hope the Fur leaders had of securing the government's cooperation was completely quashed when, a few months later, a group of them were invited to Khartoum to meet with some of the regime's most powerful players and share what information they had on the rebellion. The Fur elites saw it as a last chance to persuade the government to change course and reign in the militias who were driving young people from their communities to join the rebels. But as the Fur intermediaries were given assurances about the government's seriousness in protecting Fur communities and resolving the conflict from the likes of Al Hajj Atta al-Mannan, who was organizing the Darfur file for the government and a future governor of South Darfur, Sharif Ahmed Omar Badr, Minister of Investment and very close to President Bashir, and Salah Gosh, director of National Intelligence and Security Service (NISS), the delegation received reports from back home that Fur villages around Zalingei and Jebel Marra were being "smashed and burned."[30] Then, in a meeting with Ahmed Haroun, the state minister for the interior, it became clear why they had been brought to Khartoum. "If you are ready," he told the delegation, "we will give you support to fight the rebels." Then he added, tell the rebels that "if they don't settle the issue, we will crush them."[31] Sudanese security was not interested in negotiating with the rebels or coordinating with these Fur intermediaries to defuse the conflict. Instead, it opted for a military solution. But, unlike in 1991 and 1992, this counterinsurgency campaign would fail spectacularly in defeating the rebellion.

7.4 THE OUTBREAK OF FULL-SCALE CIVIL WAR

7.4.1 The Sudan Liberation Army Moves to North Darfur

As the Nertiti and Kass meetings failed to de-escalate the conflict, the Sudanese military organized a major military operation against the rebel bases on Jebel Marra. (See Map 7.1 at beginning of this chapter.) The SAF started to build up its forces and surrounded the mountain. In December 2002 and January 2003 the government launched a major offensive in

---

[29] Interview with Fur delegate at the Nertiti meeting, Khartoum, January 28, 2007.
[30] Interview with delegation that travelled to Khartoum, Nyala, May 25, 2005, December 8, 2005.
[31] Interview with delegation that travelled to Khartoum, Nyala, May 25, 2005, December 8, 2005.

Jebel Marra. As the Sudanese military was concentrating on clearing out Jebel Marra, it did not realize that the SLA had moved a substantial part of its rebel forces into northern Darfur and had created a new base of operations in Dar Zaghawa. The move to northern Darfur occurred after the Nertiti meeting, in which the rebels became concerned that the government was infiltrating Jebel Marra and the presence of the Zaghawa rebels in Fur territories was creating friction with local communities.[32] By September 2002, Abdalla Abaker, Minni Minawi, and some 300 rebels left for Dar Zaghawa. While in North Darfur, the rebels negotiated with Ibrahim Suleiman through tribal interlocutors but the negotiations made little headway.

According to Sharif Harir, a long-time dissident in Darfur and early adviser to the SLA, the opening of new operations in North Darfur was a "critical juncture" as "there was no government of Sudan presence" in the region.[33] In Dar Zaghawa, the SLA opened several new camps and then laid low. In February 2003, the rebels were able to liberate the town of Golo near Jebel Marra from the Sudanese military, ensuring the government's attention remain focused on this area. A month later, the SLA surprised the government with a series of attacks in North Darfur, including on Um Baru, Kornoi, and the border town of Tina. "Until [the rebels] started attacking in the north," one SAF general admitted, "we didn't realize so many were there."[34]

Part of the reason the government was in the dark about operations in Dar Zaghawa was that the SLA had neutralized the few local agents the government had left: Zaghawa tribal leaders. In February 2003, the SLA kidnapped Shartay Adam Sabi from Um Baru, whom they accused of working on behalf of the government of Sudan. When a group of Zaghawa came to meet the rebels to win the Shartay's release, the SLA displayed their impressive firepower to send a message to other tribal leaders: stay out of North Darfur and do not communicate with the government or risk being killed.[35] After this group returned to El Fasher, Dar Zaghawa was empty for the rebels. The rebels' threats proved effective. According to two generals in the Sudanese military, "The Zaghawa chiefs refused to deal with the rebels. It limited the information coming from Dar

---

[32] Interview with Minni Minawi, Abuja, Nigeria, April 10, 2006. Interview with Abdel Wahid Mohamed al-Nur, Abuja, Nigeria, April 7, 2006.

[33] Interview with Sharif Harir, Ndjamena, Chad, June 25, 2005.

[34] Interview with Lt. Gen. Ismat Abdel Rahman al-Zain and Gen. Mohamed Ahmad al-Dabi, Abuja, Nigeria. April 10, 2006.

[35] Interview with Ali Shammar, Khartoum. February 9, 2006.

Zaghawa. [Moreover], they never allowed the refugees to go to southern Darfur. They succeeded in preventing us from getting information."[36]

7.4.2 The Rebels Anger Idriss Déby

While operating in North Darfur and attacking along the Chad–Sudan border, the SLA made Chadian president Idriss Déby nervous. Since his successful insurgency out of Darfur to N'djamena in 1990, Déby had developed a close relationship with President Bashir, and both governments worked to ensure dissidents did not find sanctuary in their respective countries. With the emergence of the SLA (and with some of its leaders having fought alongside Déby in 1990 and served in the Chadian army, even though they were Sudanese), Déby was concerned that the Darfurian rebellion would threaten to disrupt his relations with Bashir and weaken his internal control as weapons and individuals would inevitably make their way to the SLA.[37]

In late 2002, Déby and the SLA leadership would engage in a heated exchange after the rebels ambushed a convoy coming from Libya and kidnapped eight individuals from the Aulayd Zeid tribe, an Arab group whose members live in both Chad and Sudan.[38] This attack would have significant repercussions as Khartoum exploited the incident to mobilize Arabs against the rebellion. Moreover, it angered Déby. Feeling pressure from Arab leaders within his country and sensitive to any negative relations between Arabs and Zaghawa in Darfur, Déby sought to end the violence between the Aulayd Zeid and the Zaghawa. When Déby traveled to Tine, Chad, for a national festival in December 2002, he called for representatives from the SLA to meet him to discuss the release of the eight Aulayd Zeid. The rebels told Déby they had no problem with the Arabs, just with the government of Sudan, and pledged to bring the abductees in fifteen days. But the rebels had deceived Déby as the nomads had already been killed. When Déby learned this, he phoned the SLA leader, Abdalla Abaker, scolding the rebels and warning them that their rebellion would just bring problems for their people and accomplish nothing. Abaker responded with a clear threat to Déby: "We may not know the way to

---

[36] Interview with Lt. Gen. Ismat Abdel Rahman al-Zain and Gen. Mohamed Ahmad al-Dabi, Abuja, Nigeria, April 10, 2006.

[37] Interview with Hassan Bargu, Khartoum, March 15, 2006. Interview with Ali Thor al-Khalla, Khartoum, August 16, 2005.

[38] A number of interviewees provided information on this important incident: Ali Thor al-Khalla, Khartoum, August 16, 2005; Hassan Bargu, Khartoum, March 15, 2006; Omda Adam Salim, Khartoum, March 28, 2006; Abdalla Safi al-Nur, Abuja, April 7, 2006.

Khartoum, but surely we know the way to N'djamena."[39] Infuriated, Déby became just as intent on destroying the rebels as his counterpart Bashir, but his security and military officials would have different ideas.

7.4.3 External Assistance from the SPLA

If the SLA had a hostile relationship with Idriss Déby, it was able to develop an important strategic alliance with the SPLA. In 2002, the SPLA began serious negotiations with the government of Sudan in Kenya under the auspices of the regional organization, the Intergovernmental Authority on Development. The government and the SPLA signed the Machakos Protocol in July 2002 in which they agreed to a framework agreement for ending their long-running war. The protocol called for the establishment of a transitional government of national unity in which power and wealth was shared between the two parties. At the end of the six-year interim period, southern Sudanese would have the right to vote in a self-determination referendum to choose to remain part of Sudan or to become independent. The protocol also included a temporary ceasefire, which was renewed in November 2002, as the parties continued to nego-tiate the modalities of a more comprehensive agreement. As the SPLA was negotiating with the government in Kenya, it made contact with the Darfurian rebels and opened a channel of communication through Ahmed Abdel Shafi, a Fur and one of the original dissidents who worked with Abdel Wahid since the early 1990s. The SPLA flew Abdel Shafi to Kenya to meet Dr. John Garang in order for the leaders of the SPLA to learn more about the rebels in Jebel Marra. The SPLA viewed the insur-gency in Darfur as another opportunity to try to spread its New Sudan ideology to northern Sudan—"Dr. John Garang never would hesitate to help marginalized people," Yassir Arman said[40]—and as a lever to be used against the government as the SPLA pressed for maximum concessions at the peace talks in Kenya.[41]

Abdel Shafi first met Dr. John Garang toward the end of November 2002 before holding more extensive discussions with the leader of the SPLA in January, and it was decided that Abdel Shafi would locate himself at SPLA headquarters in New Site, southern Sudan, for training

[39] Various interviews, including with SLA leader, Minni Minawi, Abuja, Nigeria, April 10, 2006.
[40] Interview with Yasir Arman, Khartoum, March 29, 2006.
[41] Interview with Mutrif Siddiq, Under-Secretary, Ministry of Foreign Affairs, Government of Sudan, Khartoum, August 13, 2005.

and further consultations. In March 2003, Abdalla Abaker and Minni Minawi, leaders of the rebels in Dar Zaghawa, were flown into New Site to meet Garang so that the SPLA leader could "see who he was going to be sending weapons to."[42] At this meeting, the rebels decided to change their name from the Darfur Liberation Front to the Sudan Liberation Movement/Army (SLM/A) and announced a new manifesto modeled after the SPLM's New Sudan ideology.[43] The first shipment of armaments accompanied Abaker and Minawi as they returned by plane to North Darfur, and regular shipments followed.[44] Rather than transferring the weapons to Jebel Marra, as Abdel Wahid expected, Abaker and Minni brought them to the rebels' new camp in Ain Siro, northwest of Kutum. The first time the SLA used the weapons was to capture the border town of Tina on March 27. It was the rebels' third military victory against the government in a month.

7.4.4 The Shadow of Turabi: The Government of Sudan Rejects Negotiations with the Darfur Rebels

With the SLA gaining momentum in North Darfur, Sudan's military and security shifted its attention away from Jebel Marra to the rebels' northern base in Ain Siro. As the fighting intensified, there were calls by many Darfurian leaders for negotiations, not the use of force. This was the conclusion reached at the "consultative forum on security in Darfur" held in El Fasher for the region's traditional leaders at the end of February 2003.[45] Turabi's Popular NCP piled on, issuing a statement after the conference "that political issues would not be solved by military action" and that the government complicated the problem in the region through the use of "favoritism in assigning posts" and "by freezing the federalist regime, imposing centralization by appointing governors and depriving the states of their jurisdiction."[46]

---

[42] Interview with Ahmad Abdel Shafi, Abuja, Nigeria, April 10, 2006.

[43] International Crisis Group, "Unifying Darfur's Rebels: A Prerequisite for Peace," *Africa Briefing*, October 6, 2005.

[44] Interview with Ahmad Abdel Shafi, Abuja, Nigeria, April 10, 2006. According to the SAF officers, the GOS was tracking SPLA support for the Darfurian rebels. Interview with Lt. Gen. Ismat Abdel Rahman al-Zain and Gen. Mohamed Ahmad al-Dabi, Abuja, Nigeria. April 10, 2006.

[45] International Crisis Group, "Unifying Darfur's Rebels."

[46] "Sudan: Turabi's Party Accuses Government of Security Failures in Darfur," BBC Summary of World Broadcasts, February 25, 2003.

Privately, Zaghawa, who remained in the NCP, also warned about the risks of a military solution. For example, in a memorandum written to President Bashir on April 11, 2003, and hand delivered to one of the key hardliners in the regime, Nafie Ali Nafie, on the "Resolution of the Darfur Crisis," one NCP member from the Zaghawa cautioned that the rebels should not be taken lightly as some of their fighters had military experience in the Chadian army, their numbers were increasing and they were receiving support from the civilian population. Moreover, it should be noted that the "sum of the Zaghawa believe that the government is strategically rejecting them by refusing the appointment of their sons in the regular forces and their constitutional positions." Thus, he advocated creating negotiating channels, executing a number of development projects, and allowing the participation of the Zaghawa in the division of wealth and power.[47] This advice was systematically discounted by the security cabal at the top of the regime. The author of the memorandum "found they were not trusting me. They were deceiving me. They were making decisions and laughing at me."[48]

The outcome of the February 2003 consultative conference in El Fasher led to a split between those who supported military action and those who wanted to negotiate with the rebels. Many of the Darfurians called for negotiations. But the hardliners in the regime, such as the government's minister of interior, Abd al-Rahim Mohammed Hussein, and director of the NISS, Salah Abdalla Gosh, who attended the El Fasher consultative forum, "were not happy with the outcome," as one state official observed.[49] They were not willing to make any political concessions that they feared Turabi's Popular National Congress would exploit. According to one Bashir loyalist, the Bashir group from the beginning perceived Turabi's hand was behind the rebels, especially of course the JEM, which affected their willingness to bargain.[50] As one non-Islamist presidential adviser who served at the time reflected, the hawks feared "peace would bring back Turabi, and he would slaughter the regime."[51]

This militant view was echoed by some of the leaders of Darfur's Abbala Arabs, who had the ear of Sudan's top security officials and who were concerned by the growing strength of the rebels. The Abbala leaders

---

[47] "Resolution of Darfur Crisis," April 11, 2003. Memorandum written to President Omar al-Bashir. Copy provided by author, March 2006.
[48] Interview with author of letter, "Resolution of Darfur Crisis," Khartoum, March 29, 2006.
[49] Interview, Abuja, Nigeria, April 10, 2006.
[50] Interview with Dr. Qutbi al-Mahdi, Khartoum, Sudan, January 24, 2007.
[51] Interview with Sudanese presidential adviser (2002–2004), Khartoum, March 31, 2006.

felt that if they were properly armed they could help defeat what they saw as a "Zaghawa army."[52] According to one high-ranking member of the NCP, "It is not just that the government organized the militias, but the militias came to us."[53] Thus the security hawks at the top of the regime, whose views were shaped by the previous conflict with Turabi, refused to negotiate because they saw both Turabi and Garang behind the rebellion. Moreover, they became convinced by their local Arab allies that with their help they could easily defeat the rebellion.

7.4.5 Bashir Turns to Déby to Stop the "Zaghawa Rebellion"

An aggressive counterinsurgency was also supported by Chadian President Déby. Since coming to power, Déby's government worked closely with his Sudanese counterparts to ensure dissidents did not find sanctuary in their respective countries.[54] As described in Chapter 4, at the time of the split between Turabi and Bashir, Déby was particularly concerned about the exodus of Zaghawa Islamists from the Bashir regime and the potential repercussions for his relationship with Khartoum. In fact, Déby counseled the Zaghawa in the Islamic Movement to stay with Bashir rather than joining Turabi's opposition party. With the emergence of the SLA and the JEM, Déby's worst fears were being realized.

In March 2003, the governments of Sudan and Chad decided to close the border to try to prevent the rebels from using eastern Chad as a rear base. Then on April 12, Déby traveled to Sudan to meet Bashir in El Fasher, the capital of North Darfur. Bashir's public meeting with Déby provided a revealing insight of the ethnic lens through which Bashir saw the conflict. Bashir and his security forces feared what they called the "Greater Zaghawa State," that members of the Zaghawa ethnic group, one of the strongest constituencies within the Islamic Movement, were conspiring to capture sovereign power in Sudan in addition to their group's control of Chad.[55] In fact, in his public address in El Fasher, Bashir declared, in effect, that his alliance with Déby would prevent such

---

[52] Interview with Dr. Qutbi al-Mahdi, Khartoum, April 1, 2006.
[53] Interview with Dr. Qutbi al-Mahdi, Khartoum, April 1, 2006.
[54] Interview with Daoussa Deby, N'djamena, Chad, June 25, 2005.
[55] The government of Sudan would continuously use this notion of the "Greater Zaghawa State" as propaganda to diminish the rebels as mere tribalists and to drive a wedge between the rebels from the Zaghawa and other ethnic groups in Darfur, especially the Fur.

an eventuality.[56] Unwilling to negotiate with the rebels in Darfur, Sudan's security saw strategic gains to be made from an intra-Zaghawa conflict.

The two leaders decided that the Chadian army would participate in a joint military operation against the SLA. After the meeting in El Fasher, Déby traveled straight to Tine, Chad, where he instructed his military stationed at the garrison to prepare for the operation with SAF "to destroy any rebel group in Ain Siro."[57] The Sudanese military immediately sent food rations, fuel, ammunition, and weapons to Tine to arm and equip the Chadian battalion.[58] Within the next ten days the battalion moved toward Ain Siro as the government of Sudan mobilized army units from El Fasher, Kebkabiya, al-Geneina, and Kutum. In addition, local militias in the Kutum region were being mobilized to aid in the offensive.[59]

The problem was that, though Déby was genuinely against the rebellion in Darfur, the soldiers in the Chadian battalion were more sympathetic to their Sudanese kinsmen. They knew some of the Darfurian rebels, such as Abdalla Abaker, who had fought alongside them in the Chadian army in the 1990s. Moreover, some recalled the support Sudanese Zaghawa provided to Déby's Patriotic Salvation Movement (Mouvement Patriotique du Salut; MPS) when it was based in Darfur in 1989 and 1990. They had no interest in attacking the SLA; moreover, some found it morally reprehensible.[60] Thus, as the Chadian battalion made its way to Ain Siro, contact was established with the SLA encamped in the hills. The Chadians told the SLA that they were on their way to Ain Siro but that they were not going to attack them. They entered the hills and spent about two days with the SLA.[61] On the last

---

[56] This was a clever way to propagate the poisonous idea while seeming to refute it. Several Sudanese newspapers ran headlines that reported on the meeting. See "Meeting of Two Presidents, Bashir and Idriss Déby, in El Fasher Defeated Rumours about the Plot of Formation of Greater Zaghawa State," *Al Wifaq*, April 14, 2003; "Bashir Gave Freedom to the Military to Finish Outlaws in Darfur; The Visit of Idriss Déby Gives Practical Denunciation of the Rumours of 'Greater Zaghawa State,'" *al-Ray al-Aam*, April 13, 2003.

[57] Interview with Abdul-Rahim Bahr, commander-in-chief of the Chadian Army, who led the Chadian battalion into Darfur, N'djamena, August 5, 2009.

[58] Interview with Lt. Gen. Ismat Abdel Rahman al-Zain and Gen. Mohamed Ahmad al-Dabi, Abuja, Nigeria, April 10, 2006.

[59] Amnesty International, "Sudan: Crisis in Darfur—Urgent Need for International Commission of Inquiry and Monitoring," Press Release, April 28, 2003. Available at https://www.amnesty.org/download/Documents/100000/afr540262003en.pdf (accessed October 5, 2016).

[60] Interviews, N'djamena, Chad, July 2009.

[61] Interview with Minni Minawi, Abuja, Nigeria, April 10, 2006.

day, they communicated to their superiors that "they didn't find any rebels; they only found cadavers from a battle some days ago between the rebels and the *janjawiid*" and were returning to Tine.[62] As they left,[63] the Chadians told the SLA the "government is going to attack you from all sides, including using the planes in Fasher."[64]

Shortly after the battalion left, the SAF launched its offensive, just as the Chadians said, sending in tanks and air support from El Fasher. As the government focused on Ain Siro, a mobile SLA force slipped out of the mountains and stealthily made its way to El Fasher. Early on the morning of April 25, the rebels attacked El Fasher airport and immobilized the government's air capabilities. This left the government tanks in Ain Siro vulnerable to counterattack by the rebels. As the tide turned in the rebels' favor in Ain Siro, the government soldiers called desperately to El Fasher for air cover, which never came. This major victory was one of many the rebels achieved over the next several months.

Desperate to slow the rebellion and turn the tide of the war, in the months that followed the government intensified its aerial bombardment and its use of local militias, primarily those from the Abbala Arab tribes; Abdalla Safi Nur and Musa Hilal became key players in mobilizing and overseeing local counterinsurgency operations. The regime relied on its "informal networks of ruling party insiders, former military personnel, and leaders of nomadic tribes" to recruit the *janjawiid* militias to fight the rebels.[65] For example, in South Darfur one of the key leaders of the militia was Mohammed Yacoub al Omda, who was previously granted a position of nazir by the Islamic Movement. Others were "leaders of small Arab tribes that migrated to Darfur from Chad in the past few decades and [had] been involved in local clashes with Fur and other groups over access to land in the past decade."[66]

Together the military and militias launched a brutal scorched-earth campaign against villages and civilian populations in Dar Zaghawa and

[62] Interview with Abdul-Rahim Bahr, N'djamena, Chad, August 5, 2009. In early April, a joint attack between SAF regular units, *janjawiid*, and Antonov bombers and helicopter gunships from El Fasher hit the rebels in Ain Siro, killing nine and wounding seventeen. Flint and de Waal, *Darfur: A Short History of a Long War*, p. 119.

[63] Top SAF officials claim the Chadian battalion transferred all the weapons, food, and supplies originally provided by government of Sudan to the SLA. Representatives from the SLA and Chadian government deny this.

[64] Interview with Minni Minawi, Abuja, Nigeria, April 10, 2006.

[65] Human Rights Watch, *Entrenching Impunity: Government Responsibility for International Crimes in Darfur*, New York: Human Rights Watch, 2005.

[66] Human Rights Watch, "Entrenching Impunity."

other areas of northern Darfur as the rebellion spread to South and West Darfur. Over time, the government's indiscriminate counterinsurgency campaign succeeded in slowing the rebellion and forcing a stalemate but not before the displacement of millions of Darfurians and the deaths of hundreds of thousands.

7.5 ANALYSIS OF LINK BETWEEN POLITICAL EXCLUSION AND THE SECOND DARFUR REBELLION

In the early 1990s, the Bashir government was able to effectively defeat an armed rebellion it faced in Darfur and prevent the outbreak of civil war. A decade later, facing another rebellion in Darfur that sought to continue the "revolution" started by Bolad, the government proved unable to suppress the rebellion and was confronted by a devastating and costly civil war. Why? Qualitative data gathered from in-depth interviews undertaken with a range of actors involved in the Darfur conflict illuminate the effect the split in the Islamic Movement had on the difference in outcomes. Not only did the split lead to greater political consciousness and stronger grievances among Darfurians, such that, in the words of rebel leader Minni Minnawi, "all Darfur was boiling," and increase the pool of Darfurian dissidents challenging the central government, but it also significantly altered the government's networks of control in Darfur. In the first decade of Bashir's tenure, the locus of support was among non-Arab Islamists who filled the *tanzim*. After the split, many of these brokers were purged or defected from the regime as Arab tribal leaders, especially those from the Abbala Arabs, such as Musa Hilal, rose to the fore. Though these Abbala tribal leaders would serve as effective agents in Darfur, as leaders of the so-called *janjawiid* militias that were critical for the countermobilization campaign, they were unable to act as trusted brokers between the government and members of the Fur and Zaghawa ethnic groups. Thus, unlike in the early 1990s, the government was unable to produce a counterinsurgency campaign in cooperation with the societal groups in which the rebels were embedded.

The comparative analysis of the First Darfur Rebellion with the Second Darfur Rebellion, thus, raises additional insights into how cooperative counterinsurgency works. It also sheds light on the political dynamics of exclusion and how the commitment problem prevents the rebuilding of inclusive networks after a political crisis.

7.5.1   Trusted Brokers and Cooperative Counterinsurgency

As discussed in Chapter 5, the theory of cooperative counterinsurgency helps to account for the link between political control and the use of indiscriminate violence. Cooperative counterinsurgency arises when both the government and local communities can credibly commit to work together to isolate armed rebels and protect civilians from state violence. Part of this process entails locals denouncing those who join the rebels, as Kalyvas emphasizes in his theory of selective violence,[67] but it also goes beyond this. It involves broader collaboration in which communities refrain from offering material support to the rebels and the government commits to protecting the security of local communities who assist the government. Forging this cooperation is difficult in an environment over which the government has limited control due to the weakness of the state. Growing insecurity increases uncertainty. The First Darfur Rebellion pointed to how brokers who have influence over and trust from both sides can help the government and local communities sustain cooperation under these conditions. The Second Darfur Rebellion reinforces the importance of trusted brokers, illustrating the difficulties of producing cooperative counterinsurgency in their absence.

One of the principal costs of the split in the Islamic Movement is that the Bashir group lost the trusted brothers who had served as brokers between the government and Fur communities before and during the Bolad rebellion. Of course not all non-Arab Darfurian Islamists defected or were purged after the split with Turabi. But those remaining were guilty by association and seemed to be fundamentally distrusted by the security cabal, leading the latter to discount the information and advice that the Zaghawa inside the NCP were offering. Moreover, the Fur and Zaghawa intermediaries who the government did reach out to as the second rebellion began lacked the influence that the Islamists in the *tanzim* had in the early 1990s. Consequently, as violence escalated and began to affect local communities around Jebel Marra, the Fur and Zaghawa intermediaries' entreaties to halt the violence to prevent the rebellion from gaining momentum fell on deaf ears. Suspicious of both the intermediaries and their communities, the government did little to alter its response to the rebellion, and, as the attacks continued, local communities increased their support for the rebels.

---

[67] Kalyvas, *The Logic of Violence in Civil War*.

Exacerbating the weakness of the Fur and Zaghawa intermediaries was that the individuals who now had the ear of the security cabal and served as the trusted brokers in Darfur were elites from the Abbala Arabs—the regional rivals of the Fur and Zaghawa. The interests of the Abbala Arabs were fundamentally different from those of their rivals. As previously discussed, they resented the Zaghawa's dominance in the *tanzim* in Darfur in the 1990s and now saw an opportunity to remedy their grievances regarding the lack of land and services (which again they felt the Zaghawa Islamists had blocked). Thus, they opposed policies that would restore the Zaghawa's political dominance in the region and instead voiced their support for a more hardline response to the conflict and volunteered to contribute in the counterinsurgency effort. This hardline posture resonated with the security cabal who opposed making any political concessions that would open the door for Turabi to make a comeback to power and exact revenge on his disciples who had betrayed him.

Overall, the split and the factionalization of the regime's political network led the Bashir group and its Darfurian brokers to reject negotiations and pursue war against the Darfur rebel groups. Without effective brokers from the Fur and Zaghawa, they were unable to execute cooperative counterinsurgency as in 1991, and, instead, their counterinsurgency operations escalated the conflict. As the conflict escalated, Bashir turned to Idriss Déby as a "Zaghawa ally," but this initiative backfired contributing to the surprise attack on El Fasher. As the rebels, backed by the SPLA, continued to gain ground, the government intensified its use of mass violence executed by the *janjawiid* and the Sudanese military. This strategy did manage to divide Darfur along tribal lines and keep the rebellion (mostly) confined to the western region, but at the cost of leading the UN Security Council to refer the case of Darfur to the International Criminal Court (ICC).

7.5.2 The Politics of Persistent Exclusion

An analysis of the Second Darfur Rebellion sheds light on the difficulties of producing cooperative counterinsurgency in the absence of trusted brokers from local communities. The Darfur case also sheds light on how exclusion persists. As described in Chapter 5, the split in the Islamic Movement led to a sudden exodus of Turabi supporters who were forced out of the regime as Bashir sought to eliminate the clear and present danger posed by their sheikh and his lieutenants. But, after Bashir consolidated his internal control and effectively shifted the battleground from within the regime to outside his regime, especially Darfur, one might think the optimal strategy would be to try to isolate Turabi while rebuilding the *tanzim* to prevent civil war in Darfur. This, of course, is easier said than done.

First, as described in Chapter 6, it is important to point out that Bashir tried to co-opt the Zaghawa Islamists and bring them back into the fold. He asked Déby to lean on these individuals to come back and work for the government; he also sent emissaries to meet with the leaders of the Zaghawa shura and otherwise put pressure on members of the political opposition to return to the ruling party. This bargaining failed, however, exactly because of the commitment problem that caused the rupture in the regime in the first place. Bashir recognized the benefits of regaining the support of some of the regime's most active cadres and dividing the opposition, but the commitment problem led Bashir to limit how much power he was willing to share with them. He wanted their support and allegiance but was unwilling to offer them anything more than token positions in the regime, which were largely rejected by the Zaghawa Islamists, and the exclusionary status quo continued.

7.5.3 Miscalculation

A detailed qualitative analysis of the breakdown of the Islamic Movement in Sudan and the exclusion of Turabi supporters from the regime demonstrates strong support for the strategic model of ethnopolitical exclusion and civil war. But what role, if any, did miscalculation and opportunity play? It is worth considering whether in fact the Bashir faction did anticipate that the split in the regime would lead to such an intense and costly war in Darfur (including the ICC indictments for top regime officials)— and, if they did, would it have altered their strategy.

Even if the Bashir faction did not envisage the type of war that would result in Darfur, it is clear they were well aware of the costs of the split in terms of their societal control in western Sudan but felt it was something they had to do to protect their hold on power. Moreover, as discussed, they calculated they could manage the loss of such cadres by drawing support from other groups in Darfur, such as the Abbala Arabs, and leveraging their alliance with Idriss Déby. As long as Déby denied the Zaghawa defectors from using Chad as a base to launch a rebellion, the Bashir group calculated the risk of civil war in Darfur would be low. Déby upheld his part of the deal and expelled Khalil Ibrahim when he tried to set up his JEM in N'djamena in 2001. The problem was not Déby's commitment to trying to prevent a war in Darfur but that he lacked control of his military, which, as discussed, provided crucial material support to the Darfurian rebels, especially prior to their surprise attack on El Fasher in late April 2003, a key turning point in the outbreak of the war. But even as the rebels gained support from both the Chadian military and the SPLA, the Abbala militias served as an effective counterbalance and managed to change the course of the war. While this had devastating consequences for Darfurians, in many ways, their strategy worked exactly as planned: it transformed a political rebellion into a tribal war in Darfur that failed to threaten Bashir and his allies' hold on power.

In fact, according to Sudanese officials I interviewed, the Bashir faction did not underestimate the costs of containing anti-regime dissidents in Darfur after the split with Turabi—what they underestimated was the global reaction to the war in Darfur and their counterinsurgency operations, which they felt led to the intervention of the ICC. They were confused for two reasons. First, as the Darfur conflict erupted, the Sudanese government was engaging in the internationally brokered peace talks with the SPLA in Kenya and had regular contact with high-ranking officials from the US government, who, according to the Sudanese government officials, signaled that they should "take care of the Darfur problem."[68] Second, the government of Sudan had committed countless atrocities in South Sudan, the Nuba Mountains, and the Blue Nile in their counterinsurgency operations, but this never provoked such an intense and coordinated protest.

7.6 CONCLUSION

Overall, the qualitative evidence from the Darfur case illustrates *how* ethnopolitical exclusion increases civil war risk. In addition to intensifying political grievances among Darfurians, the split in the Islamic Movement weakened the government's political network in Darfur while constraining its willingness to forge a negotiated solution as the conflict escalated. The analysis also helps to inform why the government of Sudan had to resort to what the ICC deemed genocide to counter the armed rebellion it faced in Darfur. While as de Waal rightfully notes the campaign represented "genocide by force of habit"[69]—a tried and true measure that is a regular part of the repressive repertoire of Sudan's weak central governments—it is also worth remembering how different the

---

[68] Cockett, *Sudan*.

[69] Alex de Waal, "Counter-Insurgency on the Cheap," *London Review of Books*, 26 (15) (2004): 25–27.

government's counterinsurgency campaign was against the First Darfur Rebellion. Even as the government in 1991 turned to local Arab militias to counter Bolad's rebel organization, it managed to minimize its use of indiscriminate violence. But with the breakdown of the Islamic Movement in Darfur and the loss of trusted brokers from key ethnic groups in the region, the government could no longer forge the cooperative ties with local communities necessary to isolate the rebels. As it faced a growing rebellion with societal support, it became desperate to halt the rebellion and resorted to mass killing and displacement to weaken the insurgents' support base.

PART III

TESTING THE ARGUMENT

8

Empirical Analysis of the Coup–Civil War Trap

8.1 INTRODUCTION

This chapter tests the generalizability of the key theoretical insight derived from the qualitative analysis of the breakdown of Sudan's Islamic Movement and the outbreak of the Darfur civil war: that informal powersharing confronts rulers of weak ethnically divided states with a coup–civil war trade-off. Striking alliances with rival networks of violence specialists is necessary to extend the reach of the regime and secure societal peace, but it opens the door for rivals to usurp power in a future coup d'état. Excluding these rivals eliminates their coup-making capabilities but at the cost of increased risk of civil war.

To test the generalizability of the coup–civil war trap, I turn to the hypotheses derived in Chapter 4 (see Section 4.3). Hypotheses 1–3 encapsulate the coup–civil war trap and the strategic incentives rulers have to choose ethnopolitical exclusion to hedge against coups from ethnic rivals.

H1: *Ethnic powersharing reduces civil war risk.*
H2: *Ethnic powersharing increases coup risk.*
H3: *Ethnopolitical exclusion substitutes civil war risk for coup risk for members from the targeted ethnic group.*

I then aim to test the strategic logic of ethnopolitical exclusion more directly. A key observable implication of the theory is that rulers exclude those groups with the strongest coup-making capabilities. Measuring coup-making capabilities, however, is difficult. An ideal measure would be the ethnic composition of the military, but such cross-national data are not available. The EPR dataset, which I discuss below, captures a group's control of the military, though only as a broader indicator of "state power"; it does not contain data on control of different state institutions.

As an alternative empirical strategy, I draw from the Sudan case and the fratricidal nature of the ethnopolitical exclusion that led to the outbreak of Darfur's civil war—Turabi's disciples turned on their sheikh and purged him and those who remained loyal to him. This points to one pernicious consequence of the commitment problem: your closest allies potentially represent your biggest enemy as it is these groups who are most capable of bringing about a sudden and irreversible shift in the distribution of power. It also suggests that one proxy for measuring a group's coup-making capabilities is whether members of the group are *co-conspirators* of the ruler in power. Since those groups that help a ruler come to power are most likely to control key strategic positions in the new government, we can assume that the ruler's co-conspirators have high coup-making capabilities. This leads to the fourth hypothesis I test in this chapter.

H4: Rulers are significantly more likely to target groups with strong coup-making capabilities for exclusion, including the very allies that helped them come to power—their co-conspirators—than other less threatening groups.

The rest of the chapter is as follows. The next two sections describe the suitability of the EPR dataset to capture ethnopolitical networks across time and space in Africa and measurement of key variables. The fourth section tests for the existence of the coup–civil war trade-off. The fifth and sixth sections then seek to substantiate that the coup–civil war trap is rooted in the commitment problem, drawing on evidence from "split" postcolonial regimes and interethnic co-conspirators. The seventh section probes deeper into co-conspirator civil wars, thinking through the link between camaraderie, trust, and the commitment problem, with qualitative evidence from Chad and Liberia. The final section summarizes the key findings from the large-N analysis.

8.2 EMPIRICAL STRATEGY: USING THE ETHNIC POWER RELATIONS DATASET TO CAPTURE ETHNOPOLITICAL NETWORKS IN SUB-SAHARAN AFRICA

To test the generalizability of the coup–civil war trap, I employ the Ethnic Power Relations dataset developed by Wimmer et al. (EPR 1.0).[1] The EPR dataset employs expert analysis of 100 scholars of ethnic politics to assess the distribution of central state power across different ethnic groups or categories for a subset of countries in the world in which ethnicity is politically salient from 1946 to 2005.[2] One of the advantages of the EPR dataset is it goes beyond cabinet posts and formal ministerial appointments as a measure of political power and also includes

---

[1] Wimmer et al., "Ethnic Politics and Armed Conflict." Since the production of the EPR dataset, Wimmer and Cederman have developed separate updated datasets—EPR 3.0 and EPR-ETH, respectively—that build off of EPR 1.0 but increase coverage to more recent years. In this chapter I use EPR 1.0.

[2] It only covers countries and time periods within countries "in which political objectives, alliances or disputes" are "framed in ethnic terms," thus "avoiding an ethnic lens for

representation in the presidency and senior posts in the administration, including the army, depending on their de-facto power in a given country. This is critical because, as a sizable literature has argued, real power in many African countries rests not in the formal state but in what Reno calls the "shadow state"—among those individuals who have personal ties and proximity to the ruler.[3] Thus, a country's cabinet could be largely representative—as many in fact are[4]—while the shadow state is in effect an ethnocracy. Moreover, not all cabinet positions are of equal weight. Lindemann shows that in Uganda under the rule of Yoweri Museveni, despite a generally representative cabinet, westerners, especially those from the region where Museveni comes, dominate the inner core of the cabinet, including ministers of defense, foreign affairs, internal affairs, finance, planning and economic development, commerce, agriculture, local government, and justice.[5]

For sub-Saharan Africa, EPR 1.0 covers thirty-five countries, 220 groups and 7,197 group-years.[6] It excludes data on Burkina Faso, Cape Verde, Comoros, Djibouti, Equatorial Guinea, Lesotho, Mauritius, Seychelles, São Tomé and Príncipe, Somalia, Swaziland, and Tanzania because these countries do not meet the size criteria (a population of at least 1 million and a surface area of at least 500,000 square kilometers as of 2005) or because ethnicity is considered to be of low salience. I also exclude Botswana because only one ethnic group, the San, is considered politically relevant.

Consistent with the way in which many Africanists conceive of African politics (as discussed extensively in Chapter 2), the EPR dataset assumes the state is federated across different politically relevant ethnic groups and categories. Moreover, in line with a constructivist understanding of ethnicity, the EPR does not assume that the boundaries of politically relevant groups or categories are fixed. Thus, they seek to pick up temporal changes "when the list of politically relevant categories changed from one year to the next (either because certain categories ceased to be or became

countries not characterized by ethnic politics, such as Tanzania and Korea." Wimmer et al., "Ethnic Politics and Armed Conflict," p. 325.
[3] Reno, *Warlord Politics and African States.*
[4] François et al., "How Is Power Shared in Africa?" Though again their sample tends to draw from more inclusive regimes in Africa. See discussion in Chapter 3.
[5] Stefan Lindemann, "Just Another Change of Guard? Broad-Based Politics and Civil War in Museveni's Uganda," *African Affairs,* 110 (440) (2011): 387–416.
[6] This excludes all group-years in which the group is labeled *Irrelevant* in previous year, periods of state collapse, and the first year of independence, since many variables are lagged.

relevant for the first time, or because higher or lower levels of ethnic differentiation became salient)."[7]

One potential limitation of group-level data analysis, however, is that it fails to reflect the true nature of political organization in Africa. As stressed throughout this book, politics in weak states is often organized around violence specialists and other power brokers and their network of followers, who may or may not share the same ethnic identity as their patron. These networks are fluid and can change in structure and identity over time. Often, however, they are constructed along ethnic lines. Accordingly, in using the EPR, I do not assume that politics resembles competition between different ethnic groups; instead, I use it as a measure of the ethnicity of the power brokers that control central state power and their relative density. As the power of these elites largely emanates from the strength of their political networks, we would expect in turn the distribution of power at the center to reflect the regime's societal penetration and support.[8] Conversely, if the EPR indicates that a given group is excluded from the central government, then we would expect there to be weak political networks connecting the regime with these societal groups.

These assumptions would introduce measurement error if patron–client networks in a given country are as strong across ethnic groups as within them or if regime elites generally have weak political ties with their coethnics. I am not denying such possibilities. There are a number of reasons (i.e. material, ideological or personal) why clients would align themselves with patrons from outside their ethnic groups. Similarly, we can imagine a number of potential factors that would lead conflict to break out between power brokers and their coethnics, not

[7] Wimmer et al., "Ethnic Politics and Armed Conflict," p. 326.
[8] It is important to note that the EPR dataset codes Sudan between independence and the signing of the Comprehensive Peace Agreement in 2005 as dominated by the Shaigiya, Ja'aliyin, and Danagla (Arab) with no inclusion of rival ethnic groups, including in the first decade of Al-Ingaz's reign (1989–1999) despite the diverse nature of the Islamic Movement as discussed extensively in Part II. This illustrates that while the EPR dataset is useful for picking up general patterns of power distribution, it may fail to capture the nuances of a given regime's ethnopolitical network. In the case of Sudan, the outside experts generally got it right (indeed, Al-Ingaz, like other regimes in Sudan, was disproportionately represented by riverain Arabs), but the experts probably also failed to appreciate how much support Sudan's Islamic Movement had outside the Nile River valley, especially from western Sudan. The implication is sometimes seeemingly excluded groups (as measured by EPR) can have strong ties to the central government, especially when the regime's societal penetration is buttressed by strong organizational structures, such as the Islamic Movement. If this occurs systematically in the dataset, it should bias against hypothesis 1.

least over the distribution of scarce resources given the asymmetry of wealth between those at the top and those at the bottom of the patron–client networks. While these limitations are important to keep in mind, the network benefits of coethnicity in Africa's weak states has such a strong theoretical and empirical basis that I feel it is reasonable to use ethnic representation as measured by the EPR to proxy for a regime's political network.

8.3 TESTING THE COUP–CIVIL WAR TRAP

8.3.1 Measuring Key Variables

Operating under these assumptions, the EPR dataset provides a measure of the density and breadth of the regime's political networks across different societal groups, which is necessary to test the book's core hypotheses. The first two hypotheses (H1 and H2) posit the existence of a coup–civil war trade-off in postcolonial Africa:

H1: Ethnic powersharing reduces civil war risk: The greater the representation of members of a given group in the center, the lower the likelihood of large-scale political violence between the regime and members of that group as inclusion reduces grievances and opportunity for rebellion.

H2: Ethnic powersharing increases coup risk: The greater the representation of members of a given group in the center, the lower the costs they face to displace the incumbent in a coup d'état.

To measure the density of representation, I employ the EPR's main variable, "the degree of access to power enjoyed by political leaders who claimed to represent various" politically relevant ethnic groups. (They exclude any group whose members do not have elites at the center claiming to represent them.)[9] Access to power is coded as a seven-point categorical variable. (See Appendix 2 for a data variable dictionary.) Categories include "monopoly," "dominant," "senior partner," "junior partner," "regional autonomy," "powerless," or "discriminated."[10] To examine the effect of a group's access to power and how it affects whether its members would execute a coup versus rebel, I collapse the seven-point variable into a dichotomous variable: *Inclusion*. Groupings with access to central state power (i.e. coded as "monopoly," "dominant," "senior

---

[9] See Wimmer et al., "Ethnic Politics and Armed Conflict," p. 326.
[10] For a definition of these various categories, see Wimmer, Cederman, and Min's online appendix. Available at www.epr.ucla.edu (accessed August 23, 2016).

partner," or "junior partner") are scored a 1, while all others ("regional autonomy," "powerless," or "discriminated") are scored a 0.

I also use this variable to capture the onset of a group's exclusion from the central government, *Exclude*, which indicates if a group was represented in the central government in the previous year (i.e. coded as "monopoly," "dominant," "senior partner," or "junior partner") and is excluded in the current year (i.e. coded as "powerless," or "discriminated").[11] One limitation of measuring exclusion based simply on a group's access to power in the past year with the current year is that it includes no information on what happened in the course of a year. For example, members of excluded groups can contribute to the overthrow of a dictator, such as members of the Nyankole and Banyarwanda did in the overthrow of Idi Amin in Uganda in 1979, and then find their group represented at the top of the new transitional government, in this case by Yoweri Museveni and as part of the National Executive Council, but only to lose out in the subsequent struggle for power, leading to their exclusion from power.[12] Thus, though the EPR considers these groups consistently excluded from power throughout, in fact, for a brief important period, often less than a year, they were at the heart of the new regime, and, if history had been different and they had won out in the power struggle, they would have been considered included throughout. To capture these more fluid intra-year changes, I also construct a second exclusion variable, *Exclude dynamic*, which indicates if, in the current year, a group is excluded from the central government but was included in the central government in the previous year *or* played a critical role in the seizure of power in the previous year (as measured by the variable *Co-conspirator*).

---

[11] As I am interested in purges or forcible exclusion from the central government, I do not consider changes to or from "regional autonomy" as an incidence of *Exclude*.

[12] The same is true for northerners in Côte d'Ivoire in 2000. Langer notes that the first Guéï cabinet was the most inclusive in a generation, including for northerners, who filled top seats in the new regime, such as General Lassana Palenfo, who was second-in-command and security minister. Langer writes, "It is interesting to note that the inter-ethnic political inequalities of the January 2000 government as measured by the Political Inequality Measure (PIM) was the lowest of any government in the period from 1980 to 2003. The same observation holds regarding ethnic representation within the inner circle of political power." This would begin to change, however, with Guéï's first cabinet reshuffle in May 2000, his support for the concept of l'Ivoirité, and his "purge [of] the military forces," that excluded "a significant number of officers and soldiers with a northern background." Langer, "Horizontal Inequalities." Thus, though EPR codes northerners as excluded throughout 2000, in fact, after several of their members in the military helped put Guéï in power, they were included in the heart of the new government for several months.

Exclude dynamic picks up five additional cases of excluded groups missed by *Exclude*.[13]

To determine the relationship between the density of the regime's political networks across different societal groups and the likelihood of a coup or large-scale rebellion executed by members of that group requires data on the ethnicity of those who led coup attempts (both failed and successful) and the ethnicity of those who participate in civil wars. I construct three variables to measure this: *Group successful coup* (*GroupScoup*), *Group failed coup* (*GroupFcoup*), and *Group rebel* (*GroupRebel*). *GroupScoup* and *GroupFcoup* indicate whether members of a given ethnic group executed a successful or failed coup attempt, respectively, against the incumbent in that year. To code these variables, I use data from Patrick McGowan's database on coup attempts in Africa. McGowan's definition of coups—"events in which existing regimes are suddenly and illegally displaced by the action of a relatively small group, *in which members of the military, police or security forces of the state play a key role,* either on their own or in conjunction with civilian elites such as civil servants, politicians and monarchs"—aligns closely with the organizational definition I use in this book (see Textbox 2.1).[14] Using the case materials shared by McGowan and additional secondary sources,[15] I then score *GroupScoup* and *GroupFcoup* based on the ethnicity of the leaders or executors of the coup attempts (or at least those identified as the coup-plotters by the press and secondary sources).[16] If an ethnic group's members were leaders of the successful or failed coup attempt in a given year, the group is scored a 1 on *GroupScoup* or *GroupFcoup*, respectively.[17] Otherwise it receives a zero.

Several important caveats are in order here. In undertaking this exercise, I am not suggesting that all coup-plotters are motivated by ethnic

---

[13] Igbo of Nigeria in 1966; Baganda and Southwesterners (Ankole, Banyoro, Toro, Banyarwanda) of Uganda in 1980; Gio of Liberia in 1980; and northerner (Mande and Voltaic/Gur) in Côte d'Ivoire in 2000.

[14] Emphasis added. McGowan's coup d'état dataset tracks successful coups, failed coup attempts, and coup plots for all sub-Saharan African countries between 1956 and 2004. See McGowan, "African Military Coups d'État," p. 343. Importantly, his definition does not take into consideration the level and production of violence associated with the coup, which would possibly conflate coups d'état with civil wars.

[15] Particularly useful were the *Historical Dictionaries of Africa* series by Scarecrow Press and the various years of *Africa Contemporary Record* by Holmes & Meier Publishers.

[16] The leaders of the coup are not necessarily the same as the person who becomes president after the coup.

[17] See Table A3.2, which provides information on the ethnicity of coup leaders. For case material substantiating coding decisions, see the author's website, www.philiproessler.net.

grievances; that their ethnicity is their dominant political identity; that they necessarily represent the interests of their group or even have over-whelming support from their coethnics. As is evident from a reading of the cases, coup attempts can take a variety of forms, ranging from a brazen individual acting on his own out of personal interest, to a coalition of mili-tary elites who come from a cross-section of societal groups and are driven by corporate concerns (e.g., Gambia in July 1994), to a group primarily from one ethnic group whose members are acting to preserve or restore their preeminent political position (e.g., Burundi in 1965 or Cameroon in 1984). No matter the motivation for the coup attempt, however, we can-not expect the ethnicity of the conspirators or plotters to be completely irrelevant, especially given that the analysis covers a subset of countries in which ethnicity is politically salient. To successfully execute a coup d'état requires having access to sensitive points inside a regime or at least having allies in these positions and being able to convince significant sections of the army and regime to join your movement (or at least to not resist).[18] Thus, we would expect the structure of the regime's political networks to have some mediating effect on whether an individual has the inside access or connections to lead such an attempt. Moreover, because the dissidents operate within the state itself, right under the nose of the ruler, coup-plotting requires a level of secrecy that is not necessary for other types of mobilization. High levels of trust between plotters are absolutely critical to the success of the operation as it only takes one defector to potentially subvert the scheme. Thus, we would anticipate plotters to have strong social bonds between themselves. And, in an environment in which ethnic ties are a particularly strong source of social support and reciprocity,[19] it should not be surprising to see coethnicity serve as the organizational basis for coup-plotting. Finally, a coup leader's ethnic identity may affect how a plot or attempt is perceived by other key actors, especially those who feel they will be displaced from power if the coup is successful, even if the conspirators do not have an "ethnic agenda." An incumbent may perceive or declare an "ethnic plot" even when one does not exist because of poor information or for instrumental reasons (e.g., to mobilize support from his own ethnic group).

I follow the same procedure to code *GroupRebel*. This variable captures whether members of a given ethnic group are leading and

[18] Naunihal Singh, *Seizing Power: The Strategic Logic of Military Coups* (Baltimore, Md.: Johns Hopkins University Press, 2014).

[19] Paul Collier, *Wars, Guns, and Votes: Democracy in Dangerous Places* (New York: Harper, 2009). Habyarimana et al., "Coethnicity and Trust."

significant participants in a large-scale insurgency (i.e. one that leads to a civil war) against the central government. I code the first year members of the ethnic group join the insurgency and engage in large-scale violence with the government.[20] Multiple groups may participate in a single insurgency, but they all do not necessarily become involved in the same year. For example, in the civil war in Sudan between the SPLA and the central government in Khartoum that began in 1983, members of the Dinka, Nuer, and Shilluk are coded as participating in the rebellion that led to large-scale political violence with the government's armed forces in 1983, but members of the Nuba do not become significantly involved until 1987 when the SPLA makes inroads into that community and large-scale violence breaks out in the Nuba Mountains over the next three years. For a complete list of rebellion onsets and the ethnicity of the rebels see Appendix 3.

8.4 EMPIRICAL ANALYSIS: ACCESS TO POWER AND THE COUP–CIVIL WAR TRADE-OFF

8.4.1 Bivariate Analysis of the Coup–Civil War Trade-Off

With data on the density of representation of a given ethnic group in the central government, the ethnicity of coup leaders, and the ethnicity of insurgents, we can systematically evaluate whether there is evidence of a coup–civil war trade-off in postcolonial Africa. Figure 8.1 compares the

---

[20] I consider an ethnic group to engage in large-scale violence that reaches the level of civil war if in the first three years of its participation in an insurgency the rebellion leads to 1,000 battlefield deaths, consistent with Sambanis, "What Is Civil War?," pp. 829–830. For the start date, I employ Sambanis' rule that "The start year of the war is the first year that the conflict causes at least 500 to 1,000 deaths. If the conflict has not caused 500 deaths or more in the first year, the war is coded as having started in that year only if cumulative deaths in the next three years reach 1,000." To determine whether the beginning of the insurgency led to 1,000 battlefield deaths I primarily refer to the Uppsala Battle Deaths Best Estimate, which often provides information on the insurgent groups that are active in a given conflict for each year. This allows me to make a determination about when groups enter or leave a conflict. Where the Uppsala Battle Deaths Dataset is vague about which insurgent groups are active, I also consult the UCDP/PRIO Armed Conflict Dataset (ACD) and rely on country-specific materials and interviews with country experts to evaluate which insurgencies are active and the ethnic support for the movements. Finally, if the Uppsala Battle Deaths Dataset and ACD do not identify a conflict but both the Fearon and Laitin and Sambanis datasets do, I also include the case. On the Uppsala Battle Deaths dataset, see Lacina and Gleditsch, "Monitoring Trends in Global Combat." On ACD, see Nils Petter Gleditsch, Peter Wallensteen, Mikael Eriksson, Margareta Sollenberg, and Håvard Strand, "Armed Conflict, 1946–2001: A New Dataset," *Journal of Peace Research*, 39 (5) (2002): 615–637.

mean level of successful coups and mean level of rebellions by members of an ethnic group in a given year as a function of their group's overall access to power or exclusion from power in the *previous* year. It illustrates quite starkly the trade-off rulers face: on average, ethnic exclusion reduces a group's likelihood of seizing power in a coup d'état, but at the cost of significantly increasing the likelihood of a societal rebellion that becomes a full-scale civil war.

As is evident in Figure 8.1, exclusion does not appear to have *as* substantial an effect on reducing coups as inclusion does on reducing rebellion. Why is this? I suspect this is partially a function of the fact that EPR is a measure of a group's access to political power not necessarily its representation in the military. Thus, a significant subset of the incidences of excluded groups executing coups are cases in which groups are politically excluded from the central government but still have a substantial presence in the military, such as the Kabré in Togo in the early 1960s, northerners in Benin in 1960s, Temne and Limba in Sierra Leone in the late 1960s, and the Balanta in Guinea-Bissau in the late 1970s. Most of these cases are a function of colonial policies that sought to recruit soldiers and policemen from so-called "backward groups" (i.e. those smaller, less centralized or more peripheral ethnic groups which were perceived by colonial administrators to be more reliable than other groups as soldiers because they posed less of a threat to the colonial state and lacked political and economic ambition).[21] The institutional legacy of such a colonial policy is that it ensured the military was dominated by smaller, less politically centralized ethnic groups while the larger and politically stronger ethnic groups dominated the bureaucracy (often after winning the inaugural multiparty elections after independence). We would expect that ethnic bargaining in these "split domination" regimes would be more likely to be plagued by the commitment problem, leading to regime instability and ethnic exclusion.[22] I discuss this theoretical expectation below.

Figure 8.2 provides another way to examine the effect of ethnic exclusion on a group's ability to carry out a successful coup d'état. It illustrates not only that groups excluded from the central government attempt fewer

---

[21] Horowitz, *Ethnic Groups in Conflict*. Ray tests Horowitz's conjecture and finds, using data on police forces in British colonies, that "Ethnic groups who had achieved high levels of military and political sophistication in the precolonial period were systematically excluded from the colonial security apparatus." Subhasish Ray, "The Nonmartial Origins of the 'Martial Races': Ethnicity and Military Service in Ex-British Colonies," *Armed Forces & Society*, 39 (3) (2013): 13.

[22] Horowitz, *Ethnic Groups in Conflict*.

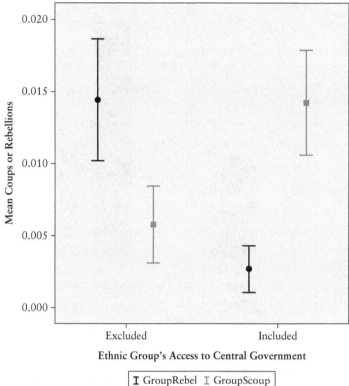

Excluded   Included

Ethnic Group's Access to Central Government

FIGURE 8.1 The Coup–Rebellion Trade-Off in Postcolonial Africa

total coups (60 percent fewer compared to groups inside the government) but also that their success rate is lower (38 percent compared to 55 percent for groups inside). Not having access to central government reduces the likelihood of a coup attempt and hinders its efficacy.

8.4.2 Regression Analysis of the Coup–Civil War Trade-Off

Moving beyond the simple, but revealing, bivariate tests, I turn to a set of logistic regressions in order to control for other potential explanatory variables that capture both group and country characteristics. I first run two sets of estimations (Models 1–7) that regress successful coups (*GroupScoup*) and group rebellions (*GroupRebel*) on an EPR group's access to central government while also including various control variables. In Models 1–7, I include group-level variables controlling for the size of the ethnic group as a proportion of population (*Group size*) and the number of ethnic groups

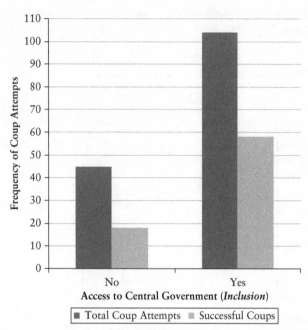

FIGURE 8.2 Access to Power and Likelihood of Executing a Successful Coup

sharing power in the central government (*Center segmentation*).[23] I then add country-level variables controlling for income level (*Log income*) and population size (*Log population*). Since data on *Log income* is missing for some group-years, which causes about 6 percent of the observations to be dropped, I run separate models (Models 2, 3, 4, 6, and 7) with the inclusion of these variables. In each of the coup models I control for time since last coup to account for coup contagion within a country.[24] In Models 3 and 7, I run the full estimation but control for country fixed effects. Finally, in Model 4 I add a variable, *Ruler ethnic group*, to control for whether the ruler of the country is of the given group. This variable allows us to check if coups from insiders are merely a function of intraethnic contests for power. In each of the models, I also control for temporal dependence (variables not shown to save space) using the cubic polynomial of the hazard for a given outcome variable.

[23] The data for these two variables come from Wimmer et al., "Ethnic Politics and Armed Conflict." and Cederman et al., "Why Do Ethnic Groups Rebel?" They find that group size and center segmentation increase the likelihood of conflict.
[24] John B. Londregan and Keith T. Poole, "Poverty, the Coup Trap, and the Seizure of Executive Power," *World Politics*, 42 (2) (1990): 151–183.

Table 8.1 reports the results of the regression analyses. In all models, *Inclusion*, is highly significant. *Inclusion* is positively associated with successful coups but negatively associated with group rebellion. The positive effect on coups is not simply due to coups from within the ruler's ethnic group (see Model 4). Two-thirds of groups involved in successful coups are different from the ruler's ethnic group. When intraethnic coups are executed, they occur at low levels of center segmentation, usually when the ruler's ethnic group is the only one represented in the central government. Other control variables also generate interesting results. Taking into account a group's access to power, members of a group or coalition are significantly more likely to attempt and successfully execute a coup the larger its size, the fewer the groups incorporated in the central government, and the poorer the country. Whereas the link between low income and coups has been reported before in the literature, the robust and significant effects of segmentation and group size on coups but not rebellion are novel findings. One reason for the strong association between group size and coups might be that large groups are more likely to have at least some representation in the military and therefore greater opportunities to employ the technology of the coup d'état. Moreover, representing a large group may increase the coup-plotters' bargaining power as other factions consider whether to resist or bandwagon as the coup attempt plays out. This also suggests that rulers are less effective at coup-proofing against large groups. I develop and test this idea in Chapter 10.

8.4.3 Can a Lot of Powersharing Neutralize Coup Risk?

What accounts for the negative effect of center segmentation in the coup models (Models 1–4)? Why does the inclusion of more groups into the central government reduce the likelihood that any given group will successfully execute a coup? This pattern is consistent with this paper's central argument that regime instability is rooted in uncertainty about rivals' future commitment to powersharing. The greater the number of groups with access to the central government, the more difficult it is for any one group to unilaterally usurp power (because, to execute a coup, the conspirators would be required to simultaneously take on multiple power-holders or coordinate with them[25]), which should reduce uncertainty. Moreover, if

---

[25] See Leonardo R. Arriola, "Patronage and Political Stability in Africa," *Comparative Political Studies*, 42 (10) (2009): 1339–1362, on the coordination problem coup-plotters face. He suggests that this coordination problem accounts for the reason coups are less likely in African countries with large cabinets.

TABLE 8.1 *Ethnopolitical Inclusion, Coups and Civil War in Africa: Independence to 2005*

	Coup (1)	Coup (2)	Coup (3)	Coup (4)	Rebellion (5)	Rebellion (6)	Rebellion (7)
Inclusion[1]	1.01**	0.88**	1.09***	0.93**	-1.38***	-1.29***	-1.27***
	(0.29)	(0.42)	(0.36)	(0.43)	(0.33)	(0.39)	(0.42)
Ruler ethnic group				0.24			
				(0.35)			
Center[1] segmentation	-0.36**	-0.35**	-1.05***	-1.00***	-0.20*	-0.22*	-0.14
	(0.16)	(0.17)	(0.22)	(0.23)	(0.11)	(0.12)	(0.18)
Log group size[1]	1.30***	1.16***	1.43***	1.46***	-0.09	-0.36	-0.28
	(0.26)	(0.30)	(0.46)	(0.46)	(0.35)	(0.38)	(0.32)
Log GDP per capita		-0.91***	-1.61***	-1.63***		-0.77**	0.88*
		(0.27)	(0.57)	(0.59)		(0.33)	(0.47)
Log country[1] population		0.13	-0.24	-0.27		-0.23	0.25
		(0.23)	(0.38)	(0.39)		(0.17)	(0.42)
Years since last coup	0.01	0.04	0.14***	0.14***			-0.19
	(0.2)	(0.03)	(0.03)	(0.03)			(0.19)
constant	-2.30***	4.79			-3.80***	3.89	
	(0.60)	(4.49)			(0.68)	(3.63)	
N	4062	6363	3806	3806	6976	6363	2888
States	35	34	22	22	34	34	15
Pseudo r²	0.10	0.13			0.06	0.08	
Country fixed effects	N	N	Y	Y	N	N	Y

All models also include cubic polynomial approximation of dependent variable to control for temporal dependence. Standard errors clustered by country (in parentheses).

[1] lagged one year *: p < 0.10; **: p < 0.05; ***: p < 0.01

a ruler is able to demonstrate his commitment to a more inclusive central government, it should help to allay rivals' fears that they will be purged in the future and in turn reduce their need to use force to defend their share of power. This suggests that one potential solution to the commitment problem at the heart of the coup–civil war trap in postcolonial Africa is more powersharing not less. Of course we have to be careful not to make too strong a causal claim about the effect of center segmentation on coup risk given the potential for endogeneity. A decline in coup risk could also open the door to powersharing. This dynamic merits further research.

8.5 TESTING THE STRATEGIC LOGIC OF ETHNOPOLITICAL EXCLUSION, PART I: REGIME BREAKDOWN IN AFRICA'S ETHNICALLY DIVIDED REGIMES

The first part of this chapter has offered systematic empirical evidence to support the claim that Africa's weak, ethnically divided states confront rulers with a coup–civil war trap. Ethnic exclusion is shown to neutralize the threat of the coup d'état from ethnic rivals but at the cost of increased civil war risk. While these empirical patterns are consistent with the strategic model of ethnopolitical exclusion, additional evidence is necessary to substantiate that it is the commitment problem causing rulers to make such a strategic choice. As discussed in Chapter 3, a number of motivations could lead a ruler to exclude their ethnic rivals, leading to an increased risk of civil war. In this section, I put forth additional evidence to support the commitment problem mechanism.

One puzzle that a strategic theory of exclusion raises is that if powersharing is so dangerous—especially real powersharing in which the ruler cedes control of key strategic parts of the regime—why do rulers adopt such a policy in the first place? Of course, many do not, as they employ preventive exclusion to avoid a future shift in the distribution of state power in favor of their rivals (as seen historically in Apartheid South Africa, Rwanda, Burundi, and Sudan).

Other times, however, powersharing is borne out of necessity. This was often the situation African states faced at independence as they inherited from colonialism what Donald Horowitz calls "split domination" regimes, in which the military and the presidency were dominated by different ethnic groups. Other cases of real powersharing arise from the interethnic alliances which are necessary to capture power in the first place. Turabi's mobilization of a diverse network of Islamists to facilitate their takeover of the Sudanese state is illustrative. An even more powerful example—the focus of Chapter 9—can be seen in former Zaire, in which an interethnic alliance between Congolese Tutsis and Katangans ended Mobutu Sese Seko's reign in power. In each of these cases, the strategic interethnic alliances at the heart of the anti-regime coalition would become the backbone of the new government.

In both split domination and co-conspirator regimes, the commitment problem and instability arising from informal powersharing should be observable. I analyze this both qualitatively and quantitatively in the next two sections. First, I draw from Horowitz's seminal work to explore the outcomes of these "split domination" regimes that emerge from colonialism. Second, I draw on an original data collection of co-conspirators to systematically test the coup-proofing theory of civil war. Mini case studies of Liberia and Chad help to illuminate the process by which the commitment problem undermines powersharing between co-conspirators.

8.5.1 Colonialism, Split Domination, and the Commitment Problem

One of the central points Donald Horowitz makes in his magnum opus, *Ethnic Groups in Conflict*, is that colonialism bequeathed African states with a legacy of what he calls "split domination—an arrangement in which the key institutions of the society are dominated by different ethnic groups."[26] He argues that split domination was "made likely in many states by recruitment practices shaped by such pervasive fears of revolt that the colonial authorities went far afield in their search for loyal officers and men."[27] This led, in some cases, for African militaries to be dominated by so-called "backward groups," "which had been bypassed by the colonial educational and economic system," and the state bureaucracy to be staffed by so-called more "advanced groups," who tended to have higher levels of state centralization and to be located closer to the center and were the beneficiaries of modernization brought about by colonialism.[28] A classic example Horowitz gives of this "split domination" is Uganda, in which the military and police were dominated by those from Northern Uganda and the civil service and educational institutions tended to be the purview of the Buganda whose kingdom is near the capital, Kampala.

Horowitz suggests that "split domination" can be managed by ethnic accommodation, in which each recognizes the other's sphere of influence.

---

[26] Horowitz, *Ethnic Groups in Conflict*, p. 457.
[27] Horowitz, *Ethnic Groups in Conflict*.
[28] Horowitz, *Ethnic Groups in Conflict*, p. 161.

But the problem with such a bargain is the commitment problem: "when one ethnic group controls the armed forces and another dominates the civilian regime . . . [e]ach of these institutions is a potential master of the other."[29] Given the leverage the ethnic networks in the military have over those networks in the government, he predicts this commitment problem will end in coups and supports this claim in a series of qualitative vignettes of Sierra Leone, Nigeria, Togo, Benin Congo (Brazzaville), and Uganda (as well as Syria). Drawing from Horowitz and others, Table 8.2 provides a summary of the instability that arises from "split domination," which map on very closely to the theoretical framework developed in Chapter 4.

Consistent with the book's central argument, we should see split domination leading to not only political instability and ethnic exclusion but also civil war. The support for this latter claim is more mixed. In some cases, such as Uganda, Nigeria, and Burundi, we see coup-proofing civil wars exactly as predicted. In other cases, such as Benin, Congo-Brazzaville, Sierra Leone, and Togo, split domination leads to bargaining failure and instability, as expected, but not large-scale political violence. Why is this? In Benin, it seems that, consistent with the coup–civil war trap, coups actually substitute for civil war, as they produce an alternation of power between ethnic groups that prevents any one group from permanent exclusion, thus helping to avert civil war. In Togo and Congo-Brazzaville, the commitment problem ushers in a coup and a significant shift in the distribution of power from southerners to northerners, but, as Horowitz notes, the new politically ascendant northerners were careful to accommodate southerners to prevent these powerful groups located near the center of power from rising up:

In both countries, northern regimes made a key decision that kept southern power alive . . . the decision not to reconstruct the civil service . . . Such [reconstruction is] costly in terms of lost expertise and run[s] the risk of creating a popular movement of ethnic opposition. The weaker military regimes in Togo and Congo (Brazzaville) did not choose to purge their civil services, which were veritable bastions of, respectively Ewe and Lari supremacy. The effect of this was to retain important centers of southern opposition within government.[30]

These negative cases are useful in further refining the coup-proofing theory of civil war and helping to develop a more precise understanding of the conditions that account for why the coup–civil war trap tips one

---

[29] Horowitz, *Ethnic Groups in Conflict*, p. 457.
[30] Horowitz, *Ethnic Groups in Conflict*, pp. 503–504.

way or the other—in favor of ethnic exclusion and civil war or power-sharing and coups. I take this up in Chapter 10.

8.5.2 Coup-Proofing Civil Wars in Uganda, Nigeria, and Burundi

On the other hand, Uganda, Nigeria, and Burundi in the first decade of independence are exemplars of countries that fall into the coup–civil war trap with their rulers choosing strategies that substitute civil war risk for coup risk. In the Uganda case, a series of failed elite bargains eventually led Idi Amin to use force to come to power against his former ally, Milton Obote. After coming to power, as discussed in Chapter 4, Amin extensively and brutally purged perceived Obote loyalists from the military and his regime. This strategy effectively consolidated Amin's hold on power and drove Obote and his supporters into exile in Tanzania. Only with the help of Tanzania was Obote able to reclaim power. In short, Amin's coup-proofing strategy worked in the short term to buy him time against what he perceived was the clear and present danger posed by his former ally but over the long term led to his downfall.

In Nigeria and Burundi, however, the commitment problem also triggered violent elite conflict and large-scale political violence, but the prevailing side was able to avoid defeat in civil war. In the Nigeria case, split domination led to two coups in 1966. (See Table 8.2.) The July 1966 countercoup would have far-reaching effects on the coup-making capabilities of the Igbo. As Siollun writes, the countercoup, led by northern officers, "permanently reversed the ethnic composition of the army. Virtually all of the Igbo soldiers were killed, permanently incapacitated or forced out of their positions. After eliminating Igbos from the army, northern soldiers consolidated their supremacy at all levels."[31] The cost of this strategy, however, was that it led to the Biafran War through the three mechanisms elucidated from the Darfur case: (1) intensified grievances and political consciousness of the Igbo, especially as they were targeted in devastating pogroms that erupted before and after the countercoup; (2) an increase in the pool of violence specialists opposing the central government and willing to take up arms against the regime, while destroying the informal networks and channels through which the government could effectively contain the armed rebellion; and (3) deepened mistrust

---

[31] Max Siollun, *Oil, Politics and Violence: Nigeria's Military Coup Culture* (1966–1976) (New York: Algora, 2009), pp. 147–148.

TABLE 8.2 *Post-Independence Split Domination Regimes and the Coup–Civil War Trap*[a]

Country	Nature of split domination	Outcome
Benin	Fon (southerners) dominate officer corps; northern inaugural president; Yoruba (in southeast) also powerful	**Coup trap with no exclusion:** Northern inaugural president increases Northern representation in military, leading to coup led by southerners in 1963, which sets in motion rotation of power via coups but no ethnoregional group is able to consolidate power and exclude others.
Burundi	Ethnically balanced cabinet and army divided between Hutu and Tutsi, though Tutsi tended to dominate officer corps	**Failed coup, ethnic exclusion, and civil war:** Hutu in military and gendarmerie attempt coup in October 1965 after Tutsi king refuses to reappoint a Hutu prime minister in wake of assassination of inaugural prime minister. Failed coup ushers in systematic exclusion of Hutu from military and government and societal-based rebellion in 1972.
Congo (Brazzaville)	Southerners (Lari and Bakongo) are politically ascendant after leading campaign for independence; but French had recruited northerners into military to balance against southerners	**Military coup, ethnic exclusion but no civil war:** Series of coups beginning in 1968, reverse power structure with northerners, especially Mbochi, locking in power and politically excluding Lari and Bakongo, but whom are allowed to remain within civil service.
Nigeria	Igbo dominate officer corps in military, but Hausa-Fulani overwhelming majority of rank-and-file; government divided between regional forces	**Coup cycle, ethnic exclusion, and civil war:** Coup, countercoup, and ethnic pogroms rock Nigeria in 1966, ending in Biafran War between Igbo-based separatist rebellion and Hausa-Fulani-dominated central government.

(continued)

TABLE 8.2 *Continued*

Country	Nature of split domination	Outcome
Sierra Leone	Mende dominate political realm and stack military officer corps; northerners (Limba and Temne) also prominent in military (mainly at junior level)	**Coup cycle, ethnic exclusion but no civil war:** Mende incumbent defeated in elections in 1967 by northern candidate. Electoral result is overturned by Mende officers in coup, leading to a northern countercoup and purge of Mende officers. Infighting then plagues northerners.
Togo	Southerners dominate politically and in civil service; northerners dominate military	**Military coup, ethnic exclusion but no civil war:** Military coup reverses power structure and marginalizes southerners politically, though they retain dominance in civil service.
Uganda	Baganda politically and economically powerful, control presidency; northerners dominant in military and police as well as in position of prime minister	**Coup cycle, ethnic exclusion, and civil war:** Baganda displaced from power as northerners consolidate control of state. Infighting then plagues northerners as power struggle plays out between Milton Obote and Idi Amin, eventually ending in societal rebellion backed by Tanzania against Amin.

[a] Most data is from Horowitz, *Ethnic Groups in Conflict*. For Burundi, Lemarchand was extremely helpful, whereas Decalo was helpful for Togo and Benin. Lemarchand, *Burundi*. Samuel Decalo, *Historical Dictionary of Benin*, 3rd edn (Lanham, Md.: Scarecrow Press, 1995). Decalo, *Historical Dictionary of Togo*.

such that any negotiated solution was off the table and the war only ended when the Biafrans, facing genocide, surrendered.

These mechanisms are personified in the leader of the Biafran Army, Chukwuemeka Odumegwu Ojukwu, born into a prominent and powerful Igbo family.[32] At the time of the countercoup, Ojukwu was the military governor of Eastern Region, having been appointed to this position after the January 1966 coup. After the 1966 countercoup, however, he

[32] For a useful background of Ojukwu, see Chinua Achebe, *There Was a Country: A Personal History of Biafra* (New York: Penguin, 2012).

would be one of the leading violence specialists in opposition to the central government, mobilizing opposition to the new regime on the grounds that it could not protect the safety of the Igbo.[33] With the loss of support of Ojukwu,[34] the central government lost its control of the Eastern Region, leading to the Biafran War. Only through the use of mass indiscriminate violence and starvation, claiming the lives of some 2 million people, could the central government subdue the Biafran secessionists.[35]

In Burundi in 1965 the strategic uncertainty arising from split domination would cause the breakdown of the Hutu–Tutsi ethnic balance that existed within the regime in the first years after independence and turned Burundi into what Horowitz called an "ethnocracy."[36] It is worth quoting Lemarchand's authoritative political history of Burundi at length again on the consequences of the actions taken by the Tutsi military elite after the failed coup:

Since most of the enlisted men (approximately one thousand out of a total of twelve hundred in 1965) were of Hutu origins, a massive ethnic purge was required. According to reliable informants, in the weeks following the 1965 attempted coup, hundreds of Hutu troops were massacred by their commanding officers. Meanwhile, as Jeremy Greenland noted, "a most bizarre 'girth by height' requirement was introduced as a patent pretext for excluding unwanted Hutu recruits from the army."[37] . . . For some Hutu elites, the handwriting was on the wall. It was now unmistakably clear to them that armed rebellion was the only meaningful alternative to Tutsi hegemony. In fact, it was around this time [after suppression of another "Hutu-coup" in 1969] that a handful of Hutu students and one deputy decided to leave the capital and take to the bush, hoping to gather enough support to instigate a major insurgency.[38]

In 1972, that insurgency, based out of Tanzania, would break out, leading to mass indiscriminate violence against Hutu, with estimates ranging at the number of lives lost from 100,000 to 200,000.[39]

---

[33] Toyin Falola and Matthew M. Heaton, *A History of Nigeria* (Cambridge: Cambridge University Press, 2008), p. 174.

[34] Ojukwu rejected the idea that he represented the Igbo but was a leader for all Easterners. See Robin Luckham, *The Nigerian Military: A Sociological Analysis of Authority and Revolt, 1960–67* (Cambridge: Cambridge University Press, 1971), p. 296.

[35] Achebe, *There Was a Country*.

[36] Horowitz, *Ethnic Groups in Conflict*.

[37] Jeremy Greenland, "Ethnic Discrimination in Rwanda and Burundi," in Willem Adriaan Veenhoven, ed., *Case Studies on Human Rights and Fundamental Freedoms: A World Survey* (The Hague: Martinus Nijhoff, 1976), pp. 98–133.

[38] Lemarchand, *Burundi*, pp. 86–87.

[39] Lemarchand, *Burundi*, p. 100.

8.6 TESTING THE STRATEGIC LOGIC OF
ETHNOPOLITICAL EXCLUSION, PART II: AFRICA'S
CO-CONSPIRATOR CIVIL WARS

Qualitative evidence from the split domination regimes that arose in postcolonial Africa offers support for the coup–civil war trap. In Nigeria, Burundi, and Uganda, military governments employed violent ethnic exclusion to try to eliminate the threat posed by rival ethnic networks in the military but at the cost of provoking coup-proofing civil wars. In other countries, however, large-scale political violence was prevented due to the coup trap ensuring a more inclusive ethnic equilibrium in Benin and Ghana. (See extensive discussion in Chapter 10.)

Irregular regime changes that occurred across sub-Saharan Africa over the next three decades, in the form of both coups and armed rebellions, however, significantly upended the power structures left by colonialism, leading to new configurations of power. For example, the collapse of the central government in Chad in the late 1970s saw the Sara, who had inherited the state at independence, chased from power by networks of violence specialists from northern Chad. In Liberia in 1980, the Americo-Liberian oligarchy was finally overturned in a coup d'état. In Sierra Leone, the Mende grip on power was forcibly transferred to the Limba. In Uganda, Idi Amin was finally ousted from power in 1979, leading to informal powersharing among violence specialists from the country's major ethnic groups. In Sudan, nontraditional political forces—first the Communists and then the Islamists—came to power in 1969 and then 1989 in military coups. In Rwanda, the Hutu ethnocracy was militarily challenged by the Tutsi-dominated RPF in the early 1990s. In former Zaire, in 1997, Mobutu and his Equateur networks were finally thrown out of power after thirty-two years in control. Though not a legacy of colonialism, of course, even the Ethiopian Empire, Abyssinia, was abolished in 1975 by the Derg. And the white-settler regime of Ian Smith conceded power to Robert Mugabe and his Zimbabwe African National Union in 1980.

These violent seizures of power would dismantle the old power structures, giving rise to new regimes of split domination, in which power was often shared between co-conspirators. Paradoxically, but very much consistent with the theoretical argument at the center of this book, powersharing between co-conspirators would be just as explosive as those divided regimes after independence. In fact, similar to the breakdown of the Al-Ingaz regime in Sudan, each of these irregular regimes described in the previous paragraph would experience violent factionalization, often leading to exclusion along ethnic lines.

In this section I offer systematic evidence to substantiate the claim that informal powersharing between co-conspirators is more likely to break down, leading to ethnic exclusion and large-scale political violence than powersharing with other less threatening groups.

8.6.1 Measuring Co-conspirators

To test the instability of powersharing between co-conspirators, I collect information on the armed actors who led, organized, or executed the coups d'état and rebellions that occurred across sub-Saharan Africa in the first five decades after independence. Co-conspirators can come from inside or outside the eventual ruler's ethnic group, depending on who contributed to the violent seizure of power. For example, in the May 1997 overthrow of Mobutu by the Alliance des Forces Démocratiques pour la Libération du Congo-Zaire (AFDL), we can identify three domestic groups of co-conspirators: (1) the Luba-Shaba, led by Laurent-Désiré Kabila; (2) the Congolese Tutsi, led by Deogratias Bugera; and (3) Other Kivu Groups, who were mobilized by Masasu Nindaga (see Chapter 9).[40] These groups remain coded as "co-conspirator" as long as the ruler they put in power remains head of state (which in this Congo case would be 2001 when Kabila was assassinated). I code this information for all African countries represented in the EPR dataset between independence and 2005. (See Appendix 3 for a list of all co-conspirators.)

Theoretically, we would expect these competing networks of violence specialists to face a particularly acute commitment problem because, after seizing power, they do not disarm but merely divide up control of the state and the regime's coercive apparatus. For example, after the overthrow of Idi Amin in 1979, the rebel coalition, the Uganda National Liberation Army (UNLA), in effect became the new national army, with the provisional government, the National Executive Council, dominated by leaders of the UNLA: Tito Okello, Chief of Defense Forces; Oyite Ojok as his deputy; and Yoweri Museveni, Minister of State for Defense. In Liberia, Thomas Quiwonkpa would become commander of the army after orchestrating Samuel Doe's rise to power. In Côte d'Ivoire, northerners would occupy key positions in the Comité National de Salut Public after overthrowing Henri Konan Bédié and placing Robert Guéï in power.

---

[40] The ethnic categories correspond to those in the EPR dataset.

8.6.2 Co-conspirators and Ethnic Exclusion: Purging the Allies Who Put You in Power

With data on co-conspirators, I test whether, consistent with H4 and the breakdown of the Islamic Movement in Sudan, we see evidence that rulers are significantly more likely to exclude their co-conspirators than other ethnic networks in their regime. Table 8.3 reports regression estimates of the determinants of ethnic exclusion for those groups included in the central government in the previous year or, for models using "Exclude dynamic" groups who contributed to the incumbent's seizure of power in the previous year.[41] Thus, the regressions specify the likelihood a group that was in power in the previous year is excluded in the current year. Models 8 and 9 use *Exclude* as the dependent variable, and Models 10 and 11 use *Exclude dynamic*. I also include a variable, *Ruler ethnic group*, which indicates whether a group controls the executive. This is an important control variable to include given the importance of ethnic support bases for incumbents in Africa and the constraints rulers face in barring or purging their own coethnics from power (see Section 3.5.1). In addition to the *co-conspirators* variable and a range of group-level and country-level control variables added to the previous models on coups and rebellions (such as *Group size*, *Center segmentation*, *Log income*, and *Log population*), I also add a variable, *Irregular replacement*, to code whether a given group was forcibly thrown out of power in the current or previous year. *Irregular replacement* allows me to test whether rulers who come to power by force are unable to credibly share power with those who dominated the *ancien régime*.

The results are consistent with the Sudan case. When controlling for *Ruler ethnic group* (REG), *Co-conspirator* is significant across all models and substantively important as well. Rulers are more than twice as likely to purge their co-conspirators as other power-holders. This is a striking finding.[42] Why would rulers expel from power the very allies who helped them come to power in the first place? Moreover, as mentioned above and starkly illustrated in the case study of the breakdown of the post-Mobutu order in the DRC, one's co-conspirators are armed and dangerous. This is a highly risky policy.

---

[41] The models only cover groups included in central government in current or previous year and those groups who contributed to the incumbent's seizure of power in the current or previous year as those that remain excluded have no possibility of being purged.

[42] Interestingly, and contrary to economic arguments that predict ethnic exclusion is more likely in low-income countries due to increased competition over distribution of state spoils, income level has no effect on the likelihood a group in the central government will be purged.

TABLE 8.3 *Co-Conspirators, Coup Attempts, and Ethnic Exclusion in Africa, Independence to 2005*

	Exclude Basic (8)	Exclude Basic (9)	Exclude Dynamic (10)	Exclude Dynamic (11)	Attempted Coup (12)	Successful Coup (13)	Exclude Dynamic (14)
Co-conspirators[1]	0.68*	0.72	0.91**	1.12**	0.70***	0.34	0.76**
	(0.39)	(0.46)	(0.43)	(0.45)	(0.26)	(0.35)	(0.33)
Ruler ethnic[1] group	-1.89***	-1.95***	-2.06***	-2.49***	0.13	0.57	-2.00***
	(0.44)	(0.50)	(0.50)	(0.52)	(0.31)	(0.27)	(0.41)
Irregular replacement	2.89***	2.85***	2.91***	3.65***	0.60	0.35	2.86***
	(0.50)	(0.56)	(0.54)	(0.51)	(0.42)	(0.93)	(0.49)
Failed coup							1.61***
							(0.33)
Center[1] segmentation	-0.38***	-0.39**	-0.42***	-0.19	-0.14	-0.20	-0.41***
	(0.14)	(0.15)	(0.15)	(0.16)	(0.09)	(0.14)	(0.14)
Log group size[1]	-0.52	-0.49	-0.41	-0.21	1.14***	1.33***	-0.53
	(0.35)	(0.41)	(0.40)	(0.43)	(0.21)	(0.24)	(0.33)
Log GDP per[1] capita		0.01	0.11	0.02			
		(0.30)	(0.57)	(0.51)			
Log country[1] population		0.05	0.08	0.35			
		(0.13)	(0.12)	(0.42)			
Years since last coup					-0.014		
					(0.02)		
Constant	-1.84***	4.79	-3.29		-1.70***	-2.32***	-1.54**
	(0.69)	(4.49)	(2.16)		(0.47)	(0.58)	(0.63)
N	4062	3837	3841	2274	6976	6976	4070
states	35	35	35	22	34	34	35
pseudo r²	0.15	0.15	0.17		0.09	0.09	0.20
Country fixed effects	N	N	N	Y	N	N	N

All models also include cubic polynomial approximation of dependent variable to control for temporal dependence. Standard errors clustered by country (in parentheses).

[1] lagged one year *: $p < 0.10$; **: $p < 0.05$; ***: $p < 0.01$.

If this is due to the strategic uncertainty that arises from the shadow of the coup d'état, we should see evidence of co-conspirators becoming locked in an internal security dilemma before the breakdown of powersharing. To test this dimension of the argument, Models 13 and 14 in Table 8.3 examine the likelihood that we see evidence of such a security dilemma. In fact, the evidence demonstrates that co-conspirators are significantly more likely to *try* to eliminate the incumbent in a coup d'état than other groups *but with a very low success rate.*[43] What is ironic about the co-conspirators' inability to successfully reclaim power as the internal rivalry plays out is it is often they who recruited the incumbent in the first place. Kérékou in Benin, Bashir in Sudan, Kabila in DRC, and Guéï in Côte d'Ivoire were all leaders by default—ranking military or rebel figures who were brought in by the conspirators for lack of a better alternative to serve as a figurehead. This suggests the emergence of a sort of incumbency advantage for these "default" rulers who are able to exploit their discretionary power to coup-proof their regimes, even as such techniques provoke violence and undermine powersharing.[44]

8.6.3 Failed Coups and Ethnic Exclusion

Consistent with the strategic logic of ethnic exclusion (i.e. that rulers exclude "where it is necessary" more than "where it is possible"), I have found that rulers are significantly more likely to exclude their co-conspirators from power than other stakeholders. One question is whether this logic applies beyond co-conspirators regimes. Theoretically we would expect it to, if formal institutions regulating the distribution of power are weak and rival power-holders possess joint control of the state's coercive apparatus. As mentioned, one challenge in testing this more broadly is gathering systematic data on the ethnic composition of the military across all African countries. However, one observable implication consistent with the strategic model of ethnic exclusion advanced is if we see evidence that, outside co-conspirators, rulers employ ethnic exclusion against other groups who pose a significant coup risk to the ruler's hold

---

[43] Of the twenty-two coup attempts by co-conspirators, only six were successful, almost half the normal coup rate by groups included in power and even lower than the rate for excluded groups illustrated in Figure 8.2. Consistent with the argument that these are preemptive coup attempts, more than 60 percent occurred while the co-conspirators were still included in the central government.

[44] For a compelling analysis of how the incumbency advantage works in authoritarian regimes, see Svolik, *The Politics of Authoritarian Rule.*

on power. In the absence of data on groups' coup-making capabilities, it is difficult to exogenously test this. One revealing endogenous implication, however, would be if we see evidence of a strong association between failed coups and ethnic exclusion, controlling for *co-conspirators*. Such a finding would be indicative of the development of an internal security dilemma between the ruler and other power-holders, and it would provide additional evidence to support the claim that rulers employ the costly strategy of ethnic exclusion to neutralize rival networks' coup-making capabilities. Having nearly been deposed by a power-holder, the incumbent employs systematic exclusion to quash the rival's capability to organize a subsequent internal challenge. To test this, in Model 14 I add the variable, *Group failed coup*, which measures whether members of a given group executed a failed coup in the current or previous year. The results reported in Table 8.3 reveal a strong association between failed coups and ethnic exclusion, even taking into account the presence of co-conspirators in the central government.

8.6.4 Co-conspirators, Coup-Proofing, and Civil War

A final set of tests seek to determine whether the exclusive coup-proofing strategies rulers use to eliminate the internal threat posed by their former allies leads to civil war. To test this overall argument, I rerun the rebellion regressions (see Models 5–7 in Table 8.1), adding *Co-conspirators*, *Ruler ethnic group*, and *Irregular replacement* to the estimations. The results are displayed in Table 8.4. When controlling for *Ruler ethnic group*, which has a significant negative effect on likelihood of group rebellion, *Co-conspirator* is highly significant and robust. Model 19 illustrates that most co-conspirators who rebel against their former patron are more likely to do so in the first three years of being purged from the central government. This result is substantively very strong. As illustrated in Figure 8.3, being a co-conspirators and excluded from the central government increases the risk of group rebellion in a given year fivefold from around 1 percent for other excluded groups to 5 percent for excluded co-conspirators. Group rebellion risk in a given year jumps to over 17 percent, however, when also taking into consideration if the co-conspirators was recently purged from power in the past three years. A final result of interest: the significance of *Group failed coup* in Models 17 and 18 suggests, moreover, this pathway is not necessarily limited to conflict between the ruler and co-conspirators but other power-holders who possess coercive capabilities.

TABLE 8.4 Co-Conspirators and Rebellion in Africa, Independence to 2005

	Group Rebel (15)	Group Rebel (16)	Group Rebel (17)	Group Rebel (18)	Group Rebel (19)
Co-conspirator[1]	1.59***	1.17***	1.39***	1.54**	0.83*
	(0.47)	(0.40)	(0.42)	(0.51)	(0.45)
Recently excluded co-conspirators					3.17***
					(2.27)
Ruler ethnic group	-1.57***	-1.38**	-1.44***	-1.73**	-1.35**
	(0.50)	(0.50)	(0.52)	(0.76)	(0.51)
Inclusion[1]	-1.29***	-1.22**	-1.28***	-1.39**	-0.98***
	(0.39)	(0.48)	(0.40)	(0.51)	(0.37)
Irregular replacement	2.55***	2.42***	2.48***	2.27***	1.83***
	(0.50)	(0.56)	(0.35)	(0.60)	(0.49)
Failed coup			1.22**	0.99*	
			(0.50)	(0.55)	
Center[1] segmentation	-0.22*	-0.24*	-0.23*	-0.05	-0.28**
	(0.14)	(0.15)	(0.11)	(0.18)	(0.13)
Log group size[1]	-0.24	-0.42	-0.28	-0.17	-0.23
	(0.37)	(0.37)	(0.35)	(0.31)	(0.34)
Log GDP per[1] capita		-0.70			
		(0.34)			
Log country[1] population		-0.20			
		(0.17)			
constant	-4.28***	2.69	-4.39		-4.69
	(0.73)	(3.80)	(0.74)		(0.69)
N	6976	6363	6976	3504	6976
States	34	34	34	17	34
Pseudo r[2]	0.10	0.11	0.11		0.12
Country fixed effects	N	N	N	Y	N

All models also include cubic polynomial approximation of dependent variable to control for temporal dependence. Standard errors clustered by country (in parentheses).

[1] lagged one year *: p < 0.10; **: p < 0.05; ***: p < 0.01.

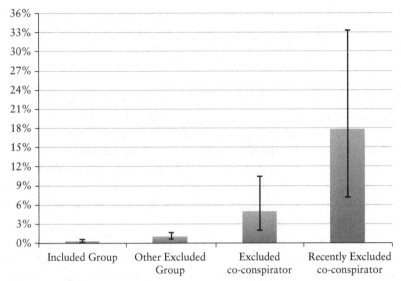

FIGURE 8.3 Predicted Probability of Group Rebellion by Recently Excluded Co-Conspirators, Independence to 2005[45]

8.7 CO-CONSPIRATORS AT WAR

8.7.1 Camaraderie, Trust, and the Commitment Problem

One puzzle that co-conspirator wars raise is what becomes of the strong levels of camaraderie and deep bonds of trust that often develop between conspirators as they work together to seize power. This is important to account for because if comrades are able to sustain trust then the commitment problem should be peacefully managed.

Part of the answer surely lies in what Hobbes described as man's "perpetual and restless desire for power."[46] After working collectively to seize

---

[45] Predicted probabilities for *Included group*, *Other excluded group*, and *Excluded co-conspirator* have been generated by running the Clarify program with model 16 in Table 8.4. *Recently excluded co-conspirator* is from model 19 in Table 8.4. Dependent variable is *Group rebel*. For each, *Irregular replacement* has been set at 0 and *Center Segmentation*, *Log group size*, *Years since last group rebellion*, *Years since last group rebellion2*, and *Years since last group rebellion3* are set at their mean. *Included group* bar was created by setting *Inclusion* at 1 and *Co-conspirator* at 0; *Other Excluded Group* bar was created by setting *Inclusion* at 0 and *co-conspirator* at 0; *Excluded co-conspirator* bar was created by setting *Inclusion* at 0 and *co-conspirator* at 1. *Recently excluded co-conspirator* bar was created by setting *Inclusion* at 0, *co-conspirator* at 1, and *Recently excluded co-conspirator* at 1.

[46] Hobbes, *Leviathan*.

the state, individual violence specialists seek to maximize their share of power and status. Such power struggles produce two key consequences that intensify the commitment problem. First, they change the identities and interests of the actors themselves. As Wendt argues, threats are a function of social interactions rather than the structural environment itself.[47] For co-conspirators, repeated conflicts over power can instigate changes in the way they start to see and relate to each other. As fraternal bonds fray, the "sense of shared history and shared future" that "safeguard against splits," in the elegant words of Dr. Ghazi Saluhuddin reflecting on the Islamists in Sudan, dissipates.[48] Camaraderie is tarnished: what was seen as selfless devotion to one's brothers is now seen as merely a tool exploited for personal gain. Betrayal, which was inconceivable in the past, is now one's foremost concern.

As elite interactions become more adversarial and mistrust increases, each side alters its expectations about the willingness of the other to reciprocate cooperation and lowers one's tolerance of the risk of exploitation.[49] This increases the stakes of the power struggle itself as each side fears that even the slightest shift in control may enable their rivals to effect a permanent change in the distribution of power. Thus, while glory and greed often generate power struggles, it is diffidence, or fear of death at the hands of his enemies,[50] that drives the use of anticipatory or preemptive force that has manifest itself in Africa's irregular regimes as coups and purges, followed by civil war.

In the next two sections, I offer brief qualitative cases of co-conspirator wars in Chad and Liberia. The cases offer additional evidence to demonstrate how the commitment problem between co-conspirators produces uncertainty, an internal security dilemma, and large-scale political violence.

8.7.2 From Allies to Enemies: Chad, 1980–1990

In 1982, Hissène Habré, the leader of the Forces Armées du Nord (FAN), and briefly former prime minister of Chad (in 1978 and 1979), seized power in an armed rebellion that was launched from Darfur with military aid from Sudan, Egypt, and the United States.[51] Critical to Habré's

---

[47] Alexander Wendt, "Anarchy is What States Make of It: The Social Construction of Power Politics," *International Organization*, 46 (2) (1992): 391–425.

[48] Interview with Dr. Ghazi Salahuddin, August 13, 2010.

[49] Jervis, "Cooperation under the Security Dilemma." Kydd, *Trust and Mistrust in International Relations.*

[50] Hobbes, *Leviathan.*

[51] Harir, "'Arab Belt' Versus 'African Belt.'"

military success was an alliance he forged with those from the Zaghawa ethnic group, whose homeland straddles the Chad–Sudan border, including parts of Darfur. After their seizure of power, this interethnic alliance between the Gouran—Habré's ethnic group—and the Zaghawa became the backbone of the new state. Habré controlled the presidency, and the army was entrusted to two Zaghawa military officers—first, Idriss Déby from 1982 to 1985 and then Hassan Djamous from 1986 to 1989. The two proved highly successful commanders in chief. In 1987, Djamous, assisted by Déby, who remained a presidential military adviser on defense and security issues, successfully recaptured the Aouzou Strip in northern Chad, which had been under Libyan control since 1973.[52]

The stunning defeat of the Libyans, however, led to a fraying of the Habré–Zaghawa alliance. Part of the friction arose from Habré's jealousy of the national acclamation Déby and Djamous received as military heroes.[53] Others attribute the conflict to control over the weapons captured in the Aouzou Strip; Habré became suspicious as the Zaghawa military commanders allegedly channeled the weapons to "their home areas of Ennedi and Biltine or sold them into the active commercial circuits in nearby Sudan."[54] After the war, Habré ordered his personal intelligence services to spy on his long-time allies. For their part, the Zaghawa elites became worried as Habré reached out to various leaders of rebellions he had faced since coming to power in 1982.[55] By August 1988, six of the twenty-four cabinet ministers were former rebel leaders.[56] Wary that their share of power was being diluted, the Zaghawa elites became further worried in late 1988 when Habré replaced Ibrahim Muhammad Itno, a Zaghawa, as head of security with the president's cousin, who privatized the security service and stacked it with other Gouran.[57] This move alarmed the Zaghawa elites, who feared that Habré was preparing to take further action against them, that might lead to their detention or death (a fate suffered by many of those who crossed Habré, including Djamous's brother-in-law, who disappeared in May 1988 after being accused of passing information to Libya).[58] To preempt their future exclusion or

[52] Burr and Collins, *Africa's Thirty Years War.*
[53] Sam C. Nolutshungu, *Limits of Anarchy: Intervention and State Formation in Chad* (Charlottesville, Va.: University Press of Virginia, 1996).
[54] William J. Foltz, "Reconstructing the State of Chad," in I. William Zartman, ed., *Collapsed States: The Disintegration and Restoration of Legitimate Authority* (Boulder, Col.: Lynne Rienner, 1995), pp. 15–32.
[55] Foltz, "Reconstructing the State of Chad."
[56] "Chad: Habré at the Turning Point." *Africa Confidential,* April 28, 1989.
[57] Nolutshungu, *Limits of Anarchy,* p. 235.
[58] Samuel Decalo, *Historical Dictionary of Chad* (Lanham, Md.: Scarecrow Press, 1997).

worse, Djamous, Déby, and Itno attempted to seize power in a coup on April 1, 1989, but their bid failed.[59] After the failed attempt, Itno was arrested and disappeared, while Djamous was killed as he and Déby fled the capital. Déby survived, however, and found refuge in Darfur, from where he was joined by other Zaghawa fleeing indiscriminate violence unleashed by the Habré government.[60] From Darfur, Déby, backed by the Sudan government, turned to armed insurgency to try to reclaim power.[61]

8.7.3 The Strategic Logic of a Shakespearean Tragedy: Liberia, 1980–1990

Liberia in the late 1980s also makes a compelling and equally tragic case of a coup-proofing civil war. In attributing the civil war to strategic uncertainty between former comrades, it challenges the conventional narrative put forth to account for the civil war. The Liberia case is often advanced as a paradigmatic example of regime breakdown and civil war rooted in the collapse of domestic economies at the end of the Cold War and the rise of new global commercial opportunities that disrupted the cooperative equilibriums underpinning order and stability in Africa's weak states.[62] There is no doubt that the loss of foreign aid from the US government and the tendency by Liberian president, Samuel Doe, to create "new, decentralized points of access to resources" created the permissive conditions for state failure. But it was the appearance of the National Patriotic Front of Liberia (NPFL), a rebel movement led by Charles Taylor, that served as "the catalyst that toppled" Doe's patronage network and triggered full-scale civil war.[63] Taylor was not the founder of the NPFL, however. Instead, the NPFL was a "continuation" of a rebellion begun by one Thomas Quiwonkpa,[64] a boyhood friend of Samuel Doe and the principal conspirator behind Doe's seizure of power in a coup in 1980. The origins of the NPFL, founded before the end of the Cold War when

---

[59] Some suggest the coup attempt was actually a purge, like that which Kiir executed against Machar in South Sudan. As Decalo notes, "Touted by Hissène Habré as an attempted coup by key Zaghawa lieutenants that helped sustain him in power ... though in reality a preemptive strike by Habré prior to a possible power-grab by the Zaghawa." Decalo, *Historical Dictionary of Chad*, p. 139.

[60] Human Rights Watch, *La Plaine des morts: le Tchad de Hissène Habré, 1982–1990*, New York: Human Rights Watch, 2013. Available at www.hrw.org/sites/default/files/reports/chad1013frwebwcover_0.pdf (accessed August 23, 2016).

[61] Decalo, *Historical Dictionary of Chad*.

[62] Reno, *Warlord Politics and African States*.

[63] Reno, *Warlord Politics and African States*.

[64] Berkeley, *The Graves Are Not Yet Full*, p. 48.

US largesse still flowed to Liberia in the form of hundreds of millions of dollars, points to the strategic causes of elite bargaining failure.

The conflict between Quiwonkpa and Doe is fitting of a Shakespearean tragedy. In fact, it still haunts the wives of the former comrades who struggle to understand the "enemy [that] went between [Samuel and Thomas] and [why] we lost them."[65] The two had been best friends and collaborated to overthrow the Americo-Liberian oligarchy that had ruled Liberia since the country's founding in 1847. Though Quiwonkpa was "the acknowledged leader" of the 1980 coup, he "used his influence to get his friend Samuel Doe accepted as nominal head of state and co-chairman" of the military junta, the People's Redemption Council (PRC).[66] In a classic example of elite accommodation, nearly identical to the Chad case, the two then parceled out control of the Liberian state: Doe served as head of state, and Quiwonkpa became the commanding general of the Armed Forces of Liberia.

Within a year, rumors swirled of threats to Doe's hold on power. Either as pretext or in response to a genuine threat, Doe maneuvered to eliminate rival power centers, including some of his key co-conspirators. The first victim was Major General Thomas Weh Syen, the deputy head of state. Syen and several others in the ruling PRC were arrested and then executed in August 1981.[67] Doe's liquidation of Syen sent shock waves through the regime about who might be next.

It was against this backdrop that a political conflict over the transition to civilian rule pit Doe and Quiwonkpa against each other. As Ellis writes, the return to civilian rule "disturbed Quiwonkpa, who feared that a move to constitutional rule would hand Doe further control of the government while his own influence would remain limited to the armed forces."[68] As Quiwonkpa pushed back, asserting that all military officers, including Doe, should step down by April 12, 1985, the president's advisers began to portray the president's "friend" as an enemy that "must be totally discredited, if not totally eliminated," albeit "*carefully*."[69] A whisper campaign

---

[65] "Liberia: Ellen Settles Row between Doe, Quiwonkpa's Wives," *The Informer* (Monrovia), August 27, 2010. Available at http://allafrica.com/stories/201008301259.html (accessed August 23, 2016).

[66] Ellis, *The Mask of Anarchy*, p. 54.

[67] Emmanuel Dolo, *Ethnic Tensions in Liberia's National Identity Crisis: Problems and Possibilities* (Cherry Hill, NJ: Africana Homestead Legacy Publishers, 2007), p. 34.

[68] Ellis, *The Mask of Anarchy*, p. 57. See also Charles Taylor's testimony at the Special Court for Sierra Leone at the Hague. "Testimony of Charles Taylor," *The Prosecutor of the Special Court v. Charles Ghankay Taylor*, Special Court for Sierra Leone, July 15, 2009, p. 24488.

[69] Letter by then minister of state, Major John G. Rancey, sent to Doe on March 22, 1983. Cited in Mark Huband, *The Liberian Civil War* (Portland, Oreg.: Frank Cass, 1998), pp. 35–36.

had already begun that claimed Quiwonkpa was planning to overthrow the Doe regime.[70] In an attempt to diminish Quiwonkpa's first-strike capabilities (or, as Taylor phrased it, "to [make] Quiwonkpa weak and unable to do anything)," Doe attempted to remove him as head of the army and transfer him to the weaker position of the secretary general of the PRC.[71] Quiwonkpa resisted the move, however, as he viewed it as a blatant violation of the powersharing deal they had made after the 1980 coup.[72] Moreover, Quiwonkpa feared that if he conceded control of the armed forces to Doe, the president would have a clear path to absolute power. In the face of what Doe viewed as insubordination, and convinced it was too dangerous to allow Quiwonkpa to remain head of the army, Doe sacked the very man who was the driving force behind his ascension to the presidency. Placed under what amounted to house arrest, Quiwonkpa was convinced he would suffer the same fate as Thomas Weh Syen.

The divorce between the former friends was complete. Doe and Quiwonkpa's relationship had completely evolved from co-conspirators to armed enemies facing off in a deadly shoot-out in which it was either kill or be killed. The depth of the mistrust and the severity of the commitment problem made reconciliation and coexistence impossible.

The shoot-out between the two sides played out at an incredible cost to the Liberian people. The first round occurred immediately after the divorce. Quiwonkpa, under pressure from his lieutenants to strike immediately, contemplated launching a reactive coup but balked. He calculated the odds of success were not in his side's favor.[73] Feeling insecure in Monrovia, he fled to his home area in Nimba County where Doe's assassins pursued him. Quiwonkpa managed to escape death and eventually fled the country, along with his key lieutenants, including Taylor. Around the same time, violence broke out in Nimba County when Quiwonkpa's supporters in the army launched a raid against government offices and the government-owned Yekepa mine.[74] Doe accused his former confidante of masterminding the attempt and punished Quiwonkpa's Gio coethnics in Nimba County. This battle "was the first open sign that the Krahn–Gio ethnic rivalry created within the armed forces by Doe's and Quiwonkpa's

---

[70] Edward Lama Wonkeryor, *Liberia Military Dictatorship: A Fiasco "Revolution"* (Chicago, Ill.: Strugglers' Community Press, 1985), pp. 90–91.
[71] "Testimony of Charles Taylor," p. 24488.
[72] Wonkeryor, *Liberia Military Dictatorship*, p. 193.
[73] "Testimony of Charles Taylor," pp. 24488–24489.
[74] Ellis, *The Mask of Anarchy*, p. 59.

competition for supreme power had spilled over from the barracks into the country itself."[75]

The second round occurred on November 12, 1985, when Quiwonkpa, leading a rebel organization that he called the NPFL, invaded Liberia from neighboring Sierra Leone. When the armed group reached Monrovia, its allies in the military stationed at the Barclay Training Center revolted. The insurgency-cum-coup nearly succeeded in toppling Doe but was eventually suppressed after hours of intense fighting. Quiwonkpa was captured, executed, and his mutilated corpse was paraded around the capital.[76] Doe's regime responded with a vengeance, conducting mass executions against hundreds of perceived Quiwonkpa loyalists in the armed forces (primarily those from the Gio and Mano ethnic groups) and killing more than 1,000 in a spree of ethnic cleansing in Nimba County.[77] Doe vanquished his former friend and co-conspirator and further consolidated his internal hold on power but at the cost of brutalizing the Gio and Mano communities, especially in Nimba County.

With their patron killed, Quiwonkpa's key lieutenants, Prince Johnson and Charles Taylor, picked up the mantle of the NPFL and launched the third round of fighting on Christmas Eve 1989 when around 100 NPFL fighters invaded Nimba County to avenge Doe's death of Quiwonkpa and get "that boy Doe off the backs of the Liberian people."[78]

8.8 CONCLUSION

This chapter has systematically tested the book's central hypotheses relying on data on ethnic powersharing from the EPR dataset as well as an original dataset on the ethnicity of key coup conspirators and insurgents across sub-Saharan Africa. The data offer strong and robust confirmatory evidence of the coup–civil war trap as well as offering evidence to support the strategic roots of ethnopolitical exclusion. Consistent with the logic that ethnopolitical exclusion is rooted in the strategic uncertainty that arises from the shadow of the coup d'état, I show that rulers are

---

[75] Ellis, *The Mask of Anarchy*, p. 58.
[76] Ellis, *The Mask of Anarchy*, p. 58.
[77] Bill Berkeley, *Liberia, A Promise Betrayed: A Report on Human Rights* (New York: Lawyers Committee for Human Rights, 1986). Berkeley, *The Graves Are Not Yet Full.*
[78] Taylor interviewed on the BBC World Service on December 31, 1989. Cited in Ellis, *The Mask of Anarchy*, p. 75.

significantly more likely to purge their co-conspirators from the central government than other powersharing holders. Vignettes from Chad and Liberia illuminate how the breakdown of camaraderie and trust kindle the commitment problem. In the next chapter, I test the relevance of this analytical framework on the most devastating war since World War II: Africa's Great War.

9

A Model-Testing Case

Explaining Africa's Great War

9.1 INTRODUCTION

In the previous chapter, I offered systematic evidence in support of a strategic theory of civil war in which rulers choose ethnopolitical exclusion to coup-proof their regimes from ethnic rivals. I have further shown that this strategic logic helps to account for the phenomenon of co-conspirator civil wars. According to the quantitative analysis, one prominent "typical case"[1] of a coup-proofing civil war between co-conspirators is Africa's Great War, the devastating armed conflict that broke out in the DRC in August 1998. A group of co-conspirators from different ethnic groups (especially the Luba-Shaba and the Tutsi-Banyamulenge) who were excluded from state power by the regime of Mobutu Sese Seko came together, with military backing from the regional governments of Rwanda, Uganda, and Angola, to capture state power through an armed rebellion in May 1997. These co-conspirators then divided state power. According to the EPR, the Tutsi-Banyamulenge would emerge as the "senior partner" in the regime (thanks to the military backing of the Rwandans) and the Luba-Shaba as "junior partner" (despite one of their own, Laurent-Désiré Kabila, becoming head of state). A year later, however, the EPR data indicates an important shift in the distribution of power. The Tutsi-Banyamulenge went from "senior partner" to "discriminated," and the Luba-Shaba went from "junior partner" to "senior partner." This shift in distribution of power preceded the outbreak of large-scale political violence between the former co-conspirators. Overall, then, the DRC case seems to represent a paradigmatic case

---

[1] Gerring, *Case Study Research*, Chapter 5.

of ethnic powersharing between co-conspirators breaking down, leading to ethnopolitical exclusion and civil war.

While it was through the large-N analysis described in Chapter 8 that I identified the DRC in the late 1990s as a likely case, I was also motivated by substantive considerations: Existing scholarship tended not to focus on the importance of internal strategic factors in accounting for the outbreak of Africa's Great War. Instead, the conflict is often seen through the lens of the Rwandan genocide and its spillover into then Zaire,[2] in which the new government in Kigali, dominated by the victorious RPF, sponsored a rebellion in Zaire to install a friendly regime and deny the perpetrators of the genocide, who fled across the border, safe haven. This alliance was undone, according to Salehyan, by the agency loss the Rwandans and Ugandans experienced after delegating authority to Kabila.[3]

This argument, however, misreads the structure of the alliance between Kabila and the RPF. After conspiring with Kabila to overthrow Mobutu, the RPF eschewed delegation and instead chose a strategy of direct intervention.[4] Its cadres took up key positions in the post-Mobutu government. The new chief of staff of the Congolese army was James Kabarebe, the rising star of the Rwandan Patriotic Army (RPA), protégé of RPF leader Paul Kagame, and military commander of the AFDL that ousted Mobutu. Other RPF elites assumed strategic positions in the Kabila regime as well, with a particularly strong presence of intelligence officers. Thus, though the heavy influence of external actors in Congo during this period may make it seem like a deviant case, Kabila's decision to allow the RPF to control the Congolese army meant that in many ways it closely resembled other incidences of powersharing between co-conspirators.

The RPF's entry into the post-Mobutu dominant coalition mitigated the information asymmetries that normally plague delegation but gave rise to a different set of strategic problems. One obvious consequence was the foreign-occupation issue that opposition leaders such as Étienne Tshisekedi exploited to increase political pressure on Kabila.[5] On the

[2] Reyntjens, *The Great African War*. Prunier, *From Genocide to Continental War*. Jason K. Stearns, *Dancing in the Glory of Monsters: The Collapse of the Congo and the Great War of Africa* (New York: PublicAffairs, 2011). René Lemarchand, *The Dynamics of Violence in Central Africa* (Philadelphia, Pa.: University of Pennsylvania Press, 2009).

[3] Idean Salehyan, "The Delegation of War to Rebel Organizations," *Journal of Conflict Resolution*, 54 (3) (2010): 493–515.

[4] This strategy reflected the RPF's beliefs that neutralizing those responsible for the 1994 genocide was too critical to entrust to anyone but its elite forces.

[5] Tshisekedi, the most prominent opposition figure, railed against the role of the RPF in Congo and pledged not to cooperate with Kabila as long as the Rwandan forces were in the country.

surface, it might seem like the breakdown of the Kabila–RPF alliance is a simple function of Kabila moving to "expel the foreigners" to strengthen his domestic legitimacy, which he surely was concerned about. For example, shortly after the AFDL captured Kinshasa opinion polls undertaken in the capital city indicated only 14 percent of those surveyed admired the new president, with most regarding him as a "hostage" to foreigners.[6] But then, after expelling the RPF, his popularity soared among the Kinois.

One problem with this explanation is that it cannot account for the sudden and unexpected expulsion of the RPF. In contrast to the RPF's claims at the time that the withdrawal was voluntary so that Congo "could sort out their own problems,"[7] the opposite was true, according to interviews with members of both the RPF and Kabila's government. Consulting with only his closest advisers, Kabila hastily made the decision to expel the Rwandans only forty-eight hours before the expulsion order was read on television. Kabila's order left the RPF's top official in Congo, James Kabarebe, "in a panic" as he scrambled to devise contingency plans.[8] If the expulsion was merely a function of Kabila's domestic legitimacy problem, why could Kabila and the RPF not come to some negotiated arrangement that would resolve the foreign-occupation problem and continue to address the RPF's security concerns but avoid a devastating regionalized civil war that nearly led to Kabila's ouster from power?

Instead, I argue, consistent with the book's central argument, that what undermined powersharing between Kabila and his allies was the strategic uncertainty related to each side's future commitment to cooperation and the consequences if there was a sudden shift in the distribution of power. For Kabila, his paramount fear was that his co-conspirators, who installed him in power and gained control of the military and other key strategic ministries, could just as easily remove him from power. In an original contribution to the political history of Africa's Great War, I show, drawing on extensive interviews in Central Africa with many of the key actors in the AFDL and with other privileged observers from the region and in the international community, that this fear and the RPF's inability to credibly commit not to remove Kabila caused the breakdown of the post-Mobutu order. Moreover, I demonstrate that Kabila's expulsion order in July 1998 represented a

---

[6] Howard W. French, "In Congo, Many Chafe Under Rule of Kabila," *New York Times*, July 13, 1997.

[7] Hrvoje Hranjski, "Rwanda Disputes Congolese Claim on Troop Expulsion," *Associated Press*, July 29, 1998.

[8] Interview with RPF official, Kigali, December 2009.

preemptive strike to thwart a coup d'état by the RPF and its allies. While Kabila recognized that expelling "foreign forces" would increase the risk of a future armed conflict, he calculated that a societal-based or foreign-based armed insurgency was less threatening—if barely—than a coup attempt from inside his government. The case study allows me to test the validity of the coup-proofing theory of civil war vis-à-vis a model of instrumental (or economic) exclusion with imperfect information as discussed in Section 3.3.

The rest of the chapter is as follows. First, I briefly describe the overthrow of Mobutu and the dominant coalition that captured the state but which broke down fifteen months later, leading to the Second Congo War. I then explore the degree to which the breakdown of the coalition was driven by economic motivations and incomplete information before exploring whether there is empirical support for the commitment problem logic.

9.2 FROM COMRADES-IN-ARMS TO BELLIGERENTS AT WAR: EXPLAINING THE POLITICAL DYNAMICS OF AFRICA'S GREAT WAR

9.2.1 The AFDL Liberates Congo

Like many revolutions, the liberation movement that coalesced against Mobutu Sese Seko, one of Africa's longest serving dictators, comprised a motley group of actors with a diverse set of proximate or long-standing grievances but whom found common ground in their opposition to the *ancien régime* and seized upon an exceptional historical opportunity in which the old order was collapsing under its own contradictions.

The principal external force was the RPF, the ruling party in neighboring Rwanda led by Major General Paul Kagame. In early 1996, the RPF faced increasingly bold incursions by thousands of *génocidaires*—the soldiers and Interahamwe militia who carried out the Rwandan genocide and then in July 1994 fled to Zaire, where Mobutu hosted and supported them. In the face of inaction by the international community against what the RPF perceived as a persistent existential threat, the Rwandan government decided to go on the offensive with the aim of eradicating the *génocidaires*, "liberating" the refugee camps where hundreds of thousands of Rwandan civilians congregated, and removing Mobutu from power. Yoweri Museveni, Uganda's president and a stalwart ally of the RPF, shared Kigali's enthusiasm for military action as the Mobutu regime allowed Ugandan rebels to operate out of Zaire's

Orientale and Kivu Provinces. Museveni and the core of the RPF had a long history of collaborating to remove regional dictators—from as far back as Idi Amin,[9] then the Obote–Okello regime in Uganda, and subsequently Juvénal Habyarimana and Rwanda's genocidal junta between 1990 and 1994. Mobutu represented the last tyrant of this old order. Museveni and Kagame enlisted allies such as the ruling Portuguese Movimento Popular de Libertação de Angola (MPLA) in Angola[10] and the Tutsi military establishment in Burundi[11] to their cause but understood that an outright invasion of Zaire would probably be a hard sell internationally: "a Congolese front was needed."[12] (See Map 9.1 for map of DRC.)

There were few domestic groups more vigorous in their opposition to Mobutu than the Tutsi of eastern Zaire, whose aspirations for full citizenship had been frustrated for decades[13] and in the 1990s were calling for ethnic solidarity against the Mobutu–*génocidaires* bloc. Thousands in the Kivus had died prior to 1994 over what became known as the "nationality question"—who was a citizen and therefore entitled to associated sociopolitical and economic rights such as land ownership—but it was the influx of genocidal ideology by Rwandan extremists and the concomitant increase in anti-Tutsi attacks that spurred an armed uprising.[14] For the RPF, the Congolese Tutsi represented an ideal ally, given shared ethnic networks, common language, previous collaboration (a fair number of Congolese Tutsi had fought with the RPF in Rwanda), and ethnic solidarity at a time when Tutsi were facing virulent racism.[15] The Banyamulenge (Tutsi from South Kivu) supplied the AFDL with

---

9 While some Banyarwanda in Uganda supported the Idi Amin regime, Fred Rwigyema, the future leader of the RPF, joined Museveni's Front for National Salvation (FRONASA) in the mid-1970s. Mamdani, *When Victims Become Killers*, pp. 167–168.

10 The MPLA's archenemy, União Nacional para a Independência Total de Angola (UNITA), had for decades received financial, political, and military support from Mobutu Seso Seko; President Dos Santos saw in the removal of the Zairean dictator a unique opportunity to weaken his nemesis.

11 The Tutsi-dominated government in Bujumbura sought, through its participation in the AFDL, to deal fatal blows to several rebel movements (mainly consisting of Hutu opponents) active in eastern Congo, most notably the FNL and the CNDD-FDD of Burundi.

12 Interview with Brig. Gen. of the Rwandan Defense Forces, July 2010.

13 Koen Vlassenroot, "Citizenship, Identity Formation and Conflict in South Kivu: The Case of the Banyamulenge," *Review of African Political Economy*, 29 (93) (2002): 499–516.

14 Stanislas Bucyalimwe Mararo, "Kivu and Ituri in the Congo War: The Roots and Nature of a Linkage," in Stefaan Marysse and Filip Reyntjens, eds., *The Political Economy of the Great Lakes Region in Africa* (Basingstoke: Palgrave Macmillan, 2005), pp. 190–222.

15 At the time, the RPF held emotional internal debates about preventing "another genocide" against its coethnics in Kivu. Interview with Patrick Mazimhaka, minister in the

MAP 9.1 Democratic Republic of the Congo

thousands of young combatants, while the Tutsi from North Kivu were represented by Deogratias Bugera, who became one of the four official "founding fathers" of the movement: "Our first requirement was [our] right to exist as human beings and as a community. [The] right to our citizenship."[16]

Kigali was eager to reach out beyond coethnics to blunt the predictable propaganda of a Tutsi conspiracy.[17] While the pro-Ugandan André Kisase Ngandu was relatively unknown, more important was the charismatic Anselme Masasu Nindaga, who had a Tutsi mother and, as a member of the RPF since the early 1990s, was trusted in Kigali. With a strong following from the disaffected young masses in eastern Congo, Masasu

---

office of the president of Rwanda during the outbreak of the Second Congo War, and other RPF leaders and officers in Kigali, December 2009.

[16] Interview (by email) with Deogratias Bugera, Secretary General of the AFDL, March 2010.

[17] Four out of ten members of the AFDL's Executive Council were Tutsi. Bugera was secretary general, while Bizima Karaha became commissioner for external affairs, Samson Muzuri was in charge of education, and Joseph Rubibi the deputy finance commissioner.

represented "something new from the east"[18]—the hope that overthrowing Mobutu would lead to a peaceful, prosperous future and could appeal to a much broader audience. The fourth Congolese pillar Museveni and Kagame recruited, on recommendation of the region's respected elder statesman, Julius Nyerere, was Laurent-Désiré Kabila.[19] Though by the mid-1990s Kabila was biding his time as a farmer in Tanzania and had never proven himself a formidable rebel leader, he brought something to the table none of the others could: name recognition, strong nationalist credentials stretching back to the Lumumbist era of the 1960s and legitimacy as a credible opponent of Mobutu who never succumbed to the old tyrants' inducements.[20] In contrast to the other AFDL leaders, Kabila, as a son of Katanga, could plausibly represent more than just key constituencies in eastern Congo.

Backed by Rwandan–Ugandan muscle and with a façade of Congolese leadership, the AFDL, as a hybrid partnership between foreign firepower and domestic dissidents, launched its rebellion in October 1996. The anti-Mobutu coalition demolished the refugee camps around Goma and Bukavu and destroyed the bases of the *génocidaires*, before setting off on an irresistible march to Kinshasa. Euphoria swept through the country; the AFDL forces were greeted as liberators. Kabila became a national hero.

9.2.2 The Rebel Alliance Becomes the Ruling Coalition

The liberation of Zaire occurred with lightning speed. From the moment the top conspirators gathered together in Kigali in early 1996 until they entered Kinshasa displacing Mobutu from power was not more than fifteen months. "The revolution was too quick . . . We never had a chance to build a strong movement . . . we were obsessed with changing Mobutu,"

---

[18] Interview with Frank De Coninck, Belgian Ambassador to Rwanda (1994–1997) and DRC (1997–2000), Rome, June 12, 2009.

[19] Laurent-Désiré Kabila was born in 1939 in Moba, a town in Katanga along Lake Tanganyika. As a Lumumbist and Marxist, Kabila spent most of his young life in rebellion against the Congolese state and its Western orientation. In the 1960s and 1970s, Kabila's revolutionary activities were centered around Fizi-Baraka in South Kivu, though it merely amounted to a local smuggling operation. Kabila became increasingly absent, however, spending most of his time in Dar es Salaam. He eventually abandoned the struggle altogether until he joined forces with the RPF in 1995.

[20] Interviews with several AFDL leaders in Kinshasa and with Rwandan security operatives in Kigali, December 2009.

one AFDL leader admitted.[21] The AFDL was a revolution with little structure or political program. The glue that kept the conspirators together was a camaraderie developed through war[22] and a strategic interdependence: Kabila, with few forces of his own, was completely dependent upon the RPF and Congolese Tutsi for his personal security and that of the state;[23] the Rwandans and Congolese Tutsi needed Kabila, a known national personality and non-Tutsi, to serve as Mobutu's successor.

After the war, this interdependence translated into an informal division of power. It was Kabila, the old nationalist lion, who assumed the presidency, with the blessing of the RPF.[24] The Congolese Tutsi had to settle for the ministry of foreign affairs, which was taken up by Bizima Karaha, who became one of Kabila's closest advisers and a key interlocutor for the regime with external allies. Bugera and Masasu, two of the other eastern AFDL "leaders,"[25] also retained positions of potential influence. Bugera stayed on as secretary general of the AFDL, while Masasu declared himself commander of the armed forces, "Afande." Other allies grabbed key political jobs in the Kivus.

The RPF, invited by Kabila, took up top positions in the realm of security and finance led by James Kabarebe[26] as chief of staff of the Forces Armées Congolaises (FAC), alongside Dan Munyuza, a key intelligence officer, and Alfred Kalisa, a Rwandan banker who in his private capacity developed close ties with Kabila.[27] Though the RPF recognized there would be costs associated with what was criticized as a "foreign occupation," they were willing to incur these to finish their war against the *génocidaires* and reform the FAC.

---

[21] Interview with Bizima Karaha, member of AFDL and DRC foreign minister in 1997 and 1998, Goma, December 14, 2009.

[22] Until this day, some of those closest to Kabila have fond views of their days as comrades-in-arms with Jamese Kabarebe and other RPF despite the later violent falling-out.

[23] Interview with Mbusa Nyamwisi, Kinshasa, December 7, 2009.

[24] Interviews with several top AFDL cadres, Kinshasa, Goma, Kigali, December 2009–March 2010.

[25] The fourth AFDL leader, Kisase Ngandu, was killed during the war against Mobutu.

[26] James Kabarebe, the great-grandson of Rwandan economic migrants, grew up in Uganda. He attended Makerere University before becoming the aide-de-camp of Paul Kagame during the civil war against the Habyarimana government. After the RPF captured the central government, Kabarebe was tapped to lead the Republican Guard and then oversee military operations against Mobutu.

[27] Uganda had a strong but more discreet presence in the regime, focusing on the intelligence services and remaining militarily present in the east. However, the Angolan military, which had also played a key role in the overthrow of Mobutu, was "dismissed" shortly

As a nationalist, Kabila resented his dependence on outside actors but knew he could not have taken Kinshasa without the RPF, and its forces remained vital for security in case Mobutists tried to reclaim power. "Kabila recognized his own forces were not yet ready. He asked us [RPF] for protection; asked for James [Kabarebe] as chief of staff. He felt he could trust us more than any other force available to him."[28] To reassure Kabila and signal the RPF's commitment to accommodation, Kabarebe personally took charge of the military education of Kabila's son, Joseph, and appointed him as his deputy.[29]

9.2.3 Kabila Expels the RPF, Triggering Africa's Great War

Fifteen months later, this remarkable alliance would come to an unceremonious end when Kabila issued the aforementioned expulsion of foreign forces from Congo late on the night of July 27, 1998.

The response by Kigali, Kampala, and their Congolese allies was swift. Within a week, a new rebellion was launched in eastern Congo by members of the 10th Brigade of the FAC, backed by the RPA's best troops. Simultaneously, Kabarebe launched a surprise attack on the other side of the country in Bas-Congo. As state-organized anti-Tutsi pogroms plunged Kinshasa into chaos, Kabila fled the capital and sought safety in Lubumbashi, leaving control of the army in the hands of his brother-in-law, General Célestin Kifwa. Facing imminent defeat, the Congolese government desperately pleaded with neighbors, Angola and Zimbabwe, to come to their aid. Luanda balked, however; it remained distrustful of Kabila, who ordered its forces out of Congo in mid-1997. Only after two weeks of shuttle diplomacy and allegedly obtaining a favorable deal on access to Congo's offshore oil fields did the Angolans join the Zimbabweans and intervene to force back Kabarebe's troops and save Kabila's regime.[30] But the war in the east continued to rage, and Africa's Great War, which would lead to the deaths of millions,[31] was under way.

---

after the capture of Kinshasa. Looking back on the exit of the Angolans, some Kabila loyalists saw the RPF's hand in this decision. Interviews in Kinshasa, December 2009.

[28] Interview with top member of the RPF, Kigali, December 16, 2009.

[29] Interviews with Rwandan political and military sources, January and November 2010.

[30] Interviews with two top envoys sent by Kabila to Luanda during those two weeks in 1998.

[31] Benjamin Coghlan, Richard J. Brennan, Pascal Ngoy, David Dofara, Brad Otto, Mark Clements, and Tony Stewart, "Mortality in the Democratic Republic of Congo: A Nationwide Survey," *The Lancet*, 367 (9504) (2006): 44–51.

As is clear, the outbreak of Africa's Great War hinged largely on the breakdown of the alliance between Kabila and the RPF. What accounts for its collapse? Why did Kabila expel the Rwandan forces in July 1998, especially if that meant imminent war? Why could a peaceful settlement not be reached? In the next few sections I assess the relevance of instrumental theories of ethnic exclusion vis-à-vis the commitment problem to account for bargaining failure between Kabila and his allies in the AFDL.

9.3 Instrumental Theories of Conflict and Africa's Great War

9.3.1 Competition over Congo's Valuable Resources

As discussed in Section 3.3, an instrumental logic of ethnopolitical exclusion and civil war attributes bargaining failure to powersharing partners' attempts to maximize their control of valuable economic rents. This is an important argument to consider as Africa's Great War would become one of the most notorious resource conflicts in the modern era. All belligerents would reap tremendous profits from the illicit exploitation of gold, diamonds, copper, cobalt, zinc, coltan, and much else.[32] Thus, some have tended to analyze the AFDL as a cartel, possibly supported by Western capital,[33] created to wrestle control over Congo's riches from the collapsing Mobutu regime.[34] Once in power, the coalition's breakdown is then seen as the consequence of the sudden availability of huge rents over which no clear agreement had been reached. With Congo's easy-to-grab riches for the taking and presenting a unique opportunity to Kigali and Kampala to fund their economic growth[35] and fuel private patronage systems,[36] some argue that Kagame and Museveni sought to increase their share of the spoils—either through a new arrangement that would have given them even more of the cake, or a definitive rupture that would enable military control of eastern Congo's minerals.

---

[32] *Final Report of the Group of Experts on the DRC Submitted in Accordance with Paragraph 5 of Security Council Resolution 1952 (2010)* (New York: UN Security Council, 2011).

[33] François Ngolet, "African and American Connivance in Congo-Zaire," *Africa Today*, 47 (1) (2000): 64–85.

[34] Nzongola-Ntalaja, *The Congo from Leopold to Kabila*.

[35] Ingrid Samset, "Conflict of Interests or Interests in Conflict? Diamonds and War in the DRC," *Review of African Political Economy*, 29 (93–94) (2002): 463–480.

[36] John F. Clark, "Explaining Ugandan Intervention in Congo: Evidence and Interpretations," *The Journal of Modern African Studies*, 39 (2) (2001): 261–287.

While it is undeniable that profits from the exploitation of coltan, gold, and diamonds have fueled and sustained the conflict at a local, national, and regional level for many years following August 1998 and that all sides discovered the profitability of fighting in the Congo during the first war, few of the key insiders I interviewed stressed that infighting over economic resources was the principal cause of regime breakdown. It was to be expected that the RPF and Congolese Tutsi would play down the role of natural resources, but what was surprising was the lack of evidence presented on this point by Kabila loyalists.[37]

This is partly explained by the disarray the mining sector was in during those early days. With the collapse of almost all economic production during the final years of Mobutu and Kabila's erratic policies with mining companies (such as reneging on contracts signed during the rebellion, including, most notoriously, with American Mineral Fields), there was no sudden windfall from natural resources in 1997 and early 1998. While surely, as has been reported,[38] some Ugandans and Rwandans expanded their commercial networks into the Congo during this time, most of their energies were concentrated on security, especially as the *génocidaires* launched incursions in Rwanda in late 1997. Moreover, as far as can be reconstructed, Kabila did not try to exploit the country's resource riches to buy off the RPF as relations worsened and conflict seemed inevitable.[39] Theoretically, this is particularly puzzling: faced with a much stronger military opponent, why did Kabila not at least offer a new power and wealth-sharing arrangement to the RPF and its allies in the course of 1998, which could have led to a soft landing that reflected the real balance of power? One possible reason, consistent with instrumental theories of conflict, is that Kabila underestimated the costs of war with the RPF. I address this possibility in the next section.

9.3.2 Instrumental Exclusion with Incomplete Information

There is no doubt that communication problems plagued the alliance from the beginning. During the creation of the AFDL, no strategic plan

---

[37] Interviews with Congolese and Rwandan elites inside and outside the AFDL, 2009–2011.

[38] United Nations, *Final Report of the Panel of Experts on the Illegal Exploitation of Natural Resources and Other Forms of Wealth of the Democratic Republic of the Congo*, New York: UNSC, 2002.

[39] Interview with Mwenze Kongolo, Kabila inner circle and minister of interior and then justice in 1997 and 1998, Kinshasa, December 10, 2009. Interview with Bizima Karaha, member of AFDL and DRC foreign minister in 1997 and 1998, Goma, DRC, December 14, 2009. Interview with Azarias Ruberwa, member of AFDL and DRC vice president from 2003 to 2006, December 6, 2009.

was developed. While there was broad agreement on working together to militarily confront Mobutu, the precise role and objectives of the different factions remained nebulous. Kabila understood Kagame's top priority was to wipe out the *génocidaires'* rear bases. He also recognized the importance the RPF placed on "reforming" the army after the overthrow of Mobutu to ensure Congolese military links with the *génocidaires* were permanently terminated.[40] But the modalities and timeline of RPF intervention in DRC were never agreed upon.

Any misunderstanding between the RPF and Kabila over their alliance was compounded over time as information-sharing broke down between the two sides. Initially, the RPF had tight control over the network of people around Kabila.[41] But one of the new president's first orders of business was to bring in people he felt he could trust to establish his autonomy vis-à-vis the RPF and their Congolese "auxiliaries." Soon after taking Kinshasa, Kabila replaced Moise Nyarugabo, a Congolese Tutsi, who served as Kabila's personal secretary since the early days of the war. To those close to Kabila, Nyarugabo was seen as Kabila's gatekeeper, and it was a "humiliation" to go through him to see the president.[42] Moreover, it was believed to be "too risky" to have a Tutsi surveilling Kabila's every decision and move. Nyarugabo's removal "was a very clear signal to everyone."[43]

As Kabila maneuvered to give himself breathing room, he used his power of appointment to move trusted individuals, including family members, to key positions. In addition to his son, Joseph, as deputy of the FAC, Mwenze Kongolo, a fellow North Katangan living in the United States, became the minister of interior and then the powerful minister of justice. In January 1998, Kabila's boyhood friend, Gaëtan Kukudji, was appointed the minister of interior, becoming the regime's official number two, leaving only foreign minister Bizima Karaha as a powerful political Banyamulenge (Congolese Tutsi) figure. According to one cabinet minister, Kakudji's takeover of the coercive apparatus coincided with the incorporation of "nonmilitary individuals, especially Katangans" into the armed forces.[44]

---

[40] Interviews with Kongolo, Faustin Munene, and Raphael Gendha in Kinshasa, December 2009.

[41] "Kabila was like a hostage inside. Tutsi were all around him. Very dangerous sign for Kabila." Interview with Mbusa Nyamwisi, Kinshasa, December 7, 2009.

[42] Interview with Celestin Kifwa, Kabila's brother-in-law and chief of staff of FAC in July–August 1998, Kinshasa, December 11, 2009.

[43] Interview with Léonard "She" Okitundu, Kabila's Minister of Human Rights, Kinshasa, December 9, 2009.

[44] Interview with Dr. Jean-Baptiste Sondji, Minister of Health and Social Welfare in 1997 and 1998, Kinshasa, December 7, 2009.

As Kabila built a shadow state dominated by his family and friends, he began to confide less in Karaha, who was one of his closest advisers in the early months and a key interlocutor with the RPF. According to one cabinet official, "In January 1998 an important signal was made to Bizima when he was downgraded a couple of spots on the protocol. The president also scaled down privileged contact with Bizima; they had fewer private lunches."[45] But as Kabila and his advisers developed their own private networks that kept information from their coalition partners, the RPF and their allies did the same. Shé Okitundu, the minister for human rights and counselor to Kabila, recalls traveling abroad with Karaha and, upon their return to Kinshasa, being picked up at the airport by an RPF official. Karaha and this official would converse in Kinyarwanda, the lingua franca of Rwanda but foreign to Okitundu, leaving him feeling humiliated and in the dark about the information exchanged.[46]

The breakdown of communication contributed to the mistrust and the uncertainty within the regime that ultimately culminated in the expulsion order. But incomplete information alone does not explain Kabila's costly decision to expel the Rwandans. Despite the breakdown in communication between the sides, the military prowess of the RPF and its allies in eastern Congo was no secret. With Kabarebe controlling the Congolese army from May 1997 until July 1998, Kabila was cognizant of the RPA's capability to mobilize militarily, especially in the East, given the amount of armaments and resources Kabarebe diverted to the FAC's 10th Brigade, which was at the frontline of the war against the Rwandan *génocidaires*.[47] Yet, despite this, in late July 1998, Kabila made the unilateral decision to throw out the Rwandans. And even before this he dared to reach out to the *génocidaires*—the RPF's archenemies.

I contend that Kabila's seemingly reckless policies can only be explained by an intensifying security dilemma between his network and the RPF and its Congolese allies. Facing what Kabila perceived was an imminent internal threat from his former comrades-in-arms, he calculated expelling the RPF as the only way out. His controversial earlier decision to reach out to the *génocidaires* thus occurs in this context. In the next section I explain how the commitment problem produced such an unthinkable outcome.

---

[45] Interview with Eddy Angulu, Minister of the Environment in 1997 and 1998, Kinshasa, December 9, 2009.
[46] Interview with Léonard "She" Okitundu, Kabila's Minister of Human Rights, Kinshasa, December 9, 2009.
[47] Interview with Gen. Faustin Munene, member of AFDL and Deputy Minister of the Interior in 1997 and 1998, Kinshasa, December 2009.

9.4 KABILA, HIS CO-CONSPIRATORS, AND THE COMMITMENT PROBLEM

Kabila and the RPF developed a strategic interdependence during the armed rebellion against Mobutu that translated into a remarkable powersharing arrangement in which Rwandans assumed key positions in the post-Mobutu regime. The actors had much to gain by sustaining their cooperation and reaping the spoils that came from controlling the Congolese state. But this camaraderie became a victim of the political conflicts that arose as the co-conspirators jockeyed over power and influence. Particularly important was a conflict that arose between Kabila and the young upstart, Masasu Nindaga, who was extremely popular in eastern Congo and a potential threat to the president's authority. Kabila's "political assassination" of Masasu helped to weaken the camaraderie that underpinned the regime and increased mistrust between the ruling elites. Rumors of conspiracies soon gave way to an internal security dilemma that pitted Kabila and his inner circle against the RPF and their Congolese allies. As mutual suspicions deepened, both camps prepared to resolve the commitment problem by taking the other side out.

9.4.1 Kabila "Assassinates" Masasu

After overthrowing Mobutu, Kabila's priority was to strengthen his political position and develop a degree of autonomy from his military backers. As described above, he exploited his discretionary authority as president to stack the regime with individuals he felt he could trust more than the violence specialists who Rwanda and Uganda recruited to fill the AFDL in 1996. This policy of "Katangisation"—the recruitment of old leftist comrades of the president but above all many relatives and coethnics from Congo's wealthy Katanga Province—suggested that while Kabila recognized the importance of his AFDL allies to his hold on power, his exclusive dependence on them left him vulnerable. Thus he started to consolidate his power, but "slowly," as it was "very dangerous to provoke the Rwandans."[48] While the incorporation of Kabila's family and friends into the coalition irked some Congolese Tutsi, it did not fundamentally affect the alliance. More destabilizing was Kabila's decision to

---

[48] Interview with Léonard "She" Okitundu, Kinshasa, December 9, 2009.

incarcerate Masasu Nindaga,[49] the charismatic young commander from the Kivus who, like Kabila, had been one of the AFDL's four "founding fathers."

Masasu had a large following within the rebel movement as he personally recruited disaffected youth from the East—known as *kadogos*—into the AFDL. Like other Congolese in the alliance, he resented Kabila's unilateral assumption of the presidency before even reaching Kinshasa.[50] In the post-Mobutu government, Masasu officially retained his title of chief of staff of the AFDL in the Ministry of Defense.[51] But consistent with Reyntjens' observation that the army "remained a hazy affair . . . [in which] no one knew who commanded whom,"[52] his position within the new military hierarchy was unclear—despite Masasu's tendency to refer to himself as commander-in-chief.[53] Nevertheless, as a strong military commander with a large, loyal following, Masasu represented a potential rival center of authority in the new regime. Masasu frequently traveled to the Kivus, maintaining close connections with his armed supporters in the East.[54] In November 1997, Kabila sought to rein in Masasu and his unauthorized activities. Fearing the *afande* might be plotting something larger, the president had him arrested and, in a slap in the face to one of the heroes of the revolution, publicly disparaged him as nothing more than a "Rwandese corporal" who played a marginal role in the AFDL.[55] Masasu was accused of providing intelligence to a foreign country, running a private militia, and setting up a shadow state in the East.[56]

Kabila's arrest of one of the most popular leaders of the revolution sent shock waves throughout the regime and society. According to one

[49] For incredible insights into the rise and fall of Masasu, see Lieve Joris, *The Rebels' Hour*, trans. Liz Waters (New York: Grove Press, 2008).

[50] Interview (by email) with Deogratias Bugera, Secretary General of the AFDL, March 2010.

[51] Government of the Democratic Republic of the Congo, "Senior Officials of the Government of the Democratic Republic of the Congo," Press Release, August 16, 1997. Available at http://reliefweb.int/report/democratic-republic-congo/senior-officials-government-democratic-republic-congo (accessed August 23, 2016).

[52] Reyntjens, *The Great African War*, p. 162. Some refer to Masasu as the first chief of staff of the FAC.

[53] Prunier, *From Genocide to Continental War*, p. 152.

[54] Interviews with former AFDL members from South Kivu in Butare, Rwanda, August 2010.

[55] Prunier, *From Genocide to Continental War*, p. 175.

[56] "Kinshasa Denounces Arrested Security Adviser," AFP, November 30, 1997. Interviews in Kinshasa, Eastern Congo and Rwanda, December 2009–August 2010.

community leader from Masasu's home area, "His arrest triggered great discontent in the East. There was a feeling that Kabila was picking off his enemies one by one."[57] One top diplomat remembered that "the political elimination of Masasu was another key sign that the influence of the East was shifting away to Katanga."[58] Violence erupted in Kinshasa between eastern forces loyal to Masasu and Kabila's Katangan soldiers, killing dozens.[59]

Masasu's "political assassination" also had a profound impact on trust between Kabila and the other co-conspirators.[60] There was a feeling that Kabila was turning "his back on the men who'd helped him to power and decided to rule by himself."[61] Even those among the pro-Kabila rank were rattled by Masasu's incarceration. "One of the biggest mistakes the president made was to arrest Masasu," General Faustin Munene, one of Kabila's lieutenants for security matters, reflected. Then, revealing the degree to which the move increased uncertainty and mistrust in the regime, he commented, "I could have been Masasu."[62]

Kabila was not intentionally trying to destabilize the ruling coalition and provoke his regime partners. He viewed Masasu's arrest as a legitimate action against a recalcitrant commander who was conducting unauthorized activities that undermined his authority. But the consequences were far-reaching. The arrest eroded trust between the co-conspirators who viewed it as politically motivated, meaning that they were equally vulnerable to such a move in the future. It also left the RPF questioning Kabila's reliability: "We lost hope in Kabila when they arrested Masasu— he represented our interest more than anyone else."[63] With the rise of mistrust, the conspirators no longer took it for granted that their partners preferred mutual cooperation, thus intensifying the commitment problem.

---

[57] Interview with South Kivu community leader, December 2009.

[58] Interview with Frank De Coninck, Rome, June 12, 2009.

[59] "Le Congo d'abord," *Jeune Afrique*, December 16, 1997.

[60] This is how a top official in the AFDL described Masasu's arrest. Personal interview, Kinshasa, December 2009.

[61] The words of Lieve Joris' Congolese Tutsi protagonist, Assani, when the young AFDL commander sees Masasu, the man who personally recruited him to join the revolution, shackled and imprisoned. Joris, *The Rebels' Hour*, p. 126.

[62] Emphasis added. Interview with Gen. Faustin Munene, member of AFDL and deputy minister of the interior in 1997 and 1998, Kinshasa, December 2009.

[63] Interview with key Rwandan security operative, December 2009.

9.4.2 The Northwest Insurgency in Rwanda

As tension increased inside the regime, it coincided with an intensification of the war between the RPF and the *génocidaires*. The latter were being squeezed by the RPA's "black ops" in Congo's interior, but had started to regroup in the rainforest and sneak back into the Kivus to link up with sleeper cells inside their homeland. During the second half of 1997, the *génocidaires*, now organized as the Armée de la Liberation du Rwanda, made increasingly audacious violent incursions into northwestern Rwanda, the home region of their late patron, President Habyarimana.[64] In response, the RPF launched a brutal counterinsurgency campaign inside Rwanda as Kagame and his generals feared the Hutu extremists might return to power particularly as fighting threatened Gitarama and the hills around Kigali, the seat of political power.[65] Inside Congo, Kabarebe increased armaments for the much-feared 10th Brigade. The escalation of the war with the *génocidaires* reinforced the strategic importance of the Congo to the RPF and strengthened Kigali's resolve to stay until they finished the job.[66] To withdraw prematurely would leave Kigali vulnerable to an existential threat. Thus, Kabila's maneuvering, in which he neutralized the RPF's allies and concentrated ever more power in the hands of a security clique, consisting of Kakudji, Kongolo, Munene, and his chef-de-cabinet, Abdoulaye Yérodia, made the Rwandans nervous that as the president became more independent they became dispensable.

9.4.3 The Coalition Keeps the Peace

In early 1998, things risked spiraling out of control. On February 23, 300 Banyamulenge soldiers led by Commander Ruhimbika Muller mutinied, occupying the Ruzizi Plain after weeks of tension in South Kivu. The mutiny was sparked by an order that Muller's soldiers redeploy to Kasai and Katanga but reflected deeper disillusionment with the regime, including its RPF representatives, about the Banyumulenge's marginalization from the ruling coalition, the lack of progress on the citizenship

---

[64] For one of the few sources on the insurgency in Rwanda in 1997 and 1998, see African Rights, *Rwanda: The Insurgency in the Northwest* (London: African Rights, 1998). See also Richard Orth, "Rwanda's Hutu Extremist Genocidal Insurgency: An Eyewitness Perspective," *Small Wars and Insurgencies*, 12 (1) (2001): 76–109.

[65] African Rights, *Rwanda*.

[66] Interviews with the RPF military leadership, December 2009–January 2010.

issue, and the removal of "their" Masasu.[67] However, before the situation could escalate further, the coalition responded, demonstrating its peacemaking potential when elite cooperation was sustained.

Signaling a unified approach to the crisis in the East, Kabarebe and his deputy, Joseph Kabila, were dispatched to South Kivu to negotiate with the mutineers. They granted personal guarantees to Muller that his men's grievances would be addressed, pledging to persuade the president to settle the nationality question, reduce insecurity, and maintain homogenous Banyamulenge military units. The timely intervention ended the mutiny, and Laurent Kabila publicly spoke out against anti-Tutsi sentiment, urging the constitutional commission he had appointed in October 1997 to deal comprehensively with the nationality question.

The nonviolent management of the mutiny demonstrated the benefits that accrued from continued cooperation between the coalition partners.[68] It also demonstrated that such cooperation was possible despite Masasu's incarceration and shifting political dynamics within the regime. Nevertheless, relations between regime factions would worsen over the next couple of months, plagued by the general environment of strategic uncertainty.

9.4.4 Conspiracies, Paranoia, and Kabila's Faustian Pact

In an environment of extreme strategic uncertainty, small incidents can have an amplified effect on relations as mistrusting elites begin to assume the worst from others in the regime. According to Jean-Baptiste Sondji, minister of health and social welfare at the time, one such incident occurred in March 1998 when, "to the astonishment of all, the [meeting of the] Council of Ministers was characterized by systematic arms searches ... On one such occasion, James [Kabarebe] was searched

---

[67] Interviews with South Kivu politicians of different ethnic groups, December 2009. See also Gauthier de Villers and Jean-Claude Willame, *République Démocratique du Congo: Chronique Politique d'un Entre-Deux-Guerres, Octobre 1996–Juillet 1998* (Paris: L'Harmattan, 1999). Ruhimbika Muller, *Les Banyamulenge entre deux guerres* (Paris: L'Harmattan, 2001).

[68] Younger Kabila's role in peacefully dealing with the mutiny made a positive impression on some from eastern Congo. Interviews in Kinshasa and Goma with several Tutsi leaders, including Azarias Ruberwa, member of the AFDL and DRC vice president from 2003 to 2006, December 6, 2009.

and a gun was discovered: that's when we understood how serious it was."[69] Two months later, according to General Munene, deputy minister of the interior, state security discovered a "very serious conspiracy" being plotted by prominent Congolese Tutsi in the regime.[70] In response to this, there was alleged to have been a secret meeting in Lubumbashi in which Kabila and several key advisers confronted the Banyamulenge, presenting evidence of the plot. The Congolese Tutsi denied everything, accusing one of Kabila's aides of trying to "get James' job."[71] Kabila responded by changing his presidential guard: "We decided to get rid of the Rwandan guys. Even David [Kabila's beloved young Rwandan bodyguard] was removed who was very close to the President."[72] Whether the plot was real or fabricated is impossible to determine, but both the plot and Kabila's reaction had a profound impact on trust between the two sides—each became convinced the other was conspiring to usurp power.

As rumors of conspiracies and plots spread and the group around Kabila became convinced the RPF and their Congolese allies were planning to steal power, it grew desperate for leverage against the RPF. The insurgency in northwest Rwanda demonstrated that, despite considerable efforts, Kigali remained vulnerable to the threat posed by the *génocidaires*. Kabila, in the context of a spiraling security dilemma and ever-shortening time horizons, did the unthinkable. Allegedly, with some help from Tanzanian security operatives, Kabila's men began providing supplies and logistical support to the *génocidaires* in the Kivus and Katanga (Kamina), at least from May 1998 onwards.[73] The RPF was flabbergasted by Kabila's audacity but, rightly or wrongly, was convinced that it had finally uncovered why it had not been able to destroy the ex-FAR/Interahamwe. James Kabarebe and Dan Munyuza, the RPF's top intelligence officer in Congo, confronted Kabila with the evidence to give him a final chance, but he evaded discussions on the topic, further infuriating the Rwandans.

---

[69] Interview with Dr. Jean-Baptiste Sondji, Minister of Health and Social Welfare in 1997 and 1998, Kinshasa, December 7, 2009.

[70] Interview with Gen. Faustin Munene, member of AFDL and deputy minister of the interior in 1997 and 1998, Kinshasa, December 10, 2009.

[71] Interview with close adviser to Kabila, December 2009.

[72] Interview with Gen. Faustin Munene, Kinshasa, December 10, 2009.

[73] Various interviews in 2009–2010. For additional evidence suggesting a Kabila–*génocidaires* link before August 1998, see Stearns, *Dancing in the Glory of Monsters*, p. 183.

9.5 ENDGAME

By July 1998, trust between the conspirators was nil, and each became convinced the other camp was preparing to make a move. In the absence of any third-party intervention (and none was forthcoming, at least from the United States, Belgium, and the UK, which seemed largely oblivious to the dynamics driving the former co-conspirators to imminent war[74]), the only way out was to eliminate the other side.

On July 13, Kabila consummated the divorce when he replaced Kabarebe as FAC chief of staff with his brother-in-law, Célestin Kifwa, who had been running the police. Kabila also gave orders to bolster security in the capital and purge the Groupe Spécial de Sécurité Présidentielle (now headed by Kifwa's son) of all pro-Rwandan elements. More power was handed to another elite force, "Police d'Intervention Rapide" (later involved in the anti-Tutsi pogroms in August 1998), while the presidential bodyguard was reinforced.[75] These moves alarmed Bizima Karaha who became convinced Kabila "would kill us."[76]

Behind the scenes, the RPF and their allies kicked into high gear their plotting to remove Kabila, a subject which was broached as early as January 1998, with Kabila's disgruntled Congolese allies the loudest advocates for this option. It was clear that Plan A was meant to be "a swift strike"—in other words, a coup d'état (a term the RPF refuses to countenance)—orchestrated by Rwanda's External Security Organization, with the help of Kampala, but implemented by disaffected Tutsi and non-Tutsi AFDL conspirators.[77] "It was meant to be short and internal, no need for war or foreign support."[78]

As the RPF and their allies made final preparations, Kabila flew to Cuba for a medical check-up. "When we were in Cuba they were feeding us information back home," one of Kabila's advisers who accompanied the president reported, "It was a frantic situation. James was preparing to take Kabila out. I encouraged the President to stay behind in Cuba, but he refused."[79]

---

[74] Interviews with various American, Belgian, and UK diplomats, Washington, DC, London, and Brussels, 2009–2011.

[75] Interviews with some of Kabila's closest security advisers, Kinshasa, December 2009.

[76] Emphasis added. Interview with Bizima Karaha, Goma, December 2009.

[77] Interviews with half a dozen leaders of what would later become the RCD and with several RPF politicians and military officers, December 2009.

[78] Interview with one of the key Congolese co-conspirators, December 2009. This was confirmed in several other interviews with protagonists.

[79] Interview with Godfroid Chamlesu, Kabila's former Minister of Defense, Kinshasa, December 9, 2009.

As a deliberate provocation to the RPF and a final push to persuade their leader to confront Kabarebe and his forces, Kabila's security in Congo even suggested that a plot "Habyarimana style"[80] was in the works, in which the Rwandans would shoot down Kabila's plane as he returned from Havana. Kabila panicked, flying back secretly, fearing a probably nonexistent plot at N'Djili Airport, and hastily convened a crisis meeting with his closest allies as he safely entered the presidential palace on July 26.

Presented with "very concrete and serious information of an immediate threat,"[81] Kabila struck first. At midnight on July 28, 1998, the undersecretary of defense appeared on state television to inform the Congolese people that President Laurent-Désiré Kabila had decided "to put an end . . . to the presence of Rwandan soldiers, who helped us during the liberation of our country. Through these soldiers, we thank all the Rwandan people for the solidarity shown to us so far. Furthermore, the head of state congratulates the nobility of soul of the people of the DRC for tolerating, hosting and facilitating these friendly soldiers' short stay in our country."[82]

9.5.1 Kabila's Preemptive Strike

The expulsion order proved to be a brilliant tactical move by Kabila. Without having to militarily confront the RPF in Kinshasa, which may have been a losing battle,[83] Kabila managed to preempt the coup using one of the key sources of leverage he had over the Rwandans: being "president of a sovereign state."[84] The RPF knew that executing a coup after Kabila had asked its forces to leave would be seen as an act of aggression, a violation of international sovereignty, and politically impossible for the international community, as well as for the Congolese population, to accept. Even Kagame had to admit that the man they treated as nothing more than a puppet had outmaneuvered them. Agonizing "over what to do—defy the order, replace Kabila, or depart—[Kagame] concluded that Kabila held the upper hand at that moment"[85] and the RPF

---

[80] Interviews with two pro-Kabila members of the government, Kinshasa, December 2009.

[81] Interview with Gen. Faustin Munene, Kinshasa, December 10, 2009.

[82] "Kabila Statement Thanks Rwandans for Solidarity," BBC Summary of World Broadcasts, July 30, 1998.

[83] "If the Rwandans had kept their cool, they could have taken power before leaving Kinshasa." Interview with key Kabila adviser, Kinshasa, December 2009.

[84] Interview with Patrick Mazimhaka, minister in the office of the president of the Rwandan government in 1998, Kigali, December 16, 2009.

[85] Robert E. Gribbin, *In the Aftermath of Genocide: The US Role in Rwanda* (Lincoln, Nebr.: iUniverse, 2005), p. 274.

had to pull out. The expulsion stopped the RPF dead in its tracks and forced the opposition alliance to turn to Plan B, in essence a repeat of the strategy used against Mobutu.[86] Within a week, an insurgency was launched in eastern Congo by the FAC's 10th Brigade, backed militarily by Rwanda and Uganda. To Kabila, a rebellion from the East was preferable to a threat from Kinshasa. What Kabila did not anticipate was James Kabarebe's audacious raid on Kitona.

9.5.2 Second Strike: The Kitona Raid

Kabarebe retreated from Kinshasa to Kigali "quite flustered and eager to strike back."[87] As mentioned, Plan B was to be an insurgency-cum-invasion; it began on August 2 when troops in the 10th Brigade mutinied in Goma and Bukavu and Rwandan and Ugandan forces entered Congo. But Kabarebe wanted to hit the government closer to the heart of power. So, on August 4, he commandereed airplanes from Goma and flew with elite RPF troops, Ugandans, and Congolese to the Kitona military base, which is clear across the country in the province of Bas-Congo and 250 miles west of Kinshasa. Kabarebe recruited Congolese soldiers (many of whom were former Mobutu soldiers stationed in "re-education camps") from Kitona and then marched toward Kinshasa, capturing the Inga Dam, the primary source of electricity for the capital, along the way.[88]

In taking the conflict to Bas-Congo, Kabarebe was trying to take Kinshasa before Kabila had time to countermobilize. In fact, the expulsion had been ordered in such a rush that the FAC defenses were completely inadequate and were overrun by Rwandan forces, the inevitable cost of saving Kabila from immediate liquidation. Kinshasa surely would have fallen too, if it were not for the last-minute intervention by Angola and Zimbabwe nearly two weeks after the Kitona invasion began. The Angolan and Zimbabwean intervention forced Kabarebe to retreat from the outskirts of Kinshasa and saved the Kabila regime.

It needs to be highlighted that Kabila expelled the RPF without any security guarantees from Angola or Zimbabwe, precisely because the hysteria after the Cuba trip left no time for this. Consequently, in the days after the expulsion, friends of the Angolan government, like

---

[86] Interview with a senior RPF politician in Kigali, December 2009.
[87] Prunier, *From Genocide to Continental War*, p. 182.
[88] Stearns, *Dancing in the Glory of Monsters*, pp. 189–190.

Pierre-Victor Mpoyo, minister for the economy and petroleum, and Munene, now had to beg Luanda for help.[89] For its part, Rwanda failed diplomatically to win backing from Angola for Kaberebe's attack on Bas-Congo, preferring instead to present regime change to Luanda as a *fait accompli*. With Kabarebe's daring and improvised second strike thwarted, the prospects of a swift conflict faded, and Africa's Great War was under way.

9.6 CONCLUSION

This chapter has employed the outbreak of Africa's Great War as a model-testing case of the coup-proofing theory of civil war, pitting it against economic theories of conflict. Drawing on original field research, I find that, consistent with the coup-proofing theory of civil war, Kabila's expulsion of Kabarebe's forces in late July 1998 represented a preemptive strike to thwart an imminent coup d'état by his comrades-in-arms. The expulsion order effectively prevented the coup, forcing Kabarebe to relocate to Bas-Congo-via-Goma, buying Kabila enough time to mobilize regional support and save his regime—if by the slimmest of margins. The Congo case provides a compelling example of a ruler purging rival networks of violence specialists from central state power to resolve the commitment problem and with an eye to increasing the barriers and costs their rival faces to usurping power via a rebellion than a coup.

The problem for Kabila, of course, is that even though he successfully thwarted his comrades-turned-enemies' bid for power, the RPF and their Congolese allies had retained control over much of the Kivus in eastern Congo due to their control of the 10th Brigade of the FAC. Thus, in an extreme example of ethnopolitical exclusion forfeiting societal and territorial control and increasing the pool of anti-regime insurgents, we see that within days of the expulsion the start of a full-scale civil war in eastern Congo.

---

[89] The Mzee had asked Angola to leave Congo after the overthrow of Mobutu, a move that some pro-MPLA cadres around Kabila ascribed to the influence of Tutsi politicians and Rwandan generals. There can be little doubt that Angola's reluctant but decisive intervention in late August 1998 was primarily the result of a security calculation—James Kabarebe's raid into Bas Congo was an offensive right on Angola's doorstep, strategically unacceptable without Luanda's permission. Interviews with three pro-Kabila members of the government, December 2009.

PART IV

EXTENSIONS

10

The Strategic Logic of Peace in Africa

10.1 INTRODUCTION

One key puzzle that arises from this book's central argument is how have some African countries avoided the vicious exclusion–conflict cycle. As illustrated in Figure 10.1, large-scale political violence tends to be concentrated in those countries with high levels of ethnopolitical exclusion, such as Sudan, Angola, Ethiopia, and Uganda. In the other half of Africa, inclusion not exclusion is the norm; these countries, such as Benin, Ghana, and Zambia, have largely avoided civil war. What accounts for Africa's two equilibriums? What policy lessons, if any, do these peaceful, inclusive states offer for Africa's most conflict-affected countries?

One possibility is that these more inclusive and peaceful states are structurally different from their conflict-affected counterparts and thus do not have the same underlying conditions (i.e. weak states with limited reach beyond the capital; society divided into geographically concentrated ethnic groups; sovereign premium) that give rise to coup-proofing civil wars. This does not seem to be the case. There have been no shortage of forceful attempts to seize power in these more peaceful states. For example, Ghana, Benin, and Togo have been three of the most coup-prone states in post-independence Africa, according to Patrick McGowan's military-intervention index.[1] Moreover, in these countries ethnicity is also politically salient[2] and geographically concentrated. What then accounts for ethnic peace in these countries?

[1] McGowan, "African Military Coups d'État."
[2] In addition to EPR, other datasets such as Posner's Politically Relevant Ethnic Groups (PREG) dataset reflect the salience of ethnicity across both sets of countries. Daniel N.

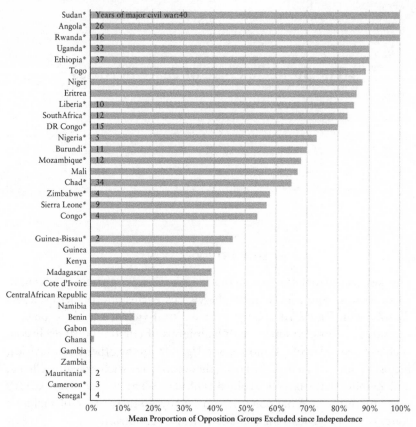

FIGURE 10.1 Africa's Two Equilibriums, Independence to 2005[3]

This penultimate chapter addresses these questions. In doing so, it draws on what Dave Ohls and I have conceived of as the threat-capabilities theory of powersharing.[4] The key intuition is that these negative

Posner, "Measuring Ethnic Fractionalization in Africa," *American Journal of Political Science*, 48 (4) (2004): 849–863.

[3] The x-axis represents the average number of group-years since independence non-ruling groups in the country were excluded from the central government, according to EPR dataset. In the case of Sudan, 100 percent of non-ruling groups have been excluded, whereas in Cameroon 0 percent of non-ruling groups have been excluded. The countries marked with an asterisk have experienced at least one armed conflict that has passed the 1,000-battlefield-death threshold according to the UCDP/PRIO Armed Conflict Dataset. The number of years of full-scale civil war is recorded near the y-axis.

[4] For a full version of the paper and a number of empirical tests supporting the threat-capabilities theory of powersharing, see Philip Roessler and David Ohls, "Self-Enforcing Powersharing in Weak States," College of William and Mary, 2016.

cases (in which weak, ethnically divided states avoid the exclusion–conflict cycle) have not escaped the coup–civil war trap, but, strikingly, rulers in these countries have made the strategic choice to accept powersharing and coup risk over civil war risk. We argue which strategic choice rulers make—exclusion and civil war risk or inclusion and coup risk—is a function of a country's ethnic geography and ethnic rivals' threat capabilities—that is their ability to effectively mobilize and credibly threaten to capture the central government *even when they are excluded from state power*. When both the ruling group and ethnic rivals possess strong threat capabilities, largely due to a group's size and proximity to the capital, ethnopolitical exclusion offers little strategic advantage as it merely trades the clear and present danger of a coup for the clear and present danger of a civil war. Under these conditions, rulers have weaker incentives to pursue ethnopolitical exclusion and tolerate coup-proofing civil wars. *In short, credible powersharing emerges when rivals gain no significant strategic advantage from ethnopolitical exclusion.* Rather than incur the high costs of mutually destructive civil wars, rivals pursue powersharing, and even accept the risk of trading power through coups. This argument highlights the value of a strategic approach to accounting for ethnopolitical bargaining outcomes in Africa's weak states.

The rest of the chapter is as follows. First, I consider the strategic limitations of ethnopolitical exclusion when rivals possess strong civil war capabilities. Second, I deduce and test a set of observable implications about the effect of threat capabilities on how the coup–civil war trap plays out. Third, I argue that empirically this helps to account for the seemingly peculiar postcolonial history, relative to the other cases analyzed in this book, of countries such as Ghana and Benin in which ethnic rivals trade power via coups but no group employs systematic ethnopolitical exclusion to try to coup-proof their regime and lock in power.

10.2 THREAT CAPABILITIES AND SELF-ENFORCING POWERSHARING

This book has argued that a key source of state failure in many African countries is the decision by rulers (or more precisely ruling groups) to hedge their bets on civil war through a strategy of ethnopolitical exclusion when confronted with the competing risks of a possible, but uncertain societal rebellion some time in the future to the clear and present danger of a coup d'état today. This is the strategic choice that the dominant coalitions around Sudan's Omar al-Bashir and DRC's Laurent-Désiré Kabila effectively made. Facing a threat from inside the government, the Bashir and Kabila regimes purged their rivals, with the aim of consolidating their hold on power and reducing their adversaries' threat capabilities. Though both ruling groups understood that exclusion would increase the likelihood of armed rebellion, they knew that their rivals' primary base of support (Darfur in the case of Sudan and eastern Congo in the case of DRC) was located some thousand kilometers from the capital. Thus, if an armed rebellion did materialize, the likelihood of it marshaling sufficient local support to take the capital was low. (The failure of Kabarebe's daring raid on Kinshasa through Bas-Congo is testament to this. With stronger support and networks among the Kinois, Kabarebe may have been able to topple the Kabila regime before Angola intervened.)

Bashir and Kabila's strategic choice would have been less clear-cut, however, if their rivals' base of support was not in Darfur or eastern Congo but, say, among large groups that surrounded the capital, in which case an armed rebellion would be practically the equivalent of a coup. Under such circumstances, Bashir and Kabila may have approached bargaining with their rivals differently and adopted a more accommodating posture to prevent the breakdown of powersharing in the first place. One implication that this counterfactual raises is that, as the short-term costs of coups and civil wars converge, the ruling group's incentive to exclude decreases. Accordingly, we would expect the commitment to powersharing to be mediated by a rival's *threat capabilities*—or mobilizational capacity to capture the capital city if excluded from state power. Unless a group possesses strong threat capabilities, the ruler is weakly constrained from excluding that group and appropriating its share of power for himself and his coethnics. However, for powersharing to be self-enforcing—such that the strong opposition group is as equally committed to the institution as the incumbent—the ruling group must also possess strong threat capabilities; otherwise the opposition will face few constraints from exploiting access to the central government to appropriate the ruling group's share of power. In other words, the costs of civil war must constrain not just the group currently in power, but constrain in expectation any actor that may seize power and become the leader in the future. If there is strong symmetry of threat capabilities between the two sides then not only does the ruling group have strong incentives to share power with the rival group, but the rival group also recognizes that there is little benefit of excluding the incumbent and his group, since it will similarly be vulnerable to an outside challenge.

The presence of mutually strong civil war capabilities does not *resolve* (initially at least) the commitment problem at the heart of the coup–civil war trap. Without agreed-upon rules or institutions regulating the distribution and transfer of sovereign power, elites embedded in each group are still vying to control the executive (and gain the international recognition and rents that come with it) and anticipate their rivals have the same intentions. This can lead to political instability and actually increase coup risk. While such irregular transfers of executive authority are costly to the ruler, who loses his seat, they are less costly to the ruling group, whose relative share of power is secured by its strong societal power (but also constrained by the strength of its rival). Consequently, under such conditions, rival groups choose to share power and reluctantly trade executive authority via coups, but which do not lead to a major redistribution of power, rather than pursuing ethnopolitical dominance, which is likely to provoke a mutually costly total war for absolute power.

Overall then, it is hypothesized that the balance of threat capabilities between the ruling group and its rivals may help to explain *how* the coup–civil war trap plays out. This represents the book's fifth core theoretical claim and produces the following hypotheses:

H5: Threat-capabilities theory of powersharing: The stronger the threat capabilities of the ruling group and a given rival group, the stronger incentives both sides have to commit to powersharing and trade coup risk for civil war risk.

H5a: When both the ruling group and the rival group have mutually strong threat capabilities, durable powersharing emerges and the ruler accepts coup risk over civil war risk.

H5b: When the ruling group's threat capabilities are high and the rival group's are low, powersharing is unlikely, and the ruler accepts civil war risk over coup risk.

H5c: When the ruling group's threat capabilities are low and the rival group's are high, unstable powersharing may emerge with intermediate levels of coup and civil war risk.

H5d: When the ruling group's threat capabilities are low and the rival group's are also low, powersharing is unlikely and the ruler accepts civil war risk over coup risk.

Table 10.1 summarizes the expected bargaining outcomes based on the balance of threat capabilities between the ruling group and a given rival group. As explained above, when the incumbent and a rival are strong (Quadrant II), the prediction is that powersharing will hold, even as it increases coup risk, as neither side sees any strategic benefit from

TABLE 10.1 *Balance of Threat Capabilities, Powersharing, and Relative Risk of Coups Versus Civil War*

	Strong opposition	Weak opposition
Strong ruling group	H5a: Powersharing and societal peace *Powersharing*: Yes *Coup risk*: High *Civil war risk*: Low	H5b: War-prone ethnocracies *Powersharing*: No *Coup risk*: Low *Civil war risk*: High
Weak ruling group	H5c: Repressive minority rule *Powersharing*: No *Coup risk*: Low *Civil war risk*: High	H5d: Unstable, violent, exclusionary regimes *Powersharing*: No *Coup risk*: Low *Civil war risk*: High

ethnopolitical exclusion and both are reluctant to bear the costs of what would be a devastating civil war.

In contrast, when groups have asymmetric threat capabilities, self-enforcing powersharing is significantly less likely. While both sides may wish to share access to the central government to avoid costly conflict, the power differential undermines such an agreement. For strong groups bargaining with weak groups (Quadrant I), the benefits of exclusion are quite high as it effectively nullifies the strategic threat from the rival group and locks in a larger control of the rents from holding office. This confronts weak ruling groups bargaining with strong groups with an acute dilemma (Quadrant III). Powersharing puts the stronger rival in a position to usurp power in a coup, likely leading to the permanent exclusion of the weak group. But employing exclusion to prevent such an outcome provokes a strategically costly civil war. Both are bad outcomes, but losing power via civil war is seen as more uncertain than in a coup in which its rival already controls a significant share of the state. This leads the weak group to resort to exclusion and high levels of repression to try to control their stronger rivals.

A similar dynamic leads powersharing to break down between mutually weak groups (Quadrant IV). As neither side possesses the mobilizational potential to hold the other to account if it reneges on powersharing, each has strong incentives to eliminate the other from state power before they are eliminated, leading to ethnic exclusion and civil war.

10.3 EMPIRICAL EVIDENCE: THE EFFECT OF BALANCE OF THREAT CAPABILITIES ON ETHNOPOLITICAL BARGAINING

To test these hypotheses, we adopt a parsimonious measure of a group's capabilities to strategically threaten the central government if excluded from state power. We include two dimensions in this calculation which we believe factor into the group's ability to credibly threaten to seize power:

• **Group size:** group's size as proportion of total population;
• **Proximity to the capital city:** the geographic distance between the center of a group's ethnic homeland and the capital city.

The power of population is inherently relative: a set number of people represents a larger share of the population in a smaller state than in a larger state and therefore represents more real power in that smaller state. For group population size as a proportion of the country's total population, we draw the data from the EPR 3.0 dataset. This results in a variable that can theoretically range from very nearly 0 (the group has only a tiny proportion of the state's population) to 1 (the group makes up the entire state population).

The power of proximity is not relative in the same way: the challenges of mobilizing forces and transporting supplies in order to project power over a certain distance is constant across countries and across groups within countries. That is, it varies at a constant rate depending on the distance, whether that distance represents the entirety of the state or just a small region. Thus, to create this measure, we begin with each group's capital city distance—the distance from its centroid (the mathematical average of all points' latitude and longitude) to the country's capital city.[5] We then standardize this capital city distance from 0 to 1 for all groups in the sample, using the group with the shortest capital city distance (the Americo-Liberians in Liberia, whose homeland is calculated as only 15 kilometers from Monrovia, the capital) and the longest capital city distance (the Makonde-Yao of Mozambique, whose homeland is in the northeast of the country and some 1,800 kilometers from Maputo, the capital) as reference points. This results in a variable that can range

---

[5] Results are substantively similar when using the minimum distance between the capital and the group's territory. For the geocoded EPR groups, see Julian Wucherpfennig, Nils B. Weidmann, Luc Girardin, Lars-Erik Cederman, and Andreas Wimmer, "Politically Relevant Ethnic Groups across Space and Time: Introducing the GeoEPR Dataset," *Conflict Management and Peace Science*, 28 (5) (2011): 423–437. Though GeoEPR is currently maintained as part of the EPR-ETH family of datasets, we found GeoEPR also matches closely with EPR 3.0 as well (not surprisingly, as they are both derived from the same base dataset, EPR 1.0) and provides valuable geospatial information on the politically relevant ethnic groups for the African countries of interest.

TABLE 10.2 *Summary Statistics (Threat Capabilities)*

Variable	Min.	Max.	Median	Mean	St. Dev.
Scaled size	0	1	0.10	0.17	0.19
Scaled (reverse) distance	0	1	0.79	0.74	0.21
Threat capabilities	0.03	0.97	0.48	0.47	0.16

from 0 (the centroid is as near to the capital as possible) to 1 (the centroid is as far from the capital as possible). Since proximity is more, not less, threatening, we then subtract this value from 1 to reverse the scale such that higher values represent greater threat capabilities.

As we have no theoretical reason to expect either of these variables to be more important than the other, we give them equal weight when calculating overall threat capabilities for each EPR group. This measure is generated by taking the arithmetic mean of the threat-by-size value and the threat-by-proximity value, resulting in a variable on the interval from 0 (least threatening) to 1 (most threatening). Summary statistics for this variable are presented in Table 10.2.

Using this coding of threat capabilities, we then construct the *Balance of threat capabilities* between the ruling group of a country for a given year vis-à-vis each given opposition group. For ease of interpretation, and because the joint effect will not necessarily be continuous,[6] the balance of threat-capabilities measure is captured through four interaction dummy variables (following Table 10.1) based on the ruling group and a given opposition group's threat capabilities. Strong groups are those in which their threat-capabilities scores are *above* the median for all groups in sub-Saharan Africa; weak groups are those in which their threat capabilities scores are *below* the median for all groups in sub-Saharan Africa. Not surprisingly, as reported in Table 10.3, low–high (LH) and low–low (LL) dyads are least common, while high–high (HH) and high–low (HL) dyads (where the ruling group is strong) are most common.

---

[6] What matters in expectation is not only the relative threat capabilities of the ruler and opposition but, when threat capabilities are asymmetric, whether it is the ruler or opposition that has the stronger threat capabilities. A pure continuous interaction term does not allow us to unpack this categorical effect and risks inaccurately labeling asymmetric dyads with one exceptionally strong side as having mutually high threat capabilities.

TABLE 10.3 *Distribution of Ruling Group-Rival Group Dyads by Balance of Threat Capabilities Across Sub-Saharan Africa, Independence to 2009*

	Strong opposition	Weak opposition
Strong ruling group	*HH threat capabilities* N = 2,088 *Proportion of dyads:* 33% *Example:* Ewe vs. Asante (Akan) in Ghana between 1981 and 2000	*HL threat capabilities* N = 2,242 *Proportion of dyads:* 37% *Example:* Shaigiya, Ja'aliyin, and Danagla (Arab) vs. Dinka between independence and 2011
Weak ruling group	*LH threat capabilities* N = 681 *Proportion of dyads:* 11% *Example:* Afrikaners vs. Black Africans in South Africa between 1947 and 1994	*LL threat capabilities* N = 1,079 *Proportion of dyads:* 18% *Example:* Krahn vs. Gio in Liberia between 1980 and 1990

To systematically test the relationship between balance of threat capabilities, powersharing, and coups and civil war after controlling for key confounds, we employ logistic regression with standard errors clustered by country to account for non-independence of ongoing political relationships within states, and with the cubic polynomial of each outcome variable to account for temporal dependence.[7] In addition to models containing only the balance of capabilities parameters, we include specifications containing a number of control variables that account for alternative explanations of elite bargaining, political violence, and governance outcomes, including: *GDP per capita, Log country population, Number of ethnic groups, Institutionalized regime* (dummy measure of whether a given country is governed by a single-party regime, multiparty regime, or democracy versus military government[8]), *Former French colony, Cold*

---

[7] This is especially pertinent for the powersharing models given the stickiness of inclusion and exclusion from year to year. Of the groups included in power in the previous year, some 99 percent are also included in power in the next year. On controlling for temporal dependence generally in regression analysis, see David B. Carter and Curtis S. Signorino, "Back to the Future: Modeling Time Dependence in Binary Data," *Political Analysis*, 18 (3) (2010): 271–292.

[8] Beatriz Magaloni, "Credible Powersharing and the Longevity of Authoritarian Rule," *Comparative Political Studies*, 41 (4–5) (2008): 715–741. Beatriz Magaloni, Jonathan Chu, and Eric Min, "Autocracies of the World, 1950–2012" (Stanford University, 2013).

War, Years since last coup, Ongoing rebellion, Post-conflict dyad, Past coup dyad, and *Year variable.*

The results from the logistic regressions are summarized in Table 10.4 using the Clarify statistical software and keeping all control variables at representative levels.[9] Overall, they are highly consistent with theoretical expectations. When both the ruling and a given rival group have high threat capabilities (above the median for sub-Saharan Africa), powersharing is statistically significantly more likely to endure, generally reducing armed rebellion but coming with a higher risk of coups. In contrast, when a given opposition group has weak threat capabilities, ruling groups are significantly less likely to include their rivals in the central government. This nullifies coup risk and increases rebellion risk. For weak ruling groups bargaining with strong groups, the results point to the strategic dilemma resulting from such conditions—neither inclusion nor exclusion is very appealing as both potentially can permanently displace them from power. In such a situation, no dominant strategy of inclusion or exclusion appears to emerge, and, accordingly, weak ruling groups bargaining with strong groups tend to face relatively high risks of both coups and civil wars.

10.4   DISCUSSION AND SENSITIVITY ANALYSIS

10.4.1 Testing the Robustness of the Results Employing an Alternative Measure of Ethnic Geography

The balance of threat capabilities between the ruling group and a given opposition group has a robust and consistent effect on ethnic powersharing: when the ruling group and opposition group both have high threat capabilities, rivals are significantly more likely to share power. Notably, this is true despite the fact that such circumstances also bring an elevated coup risk and (in some empirical cases) feature frequent coups. Even as these groups trade control of the executive, they do not fundamentally

---

[9] For full regression models, see Roessler and Ohls, "Self-enforcing Powersharing in Weak States." These predicted probabilities are generated using statistical models with all control variables and setting the variables to their mean values and temporal dependence cubic polynomial variables to their median values. The right skew of the latter leads to distorted (unrealistically low) predicted probabilities of all outcomes when estimated using mean values.

TABLE 10.4 *Balance of Threat Capabilities and Predicted Probabilities of Powersharing, Coups, and Armed Rebellion*

	Strong opposition	Weak opposition
Strong ruling group	H1 P(Powersharing): 57.4% P(Successful coup): 0.6% P(Armed rebellion): 0.4%	H2 P(Powersharing): 44.1% P(Successful coup): 0.0% P(Armed rebellion): 0.9%
Weak ruling group	H4 P(Powersharing): 47.4% P(Successful coup): 0.5% P(Armed rebellion): 1.2%	H3 P(Powersharing): 36.9% P(Successful coup): 0.1% P(Armed rebellion): 1.3%

change the distribution of power and thus are generally able to avoid costly civil wars.[10]

Using ethnic geography as a parsimonious measure of threat capabilities is not without limitations, however. Ethnicity's constructivist foundations—which accept that ethnic boundaries (and groups) are not fixed and that individuals possess multiple identities whose salience is situational—pose two possible challenges to the credibility of the empirical results.[11] First, identifying a stable and objective set of politically relevant ethnic groups is difficult, as a number of different ethnic and ethnoregional cleavages in a country could be seen as salient and lead to competing units of analysis.[12] For example, in Uganda one could categorize northerners as a single ethnoregional grouping or disaggregate the region into distinct ethnic groups (e.g., Acholi, Alur, Kakwa, Lango, Lugbara, Madi, and Teso). Which coding one chooses has material consequences on the groups included in the sample and the threat-capabilities scores assigned to those groups. Second, competition for state power and the coups and civil war that arise from this could shape the existence and

---

[10] The mispredictions of civil wars when the ruling group and opposition both have high threat capabilities are theoretically consistent with the argument put forth in this chapter as they have led to highly destructive and in some cases existential civil wars, such as the Biafran War in Nigeria in the late 1960s, Uganda in the early 1980s, and Rwanda in the early 1990s, leading to the Rwandan genocide. In Rwanda, the Hutu extremists chose extermination as the solution to the coup–civil war trap.

[11] Chandra, "Introduction."

[12] Fearon, "Ethnic and Cultural Diversity by Country."

intensity of a country's ethnic divisions, making identifiably different ethnic groups endogenous to political structures and events.[13]

To address both of these concerns and mitigate the problems that may arise from ethnicity's endogeneity to postcolonial politics, we check the sensitivity of the findings to alternative means of selecting relevant ethnic groups and their boundaries. For an alternate set of ethnic units of analysis, we rerun the analysis using data from Fearon's dataset of ethnic and cultural diversity across the globe, which provides information on the relative size of all ethnic groups that make up at least 1 percent of the population in 160 countries.[14] Of the thirty-five countries covered in both datasets, EPR identifies 217 ethnic groups, and Fearon identifies 292 ethnic groups. The key difference in the datasets is the level of aggregation they choose to demarcate ethnic-group boundaries; EPR tends to identify the relevant boundaries at a higher level of aggregation than Fearon. In the case of Northern Uganda mentioned previously, EPR codes the relevant social boundary as northerners (Langi, Acholi, Teso, Madi, Kakwa-Nubian, Lugbara, Alur) whereas Fearon's dataset includes each of these subgroups as individual units.[15] These differences in identifying relevant ethnic boundaries between the EPR dataset and Fearon's dataset are precisely the reason why it is important to check that the robustness of the results are not an artifact of which data source is used. We then calculate threat-capabilities' scores for each Fearon group based on relative population and group distance to capital city.[16] Using Fearon data, balance of threat-capabilities' dyads break down as reported in Table 10.5.

Using Fearon's data on ethnic groups leads to a similar set of HH dyads but a higher number of LH and LL dyads (a result of its tendency to rely on lower levels of group aggregation). To identify powersharing, coups, and group rebellion, we rely on the same data sources as above

---

[13] Fearon and Laitin, "Violence and the Social Construction of Ethnic Identities." Benn Eifert, Edward Miguel, and Daniel N. Posner, "Political Competition and Ethnic Identification in Africa," *American Journal of Political Science*, 54 (2) (2010): 494–510.

[14] Fearon, "Ethnic and Cultural Diversity by Country."

[15] Though the EPR, taking into account identity changes, recategorizes the relevant ethnic groups over time as region becomes less salient and ethnic identities more so.

[16] Data on relative group size come from Fearon's data. For distance to capital city, we use the GeoEPR-ETH dataset when the Fearon and EPR groups match. When there is a mismatch (often due to Fearon identifying a subset of a larger ethnic category), we rely on maps from Ethnologue, which reports spatial concentrations of ethnic groups in many African countries, to identify capital city distance.

TABLE 10.5 *Distribution of Dyads Using Fearon (2003) Data on Ethnic Geography, Independence to 2009*

	Strong opposition	Weak opposition
Strong ruling group	*HH threat capabilities* *N* = 2,206 *Proportion of dyads:* 31%	*HL threat capabilities* *N* = 1,850 *Proportion of dyads:* 26%
Weak ruling group	*LH threat capabilities* *N* = 1,202 *Proportion of dyads:* 17%	*LL threat capabilities* *N* = 1,800 *Proportion of dyads:* 26%

and conduct additional research when necessary to identify whether a given subgroup was a participant in a coup or rebellion.

The results from the estimated logistic regression models of *Ethnic powersharing, GroupSCoup,* and *Group Rebellion,* with all controls using the dyads defined by Fearon's groups as the unit of analysis, are reported in Table 10.6. Results are very similar to those using the EPR ethnic group configurations. Ruling groups are significantly more likely to include a given rival into their central government when both possess strong threat capabilities, significantly reducing civil war risk but increasing coup risk.

10.4.2 Restricting the Analysis to Group Configurations at Independence

The second potential concern is that the results suffer from endogeneity bias as competition for state power leads to changes in ethnic geography consistent with the purported hypotheses. Although plausible, this critique encounters significant theoretical and empirical limitations. Theoretically, while the effect of civil war on ethnic divisions is well discussed in the literature, there is almost no research suggesting endogenous construction of large identity groups from coups. Why these forms of violent conflict would have opposite effects on the construction of identity is not obvious.

Similarly, there are contradicting theories of whether access to power and the rents that come from power should lead to group enlargement[17] or group narrowing.[18] According to the EPR dataset, the active cases

---

[17] Posner, *Institutions and Ethnic Politics in Africa.*
[18] Bates, "Modernization, Ethnic Competition." Bueno de Mesquita et al., *The Logic of Political Survival*; Caselli and Coleman, "On the Theory of Ethnic Conflict."

TABLE 10.6 *Balance of Threat Capabilities and the Likelihood of Ethnic Inclusion, Coups, and Civil War Using Ethnic Configurations from Fearon (2003)*

	Ethnic powersharing		Successful coup		Rebellion onset	
HH threat capabilities	0.66*** (0.21)		0.52** (0.22)		−1.38*** (0.39)	
HL threat capabilities		−0.42* (0.24)		−0.89** (0.36)		1.26*** (0.38)
LH threat capabilities		−1.03*** (0.33)		−0.30 (0.32)		1.71*** (0.53)
LL threat capabilities		−0.78** (0.36)		−0.34 (0.45)		1.15* (0.62)
Log GDP per capita	0.25* (0.14)	0.28** (0.14)	−0.69 (0.39)	−0.74* (0.38)	−0.56** (0.25)	−0.56** (0.26)
Log country population	0.22* (0.13)	0.24* (0.14)	−0.06 (0.23)	−0.08 (0.22)	−0.28 (0.21)	−0.24 (0.22)
Ethnic fractionalization	0.38 (1.02)	0.78 (0.94)	−0.61 (0.86)	−0.78 (0.92)	−2.11** (1.04)	−1.99** (0.95)
Institutionalized regime	0.41 (0.25)	0.39 (0.26)	0.78 (0.47)	0.79* (0.46)	−0.08 (0.34)	−0.08 (0.31)
Former French colony	0.55 (0.37)	0.59 (0.37)	0.52 (0.34)	0.53 (0.35)	−1.07* (0.56)	−1.10** (0.56)
Pastcoup			2.19*** (0.44)	2.11*** (0.46)		
Pastconflict					0.45 (0.36)	0.38 (0.36)

	(1)	(2)	(3)	(4)	(5)	(6)
Cold War	0.58	0.59	0.83	0.84	1.25*	1.17
	(0.51)	(0.51)	(0.84)	(0.84)	(0.75)	(0.72)
Ongoing rebellion					-0.32	-0.42
					(0.84)	(0.88)
Year	0.04**	0.04**	-0.05	-0.05*	0.03	0.03
	(0.02)	(0.02)	(0.03)	(0.03)	(0.03)	(0.033)
t	-1.70***	-1.69***	-0.15	-0.15	-0.10	-0.08
	(0.16)	(0.16)	(0.10)	(0.10)	(0.15)	(0.15)
t_2	0.07***	0.07***	0.01	0.01	0.01	0.00
	(0.01)	(0.01)	(0.01)	(0.01)	(0.01)	(0.01)
t_3	-0.00***	-0.00***	-0.00	-0.00	-0.00	-0.00
	(0.00)	(0.00)	(0.00)	(0.00)	(0.00)	(0.00)
constant	-73.32	-72.57	101.94	105.40	-57.65	-62.87
	(35.33)	(35.63)	(53.15)	(54.70)	(57.44)	(59.21)
N	6542	6542	6436	6436	6436	6436
states	34	34	34	34	34	34
pseudo r²	0.77	0.78	0.10	0.10	0.07	0.07

*: $p < 0.10$; **: $p < 0.05$; ***: $p < 0.01$.

TABLE 10.7 *Balance of Threat Capabilities and the Likelihood of Ethnic Inclusion, Coups, and Civil War with Independence Group Configurations*

	Ethnic powersharing		Successful coup			Rebellion onset
	1	2	3	4	5	6
HH threat capabilities	0.54** (0.26)		1.43** (0.64)		-0.66 (0.49)	
HL threat capabilities		-0.43 (0.31)		-2.78*** (1.05)		0.59 (0.50)
LH threat capabilities		-0.47 (0.41)		-0.39 (0.63)		1.12** (0.54)
LL threat capabilities		-0.92** (0.46)		-1.82*** (0.60)		0.44 (0.76)
Log GDP per capita	0.48* (0.26)	0.55* (0.29)	-0.29 (0.48)	-0.44 (0.46)	-0.88** (0.37)	-0.92** (0.4))
Log country population	0.02 (0.13)	0.07 (0.13)	-0.04 (0.22)	-0.02 (0.19)	-0.19 (0.20)	-0.15 (0.21)
Number of ethnic groups	-0.03 (0.06)	-0.07 (0.08)	-0.20** (0.09)	-0.18* (0.10)	0.10 (0.07)	0.11 (0.08)
Institutionalized regime	0.47 (0.31)	0.41 (0.34)	0.49 (0.46)	0.44 (0.46)	-0.52 (0.42)	-0.52 (0.43)
Former French colony	0.40 (0.39)	0.37 (0.39)	0.47 (0.47)	0.47 (0.46)	-0.12 (0.74)	-0.16 (0.75)
Cold War	1.05* (0.59)	1.04 (0.60)	0.63 (0.70)	0.60 (0.70)	0.81 (0.85)	0.75 (0.83)
Past coup			1.09 (0.75)	0.86 (0.77)		
Past conflict					-0.06 (0.56)	-0.07 (0.56)
Ongoing rebellion					-0.10 (0.76)	-0.10 (0.74)
Year	0.06*** (0.02)	0.06*** (0.02)	-0.02 (0.03)	-0.02 (0.03)	0.01 (0.03)	0.01 (0.03)
t	-1.63*** (0.17)	-1.63*** (0.17)	-0.21** (0.10)	-0.23** (0.11)	-0.15 (0.14)	-0.16 (0.14)
$t2$	0.07*** (0.01)	0.07*** (0.01)	0.01* (0.01)	0.01* (0.01)	0.01 (0.01)	0.01 (0.01)
$t3$	-0.00*** (0.00)	-0.00*** (0.00)	-0.00 (0.00)	-0.00* (0.00)	-0.00 (0.00)	-0.00 (0.00)
constant	-119.08 (44.54)	-118.92 (43.75)	36.39 (60.01)	36.68 (62.28)	-25.84 (56.42)	-26.09 (58.71)
N	5388	5388	4875	4875	4875	4875
states	35	35	35	35	35	35
pseudo r²	0.79	0.79	0.13	0.15	0.04	0.05

*: $p < 0.10$; **: $p < 0.05$; ***: $p < 0.01$.

of fractionalization in postcolonial Africa are consistent with the latter group-narrowing hypothesis, which biases the results against us. The EPR dataset codes fifteen instances of larger ethnic coalitions splitting into smaller ethnic divisions (with thirty-seven resulting groups), of which 93 percent (all but one) occurred when the group was in, or coming into, power. Ethnic recombination is less common, with only five incidents (from twelve original groups).

Nonetheless, to limit the potential bias that may arise as ethnic configurations change during the postcolonial period, we rerun the estimations used to report Figure 10.4 but only using ethnic configurations as they exist at independence, which reduces the total observations by about 7 percent. Restricting the data analysis to only groups as they exist at independence excludes any incidences of fractionalization and amalgamation as a result of post-independence politics.

The results are reported in Table 10.7. The results are nearly identical, especially on the effect on powersharing and coup risk, increasing our confidence that the empirics are not merely driven by postcolonial changes in ethnic geography.

10.5 IMPLICATIONS

10.5.1 Additional Insights into the Coup–Civil War Trap

The threat-capabilities theory of powersharing offers additional insights into two striking empirical regularities that have been identified in previous parts of this book. The first is the existence of the coup–civil war trap. The coup-proofing model of civil war makes intuitive sense, and there is no shortage of evidence of rulers employing ethnopolitical exclusion to substitute civil war risk for coup risk. But what is striking about Figure 8.1, illustrating the coup–civil war trade-off, is that not all rulers in postcolonial Africa have pursued ethnopolitical exclusion as a coup-proofing strategy. In fact, quite paradoxically, some rulers have committed to powersharing even at the cost of increased coup risk. Why have these rulers adopted what seems like an irrational political strategy? The threat-capabilities theory of powersharing helps to account for this counterintuitive outcome. When rivals possess particularly strong mobilizational capabilities, rulers—or at least their ruling groups[19]—may see coups, not civil war, as the lesser of two evils.

---

[19] It is important to distinguish between the interests of the ruler and the interests of the ruling group in which the ruler is embedded and on whose support the ruler is dependent

In countries where multiple groups with strong threat capabilities dominate politics, we expect peaceful, if uneasy, powersharing to endure. Though any one group may prefer to dominate the central government, its ability to do so is constrained by the costs and strategic benefit of exclusion. In contrast to countries dominated by dyads with asymmetric threat capabilities, where the costs of civil war tend to be asymmetric and disproportionately borne by the excluded group, when both groups have high threat capabilities it is likely the costs of the civil war will be symmetric as well. Under these circumstances, rivals may prefer coup risk, which is a potentially less costly way of changing power, than a bloody civil war for exclusive control of the central government (as seen in the genocidal conflict in Rwanda in 1994).

Two paradigmatic cases illustrating how strong symmetric threat capabilities underwrite powersharing, even as groups trade power via coups, are Ghana and Benin. Both countries are relatively small in area (below the median for Africa) yet are divided between four relatively large ethnic or ethnoregional blocs,[20] giving each group relatively strong threat capabilities.[21] Throughout the postcolonial period, ethnic identities have been politically salient and have structured how competition for state power has played out.[22] In Benin in the first decade after independence, the country was severely divided along "ethnoregional lines" between the Fon in the Southwest, the Nagot-Yoruba in the East, and the Bariba

---

upon to stay in power. While rulers may prefer to use exclusion to substitute coup risk for civil war risk to protect their personal hold on power, under conditions of mutually strong threat capabilities, this offers little political or strategic advantage for the ruling group as a whole, whose relative share of power is not only secured by its societal power but is also constrained by the strength of its rival. Consequently, in the face of a devastating civil war—the costs of which would be borne by the group's members—the ruling group is unlikely to support the ruler's rejection of powersharing in a bid to consolidate his personal hold on power.

[20] In Benin, the EPR dataset identifies the key groups as: Northern (15 percent of the population), Southwestern (15 percent), Southeastern (18.5 percent), and South/Central (33 percent). In Ghana, Ewe (13 percent of population), Asante (Akan) (15 percent), Northern Groups (23.5 percent), and Other Akans (34.5 percent).

[21] In Benin, all groups have high threat capabilities, except the northern group; its score falls just below the Africa median (0.45 vs. 0.48); it is relatively large in size (66 percentile for Africa) but relatively far from the capital (36 percentile for Africa).

[22] David R. Smock and Audrey C. Smock, *The Politics of Pluralism: A Comparative Study of Lebanon and Ghana* (Cambridge: Cambridge University Press, 1975). Naomi Chazan, "Ethnicity and Politics in Ghana," *Political Science Quarterly*, 97 (3) (1982): 461–485. Dov Ronen, *Dahomey: Between Tradition and Modernity* (Ithaca, NY: Cornell University Press, 1975). Chris Allen, Joan Baxter, Michael S. Radu, and Keith Somerville, *Benin, The Congo, Burkina Faso: Politics, Economics and Society* (London and New York: Pinter, 1989). Decalo, *Historical Dictionary of Benin*.

in the North.[23] The locus of power shifted between these ethnoregional blocs as executive control traded hands between them.[24] In Ghana's early postcolonial governments, the ethnic power base also shifted significantly from regime to regime, starting with the privileged position of southern Akan groups under Kwame Nkrumah and ending with the Ewe-based ruling clique under Jerry Rawlings.[25]

As bargaining over state power played out in these countries, rulers did not operate much differently than their counterparts in other African states. Seeking to maximize their power vis-à-vis their rivals, rulers sought to increase the share of rents and political positions controlled by their coethnics and other allies.[26] Where these cases differ, however, is how these strategic interactions played out. Nearly each time a ruler in Ghana or Benin in the 1960s and 1970s pursued such a policy in an attempt to entrench their hold on power, they were thrown out of power in a coup d'état, leading to a new, but *ethnically inclusive*, political configuration.[27]

Thus, in these cases, the coup (backed up by the threat of a costly civil war) would serve as the mechanism to uphold powersharing. A paradigmatic example of this is seen in Benin in the first few years after independence. Benin's inaugural president, Hubert Maga, hailed from the northern part of the country and formed an unstable alliance with various leaders from the South. But, as these alliances frayed due to political conflicts between rival ethnic elites, Maga moved to consolidate his hold on power by promoting "Northerners in large numbers . . . throughout the entire governmental system, and the gendarmerie, in particular, was packed with Baribas who often regarded themselves as Maga's private militia."[28] But in the face of what were perceived as discriminatory practices combined with austerity measures in the public sector, southerners, led by the trade unions, launched a general strike and paralyzed the country's two largest cities,

---

[23] Samuel Decalo, "Benin: First of the New Democracies," in John F. Clark and David E. Gardinier, eds., *Political Reform in Francophone Africa* (Boulder, Col.: Westview Press, 1997), p. 44.

[24] In the first five governments between 1960 and 1965, executive power went from a northerner to a Fon to a Yoruba to a northerner to a Fon. See Decalo, *Historical Dictionary of Benin.*

[25] Chazan, "Ethnicity and Politics in Ghana."

[26] Chazan, "Ethnicity and Politics in Ghana." Decalo, *Historical Dictionary of Benin.*

[27] Both countries would experience five successful interethnic coups (in which at least some of the coup conspirators hailed from a different ethnic group as the head of state) in the first couple of decades after independence.

[28] Samuel Decalo, "Regionalism, Politics, and the Military in Dahomey," *The Journal of Developing Areas*, 7 (3) (1973): 449–478, at p. 458.

Porto Novo and Cotonou. As the conflict intensified, "Colonel Christopher Soglo, Chief of Staff of the Army, announced that the armed forces were taking over power *in order to avert civil war.*"[29] This in turn swung the pendulum of power in favor of the South, though subsequent coups by northerners, who maintained a strong influence in the military, prevented southerners from monopolizing power.[30] The societal balance of power helped to preserve peace through durable but uneasy powersharing.

10.5.2 The Structural Roots of Co-conspirator Civil Wars

The second empirical regularity identified in Part III is the prevalence of co-conspirator wars in postcolonial Africa, which seem to be particularly likely from the 1980s onward. The threat-capabilities theory of power-sharing also helps to account for this pattern. A number of these inter-ethnic co-conspirator were from or included peripheral groups, almost all of which were excluded from power since independence but, taking advantage of poor governance, persistent economic decline, and often external support, managed to penetrate or fight their way to the center. Examples include the Islamists in Sudan; the Congolese Tutsi and Katanga in DRC; the Toubou and Zaghawa and then the Zaghawa and Hadjerai in Chad; the Tigray and Eritreans in Ethiopia; the Nyankole, Baganda, and Acholi and then the Nyankole and Baganda in Uganda; the Krahn, Gio, and Mano in Liberia; and the Shona and Ndebele in Zimbabwe. Strikingly, each of these alliances would suffer a violent rupture in the post-liberation period save the Baganda–Nyankole alliance at the heart of the National Resistance Movement, in which both groups have strong threat capabilities. The threat-capabilities theory of powersharing offers additional insights into why this is the case. Given each side's remoteness from the capital, their members know that if they are excluded from government the chances of them reclaiming power are low, so they have strong incentives to prevent their exclusion. And consolidating power by excluding their co-conspirators is tempting, given their partners' weak threat capabilities. Thus, weak threat capabilities between co-conspira-tors increases strategic uncertainty as both sides calculate the other has strong incentives to employ ethnic exclusion to lock in power.

---

[29] Ronald Matthews, *African Powder Keg: Revolt and Dissent in Six Emergent Nations* (London: Bodley Head, 1966), p. 152.
[30] Decalo, "Regionalism, Politics, and the Military in Dahomey." Ronen, *Dahomey*; Allen et al., *Benin, The Congo, Burkina Faso.*

TABLE 10.8 *State Size, Ethnopolitical Exclusion, Rebellion, and Coups in Africa*

State size	Percentage of included opposition groups	Mean rebellions by opposition groups	Mean coups by opposition groups
Below Median	59%	0.008	0.010
Above Median	29%	0.012	0.003

10.5.3 Africa's Big State Problem

A third contribution of the threat-capabilities model of powersharing is that it helps to account for Africa's big states problem[31]—that is, why the region's largest countries, such as Sudan, DRC, Angola, Chad, and Ethiopia, have been disproportionately plagued by ethnopolitical exclusion and civil war. In fact, as illustrated in Table 10.8, large states in the region tend, on average, to include half as many ethnic rivals in the central government as small states and experience 50 percent more group rebellions.

In his seminal book on political topography in Africa, Jeffrey Herbst argues that African conditions of low and unevenly distributed populations "privilege nations that are relatively small."[32] Herbst emphasizes that smallness reduces the costs of state consolidation. Interestingly, state consolidation has not necessarily translated into political consolidation: small states are more than three times more likely to experience coups than large ones. The analysis in this chapter offers an alternative logic to account for these patterns: size reduces ethnic rivals' capabilities to use the threat of force to hold the ruling group accountable if it rejects inclusive governance.

10.6 CONCLUSION

One of the enduring puzzles in political science is why ethnic politics leads to large-scale political violence in some countries but is largely

---

[31] Clapham, *Africa and the International System*. Christopher S. Clapham, Jeffrey Herbst, and Greg Ira Mills, eds., *Big African States* (Johannesburg: Witwatersrand University Press, 2006); Elliott Green, "On the Size and Shape of African States," *International Studies Quarterly*, 56 (2) (2012): 229–244.

[32] Herbst, *States and Power in Africa*, p. 140.

peaceful in others. This is especially true in Africa. While ethnicity is politically salient in most countries, only some (e.g., Sudan, DRC, and Chad) have been wracked by high levels of ethnopolitical exclusion and civil war, whereas others (e.g., Ghana, Malawi, and Benin) have been characterized by ethnic powersharing and durable ethnic peace. This chapter puts forth a theory to account for durable powersharing in Africa. Counterintuitively, it finds that ethnic powersharing is a positive function of the civil war capabilities of both the ruling and rival groups— that is, their mobilizational potential to forcibly seize power when they are excluded from the central government. When both are strong, both prefer to accept the risk of coups to the risk of civil wars and neither is willing to systematically exclude the other from government; continuous, if fluid, powersharing emerges. Extensive quantitative evidence supports the theoretical argument and provides novel empirical insights into how the coup–civil war plays out across postcolonial Africa. It also sheds further light on the strategic relationship between coups and civil war. Coups are significantly more likely from groups that can credibly back them up with the threat of a strong civil war.

The threat-capability theory of powersharing helps to account for why some African countries have been plagued by large-scale ethnopolitical violence and others have been characterized by durable ethnic peace. It also illuminates why the violent, exclusionary equilibrium has proven to be so vicious and persistent for, say, Sudan, Chad, Ethiopia, and DRC as these countries have highly dispersed or unequal societal configurations, which are difficult to change. Even more, like the slave-trade wars in the seventeenth through nineteenth centuries,[33] the violence in these countries has tended not to lead to nation-building and societal consolidation but ethnic fractionalization,[34] further exacerbating the strategic problems that undermine powersharing.

---

[33] Nunn, "The Long-Term Effects of Africa's Slave Trades."
[34] Jeffrey Herbst, "War and the State in Africa," *International Security*, 14 (4) (1990): 117–139. Fearon and Laitin, "Violence and the Social Construction of Ethnic Identities."

II

Conclusion

The study of civil war, or the outbreak of large-scale political violence between a central government and an armed domestic opposition, has been at the center of the international development agenda over the past twenty years. As one of the dominant sources of excess mortality, population displacement, and economic underdevelopment in the post-World War II era, scholars and practitioners alike have sought to better understand how violent conflicts begin, with the goal of developing more effective conflict management and prevention policies. Much has been written on this important subject.[1] Whereas existing research does well to explain why some countries are more vulnerable to civil war than others or the microlevel processes driving individuals to join a rebellion, we have fewer systematic explanations of the politics of civil war onset—that is, how political bargaining over state power ends in large-scale political violence. This book fills this critical gap in the literature. It builds a mesolevel theory of civil war that privileges the importance of the informal institutions that represent the superstructure of weak states, in which rulers strike alliances with violence specialists embedded in different societal groups as a means to extend their control beyond their own ethnic group. Such interethnic alliances reduce civil war risk by sharing access to scarce states resources, which are essential not only for rivals to keep their own political networks intact but also as a political instrument to cultivate local support and information necessary for the government to effectively countermobilize in the face of societal dissidence.

---

[1] See literature review in Chapter 2.

Extensive qualitative evidence from Sudan's Darfur has illustrated how interethnic political networks facilitate the production of cooperative counterinsurgency. One of the key takeaways is that inclusion empowers trusted brokers from rival groups who can credibly bridge the gap between state and society. Key to their credibility is their ability to not only provide patronage to their clients and coethnics but also to protect them from state violence. I have shown how this helps to account for the divergent conflict outcomes in Darfur in the early 1990s to the early 2000s. In the early 1990s, the Islamic Movement had extensive networks in Darfur, especially among non-Arab ethnic groups. Islamists in these networks possessed the leverage to constrain the government's use of indiscriminate violence against their coethnics and in turn convinced local communities to refrain from abetting or assisting the insurgents. Peace prevailed. However, after the split in the Islamic Movement in late 1999 and the dismantling of its networks in Darfur, non-Arab Darfurian brokers lacked leverage over the regime, which, in turn, weakened their local influence. Their efforts to stave off a devastating civil war proved in vain.

The puzzle at the heart of any meso-level theory of civil war, then, is why, if these interethnic bargains and alliances are the key to societal peace, do rulers fail to forge them at the risk of large-scale political violence. I have argued that three broad theoretical frameworks—one rooted in an instrumental, or economic, logic; one based on cultural factors; and the final connected to the strategic environment—help to account for the phenomenon of ethnopolitical exclusion.

According to an instrumental logic, exclusion is a means to maximize the economic rents rulers and their allies extract from controlling the state. The fewer groups and power brokers included in the central government, the more spoils to go around for those inside. Instrumental exclusion produces large-scale political violence when the ruler miscalculates the mobilizational capabilities of those targeted for exclusion. An alternative logic suggests that rulers structure their regimes and alliances based on what they see as culturally appropriate. For ethnonationalists, who feel a strong attachment to their group and value (and are valued for) advancing the interests and wellbeing of their group, exclusion is a means to credibly signal they are committed to taking care of their own.

Instrumental and cultural explanations of regime formation have been at the heart of the comparative politics literature.[2] And rightfully so, as there is no shortage of evidence illustrating how elites manipulate their

[2] Bueno de Mesquita et al., *The Logic of Political Survival.* Weber, *Economy and Society.*

political control to maximize economic wealth and how their social identity mediates their political strategies. But, as this book has extensively argued, strategic forces can have just as powerful, if not even more powerful, effects on regime formation and ethnopolitical exclusion.

The strategic dynamic at the heart of weak states is that in the absence of strong institutions or third-party enforcers, rivals must rely on the threat of force to induce powersharing. The problem is that whereas the threat of force is necessary to defend one's share of power, it can also be used for offensive purposes: to eliminate rivals, appropriate their share of power, and lock in a larger share of power for the attacking group. The inability of rival societal groups to credibly commit not to exploit their force capabilities to capture sovereign power for themselves represents the key cause of regime instability in weak states. This commitment problem has been exacerbated by the international community's use of sovereign power (i.e. executive control of the government) as a means to assign legitimacy and allocate economic and military assistance. Following from this strategic logic, ethnopolitical exclusion represents an inefficient solution to the commitment problem that plagues powersharing in weak states as it leads rulers to substitute civil war risk for coup risk.

I have derived this strategic logic of ethnopolitical exclusion from an in-depth qualitative analysis of the breakdown of the Islamic Movement in Sudan and the outbreak of the 2002–2003 Darfur civil war. The breakdown of trust and a sense of a "shared future" between Sudan's top Islamists opened the door for the commitment problem to dominate strategic interactions. As uncertainty increased, the regime factionalized along ethnoregional lines, and Sudan's president, Omar al-Bashir, used force to eliminate his sheikh, Hassan al-Turabi, and Turabi loyalists from the central government, though at the cost of increasing the opportunity for civil war in Darfur. The Sudan case illuminates the coup–civil war trade-off that confronts rulers in weak, ethnically divided states.

Beyond the Sudan case, I have employed the EPR dataset and original data on the ethnicity of coup conspirators and rebel movements to test the generalizability of the coup–civil war trap and the strategic logic of ethnopolitical exclusion across sub-Saharan Africa. Consistent with the political networks hypothesis (H1), ethnic powersharing reduces the risk of civil war from members of groups included in the central government, but, consistent with the notion of the coup–civil war trap (H2), groups included in the central government are more likely to be able to usurp power in a coup. This evidence also supports the hypothesis that rulers employ ethnopolitical exclusion as a coup-proofing strategy (H3). Qualitative evidence from

Sudan, Liberia, Chad, and the DRC illuminate the mechanics of ethnopolitical exclusion as a coup-proofing strategy. Finally, I have shown that the strategic logic of ethnopolitical exclusion, more than an instrumental or cultural logic, can explain the tragic phenomenon of co-conspirator civil wars in postcolonial Africa, in which the very comrades-in-arms who came together to overthrow a dictatorial incumbent ended up turning on each other with devastating consequences (H4). Though rarely analyzed in this way, Africa's Great War that erupted in the DRC in August 1998 is a paradigmatic case of a co-conspirator civil war. Original fieldwork in the DRC and Rwanda illustrates how the expulsion order by Congo's president, Laurent-Désiré Kabila, against his comrades in the RPF in late July 1998 represented a preemptive strike to coup-proof his regime at the price of triggering the most devastating war since World War II.

Overall, the book offers extensive qualitative and quantitative evidence in support of a strategic theory of civil war in postcolonial Africa. But one key puzzle that follows from this analysis is that, as prevalent as ethnic-based civil war has been in postcolonial Africa, not every African country has experienced ethnic exclusion and large-scale political violence. In fact, as explained at the outset of this book, half of African states have never had a civil war and durable ethnic powersharing has prevailed. What accounts for these counter-cases of durable ethnic powersharing and societal peace? How have rulers in these countries managed to overcome the commitment problem that has provoked some of Africa's most devastating civil wars?

In the book's penultimate chapter I explore these questions. One of the striking implications of the existence of a coup–civil war trap, as illustrated in Figure 8.1, is that some rulers have accepted coup risk over civil war risk. Why would rulers continue to commit to ethnic powersharing if it enables one's ethnic rivals to seize power in a coup d'état? This puzzle is illuminated by the cases of Benin and Ghana where postcolonial politics was dominated by interethnic coups but no ruler embraced the "Idi Amin option," in which the military and other organs of the state were violently purged to prevent future coups from ethnic rivals.

One potential explanation, internally consistent with the coup–civil war trap, is that rulers are more likely to commit to powersharing as the strategic costs of civil war increase. When ethnopolitical exclusion merely substitutes the risk of a coup for the risk of a devastating civil war that threatens to bring down the incumbent government, then we would expect the ruler's incentive structure to change. As rulers become less accepting of civil wars, they have stronger incentives to commit to powersharing. Powersharing is only self-enforcing, however, if the opposition faces the same incentive structure—that it too would face a strategically costly civil war if it tried to monopolize power in a coup. This suggests that in weak states powersharing is self-enforcing when both the ruling group and opposition group possess strong threat capabilities (H5). Consistent with this claim, I have shown that ethnic geography (i.e. a group's size and proximity to the capital) as a measure of a group's threat capabilities significantly predicts the durability of powersharing. As the ruling and opposition groups' size and proximity to the center increases, powersharing is significantly more likely and the groups are willing to accept coup risk over civil war risk.

The threat-capabilities theory of powersharing sheds new light on why Africa's small states, like Ghana, Benin, Gambia, and Togo have been consumed by coups but not civil wars and Africa's large states, like Sudan, Chad, the DRC, and Angola have been much more likely to experience civil war and few ethnic transfers of power via coups. It also helps to inform the seemingly anomalous cases of Rwanda and Burundi; though small states, the extreme disparity in population size between Hutu and Tutsi has undermined self-enforcing powersharing.

11.2 CONTRIBUTIONS

Overall, this book advances the study of ethnic politics, coups, and civil war in several significant ways. First, building on the body of work of Wimmer and Cederman,[3] it accounts for the strong relationship between ethnopolitical exclusion and civil war. Wimmer, Cederman, and colleagues rightfully emphasize the importance of political and economic grievances as a key mechanism linking ethnic exclusion with armed rebellion.[4] Groups barred from the central government are denied access not only to state power but also to control of key economic rents needed for survival and security. Less emphasis, however, has been placed on how ethnic exclusion creates an opportunity structure for large-scale political violence by facilitating insurgency formation and undermining the government's counterinsurgency capabilities. Regarding insurgency formation, ethnic exclusion creates a pool of dissidents who often share a geographic homeland and strong social institutions (e.g., common language, norms of reciprocity)

---

[3] Wimmer et al., "Ethnic Politics and Armed Conflict." Cederman et al., "Why Do Ethnic Groups Rebel?" Cederman et al., "Horizontal Inequalities." Wimmer, *Waves of War.* Cederman et al., *Inequality, Grievances, and Civil War.*

[4] Cederman et al., *Inequality, Grievances, and Civil War.* Wimmer, *Waves of War.*

that provide would-be rebels with the terrain and social capital needed to establish an armed organization. Simultaneously, ethnic exclusion hinders the government's support from members of the excluded group, limiting its ability to extract local information but also the group's ability to constrain the government from resorting to indiscriminate violence.[5]

The second contribution is that it offers a complete, integrated theory of why rulers adopt a political strategy of ethnopolitical exclusion at the cost of increasing the risk of civil war. In doing so, it directly addresses Blattman and Miguel's critique of the civil war literature that "one of the most dominant rational explanations for civil war, conflict as the result of commitment problems that prevent socially desirable agreements between fighting sides, has barely been examined."[6] I argue that one of the primary channels by which the commitment problem leads to bargaining failure and civil war in weak states is via the shadow of the coup d'état. Fearful that bringing their rivals into the central government will increase their capabilities to bring about a sudden, permanent shift in the distribution of power in the future, rulers tend to undersupply how much real power they share, leading to bargaining failure and conflict.

In offering an integrated theory about how the commitment problem prevents rulers from striking the bargains necessary to avert civil war, this book also is one of the first to systematically unravel the strategic relationship between coups and civil wars in weak states. Most of the existing literature has tended to study these two phenomena in isolation. But this artificial division within the conflict literature has hindered our theoretical understanding of the politics of political survival in weak states. In this book, I conceive of coups and civil wars as substitutes or competing risks. Both represent anti-regime technologies that dissidents may use to challenge the ruler's hold on power, but they differ in that coup conspirators leverage partial control of the state (and the resources and matériel that come with access to the state) in their bid to capture political power, whereas rebels or insurgents lack such access and have to build a private military organization to challenge the central government and its military. The difference in organizational basis matters because it affects the mobilizational costs necessary to credibly threaten the ruler's hold on power. Partial control of the state, especially the most strategic points of the regime (such as, military and finance), lowers the mobilizational costs dissidents must overcome to seize power in a coup. In

[5] Mason, "The Political Economy of Death Squads." Goodwin, *No Other Way Out.* Kalyvas, *The Logic of Violence in Civil War.*
[6] Blattman and Miguel, "Civil War."

contrast, for those outside of the regime, the burden of mobilization is much greater; unable to rely on partial control of the state, these dissidents must build, finance, and equip their own private army. These asymmetric mobilizational costs produce asymmetric risks for the ruler and create an incentive structure for rulers to generally choose political strategies that substitute civil war risk for coup risk—except when a group possesses exceptionally strong civil war capabilities, which, as explained in Chapter 10, reduce the advantages of using ethnopolitical exclusion as a strategy of political survival.

In conceiving of coups and civil wars as substitutes, another innovation to come out of the book is the model of the coup–civil war trap. In weak states, rulers need to strike alliances with elites embedded in rival ethnic groups to secure societal peace, but this opens the door for rivals to usurp power in a future coup d'état; excluding ethnic rivals eliminates their coup-making capabilities but at the cost of increased risk of civil war. One counterintuitive implication of the coup–civil war trap is that coups, as substitutes for civil war, can effectively prevent the outbreak of large-scale political violence. The history of Ghana and Benin provide evidence as to how interethnic coups averted the costly ethnic-based civil wars that devastated other African countries, such as Uganda, Sudan, and Chad. But these interethnic coups need to be backed up by the credible threat of a devastating civil war or they will be nullified through ethnopolitical exclusion. Counterintuitively, this finds that civil war capabilities predict coup risk.

This counterintuitive finding has motivated a novel theory of power-sharing in weak states based on the balance of threat capabilities between rulers and their rivals. Existing research tends to focus on the importance of either formal institutions[7] or external intervention.[8] While both factors can serve as key levers to reduce uncertainty, most powersharing regimes since World War II have emerged without external intervention, and in most weak states informal institutions have greater influence than formal ones.[9] Under such conditions, in which societal groups cannot rely on strong institutions or external actors to hold rulers accountable, the distribution of power is ultimately determined by the threat of force. But

---

[7] Arend Lijphart, *Democracy in Plural Societies: A Comparative Exploration* (New Haven, Conn.: Yale University Press, 1977); Magaloni, "Credible Powersharing." Pippa Norris, *Driving Democracy: Do Powersharing Institutions Work?* (Cambridge: Cambridge University Press, 2008).

[8] Caroline A. Hartzell and Matthew Hoddie, *Crafting Peace: Powersharing Institutions and the Negotiated Settlement of Civil Wars* (University Park, Pa.: Pennsylvania State University Press, 2007). Walter, *Committing to Peace.*

[9] Helmke and Levitsky, "Informal Institutions." Reno, *Warlord Politics and African States.*

the key question is when does the threat of force lead to a peaceful and productive equilibrium underwritten by powersharing and when does it merely reproduce the exclusion–conflict cycle? I have demonstrated that one source of credible powersharing rests in a group's societal power, in which a given group possesses the mobilizational potential to credibly threaten to recapture state power from its societal base *if it is excluded from the central government*. Unless a group possesses strong threat capabilities, the ruler is weakly constrained from excluding that group and appropriating its share of power for himself and his coethnics. However, for powersharing to be self-enforcing, the ruling group similarly must possess strong threat capabilities—otherwise the opposition will face few constraints from exploiting access to the central government to appropriate the ruling group's share of power.

The final contributions of the book are substantive and methodological. Given their scale, the Darfur civil war and Africa's Great War have attracted quite a bit of attention relative to other African conflicts. There is no shortage of excellent scholarship on these conflicts that has informed the research in this book. But almost exclusively these monographs are contemporary political histories, offering different narratives on the key events leading to war and insights on how the wars have played out. In focusing singularly on these conflicts, these books tend to emphasize their particularistic and exceptional dimensions. Rarely are these conflicts studied from a comparative perspective and employed to generate or test theories of political violence.[10] This is a detriment both to our understanding of these important conflicts and to political science as these conflicts may contain important insights that advance our understanding of the causes of civil war. This book has sought to fill this gap and integrate the study of Darfur and Congo into the civil war research program. In doing so, I have leveraged a mixed-methods research design and hope to have illustrated the value of such an approach.

Though inductive theorizing is widely used in political science, rarely are scholars explicit about it. This is problematic if it means that scholars are testing and deriving their hypotheses from the same case. In this book, I have followed Evan Lieberman's call for political scientists "to provide a more transparent accounting of their research" with the goal of facilitating analytic and inferential clarity.[11] In contrast to most nested research designs, I began with a small-N analysis and then moved to large-N analysis. While

---

[10] For an exception on Congo, see Autesserre, *The Trouble with the Congo*.
[11] Lieberman, "Nested Analysis."

the Darfur case provided inspiration for the political networks hypothesis, the idea of cooperative counterinsurgency, and the coup-proofing theory of civil war, it was in operationalizing the coup-proofing theory of civil war for large-N testing that I conceived of the coup–civil war trap as a broader phenomenon rooted in the historical development of the state in Africa. Thus, the movement from small-N to large-N and the theoretical and conceptual precision that is necessary to move between methodological levels contributed to the development of a more powerful theoretical framework that helped to account for the strategic logic of coups and civil war in Africa but also the roots of powersharing and peace. But it was only because of the in-depth study of the Darfur case that I conceived of the building blocks of the theory in the first place.

11.3 AVENUES FOR FUTURE RESEARCH

The argument and evidence advanced in this book raise a number of avenues for future research. Two avenues probably on the forefront of most readers' minds are: (1) the relevance of the coup–civil war trap beyond Africa; and (2) given the important political and economic changes that have occurred across sub-Saharan Africa over the past ten to twenty years, such as democratization, end of the capital city rule, and a new era of state-building, whether African states are escaping the coup–civil war trap. In the last section of the book, I aim to motivate further research on these two dimensions. Before doing so, I want to briefly address two other important avenues for future research: intraethnic bargaining and its impact on powersharing and the role of external factors, especially strategic interactions with neighboring states.

11.3.1 Bringing Intraethnic Bargaining into the Study of the Coup–Civil War Trap

Building from the work of North et al., who follow from an extensive literature in comparative politics on the role of informal political institutions in weak states, this book models politics as between competing violence specialists who sit atop of political networks embedded in different social groups. In the African context, these networks are often organized along ethnic lines, though need not be, as illustrated by Sudan's Islamic Movement. But even within Sudan's Islamist organization, ethnicity's dense and durable social connections, strong norms of reciprocity, geographic proximity, and shared histories ensured that it represented an alternative basis of collective mobilization that would structure political bargaining as the Islamic Movement broke down.

Given the importance of ethnicity as a vehicle for political mobilization in postcolonial Africa, this book has focused primarily on bargaining between competing ethnopolitical networks as illustrated in Figure 2.1. As I have stressed throughout, such interethnic bargaining is critical to the ruler's ability to broadcast power in a weak state because the same norms, institutions, and technologies that facilitate intraethnic cooperation represent barriers to controlling other networks. Striking alliances with rival violence specialists thus serves as a low-cost solution to the problem of political control in weak states.

But, as illustrated in Figure 3.1, ethnic bargaining represents a two-level game; as rulers reach out to ethnic rivals, they are simultaneously bargaining with their coethnics. I have given priority to interethnic bargaining, assuming that the ruler and his coethnics should have similar strategic preferences; they recognize the importance of avoiding costly civil wars with their ethnic rivals but are wary of giving away too much power that their rivals may exploit in a future coup d'état.

In future research, however, it would be important to further analyze the relationship between intraethnic and interethnic bargaining. While a ruler and his coethnics may agree upon the strategic approach to bargaining with rivals, they may not agree upon the distribution of power within their own network. Given the incredible inequalities within each network and the power and status premium that goes to he who wears the crown, coethnics face the same commitment problem as they do when bargaining with ethnic rivals. The uncertainty and network factionalization that arises from this could weaken the threat capabilities of the incumbent group and thus destabilize interethnic bargaining.

How do coethnics manage the commitment problem that arises from bargaining in a highly uncertain environment? Are they better able to manage the distribution of power through shared social institutions?[12] What is the effect of interethnic bargaining on intraethnic bargaining? Does the shadow of the coup d'état from ethnic rivals contribute to intraethnic cooperation, helping to reduce infighting among coethnics? Overall, bringing intraethnic bargaining into the study of the coup–civil war trap may lead to some fascinating new insights into the politics of weak states.

---

[12] Fearon and Laitin, "Explaining Interethnic Cooperation."

11.3.2 Regional Politics and the Coup–Civil War Trap

Another important avenue for future research is to model the impact of regional and international politics on the coup–civil war trap. For reasons of parsimony, in this book I have focused primarily on the domestic politics of interethnic bargaining and its effect on coups and civil war. This parsimonious approach has the benefit of accounting for important political phenomenon in postcolonial Africa with few variables. In fact, in Chapter 10, I show the power of ethnic geography—measured by size and distance to the capital—in accounting for patterns of ethnic powersharing, coups, and civil war. But, of course, Africa's political systems are not self-contained; they are rooted in both international and regional systems, which have had profound effects on the domestic politics of African states.[13] In particular, as Christopher Clapham has argued, when it comes to civil war, neighboring states, not global powers, have had the most profound impact.[14]

There are a number of important avenues for future research on the intersection between external factors and the coup–civil war trap. One is how external support and alliances affect a group's threat capabilities and thus bargaining over state power.[15] If a balance of threat capabilities is key for ethnic powersharing and peace, then the potential intervention of a third party could disrupt this balance and increase the risk of bargaining failure. For example, in the case of South Sudan discussed at the outset of this book, Kiir's strategic choice to purge Riek Machar from the regime was very costly given the relatively high threat capabilities of Machar's ethnic group, the Nuer. But Kiir was able to survive this costly civil war because of the decisive military intervention from Uganda. This is a potential case, then, where regional intervention may have undermined powersharing that would have been induced from a costly civil war.

The South Sudan case points to another potential avenue of research on the external politics of the coup–civil war trap: how elite bargaining within weak states structures and is structured by interstate competition between regional powers. The fallout between Salva Kiir and Riek Machar drew Uganda into its civil war. But the problem of such a

---

[13] Clapham, *Africa and the International System.*
[14] Clapham, *Africa and the International System.* See also Salehyan, "Transnational Rebels." Kristian Skrede Gleditsch, Idean Salehyan, and Kenneth Schultz, "Fighting at Home, Fighting Abroad," *Journal of Conflict Resolution,* 52 (4) (2008): 479–506.
[15] For one study on a similar question, see Cetinyan, "Ethnic Bargaining."

development is that it potentially disrupts the regional balance of power as it increases uncertainty among rival states about the regional state's agenda and the effect this will have on other states' spheres of influence. This has the potential to lead to a regionalized civil war.

There has been a recent surge in the study of the nexus between internal conflict and external conflict,[16] but this important dimension— how elite bargaining within regimes affects regional competition and vice versa—has been understudied. Drawing on additional field research in the DRC, Rwanda, and Angola, Harry Verhoeven and I have extended the analysis of the breakdown of the post-Mobutu order to better account for the nexus between regional politics and the coup–civil war trap and more precisely elucidate how the Second Congo War would become Africa's Great War. We explain that, while the Kabila–RPF alliance was key to the overthrow of Mobutu and represented the linchpin of a new Central Africa, it sowed the seeds of the second war not only by disrupting the collective security regime that the Pan-Africanist coalition against Mobutu was supposed to usher in but also by ensuring that, as camaraderie dissolved, the two sides faced a vicious and unrelenting strategic problem that threatened not only Congo's internal security but also the geopolitical order in Central Africa.[17]

11.4 BEYOND AFRICA: INSIGHTS FROM THE COUP–CIVIL WAR TRAP FOR UNDERSTANDING STATE FAILURE IN IRAQ AND SYRIA

In considering the relevance of the coup–civil war trap beyond the states of sub-Saharan Africa, it is worth reviewing the scope conditions that give rise to the phenomenon:

Weak states: Violence is dispersed among powerful individuals. The organizational capacity of the state (and its institutions, such as an impersonal bureaucracy) to enforce the rule of law, monitor and

---

[16] Salehyan, "Transnational Rebels." Gleditsch et al., "Fighting at Home, Fighting Abroad." Salehyan, *Rebels without Borders*. Kenneth A. Schultz, "The Enforcement Problem in Coercive Bargaining: Interstate Conflict over Rebel Support in Civil Wars," *International Organization*, 64 (2) (2010): 281–312; Jeff D. Colgan, "Domestic Revolutionary Leaders and International Conflict," *World Politics*, 65 (4) (2013): 656–690.

[17] Roessler and Verhoeven, *Why Comrades Go to War*.

control society, and sanction the use of violence is low. Rival violence specialists use the threat of force to uphold distribution of power.

Strong, geographically concentrated social groups: Society is divided into groups that possess strong social ties and institutions (such as shared norms of reciprocity, common language, common history) and are clustered spatially.

High-value political center: These social groups are situated in a political entity from which exit is very costly and control of the capital, or political center, leads to international recognition, economic rents, and discretionary authority over key administrative and coercive instruments.

The first two conditions necessitate the importance of powersharing for the ruler to extend his political control beyond his own social group. Unable to rely on a strong impersonal bureaucracy to exert the state's authority over other societal groups and the costs of trying to forcibly do so, striking alliances with other societal power brokers represents a solution to the strong society–weak states problem. The third condition increases the prize for capturing and controlling sovereign power and the incentives for rivals to use force to do so.

While these scope conditions map on to the African state very well, they should just as well apply to other ethnically divided weak states in the post-World War II era.[18] Two such prime cases that are dominating international affairs as this book goes to press (2016) are Iraq and Syria.[19] It is beyond the scope of the book to systematically apply the coup–civil war trap to these cases, but at first glance there are strong indications this book's analytical framework informs the outbreak of large-scale political violence in both cases.

11.4.1 Iraq: Al-Maliki's Fateful Bet on Civil War

In Iraq, according to the EPR dataset and an extensive qualitative scholarship, the primary ethnoregional fault lines have been between Shia Arabs (63 percent of the population), Sunni Arabs (19 percent),

---

[18] Donald Horowitz's magnum opus, which draws empirical evidence from postcolonial countries in Africa, Asia, and the Middle East, is a testament to this. Horowitz, *Ethnic Groups in Conflict*.

[19] According to the EPR dataset between 1946 and 2005, outside of Africa there have only been fourteen *Ethnic transfers of power* (ETOP) versus sixty-six within sub-Saharan Africa. Of these fourteen cases, four have been in Syria (three) and Iraq (one). An ETOP is considered to have occurred when the politically dominant ethnic group (as coded as "Senior Partner," "Dominant," or "Monopoly") is replaced by an ethnic rival.

and Kurds (17 percent).[20] After World War II, powersharing prevailed between the Sunni and Shia as several national institutions, including the Hashemite monarchy and the Communist and Baath parties, managed to attract followers from both ethnoreligious groups.[21] A series of coups upset this balance, however, from 1963 onward. The rise to power of a restructured Baath Party in the hands of Hassan al-Bakr and his cousin, Saddam Hussein, in 1968 consolidated Sunni power in Iraq as al-Bakr and Saddam sought to leverage family and hometown ties as a "community of trust" to coup-proof their governments.[22] Accordingly, under Saddam, "[t]he most important posts went to his half brothers and cousins, members of the Bejat clan of the Albu Nasir tribe from Tikrit. 'If you want to know how we rule Iraq,' reflected one of Saddam's relatives in later years, 'we do it just the same way as we used to run Tikrit.' "[23] The consolidation of Sunni rule at the expense of Shia Arabs and Kurds provoked several episodes of large-scale political violence, especially after the First Gulf War when Saddam brutally crushed Shia and Kurd uprisings, leading to tens of thousands of deaths and millions displaced.[24]

As is well known, in 2003 the US intervention in Iraq, overthrow of Saddam and, especially, its program of de-Baathification completely upended the power structure, provoking a series of insurgencies with Sunni Arabs now at the forefront of the opposition.[25] There was a hope that the transition to an elected parliamentary government in 2005 and 2006 would help to quell the rebellion by contributing to ethnic powersharing, with a Shia prime minister, Kurdish president, and Sunni vice

[20] Amatzia Baram, "Neo-tribalism in Iraq: Saddam Hussein's Tribal Policies, 1991–96," *International Journal of Middle East Studies*, 29 (1) (1997): 1–31. Said K. Aburish, *Saddam Hussein: The Politics of Revenge* (New York: Bloomsbury 2000). Efraim Karsh and Inari Rautsi, *Saddam Hussein: A Political Biography* (New York: Grove Press, 2002). Sandra Mackey, *The Reckoning: Iraq and the Legacy of Saddam Hussein* (New York: Norton, 2003).

[21] Adeed Dawisha, *Arab Nationalism in the Twentieth Century: From Triumph to Despair* (Princeton, NJ: Princeton University Press, 2003), p. 174.

[22] James T. Quinlivan, "Coup-Proofing: Its Practice and Consequences in the Middle East," *International Security*, 24 (2) (1999): 131–165.

[23] Patrick Cockburn, *Muqtada: Muqtada al-Sadr, the Shia Revival, and the Struggle for Iraq* (New York: Scribner, 2008), p. 34.

[24] Middle East Watch, *Endless Torment: The 1991 Uprising in Iraq and Its Aftermath* (New York: Middle East Watch, 1992).

[25] According to the US deputy chief of planning at Central Command, Colonel John Agoglia, the day that Ian Bremer, US viceroy in Iraq, announced that his de-Baathification program included officers in the Iraqi Army under Saddam was the day "that we snatched defeat from the jaws of victory and created an insurgency." Thomas E. Ricks, *Fiasco: The American Military Adventure in Iraq* (New York: Penguin, 2006), p. 163.

president. But Iraq's elected prime minister, Nouri al-Maliki, from 2006 to 2014 undermined powersharing by consolidating power in the hands of the Shia at the expense of other groups. One consequence of this is that it weakened the government and Sunni communities' ability to produce cooperative counterinsurgency[26] and opened the door for the Iraq and Syria-based terrorist organization, Islamic State of Iraq and Syria (ISIS), a predominantly Sunni-backed militant organization, to make significant inroads into Iraq and control large swathes of the country.

Several observers have suggested that part of the motivation for al-Maliki's exclusive rule along sectarian lines, especially within the military and special forces, was to coup-proof his regime.[27] As two former US intelligence officials commented, "al-Maliki's 'Shiafication' of the Iraqi security forces has been less about the security of Iraq than the security of Baghdad and his regime."[28] Thus, al-Maliki seems to represent another case of a ruler in a weak state choosing ethnopolitical exclusion to substitute civil war risk for coup risk.[29]

The problem for al-Maliki is that, though the Shia Arabs are a strong majority in Iraq, the Sunni make up a sizable minority with geographic

[26] In direct support of the importance of cooperative counterinsurgency as a mechanism by which ethnic powersharing contributes to societal peace, two former American officials note the devastating consequences al-Maliki's marginalization of the Sunni had: "It's no accident that there exists today virtually no Sunni popular resistance to ISIS, but rather the result of a conscious al-Maliki government policy to marginalize the Sunni tribal 'Awakening' that deployed more than 90,000 Sunni fighters against al Qaeda in 2007–2008. These 90,000 'Sons of Iraq' made a significant contribution to the reported 90 percent drop in sectarian violence in 2007–2008, assisting the Iraqi security forces and the United States in securing territory from Mosul to the Sunni enclaves of Baghdad and the surrounding Baghdad 'belts.' As the situation stabilized, the Iraqi government agreed to a plan to integrate vetted Sunni members of the Sons of Iraq into the Iraqi army and police to make those forces more representative of the overall Iraqi population. But this integration never happened." Derek Harvey and Michael Pregent, "Who's to Blame for Iraq Crisis?" CNN.com, June 12, 2014. Available at http://edition.cnn.com/2014/06/12/opinion/pregent-harvey-northern-iraq-collapse (accessed August 23, 2016). See also Tim Arango, "Uneasy Alliance Gives Insurgents an Edge in Iraq," *The New York Times*, June 18, 2014. Available at www.nytimes.com/2014/06/19/world/middleeast/former-loyalists-of-saddam-hussein-crucial-in-helping-isis.html (accessed August 23, 2016).

[27] See also Joshua Keating, "Iraq's Built-to-Fail Military," *Slate*, June 19, 2014. Available at www.slate.com/blogs/the_world_/2014/06/19/how_maliki_s_paranoia_created_iraq_s_dysfunctional_military.html (accessed August 23, 2016).

[28] Harvey and Pregent, "Who's to Blame for Iraq Crisis?"

[29] Steve Saideman, drawing from "The Enemy Within," my 2011 piece in *World Politics*, directly makes this argument. Steve Saideman, "Coup-Proof? Trading One Kind of Insecurity for Another," Political Violence at a Glance blog, June 20, 2014. Available at http://politicalviolenceataglance.org/2014/06/20/coup-proof-trading-one-kind-of-insecurity-for-another (accessed August 23, 2016).

proximity to the ethnically mixed capital of Baghdad. This ethnic geography combined with ISIS's financial and military support from wealthy foreign states ensured that the civil war al-Maliki provoked was a devastating one. Consistent with the threat-capabilities theory of powersharing, however, the ISIS threat alarmed Shias that Baghdad may be overrun, forcing them to abandon support for al-Maliki and back a Shia leader who promised to restore powersharing with Sunnis.[30] Whether a credible arrangement can be made with Sunni power brokers sufficient to reverse the tide of the war is yet to be seen.

11.4.2 Syria: Al-Assad Tries to Crush Syria's Arab Spring

One could also apply the coup–civil war framework to Syria, which is divided between the ethnoreligious groups—the Sunni Arabs (62 percent of the population), the Alawi (12 percent), Sunni Kurds (10 percent), Christians (10 percent), and Druze (3 percent). Since 1966, the Alawis have been the ruling group in Syria, entrenching themselves in power in an ethnocracy. Like other minority groups in Syria, the Alawis were the beneficiaries of disproportionate representation in the army under French colonial rule as a way to balance "against the nationalist tendencies of the Arab-Sunni majority."[31] As Horowitz describes it, "The ethnic history of the post-war period is the story of how some of these groups, powerful in the army, gradually displaced the Sunni civilian political elite and then were themselves eliminated from military leadership, one at a time: first the Kurds, then the Sunni, and then the Druze, until only the Alawi remained."[32]

The Alawis' ethnic dominance of the Syrian state reduced the coup risk posed by their communal rivals but presented them with the challenge of maintaining societal control of a hostile and resentful majority. Between 1976 and 1982, this combination provoked an armed uprising by Sunni Islamists led by the Muslim Brotherhood. The Syrian government finally was able to crush the rebellion but only through the use of indiscriminate mass violence when it razed the Syrian city of Hama in 1982, killing an estimated 20,000 people.[33] Thirty years later, the Arab Spring again inspired societal mobilization against the Syrian government. Refusing to

---

[30] Priyanka Boghani, "Can Haider al-Abadi Bridge Iraq's Sectarian Divide?" PBS.org, October 21, 2014. Available at www.pbs.org/wgbh/pages/frontline/iraq-war-on-terror/losing-iraq/can-haider-al-abadi-bridge-iraqs-sectarian-divide (accessed August 23, 2016).

[31] Mahmud A. Faksh, "The Alawi Community of Syria: A New Dominant Political Force," *Middle Eastern Studies*, 20 (2) (1984), p. 143.

[32] Horowitz, *Ethnic Groups in Conflict*, pp. 492–493.

[33] Raphaël Lefevre, *Ashes of Hama: The Muslim Brotherhood in Syria* (Oxford: Oxford University Press, 2013).

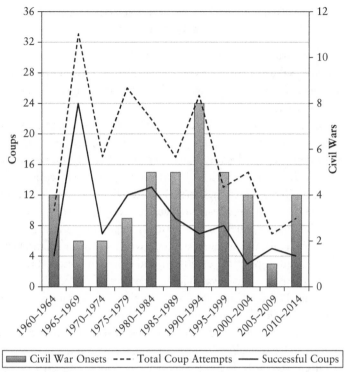

Civil War Onsets --- Total Coup Attempts —— Successful Coups

FIGURE 11.1 The Coup–Civil War Trade-Off in Sub-Saharan Africa, Independence to 2005[35]

step down or significantly give up power, Bashar al-Assad instead sought to crush the antigovernment protest, leading to civil war. As the International Crisis Group analyzed the regime's calculations in 2011, several months into the uprising, al-Assad and his Alawi loyalists felt the only credible solution to the conflict was to crush the rebellion—or at least to use all means to keep it at bay—or else face their own demise. "Assad essentially pledged to go down fighting. He will not do so alone . . . many regime supporters are terrified about their future and thus liable to resist till the bitter end. A majority of Alawite officials, security officers and ordinary citizens, along with segments of the Christian community and some secularists, have become convinced that *their fate is either to kill or be killed*."[34]

[34] Emphasis added. International Crisis Group, "Unchartered Waters: Thinking Through Syria's Dynamics," *Middle East Briefing*, November 24, 2011.
[35] In Figure 11.1, the primary y-axis counts the number of total (successful and failed) coup attempts, and the secondary y-axis counts the number of civil war onsets for each

11.5 POLICY IMPLICATIONS: ENDING THE COUP–CIVIL WAR TRAP IN AFRICA

Vignettes from Iraq and Syria suggest that the coup–civil war trap is not unique to sub-Saharan Africa, even if it has been particularly prominent in that region. What is the way out for African countries stuck in the coup–civil war trap?

The aggregate picture of the coup–civil war trap across sub-Saharan Africa since independence is quite intriguing (see Figure 11.1). During the first post-independence decade, there were significantly more coups than civil wars as the military locked in power in preventive coups in many countries (e.g., Togo, Uganda, Sierra Leone, Nigeria, Benin, and Sudan). Over the next several decades, however, a reversal in the proportion of coups and civil wars occurred as some rulers, depending on the threat capabilities of their rivals, more aggressively moved to protect themselves from coups through ethnopolitical exclusion and other measures, but in doing so increased the risk of civil war. Violent seizures of power through (often peripheral-based) interethnic coalitions in the 1970s, 1980s, and 1990s failed to reverse this trend, as explained in Chapter 8; they merely factionalized, provoking ethnic-based wars between co-conspirators and former allies (such as in Uganda, Zimbabwe, Liberia, Chad, Sudan, Guinea-Bissau, and the DRC). Recently it looked as if both coups and civil wars were trending toward zero, though that pattern has been disrupted by the turbulent past five years. These episodes of large-scale political violence borne out of bargaining failure over state power, such as South Sudan at end of 2013, the Côte d'Ivoire crisis in 2011, and the collapse of order in the CAR in 2013, reveal that the coup–civil war trap is a not a thing of the past.

What is the way out of the vicious trap? Deeply rooted in the sociopolitical foundations of the African state, overcoming the coup–civil war trap will not occur overnight. Instead, it will require a significant change over time along three key dimensions: (1) the rules of the game; (2) the structure of the state; and (3) the basis of societal mobilization. Importantly, significant change across all three dimensions has occurred over the past fifteen years. For example, on the changing rules of the game, the African Union has outlawed coups, and elections are now the modal source of political

five-year period since 1960. As civil wars tend to be rarer than coups, given the higher mobilizational costs required to successfully build and sustain an insurgency, I use different scales for the two. Data on coup attempts is from Powell and Thyne and the civil war data from Fearon and Laitin's dataset, with recent updates by the author.

change. On the changing structure of the state, a number of African regimes, backed by Chinese loans and investment, are aiming to strengthen the infrastructural and extractive capacity of the state and extend its reach into the periphery. Finally, on the changing basis of social mobilization, urbanization, technological diffusion, and generational change are strengthening interethnic social ties and bases of trust, while leading an increasing number of individuals to reject political appeals along ethnic lines. This broadening of social identification and social movements increases society's threat capabilities and capacity to hold incumbents to account if they violate the letter or spirit of constitutionalism.

Another fruitful avenue for future research is to explore how these changes as well as others, such as the embrace of formal powersharing as a mode of governance,[36] improved macroeconomic performance,[37] embrace of federalism or decentralized rule,[38] acceptance of state partition in Sudan and Ethiopia, are transforming the coup–civil war trap. Additional research is necessary to systematically address this question. But it is worth discussing potential change on the first dimension—the rules of the game—as the African Union has sought to stamp out unconstitutional transfers of power and put an end to the capital city rule.

11.5.1 The End of the Capital City Rule

The early 1990s saw a devastating civil war erupt in Sierra Leone. By the mid-1990s, the military junta that had seized power in 1992 was under intense regional and international pressure to hand over control to an elected government. Multiparty elections were held in the first part of 1996, and the newly elected leader, Ahmed Tejan Kabbah, sought to make good on his election promise to end the war. In October 1996, the Kabbah government signed a peace agreement in Abidjan with the Revolutionary United Front (RUF). The agreement had no real effect, however, as Kabbah failed to secure the support of the military and was quickly overthrown in a coup d'état in May 1997. The new military regime, led by Johnny Koroma, reached out to the rebels

---

[36] Hartzell and Hoddie, *Crafting Peace*, p. 10. Andreas Mehler, "Peace and Power Sharing in Africa: A Not So Obvious Relationship," *African Affairs*, 108 (432) (2009): 453–473.

[37] Shantayanan Devarajan and Wolfgang Fengler, "Africa's Economic Boom: Why the Pessimists and the Optimists are Both Right," *Foreign Affairs*, 92 (3) (2013): 68–81.

[38] Lindemann, "Just Another Change of Guard?" Christophe van der Beken, *Unity in Diversity: Federalism as a Mechanism to Accommodate Ethnic Diversity—The Case of Ethiopia* (Berlin: LIT, 2012).

and incorporated them into government, with the RUF leader, Foday Sankoh, appointed as Koroma's deputy. The alliance allowed the RUF to operate unchecked, exacting a huge cost for the country's civilian population.[39]

But the military's seizure of power in Sierra Leone prompted an unprecedented response from the OAU. Unlike in the past when it abided by the "capital city rule" and recognized whichever group controlled the central government, the OAU, at its summit meeting in Harare, Zimbabwe, in the days after Koroma's seizure of power, took the remarkable step of not only calling for the return of the elected government of Kabbah but also tasking the Economic Community of West African States (ECOWAS) to achieve this goal and calling on African states and the broader international community not to recognize the military regime.[40] Less than a year later, a Nigerian-led ECOWAS force (the Economic Community of West African States Monitoring Group [ECOMOG]) had forcibly removed the junta and reinstated Kabbah as president.

On the heels of the successful reinstatement of the constitutional government in Sierra Leone, the OAU adopted the "Declaration on a Framework for Response to Unconstitutional Changes of Government," known as the Lomé Declaration, which condemned the coup d'état as a means for acquiring power, though only against democratically elected governments. But, like in the Sierra Leone case, the OAU set out a set of steps the organization would follow in response to coups and other types of unconstitutional changes of government, including public condemnation and refusal of recognition; suspension from OAU policy organs; and, eventually, targeted sanctions if the offending government refused to restore constitutional order.[41]

These anti-coup measures would be enshrined, and even expanded, in the constitution of the new African Union (AU; which formally replaced the OAU in 2002), in which the member-states pledged not only to reject coups against democratically elected governments but all "unconstitutional changes of government." Furthermore it empowered the AU to employ force and other measures to sanction the forcible seizure of

---

[39] John L. Hirsch, *Sierra Leone: Diamonds and the Struggle for Democracy* (Boulder, Col.: Lynne Rienner, 2001).

[40] For an excellent article highlighting this decision as precedent-setting, see Eki Yemisi Omorogbe, "A Club of Incumbents? The African Union and Coups d'État," *Vanderbilt Journal of Transnational Law*, 44 (2011): 123–154.

[41] Omorogbe, "A Club of Incumbents?"

power and reinstate the constitutional government.[42] Since the AU has come into existence, it has suspended no fewer than ten members, including Egypt after the military's counterrevolution against the Mohamed Morsi government.[43]

The events in Mali in 2012 are emblematic of the new political reality for violence specialists. On March 21, 2012, Captain Amadou Sanogo led a coup d'état against President Amadou Toumani Touré and installed a military junta in power. But, in the face of immediate sanctions and suspension from ECOWAS and the AU, as well as condemnation from other international organizations and foreign governments, Sanogo was forced to almost immediately cede sovereign power to Dioncounda Traoré, the president of the national assembly of Mali, who was appointed interim president of the country on April 12, 2012. Despite the handover of power, Sanogo and his military junta sought to wield power from behind the scenes. In May, Traoré was beaten by thugs in his office and evacuated to France for medical treatment; in December 2012, the military under the direction of Sanogo arrested the interim prime minister.[44] While Sanogo sought to continue to retain his de-facto hold on power, he was never able to convert that into de-jure power either through multiparty elections or otherwise, without once again incurring the wrath of the AU and other international actors. Sanogo's lack of sovereign power would prove decisive because, despite his strong objections to a French military intervention, he lacked the authority to block President Traoré from inviting France to deploy forces to help the government reverse the gains made by Islamic militants in the northern part of the country after the coup. The French military intervention was a significant boost to the power of Traoré vis-à-vis Sanogo.[45] On the heels of the French military intervention, two rounds of presidential elections were held in July and August 2013. The elected government further emasculated Sanogo's power, and, in

---

[42] Omorogbe, "A Club of Incumbents?"

[43] Central African Republic was suspended in 2003; Togo was suspended in 2005; Mauritania in 2005 and then again in 2008; Guinea in 2008; Madgascar in 2009; Niger in 2010; Côte d'Ivoire in 2010; Mali in 2012; Guinea-Bissau in 2012; Egypt in 2013; and Central African Republic in 2013.

[44] Adam Nossiter, "Mali's Prime Minister Resigns after Arrest, Muddling Plans to Retake North," *The New York Times*, December 11, 2012. Available at www.nytimes.com/2012/12/12/world/africa/malis-prime-minister-arrested-by-military.html?_r=0 (accessed August 23, 2016).

[45] Leela Jacinto, "Is Mali's Captain Sanogo Losing Control of the Ship?" France24.com, January 17, 2013. Available at www.france24.com/en/20130116-mali-captain-amadou-sanogo-army-coup-power-france-intervention (accessed August 23, 2016).

November 2013, he was arrested and charged with kidnapping and murdering military officers deemed disloyal to him.[46]

The sequence of events in Mali—from coup to transitional governments to multiparty elections—reflects the constraints that violence specialists in Africa increasingly face; unlike in the past, international recognition is contingent upon how a group acquired power. Unless acquired through elections or some other constitutional process, capturing the capital city is no longer the prize it once was.[47]

11.5.2 The Limits of Africa's New Anti-coup Rule

The new anti-coup rules have gone a long way to weakening the capital city rule that governed the postcolonial order; coups no longer represent the path to sovereign power they once did. Does this exogenous change—a sudden increase in the costs of capturing sovereign power by force—help to account for the recent decline in both coups and civil wars? Based on this book's central theoretical argument, we would expect this change not to be inconsequential. As the shadow of the coup d'état recedes, the commitment problem that underpins the coup–civil war trap should decrease in severity, reducing the strategic costs of ethnic powersharing.

While certainly the emergence of an anti-coup rule is an important and positive development—and emblematic of the more democratic era that has characterized African politics over the past quarter of a century—there are several reasons why caution is warranted. First, though the rule has increased the costs of irregular seizures of power, it has not eliminated politics by force. Violence specialists may still use force to displace the head of state and do well out of the new political dispensation that arises. But, according to the African Union's anti-coup rules, they are unable to become the sovereign power after the coup, even if they subject their newfound authority to multiparty elections;[48] the AU has

---

[46] "Leader of Mali Coup Charged with Conspiracy to Murder after Bodies Discovered," *Reuters*, April 24, 2014. Available at www.reuters.com/article/2014/04/24/us-mali-sanogo-idUSBREA3N14P20140424 (accessed August 23, 2016).

[47] Hein Goemans and Nikolay Marinov, "Coups and Democracy," *British Journal of Political Science*, 44 (4) (2014): 799–825.

[48] This is clearly spelled out in the African Charter on Democracy, Elections and Good Governance put forth in 2007: "perpetrators of unconstitutional change of government shall not be allowed to participate in elections held to restore the democratic order." This was put in place after several coup conspirators (in Togo 2005 and Mauritania

condemned these post-coup elections that involved the coup perpetrators as merely a "continuation of [the] illegal seizure of power."[49]

This principle and rule were put to the test, however, with events that unfolded in Egypt in 2013 and 2014. Consistent with its more assertive posture on irregular changes of government, the AU was out in the lead condemning the military coup that overthrew Egypt's first democratically elected government, even as the United States and the EU were more ambivalent and accepting of the coup. The AU suspended Egypt in an emergency meeting of the Peace and Security Council (PSC) on July 5, 2013. In the wake of the coup, the Egyptian military government embraced multiparty elections to select a new government, though it barred the Muslim Brotherhood, which controlled the government prior to the coup, from participating. In defiance of the AU, Abdel Fattah el-Sisi, the military leader of the coup against the democratically elected government of Mohamed Morsi, participated in the election and won with 96 percent of the vote.

After the election, the AU faced a difficult choice. It was under intense diplomatic pressure from Egypt to lift its suspension. Moreover, both the EU and the United States recognized Sisi as the new head of state of Egypt.[50] In disregard of its own principle and legal resolution on the illegitimacy of elections that involved coup perpetrators, the AU, in a meeting of the PSC in June, voted to end Egypt's suspension from the AU. This has led some observers to question whether this decision will undermine the AU's investment in ending politics by force in Africa. As the respected South African think tank, the Institute for Strategic Studies noted, "The AU also faces the prospect of setting a precedent that undermines the legitimacy of this rule for application in future cases. In the event of the occurrence of an unconstitutional change of government in another AU member state, there is now a serious risk that those responsible will cite Egypt's example to justify the legitimacy of their participation in elections held to restore constitutional order."[51]

2008) sought to validate their capture of sovereign power through subsequent elections. Goemans and Marinov, "Coups and Democracy."

[49] Goemans and Marinov, "Coups and Democracy."

[50] Solomon Dersso, "Egypt vs. African Union: A Mutually Unhappy Ending?" AlJazeera. com, July 14, 2014. Available at www.aljazeera.com/indepth/opinion/2014/07/egypt-vs-african-union-mutually-u-2014714687899839.html (accessed August 23, 2016).

[51] Institute for Strategic Studies, "Far-reaching Implications of the PSC's Decision on Egypt," Peace and Security Council Report, July 3, 2014. Available at www.issafrica. org/pscreport/on-the-agenda/far-reaching-implications-of-the-pscs-decision-on-egypt (accessed August 23, 2016).

Another important limitation of the AU's attempts to end politics by force is that its policy to strengthen constitutionalism has largely been one-sided. It has sanctioned and targeted rivals of the incumbents for breaches of democratic norms but rarely the incumbents themselves.[52] First, there was no retroactive policy against rulers who originally came to power by force (which represented a majority of the heads of states at the time of the AU's founding in 2002). Second, though the AU's Charter on Democracy, Elections and Good Governance also classifies as an "illegal means of accessing or maintaining power . . . any amendment or revision of the constitution or legal instruments, which is an infringement on the principles of democratic change of government," the AU has rarely sanctioned African heads of state for violating this rule, such as rigging elections, arresting political rivals, or violating term limits.

One consequence of this biased regime of constitutionalism put in place by the member-states of the AU is that it has made some rulers less accountable. Knowing their rivals' hands are tied by the anti-coup policies of the AU and foreign powers, such as the United States, the incumbents have more room to amass personal power.[53] Moreover, as shown in Chapter 10, the credible threat of losing power from excluded groups represents an important constraint on the ruler's decision to monopolize power. If that credible threat is nullified by anti-coup measures but alternative accountability mechanisms are not put in place to uphold powersharing (e.g., strict term limits and free and fair elections), then this risks entrenching personal rule and exacerbating political instability as rivals mobilize to defend themselves from the arbitrary rule of the incumbent.

Let us return to where this book started: the case of South Sudan. The AU's one-sided regime of constitutionalism may help to account for Salva Kiir's bold and reckless play against his rivals. Unwilling to strengthen the ruling party's formal institutions for fear of the costs to his political survival, Kiir concentrated more power in his own hands.[54] The consequence of this was that the only way his rivals could hold him to account was through the use of force, which they resorted

---

[52] Of course this aligns precisely with the interests of the sitting heads of state who represent the key decision-makers in the AU. Hence Omorogbe's aptly titled review article on the anti-coup measures. Omorogbe, "A Club of Incumbents?"
[53] On coups as accountability mechanisms, see Svolik, *The Politics of Authoritarian Rule.*
[54] Roessler, "Why South Sudan Has Exploded in Violence."

to when violence erupted in the presidential guard. With strong threat capabilities, Machar and his followers were able to mobilize a formidable rebel force that was on its way to attack Juba if it were not for the intervention of the Ugandan military green-lighted by the US government. While external intervention buffered Salva Kiir from the military consequences of personalizing power, statements from regional states and the US government made it clear that Kiir also was protected legally from Riek's rebellion. For example, Uhuru Kenyatta, President of Kenya, in a special summit of the Intergovernmental Authority on Development (IGAD) on December 27, 2013, declared, "Let it be known that we in IGAD will not accept the unconstitutional overthrow of a duly and democratically elected government in South Sudan."[55] A few days later, the AU's PSC released a statement after its 411th meeting, which, addressing the South Sudan crisis, reiterated that the "AU's relevant instruments on the rejection of unconstitutional changes of Government."[56]

Similar pressure on Kiir in the lead-up to the outbreak of the war may have averted the crisis to begin with. The challenge for the AU, IGAD, and interested member-states in the international system is that whereas unconstitutional changes of government by force are easily observable and indisputable, other "infringement(s) on the principles of democratic change of government" by the incumbent fall into a gray zone on whether they violate the letter or spirit of the law. Was Salva Kiir's dismissal of Riek Machar as vice president legal, based on the president's constitutional mandate to form and dissolve the government, or an infringement of democratic governance? Similar questions are raised when it comes to violation of term limits by incumbents who do so through constitutional referenda. Not wanting to constrain their own power but also not wanting to wade into the domestic politics of countless of their member-states, the rulers who make up the AU

---

[55] Erin Conway-Smith, "South Sudan Government Agrees to Stop Fighting; Rebels Stay Mum," *Los Angeles Times*, December 27, 2013. Available at http://articles.latimes.com/2013/dec/27/world/la-fg-wn-south-sudan-fighting-rebels-20131227 (accessed August 23, 2016).

[56] African Union, Communiqué, Peace and Security Council, 411th Meeting at the Level of Heads of State and Government, Banjul, The Gambia, December 30, 2013. Available at www.peaceau.org/uploads/psc-com-411-south-sudan-30-12-2013.pdf (accessed August 23, 2016).

have taken a soft stance on incumbent's semi-legal or illegal means of accessing or maintaining power. But until accountability mechanisms constraining incumbents are as strong as the mechanisms sanctioning the use of force by the opposition, rulers will continue to exploit this unbalanced regime of constitutionalism to consolidate their hold on power with deleterious consequences for the institutionalization of powersharing and democracy in Africa.

Appendix 1

A Note on the Book's Qualitative Methods

A central methodological pillar of this book has been qualitative research in Sudan and the DRC to unravel the causal and empirical relationships between informal institutions of political rule, namely elite powersharing and the political networks in which elites are embedded, and coups and civil war. The qualitative research relied heavily on intensive semi-structured one-on-one interviews, primarily with elites. I received institutional review board approval from the appropriate offices at University of Maryland, Oxford University, and the College of William and Mary prior to undertaking field research. For the Sudan chapters, research was conducted in Khartoum, North Darfur, South Darfur, and West Darfur as well as in Asmara, Eritrea, N'djamena, Chad, and Abuja, Nigeria. Interviews were also conducted with Sudanese in the UK, the United States, and Europe. For the Congo chapter, research was conducted in Kinshasa and Goma as well as in Kigali, Rwanda. When possible, interviews were conducted in English; otherwise, a local translator was used. In Congo, most interviews were conducted in French, with Harry Verhoeven translating.

I employed qualitative methods in two ways. The first was primarily exploratory. When I set off to Sudan, I was interested in the mediating effect informal political institutions have on state authority and violence and suspected that understanding this would help to explain the onset of the Darfur civil war. Thus, the first task was understanding the institutional base of the Al-Ingaz regime and the sequence of events leading to the outbreak of full-scale civil war in Darfur. With little secondary literature (in English) on either of these variables, given the newness of the

Darfur conflict[1] and the shadowy nature of Sudan's Islamic Movement, the first part of my field research in Sudan was devoted to reconstructing the sequence of events leading to the Darfur civil war and the institutional origins and structure of Sudan's Islamic Movement. To do so, I relied on non-probability purposive sampling among several key groups: those in the Islamic Movement both at the upper echelon and within the *tanzim* in Darfur as well as those involved in the civil war from all sides (the rebels, national, state, and local governments, *janjawiid* militias, local communities, foreign governments, and the SPLA). In reconstructing events, I prioritized the accounts of those individuals who were actually present and sought to substantiate information offered by at least one other person who was involved or who would have direct personal knowledge of an event.[2]

To identify important political players and gain access to them, I employed the snowballing, or chain-referral, method.[3] This can be remarkably effective and efficient as it quickly connects one with the key decision-makers or individuals involved in a given event. But it can also be problematic as it may lead to those with strong social connections to be more likely to be referred, and it can lead to certain individuals within a given network to be more represented than others. I was more concerned about the latter than the former given that we would expect social connections to correlate with political influence, and I was fundamentally interested in events involving the countries' most important political players.[4] (The bigger challenge was gaining access to the most

---

[1] I conducted most of my field research in Sudan before and during the publication of Flint and de Waal's excellent book on the Darfur civil war. Having not seen their book as I was trying to reconstruct the events leading to the onset of the conflict through qualitative interviews, it would be striking the degree to which our two accounts would independently corroborate each other. Even more is that I connected with the interviewees in my book completely independently from Flint and de Waal. I would later use their original version and its updated edition to substantiate key events and to fill in important gaps. See Flint and de Waal, *Darfur: A Short History of a Long War* and *Darfur: A New History of a Long War*.

[2] On the benefits of using elite interviewing "to establish the decision and actions that lay behind an event or series of events," see Ois Tansey, "Process Tracing and Elite Interviewing: A Case for Non-probability Sampling," *PS: Political Science and Politics*, 40 (4) (2007): 765–772, at pp. 766–767.

[3] Patrick Biernacki and Dan Waldorf, "Snowball Sampling: Problems and Techniques of Chain Referral Sampling," *Sociological Methods and Research*, 10 (2) (1981): 141–163.

[4] An important exception was individuals who were important but who have since fallen out of favor and are marginalized both politically and socially. I did manage to interview one key elite from prison. For others, unfortunately, this made it impossible to meet them as my contacts refused or failed to arrange a meeting with them.

networked as inevitably they have many demands on their time.) To over-come the risk of drawing too much from certain networks of individuals (the Bashir faction, the Turabi faction, the Kabila faction, the RPF, etc.), I sought to be as comprehensive as I could be: talking to people on all sides and being conscious of groups of people to whom I was not able to gain access and seeking them out. I also sought to exploit the divisions that I was studying in the Islamic Movement in Sudan and the AFDL in Congo to gain parallel perspectives on the same events and to represent both sides accurately.

Once I developed an in-depth understanding of the Islamic Movement and political violence in Darfur in 1991 and 2002–2003, I refined my theo-retical model: how informal institutions facilitate societal peace (develop-ing the cooperative counterinsurgency hypothesis); the strategic problems that lead to the breakdown of informal powersharing; the logic by which rulers choose strategies of ethnopolitical exclusion and the mechanisms by which it leads to civil war. I then went back to Sudan to conduct additional interviews, this time with the intention of using elite-level interviews for causal process tracing in order to determine whether these hypothesized causal processes were empirically supported.[5] It also allowed me to probe the feasibility of rival explanations and the use of counterfactuals to analyze the importance of certain mechanisms. One counterfactual that I explored with a number of interviewees was whether the Darfur civil war would still have occurred if the Islamic Movement did not factionalize between the Bashir camp and the Turabi camp. I do not systematically incorporate these discussions in my write-up of the within-Sudan comparison, but it nonetheless informed different aspects of the qualitative analysis.

Given the strategic nature of the theory at the center of this book, the other advantage of leveraging elite-level interviews is to try "to get in the heads" of the key decision-makers and to seek to illuminate why, con-fronted with a given strategic situation, they made the choices they did. There is always a risk of deception or self-reporting bias when trying to validly extract what one did and why; thus, critical to reducing system-atic error was triangulating from multiple sources on how the situation was assessed and why a given decision was made (as often key decisions were decided among a group of people, however small).

While the within-Sudan comparison relied on both exploratory and process-tracing qualitative analysis, making it a true theory-building

---

[5] George and Bennett, *Case Studies and Theory Development*. Tansey, "Process Tracing and Elite Interviewing."

case, the case study of the DRC relied solely on process-tracing—that is, using the DRC case to test the coup-proofing theory of civil war by using elite-level interviews to substantiate whether the purported mechanisms by which ethnic powersharing breaks down leading to civil war are actually observed. The case study was also used to address potential rival causal mechanisms. As there was much more written about the overthrow of Mobutu and Africa's Great War prior to the beginning of field research, we could more readily observe who the key elites were,[6] though we uncovered unidentified ones through our qualitative research, the configuration of political power, and the sequence of events leading to regime breakdown and civil war. (Again we also uncovered key events and political arrangements that were underexplored in the existing literature.) Central to our qualitative research thus was better understanding the strategic decisions made by key elites and isolating the degree to which they were consistent or inconsistent with the coup-proofing theory of civil war. To gain access to these key individuals we once again relied on the snowballing, or chain-referral, method with due diligence to tap into multiple political networks and reconnect with individuals who have since been politically and socially marginalized but who were once central to the political game.

---

[6] Especially helpful in this regard was De Villers and Williame, *République Démocratique du Congo.*

Appendix 2

Data Variable Dictionary

Center segmentation: The number of groups represented in the central government. Source: EPR dataset.

Co-conspirator: A dummy variable indicating if members of a given ethnic group led, organized or played another prominent role in the violent seizure of power by the current incumbent. For list of co-conspirators, see Appendix 3.

Cold War: A dummy variable indicating if year is 1990 or before.

Country area: Size of the country in square kilometers.

Ethnic dominance: A dummy variable indicating if for a given country-year a group is coded as "dominant." Source: EPR dataset.

Ethnic fractionalization: The probability that two individuals selected at random from a country will be from different ethnic groups. Source: Fearon 2003.

Ethnocracy: A dummy variable indicating if for a given country-year a group is coded as "monopoly." Source: EPR dataset.

Ethnic transfer of power: A dummy variable indicating when the politically dominant ethnic group (as coded as "senior partner," "dominant," or "monopoly") is replaced by another ethnic group.

Exclude basic: A dummy variable indicating if for a given country-year a group is coded as "discriminated" or "powerless" but in the previous year was coded as "monopoly," "dominant," "senior partner," or "junior partner." Source: EPR dataset.

Exclude dynamic: A dummy variable indicating if for a given country-year a group is coded as "discriminated" or "powerless" but in the previous year was coded as "monopoly," "dominant," "senior partner," or "junior partner" or coded as "co-conspirator." Source: EPR dataset and author codings.

Former French colony: A dummy variable indicating if a given country was colonized by France.

Group attempted coup: A dummy variable indicating whether members of a given ethnic group executed a successful or failed coup d'état in the current year. Source: McGowan 2003 for list of coups. Ethnicity of conspirators coded by author. See Appendix 3 for coup leaders and their ethnicities.

Group failed coup: A dummy variable indicating whether members of a given ethnic group executed a failed coup d'état in the current year. Source: McGowan 2003 for list of coups. Ethnicity of conspirators coded by author. See Appendix 3 for coup leaders and their ethnicities.

Group peace years: Number of years since group was last involved in civil war. Source: Fearon and Laitin (2003), Sambanis (2004), Lacina and Gleditsch (2006), and author's codings.

Group rebel: A dummy variable indicating the onset of large-scale violence between members of a given ethnic group and the central government. See Footnote 20 in Chapter 8 for how civil war onset at the group-level is coded. Source: Coded by author. See Appendix 3 for list of rebellion onsets and the ethnicity of the rebels.

Group successful coup: A dummy variable indicating whether members of a given ethnic group executed a successful coup d'état in the current year. Source: McGowan 2003 for list of coups. Ethnicity coded by author. See Appendix 3 for coup leaders and their ethnicities.

High–high (HH) threat capabilities: A dummy variable indicating whether a given group has threat capabilities above the median level of sub-Saharan Africa and the ruling group in power in the given year also has threat capabilities above the median level.

High–low (HL) threat capabilities: A dummy variable indicating whether a given group has threat capabilities below the median level of sub-Saharan Africa and the ruling group in power in the given year has threat capabilities above the median level.

Inclusion: A dummy variable indicating an ethnic group's access to or exclusion from the central government. Scores are derived from the EPR's categorical variable on access to power. Groups coded as "monopoly," "dominant," "senior partner," or "junior partner" on the EPR index in a given year are scored 1. Groups coded as "regional autonomy," "powerless," or "discriminated" are scored 0. Source: EPR dataset.

Inclusive powersharing: A dummy variable indicating if for a given country-year there are no groups excluded from access to the central government (i.e. coded as a 0 on *Inclusion)* and no group is "monopoly" or "dominant." Source: EPR dataset.

Institutionalized regime: Dummy measure of whether in a given year a country is governed by a single-party regime, multiparty regime, or democracy versus military government. Source: Autocracies of the World dataset.

Irregular replacement: A dummy variable indicating if for a given group, (1) the ruler of the country was a member of the group in the current or previous two years and (2) during that time the ruler was removed from power in a coup, rebellion or through other forcible means by members of a rival ethnic group. See Appendix 3.

Log country area: Natural log of the country's area in square kilometers. Source: Wikipedia.org.

Log group size: Natural log of the group's proportion of the population. Source: EPR dataset.

Log income: Natural log of the country's gross domestic product per capita (constant US$, 2000). Source: World Bank 2009.

Log population: Natural log of the country's total population. Source: World Bank 2009.

Low–high (LH) threat capabilities: A dummy variable indicating whether a given group has threat capabilities above the median level of sub-Saharan Africa and the ruling group in power in the given year has threat capabilities below the median level.

Low–low (LL) threat capabilities: A dummy variable indicating whether a given group has threat capabilities below the median level of sub-Saharan Africa and the ruling group in power in the given year also has threat capabilities below the median level.

Number of (politically relevant) ethnic groups: A count variable of the number of politically relevant groups at independence for a given country. Source: EPR dataset.

Ongoing rebellion: A dummy variable indicating whether there is an ongoing rebellion in the country in the previous year.

Past conflict: A dummy variable indicating whether a given group engaged in a large-scale civil war against the central government in the past.

Past coup: A dummy variable indicating whether a given group executed a successful coup in the past.

Powersharing but some exclusion: A dummy variable indicating if for a given country-year no group is "Monopoly" or "Dominant," but at least one or more politically relevant groups is excluded. Source: EPR dataset.

Recently excluded co-conspirator: A dummy variable indicating if a group is coded as a "co-conspirator" and coded as "Exclude dynamic" in the previous three years.

Ruler ethnic group (REG): A dummy variable indicating if the ruler of the country is a member of a given ethnic group. Source for ethnic group codings: Fearon 2003. Source for ruler's ethnic group: Fearon, Kasara and Laitin 2007 and author's codings.

Ruler's threat capabilities: A measure of the threat capabilities of the ruling group for a given year.

Threat capabilities: A normalized measure from 0 to 1 of a given group's size as a proportion of total population *and* the inverse of the log distance to the capital city from the center of the ethnic group's homeland.

Years since coup: Number of years since any group in the country successfully executed a coup. Source: McGowan 2003 and author's codings.

Years since last excluded: Number of years since group was last excluded from central government. Source: EPR dataset.

Appendix 3

Data on Ethnic Transfers of Power and Ethnicity of Coup Conspirators and Insurgents

TABLE A3.1 *Ruling Group Changes in Sub-Saharan Africa, Independence to 2005*

Country	Ruling group(s)	Years	Cause of loss of power	New ruling group(s)	Type of change
Angola	Mbundu-Mestico	1975–2005	–	–	
Benin	Northern (Bariba, Gurmanché/Betamaribe, etc.)	1960–1963	Coup d'état	South/Central (Fon) and Southeastern (Yoruba/Nagot and Goun)	Irregular replacement
Benin	South/Central (Fon) and Southeastern (Yoruba/Nagot and Goun)	1964–1965	Coup d'état	South/Central (Fon)	Irregular replacement
Benin	South/Central (Fon)	1966–1967	Coup d'état	Northern (Bariba, Gurmanché/Betamaribe, etc.)	Irregular replacement
Benin	Northern (Bariba, Gurmanché/Betamaribe, etc.)	1968–1989	National conference	South/Central (Fon)	Negotiated replacement

(continued)

TABLE A3.1 *Continued*

Country	Ruling group(s)	Years	Cause of loss of power	New ruling group(s)	Type of change
Benin	South/Central (Fon)	1990–1995	Election	Northern (Bariba, Gurmanché/Betamaribe, etc.)	Negotiated replacement
Benin	Northern (Bariba, Gurmanché/Betamaribe, etc.)	1996–2005	—	—	
Burundi	Tutsi and Hutu	1962–1965	Failed coup d'état	Tutsi	Narrowing
Burundi	Tutsi	1966–2001	Peace agreement	Tutsi and Hutu	Expansion
Burundi	Tutsi and Hutu	2002–2005	—	—	
Cameroon	Fulani (and other northern Muslim peoples)	1960–1982	Handover of power	Beti (and related peoples)	Negotiated replacement
Cameroon	Beti (and related peoples)	1983–2005	—	—	
CAR	Riverine groups (Mbaka, Yakoma, Banziri, etc.)	1960–1981	Coup d'état	Yakoma	Irregular replacement
CAR	Yakoma	1982–1993	Election	Sara	Negotiated replacement
CAR	Sara	1994–2002	Rebellion	Baya	Negotiated replacement
CAR	Baya	2003–2005	—	—	Irregular replacement

Country	Ethnic group	Year	Event	Successor group	Transition type
Chad	Sara	1960–1978	Rebellion	None (state collapse)	Irregular replacement
Chad	None (State collapse)	1979	Rebellion	Toubou	Irregular replacement
Chad	Toubou	1980–1990	Rebellion	Zaghawa, Bideyat	Irregular replacement
Chad	Zaghawa, Bideyat	1991–2005	–	–	
Congo	Lari	1960–1963	Coup d'état	Bakongo	Irregular replacement
Congo	Bakongo	1964–1968	Coup d'état	Mbochi	Irregular replacement
Congo	Mbochi	1969–1990	National conference	Lari/Bakongo	Negotiated replacement
Congo	Lari/Bakongo	1991	Election	Nibolek (Bembe, etc.)	Negotiated replacement
Congo	Nibolek (Bembe, etc.)	1992–1997	Rebellion	Mbochi	Irregular replacement
Congo	Mbochi	1998–2005	–	–	
Côte d'Ivoire	Baule (Akan)	1960–1999	Coup d'état (followed by election)	Kru	Irregular replacement
Côte d'Ivoire	Kru	2000–2005	–	–	
DRC	None (irrelevant)	1960–1965	Coup d'état	Ngbandi	Irregular replacement
DRC	Ngbandi	1966–1996	Rebellion	Tutsi-Banyamulenge	Irregular replacement
DRC	Tutsi-Banyamulenge	1997	Purge	Luba-Shaba	Narrowing
DRC	Luba-Shaba	1998–2002	Peace agreement	Luba-Shaba and Lunda-Yeke	Expansion
DRC	Luba-Shaba and Lunda-Yeke	2003–2005	–	–	
Eritrea	Tigrinya	1993–2005	–	–	
Ethiopia	Amhara	1946–1991	Rebellion	Tigray	Irregular replacement
Ethiopia	Tigray	1992–2005	–	–	

(continued)

TABLE A3.1 *Continued*

Country	Ruling group(s)	Years	Cause of loss of power	New ruling group(s)	Type of change
Gabon	Estuary Fang	1960–1967	Handover of power	Mbede (Bateke, Obamba)	Negotiated replacement
Gabon	Mbede (Bateke, Obamba)	1968–2005	–	–	
Gambia	Wolof	1965–1993	Coup d'état	Coalition (ethnicity irrelevant)	Irregular replacement
Gambia	Coalition (ethnicity irrelevant)	1994–2005	–	–	
Ghana	Other Akans	1957–1965	Coup d'état	Ga-Adangbe	Irregular replacement
Ghana	Ga-Adangbe	1966–1969	Coup d'état (then election)	Other Akans	Irregular replacement
Ghana	Other Akans	1970–1971	Coup d'état	Asante (Akan)	Irregular replacement
Ghana	Asante (Akan)	1972–1981	Coup d'état	Ewe	Irregular replacement
Ghana	Ewe	1982–1999	Election	Asante (Akan)	Negotiated replacement
Ghana	Asante (Akan)	2000–2005	–	–	
Guinea	Malinké	1958–1983	Coup d'état	Susu	Irregular replacement
Guinea	Susu	1984–2005	–	–	
Guinea-Bissau	Cape Verdean	1974–1980	Coup d'état	Papel	Irregular replacement
Guinea-Bissau	Papel	1981–1999	Rebellion (then election)	Balanta	Irregular replacement

Country	Ethnic group	Years	Event	Ethnic group	Outcome
Guinea-Bissau	Balanta	2000–2005	–	–	
Kenya	Kikuyu-Meru-Emb	1963–1978	Handover of power	Kalenjin-Masai-Turkana-Samburu	Negotiated replacement
Kenya	Kalenjin-Masai-Turkana-Samburu	1979–2002	Election	Kikuyu-Meru-Emb	Negotiated replacement
Kenya	Kikuyu-Meru-Emb	2003–2005	–	–	
Liberia	Americo-Liberians	1946–1980	Coup d'état	Krahn	Irregular replacement
Liberia	Krahn	1980–1989	Rebellion	None (state collapse)	Irregular replacement
Liberia	None (state collapse)	1990–1996	Rebellion	Americo-Liberians	
Liberia	Americo-Liberians	1997–2003	Handover of power/transitional government	Gio, Mano, Krahn (Guere), Americo-Liberians, Mandingo	Negotiated replacement
Liberia	Gio, Mano, Krahn (Guere), Americo-Liberians, Mandingo	2004–2005	–	–	
Madagascar	Cùtiers	1960–1972	Coup d'état	Highlanders	Irregular replacement
Madagascar	Highlanders	1973–1975	Assassination and appointment of new head of state	Cùtiers	Irregular replacement
Madagascar	Cùtiers	1976–1992	Election	None (irrelevant)	
Madagascar	None (irrelevant)	1993–2005	–	–	

(continued)

TABLE A3.1 *Continued*

Country	Ruling group(s)	Years	Cause of loss of power	New ruling group(s)	Type of change
Malawi	Chewa and Ngoni	1964–1993	Election	Lomwe (Nguru), Mananja-Nyanja, and Yao	Negotiated replacement
Malawi	Lomwe (Nguru), Mananja-Nyanja, and Yao	1994–2005	–	–	
Mali	Blacks (Mande, Peul, Voltaic, etc.)	1960–2005	–	–	
Mauritania	White Moor (Beydan)	1960–2005	–	–	
Mozambique	Tsonga-Chopi	1975–2005	–	–	
Namibia	Ovambo	1990–2005	–	–	
Niger	Djerma-Songhai	1960–1990	National conference	Hausa	Negotiated replacement
Niger	Hausa	1991–1994	Election	Hausa and Djerma-Songhai	Negotiated replacement
Niger	Hausa and Djerma-Songhai	1995	Coup d'état	Djerma-Songhai	Narrowing
Niger	Djerma-Songhai	1996–2005	–	–	
Nigeria	Hausa-Fulani and Muslim Middle Belt	1960–1999	Election	Yoruba	Negotiated replacement
Nigeria	Yoruba	2000–2005	–	–	
Rwanda	Hutu	1962–1994	Rebellion	Tutsi	Irregular replacement

Rwanda	Tutsi	1995–2005	–	–	
Senegal	Serer	1960–1980	Handover of power	Wolof	Negotiated replacement
Senegal	Wolof	1981–2005	–	–	
Sierra Leone	Mende	1961–1967	Coup d'état	Limba	Irregular replacement
Sierra Leone	Limba	1968–1991	Coup d'état	None (state collapse)	Irregular replacement
Sierra Leone	None (state collapse)	1992–1995	Coup d'état (then election)	Mende	
Sierra Leone	Mende	1996	Coup d'état	None (state collapse)	Irregular replacement
Sierra Leone	None (state collapse)	1997–2001	Peace process (then election)	Mende	
Sierra Leone	Mende	2002–2005	–	–	
South Africa	Afrikaner	1947–1993	Election	Xhosa	Negotiated replacement
South Africa	Xhosa	1994–2005	–	–	
Sudan	Shaigiya, Ja'aliyin, and Danagla (Arab)	1956–2005	–	–	
Togo	Ewe (and related groups)	1960–1966	Coup d'état	Kabré (and related groups)	Irregular replacement

(continued)

TABLE A3.1 *Continued*

Country	Ruling group(s)	Years	Cause of loss of power	New ruling group(s)	Type of change
Togo	Kabré (and related groups)	1967–2005	–	–	–
Uganda	Northerners (Langi, Acholi, Teso, Madi, Kakwa-Nubian, Lugbara, Alur) and Baganda	1960–1965	Coup d'état	Northerners (Langi, Acholi, Madi, Kakwa-Nubian, Lugbara, Alur)	Narrowing
Uganda	Northerners (Langi, Acholi, Madi, Kakwa-Nubian, Lugbara, Alur)	1966–1971	Coup d'état	Far Northwest Nile (Kakwa-Nubian, Madi, Lugbara, Alur)	Irregular replacement
Uganda	Far Northwest Nile (Kakwa-Nubian, Madi, Lugbara, Alur)	1972–1973	Purge	Kakwa-Nubian	Narrowing
Uganda	Kakwa-Nubian	1974–1979	Rebellion/ foreign invasion/ election	Northerners (Langi, Acholi, Teso)	Irregular replacement
Uganda	Northerners (Langi, Acholi, Teso)	1980–1985	Rebellion	Southwesterners (Ankole, Banyoro, Toro, Banyarwanda)	Irregular replacement

				Southwesterners (Ankole, Banyoro, Toro)	Narrowing
Uganda	Southwesterners (Ankole, Banyoro, Toro, Banyarwanda)	1986–1989	Purge	Southwesterners (Ankole, Banyoro, Toro)	Narrowing
Uganda	Southwesterners (Ankole, Banyoro, Toro)	1990–2005	–	–	
Zambia	Bemba speakers, Tonga-Ila-Lenje, Nyanja speakers (Easterners), and Lozi (Barotse)	1964–2005	–	–	
Zimbabwe	Europeans	1965–1979	Peace agreement/ election	Shona	Negotiated replacement
Zimbabwe	Shona	1980–1981	Purge	Shona (minus Ndau)	Narrowing
Zimbabwe	Shona (minus Ndau)	1982–1987	Purge	Shona (minus Manyika and Ndau)	Narrowing
Zimbabwe	Shona (minus Manyika and Ndau)	1988–1991	Reconciliation	Shona	Expansion
Zimbabwe	Shona	1992–2005	–	–	

TABLE A3.2 *Ethnicity of Conspirators of Failed and Successful Coups and Successful Rebellions, Independence to 2005*

Event	Country	Date	Conspirator(s)	Ethnic category (and EPR status) of conspirators at time of event
Failed coup	Angola	May 27, 1977	Commander Nito Alves (former interior minister)	Mbundu-Mestico (Monopoly)
Successful coup	Benin	October 28, 1963	Col. Christophe Soglo, army commander, and members of military	South-central (Fon) (Junior Partner)
Successful coup	Benin	November 29, 1965	Gen. Soglo, army commander	South-central (Fon) (Senior Partner)
Successful coup	Benin	December 22, 1965	Gen. Soglo, army chief of staff, Maj. Alphonse Alley, who became chief of staff under Soglo, and military elements	South-central (Fon) (Senior Partner); Basila (Irrelevant)
Successful coup	Benin	December 17, 1967	Capt. Kérékou and Maj. Kouandété	Northern (Bariba, Gurmanché/Betamaribe, etc.) (Powerless)
Successful coup	Benin	December 10, 1969	Lt. Col. Maurice Kouandété	Northern (Bariba, Gurmanché/Betamaribe, etc.) (Senior Partner)
Failed coup	Benin	February 23, 1972	Col. Maurice Kouandété	Northern (Bariba, Gurmanché/Betamaribe, etc.) (Senior Partner)
Successful coup	Benin	October 26, 1972	Maj. Mathieu Kérékou supported by a troika of Fon junior officers	Northern (Bariba, Gurmanché/Betamaribe, etc.) (Senior Partner); South/Central (Fon) (Junior Partner)
Failed coup	Benin	January 21, 1975	Capt. Janvier Assogba, Minister of Civil Service and Labor	South/Central (Fon) (Junior Partner)

Failed coup	Benin	May 27, 1992	Capt. Pascal Tawes	Northern (Bariba, Gurmanché/ Betamaribe, etc.) (Junior Partner)
Failed coup	Burundi	October 18, 1965	Members of army and gendarmerie	Hutu (Senior Partner)
Successful coup	Burundi	July 8, 1966	Prince Charles Ndizeye, Crown Prince	Tutsi (Dominant)
Successful coup	Burundi	November 28, 1966	Young Tutsi army officers, led by Capt. Micombero	Tutsi (Dominant)
Successful coup	Burundi	November 1, 1976	Burundi armed forces, under the leadership of Col. Bagaza	Tutsi (Dominant)
Successful coup	Burundi	September 3, 1987	Maj. Pierre Buyoya (a Tutsi), installed as president with the full support of the army	Tutsi (Dominant)
Failed coup	Burundi	March 4, 1992	Cyprien Mbonimpa (former foreign minister) and others	Tutsi (Senior Partner)
Failed coup	Burundi	July 3, 1993	Senior military officers	Tutsi (Senior Partner)
Failed coup	Burundi	October 21, 1993	Col. Jean Bikomagu	Tutsi (Senior Partner)
Failed coup	Burundi	April 25, 1994	Members of Burundi's army, including at least four army captains	Tutsi (Dominant)
Successful coup	Burundi	July 25, 1996	Defense Minister Sinsoyiheba, Pierre Buyoya and the Army	Tutsi (Dominant)
Failed coup	Burundi	April 19, 2001	Lt. Gaston Ntakarutimana	Tutsi (Dominant)
Failed coup	Burundi	July 23, 2001	Army soldiers	Tutsi (Dominant)
Failed coup	Cameroon	April 6–9, 1984	Col. Saleh Ibrahim and members of the Presidential Republican Guard	Fulani (and other northern Muslim peoples) (Junior Partner)

(continued)

TABLE A3.2 *Continued*

Event	Country	Date	Conspirator(s)	Ethnic category (and EPR status) of conspirators at time of event
Successful coup	CAR	January 1, 1966	High-level army officers, led by Col. Jean-Bedel Bokassa (army chief of staff) and Lt. Col. Alexander Banza	Bokassa is riverine groups (Mbaka, Yakoma, Banziri, etc.) (Dominant); Banza is northern groups (Baya, Banda, Mandjia, Sara) (Powerless)
Failed coup	CAR	December 7, 1974	Inspector General of the Gendarmerie, Gen. Lingoupou	Northern groups (Baya, Banda, Mandjia, Sara) (Powerless)
Failed coup	CAR	February 1, 1976	Three army officers, Cdr. Fidel Obrou (Bokassa's son-in-law), Lt. Satao, and Martin Meya (Obrou's brother) were named as the ringleaders	Northern groups (Baya, Banda, Mandjia, Sara) (Powerless)
Successful coup	CAR	September 20, 1979	Mr. David Dacko, with the aid of CAR and French troops	Riverine groups (Mbaka, Yakoma, Banziri, etc.) (Dominant)
Successful coup	CAR	September 1, 1981	Army, led by Gen. André Kolingba	Riverine groups (Mbaka, Yakoma, Banziri, etc.) (Dominant)
Failed coup	CAR	March 3, 1982	Gen. François Bozize, Gen. Mbaikuna, and M. Patasse	Northern groups (Baya, Banda, Mandjia, Sara) (Powerless)
Failed coup	CAR	May 18, 1996	About 200 army soldiers led by Sgt. Cyriaque Souke	Yakoma (Junior Partner)
Failed coup	CAR	May 28, 2001	Rebellious soldiers led by the CAR's former ruler, Gen. André Kolingba	Yakoma (Junior Partner)
Successful coup	CAR	March 15, 2003	The coup leader was François Bozize, former army commander	Baya (Junior Partner)

Successful coup	Chad	April 13, 1975	Units of the army and gendarmerie, led by Gen. Noel Odingar, armed forces chief of staff	Sara (Dominant)
Failed coup	Chad	April 1, 1977	Some sixty soldiers ("Nomad Guards") supported by armored cars and led by Sub-Lt. Brahim Abakar Koumba	Arabs (Powerless)
Successful rebellion	Chad	June 7, 1982	Hissène Habré and the FAN	Toubou (Discriminated); Zaghawa, Bideyat (Irrelevant); Hadjerai (Irrelevant)
Failed coup	Chad	April 1, 1989	Interior Minister Ibrahim Mahamat Itno, Habré's security adviser and former chief of staff Idriss Déby, and Hassan Djamous of the Chadian National Armed Forces	Zaghawa-Bideyat (Junior Partner)
Successful rebellion	Chad	1990	The MPS led by Idriss Déby and his deputy, Maldoum Abbas	Zaghawa-Bideyat (Discriminated); Hadjerai (Discriminated)
Failed coup	Chad	October 13, 1991	Maldom Bada Abbas	Hadjerai (Junior Partner)
Successful coup	Congo	August 15, 1963	A large crowd of demonstrators, supported by trade-union leaders, the police commander, and elements of the army led by Capt. David Maoutsaka and Capt. Félix Mouzabakany	Bakongo (Junior Partner)
Failed coup	Congo	June 27, 1966	Capt. Marien Ngouabi and elements of the Congolese army	Kouyou (Irrelevant)

(continued)

TABLE A3.2 *Continued*

Event	Country	Date	Conspirator(s)	Ethnic category (and EPR status) of conspirators at time of event
Failed coup	Congo	July 31, 1968	Paramilitary civic guards	Not clear
Successful coup	Congo	August 3, 1968	Elements of the army (mainly paratroopers) overthrew the government and rescued Marien Ngouabi from prison	Kouyou (Irrelevant)
Failed coup	Congo	March 22, 1970	Lt. Pierre Kikanga	Lari/Bakongo (Powerless)
Failed coup	Congo	February 22, 1972	Lt. Ange Diawara	Lari/Bakongo (Powerless)
Failed coup	Congo	March 18, 1977	Army Capt. Berthelemy Kikadidi	Lari/Bakongo (Powerless)
Successful rebellion	Congo	October 4, 1997	Denis Sassou-Nguesso's Cobra militia	Mbochi (Powerless)
Successful coup	Côte d'Ivoire	December 24, 1999	Non-commissioned officers, led by Staff Sgt. Ibrahim ("Ib") Coulibaly, oust Bédié in a bloodless coup d'état; Gen. Guéï is asked to lead the junta	Southern Mande (Discriminated); Kru (Powerless); northerner (Mande and Voltaic/Gur) (Discriminated)
Failed coup	Côte d'Ivoire	September 18, 2000	Twenty-six persons, including six military officers (among them Gen. Palenfo and Gen. Coulibaly)	Northerner (Mande and Voltaic/Gur) (Discriminated)
Failed coup	Côte d'Ivoire	January 7–8, 2001	Government claimed they were from "the north"	Northerner (Mande and Voltaic/Gur) (Discriminated)

Failed coup	Côte d'Ivoire	September 19, 2002	Ibrahim "Ib" Coulibaly and about 750–800 soldiers, mainly northern ranks and NCOs known to be loyal to former leader Gen. Robert Guéï	Northerner (Mande and Voltaic/Gur) (Discriminated)
Successful coup	DRC	September 14, 1960	200 paratroopers of the Congolese Army under the command of Col. Mobutu	Ngbandi (Irrelevant)
Successful coup	DRC	November 25, 1960	Gen. Mobutu, commander-in-chief of the army, with the support of senior officers and the army	Ngbandi (Irrelevant)
Failed coup	DRC	November 19, 1963	Unnamed soldiers and supporters of the Conseil National de Libération, which is led by C. Gbenye	Not clear
Successful rebellion	DRC	May 17, 1997	AFDL, chaired by Laurent Kabila and supported by groups from eastern DRC	Luba-Shaba (Powerless); Tutsi-Banyamulenge (Discriminated); Other Kivu Groups (Powerless)
Successful coup	DRC	January 16, 2001	Rachidi Kasereka, Col. Eddy Kapend, the DRC chief of staff, Newej Yau, Commander of the Kinshasa Military Region, and possibly Angolans and the recently fired generals	Rachidi was Nandi (Other Kivu Groups) (Junior Partner); Kapend and Nawej were Lunda-Yeke (Junior Partner)
Failed coup	DRC	March 28, 2004	Ex-officers of the army of the late President Mobutu Sese Seko	Ngbandi (Junior Partner)
Failed coup	DRC	June 11, 2004	Maj. Eric Lenge	Luba-Shaba (Senior Partner)

(*continued*)

TABLE A3.2 *Continued*

Event	Country	Date	Conspirator(s)	Ethnic category (and EPR status) of conspirators at time of event
Failed coup	Ethiopia	December 13–17, 1960	Imperial Bodyguard, led by Brig. Gen Mengistu Neway and his younger brother Germame Neway	Amhara (Dominant)
Successful coup	Ethiopia	September 12, 1974	The armed forces, under the leadership of Gen. Andom, Gen. Abate, and Gen. Mengistu	Andom is Tigray (Discriminated); Mengistu and Abate, Amhara (Dominant)
Successful coup	Ethiopia	November 22–23, 1974	Provisional military government's security forces loyal to Maj. Haile Mengistu Mariam	Amhara (Dominant)
Successful coup	Ethiopia	February 3, 1977	Cols. Mengistu and Atnafu and troops loyal to them	Amhara (Dominant)
Successful coup	Ethiopia	November 12, 1977	Col. Mengistu and his troops	Amhara (Dominant)
Failed coup	Ethiopia	May 16, 1989	Gen. Merid Neguisse, armed forces chief of staff and Gen. Amha Desta, air-force commander	Merid's ethnicity is unknown; Desta is Amhara (Dominant)
Successful rebellion	Ethiopia	1991	EPRDF, a coalition of the TPLF, EPLF, and OLF	Tigray (Discriminated); Eritrean (Discriminated); Oroma (Discriminated)
Failed coup	Gabon	February 17–20, 1964	The group of 150 troops from the 400 strong Gabonese Army was led by Lt. Daniel M'bene and Lt. Ndo Edeu with J. H. Aubame in charge	Northern Fang (Powerless)

Outcome	Country	Date	Description	Ethnic identity
Failed coup	Gambia	July 30, 1981	Some 358 members of the field force in alliance with discontented urban civilians led by Mr. Kukoi Samba Sanyang	Diola (Junior Partner)
Successful coup	Gambia	July 22–23, 1994	Soldiers of the Gambia National Army led by four very young and well-trained lieutenants: Yahya Jammeh (twenty-nine at the time of the coup), Sadibou Hydara (twenty-nine), Sana Sabally (twenty-eight), Yankuba Touray (twenty-seven), and Edward Signateh (twenty-four)	Jammeh is Diola (Junior Partner); Sadibou Hydara is Mandinka (Junior Partner); Sana Sabally is Fula (Junior Partner); Yankuba Touray is Bambara (Irrelevant); Edward Signateh is Mandinka (Junior Partner).
Failed coup	Gambia	November 11, 1994	Finance Minister Bakary Dabo	Mandinka (Irrelevant)
Failed coup	Ghana	January 2, 1964	Police Constable Seth Ametewee	Ewe (Junior Partner)
Successful coup	Ghana	February 24, 1966	Group of army officers, led by Col. E. K. Kotoka, Police Inspector General J. W. K. Harley, and A. A. Afrifa	Kotoka and Harley are Ewe (Junior Partner); Afrifa is Asante (Akan) (Junior Partner)
Failed coup	Ghana	April 17, 1967	120 members of the Reconnaissance Regiment commanded by Lt. Samuel B. Arthur	Other Akans (Junior Partner)
Successful coup	Ghana	January 13, 1972	Army officers led by Col. Acheampong	Asante (Akan) (Junior Partner)

(continued)

TABLE A3.2 *Continued*

Event	Country	Date	Conspirator(s)	Ethnic category (and EPR status) of conspirators at time of event
Successful coup	Ghana	July 5, 1978	Senior officers in the Supreme Military Council led by Gen. Fred Akuffo and Brig. Odartey-Wellington	Other Akans (Junior Partner)
Failed coup	Ghana	May 15, 1979	About sixty air-force men led by Flight Lt. Rawlings	Ewe (Junior Partner)
Successful coup	Ghana	June 4–6, 1979	Maj. Mensah, Flight Lt. Rawlings, and junior air-force officers and ranks	Mensah and Rawlings are Ewe (Junior Partner)
Successful coup	Ghana	December 31, 1981	Flight Lt. Rawlings, Sgt. Alolga Akata-Pore and a group of ex-soldiers and elements of the army and air force, including ranks and NCOs	Rawlings is Ewe (Junior Partner); Akata-Pore is northern groups (Mole-Dagbani, Gurma, Grusi) (Junior Partner)
Failed coup	Ghana	November 24, 1982	Soldiers loyal to Sgt. Alolga Akate-Pore, a member of the Provisional National Defense Council	Northern groups (Mole-Dagbani, Gurma, Grusi) (Junior Partner)
Failed coup	Ghana	June 19, 1983	A group of Ghanaian soldiers that had escaped to Togo after the November 1982 coup attempt led by Lt. Col. Ekow Dennis, Capt. Edward Adjei Sgt. Malik	Northern groups (Mole-Dagbani, Gurma, Grusi) (Junior Partner)

Failed coup	Ghana	March 23–25, 1984	Ghanaian military exiles led by Lance Corporal Halidu Gyiwah, Corporal Martin Ajumba, Sgt. Malik who had escaped the country after the last coup attempt	Northern groups (Mole-Dagbani, Gurma, Grusi) (Junior Partner)
Failed coup	Guinea	November 22, 1970	Portuguese	Portuguese (Foreign)
Successful coup	Guinea	April 3, 1984	The armed forces of Guinea (army, navy, air force, gendarmerie and people's militia) led by French-trained Col. Lansana Conté and supported by Col. Diarra Traoré	Conté is Susu (Junior Partner); Traoré is Malinké (Senior Partner); Peul (Junior Partner)
Failed coup	Guinea	July 4, 1985	Col. Diarra Traoré	Malinké (Junior Partner)
Failed coup	Guinea	February 3, 1996	2,000 lower-ranked troops; Maj. Gbago Zoumanigui was the apparent ringleader	Zoumanigui is Toma (Irrelevant); others Malinké (Powerless)
Successful coup	Guinea-Bissau	November 15, 1980	Brig. Gen. Joao Vieira supported by Balanta soldiers	Vieira is Papel (Irrelevant); soldiers are Balanta (Powerless)
Failed coup	Guinea-Bissau	March 17, 1993	Mario Soares, a senior officer of the National Marine	Unknown
Failed coup	Guinea-Bissau	June 7, 1998	Brig. Ansumane Mane, supported by Balanta soldiers	Mane is Mandinka (Irrelevant); soldiers are Balanta (Junior Partner)
Successful rebellion	Guinea-Bissau	May 7, 1999	Brig. Ansumane Mane supported by Balanta soldiers	Mane is Mandinka (Irrelevant); soldiers are Balanta (Junior Partner)
Successful coup	Guinea-Bissau	September 14, 2003	Gen. Verissimo Correia Seabre, army chief of staff	Papel (Powerless)

(continued)

TABLE A3.2 *Continued*

Event	Country	Date	Conspirator(s)	Ethnic category (and EPR status) of conspirators at time of event
Failed coup	Kenya	August 1, 1982	About 200 junior members of the Kenya Air Force led by Senior Private Hezekiah Ochuka and Senior Sgt. Pancras Oteyo	Luo (Discriminated)
Failed coup	Liberia	June 22, 1955	S. David Coleman	Americo-Liberian (Monopoly)
Successful coup	Liberia	April 12, 1980	Seventeen NCOs led by twenty-eight-year-old Master Sgt. Samuel Doe, Thomas Quiwonkpa, and Weh Syen	Doe is Krahn (Discriminated); Quiwonkpa is Gio (Discriminated); Syen is Kru (Discriminated)
Failed coup	Liberia	April 1, 1985	Moses M. D. Flanzamation (Deputy Commander of the Presidential Guard)	Unknown
Failed coup	Liberia	November 12, 1985	Brig. Gen. Thomas Quiwonkpa and supporters	Gio (Discriminated)
Failed coup	Liberia	September 15, 1994	Former Lt. Gen. Charles Julue	Krahn (State collapse)
Successful coup	Madagascar	May 18, 1972	Gen. Ramanantsoa	Highlanders (Powerless)
Failed coup	Madagascar	December 31, 1974	Col. Brechard Rajaonarison	Côtiers (Junior Partner)
Failed coup	Madagascar	February 11, 1975	Elements of the Mobile Police Commando Unit led by Capt. Jean Bora, Maurice Alphonse, and Laza Petit-Jean and members of the Parti Socialiste Malgache under the leadership of Col. Rajaonarison	Côtiers (Junior Partner)

Outcome	Country	Date	Description	Ethnic group
Successful coup	Mali	November 19, 1968	A national liberation committee, led by Lt. Moussa Traoré (later Brig. Gen.), took over the country and jailed President Keita	Blacks (Mande, Peul, Voltaic, etc.) (Monopoly)
Successful coup	Mali	March 25, 1991	Lt. Col. Amadou Toumani Touré, troops loyal to him, and thousands of civilian protestors	Blacks (Mande, Peul, Voltaic, etc.) (Monopoly)
Successful coup	Mauritania	July 10, 1978	Army led by Lt. Col. Mustapha Ould Salek	White Moor (Beydan) (Senior Partner)
Successful coup	Mauritania	January 4, 1980	Mohamed Ould Haidalla, the ruling Military Committee of National Salvation, with the tacit support of the army	White Moor (Beydan) (Senior Partner)
Failed coup	Mauritania	March 16, 1981	Soldiers led by four officers (Lt. Col. M. Ould Abdel Kader, Lt. Col. A. Salem Ould Sidi, Lt. M. Niang, and Lt. M. Doudou Seck)	White Moor (Beydan) (Senior Partner)
Successful coup	Mauritania	December 12, 1984	Lt. Col. Maaouya Ould Sid'Ahmed Taya (Sidi Ahmed Taya) and the Army	White Moor (Beydan) (Senior Partner)
Failed coup	Mauritania	June 8–10, 2003	Ould Hannena	White Moor (Beydan) (Senior Partner)
Failed coup	Mozambique	December 17–18, 1975	Troops of the Machava Battalion	Not clear

(continued)

TABLE A3.2 *Continued*

Event	Country	Date	Conspirator(s)	Ethnic category (and EPR status) of conspirators at time of event
Successful coup	Niger	April 14, 1974	The 2,500-man army led by Lt. Col. Seyni Kountche and Maj. Sani-Souna Sido	Kountche is Djerma-Songhai (Dominant)
Failed coup	Niger	March 14–15, 1976	Maj. Moussa Bayere and Capt. Sidi Mohammed	Bayere is Hausa (Powerless); Mohammed is Taureg (Powerless)
Failed coup	Niger	October 5–6, 1983	Mahamane Sidikou and Amadou Oumarou	Sidikou is Djerma-Songhai (Dominant); Oumarou is Fulani (Powerless)
Successful coup	Niger	January 27, 1996	Coup leader Col. Ibrahim Bare Mainassara and members of the military	Hausa (Senior Partner)
Successful coup	Niger	April 9, 1999	Daouda Malam Wanke, head of presidential guard	Hausa (Powerless)
Successful coup	Nigeria	January 15, 1966	Five army majors led by the young Maj. Chakwuma Kaduna Nzeogwu	Igbo (Regional Autonomy)
Successful coup	Nigeria	July 29, 1966	Troops from both the Middle Belt and North did the coup; Lt.-Col. Muritala Mohammed, later to become head of state via a coup in 1975, was one of the principal architects	Hausa-Fulani and Muslim Middle Belt (Dominant)
Successful coup	Nigeria	July 29, 1975	Gen. Hassan Katsina	Hausa-Fulani and Muslim Middle Belt (Senior Partner)

Failed coup	Nigeria	February 13, 1976	Lt. Col. Bukar Suka Dimka (head of the Nigerian Army Signal Training Corps)	Hausa-Fulani and Muslim Middle Belt (Senior Partner)
Successful coup	Nigeria	December 31, 1983	Maj. Gen. Mohammed Buhari and Maj. Gen. Tunde Idiagbon, Brig. Sani Abacha and senior members of the Nigerian armed forces including Maj. Gen. Ibrahim Babangida, who became army chief of staff after the coup	Hausa-Fulani and Muslim Middle Belt (Senior Partner)
Successful coup	Nigeria	August 27, 1985	Gen. Babangida	Hausa-Fulani and Muslim Middle Belt (Dominant)
Failed coup	Nigeria	April 22, 1990	Maj. Gideon Orkar (and others from southern Nigeria)	Tiv (Powerless)
Successful coup	Nigeria	November 17, 1993	Gen. Sani Abacha and the Nigerian Armed Forces	Hausa-Fulani and Muslim Middle Belt (Dominant)
Successful coup	Rwanda	July 5, 1973	Army colonels, led by Maj. Gen. Juvénal Habyarimana, Defense Minister, and the National Guard (Army)	Hutu (Monopoly)
Successful rebellion	Rwanda	June 1994	RPF under military leadership of Paul Kagame	Tutsi (Discriminated)
Failed coup	Sierra Leone	March 21, 1967	Brig. David Lansana	Mende (Dominant)

(continued)

TABLE A3.2 *Continued*

Event	Country	Date	Conspirator(s)	Ethnic category (and EPR status) of conspirators at time of event
Successful coup	Sierra Leone	March 23, 1967	Senior army officers headed by Lt. Col. Genda and Lt. Col. Juxon-Smith, Maj. S. B. Jumu, Maj. A. Charles Blake, and Maj. B. I. Kaisamba plus Mr. L. William Leigh, Commissioner of Police; Assistant Commissioner Alpha Kamara, and units of the army and police	Juxon-Smith is Creole (Powerless); Most Others Mende (Dominant)
Successful coup	Sierra Leone	April 18, 1968	Brig. John Bangura and members of the Anti-Corruption Revolutionary Movement (ACRM)	Northern groups (Temne, Limba) (Powerless)
Failed coup	Sierra Leone	March 23, 1971	Brig. John Bangura and other officers	Bangura is Temne (Junior Partner); a number of other officers are Mende (Powerless)
Failed coup	Sierra Leone	March 23, 1987	A group of rebel senior officers, led by Gabriel Mohamad Tennyson Kaikai	Mende (Powerless)
Successful coup	Sierra Leone	April 30, 1992	Junior officer members of the Sierra Leone Army led by Capt. Valentine Strasser, Solomon Musa, and Julius Bio	Strasser is Creole (Junior Partner); Musa and Bio are Mende (Powerless)

Failed coup	Sierra Leone	December 29, 1992	Supporters of ex-president Joseph Monoh, allegedly led by Sgt. Lamin Bangura	Limba (State collapse)
Failed coup	Sierra Leone	October 2–3, 1995	Capt. Alie Badara Koroma	Not clear
Successful coup	Sierra Leone	January 16, 1996	Julius Maada Bio, who had been Strasser's closest associate in the military junta, and Lt. T. M. Brima	Bio is Mende (Senior Partner); Brima is Kono (Powerless)
Successful coup	Sierra Leone	May 25, 1997	Johnny Paul Koroma and Armed Forces Revolutionary Council (AFRC)	Limba (Junior Partner)
Failed coup	Sierra Leone	May 22, 2000	Mutinous soldiers who support the former military junta of Maj. Johnny Paul Koroma	Not clear
Successful coup	Sudan	November 17, 1958	Troops under command of Gen. Ibrahim Ahmed Abboud	Shaigiya, Ja'aliyin and Danagla (Arab) (Dominant)
Failed coup	Sudan	March 4–9, 1959	Brig. Muhyi al-Din Abdullah and Brig. Abdal-Rahim Shannan	Shaigiya, Ja'aliyin and Danagla (Arab) (Dominant)
Failed coup	Sudan	May 21–22, 1959	Brig. Muhyi al-Din Abdullah and Brig. Abdal-Rahim Shannan	Shaigiya, Ja'aliyin and Danagla (Arab) (Dominant)
Failed coup	Sudan	November 9, 1959	Mutiny at Infantry School in Omdurman	Not clear
Failed coup	Sudan	December 18, 1966	Khalid Hussein al-Kid	Shaigiya, Ja'aliyin and Danagla (Arab) (Dominant)

(continued)

TABLE A3.2 *Continued*

Event	Country	Date	Conspirator(s)	Ethnic category (and EPR status) of conspirators at time of event
Successful coup	Sudan	May 25, 1969	Some 400 army troops led by young officers of the rank of Maj. and Col. under the overall leadership of Col. Nimeiry	Shaigiya, Ja'aliyin and Danagla (Arab) (Dominant)
Failed coup	Sudan	July 21–23, 1971	Maj. Hashim al-Ata	Shaigiya, Ja'aliyin and Danagla (Arab) (Dominant)
Failed coup	Sudan	September 5, 1975	Lt. Col. Hassan Hussein Osman	Other Arab groups (Powerless)
Failed coup	Sudan	July 2, 1976	Mohammed Nour Saad and Sadiq al-Mahdi	Other Arab groups (Powerless); Shaigiya, Ja'aliyin and Danagla (Arab) (Dominant)
Failed coup	Sudan	February 3, 1977	Mr. Philip Abbas Gabosha	Nuba (Powerless)
Failed coup	Sudan	July 2–3, 1978	Army units and others loyal to Northern Front	Unknown
Failed coup	Sudan	May 15–16, 1983	105th Battalion (Southern) of the 1st Division led by Kerubino Kuanyin Bol	Dinka (Discriminated)
Successful coup	Sudan	April 6, 1985	Gen. Sawar al-Dahab and top officers of the Sudanese military	Shaigiya, Ja'aliyin and Danagla (Arab) (Dominant)
Successful coup	Sudan	June 30, 1989	A group of army officers led by Brig. Gen. Omar Hassan Ahmad al-Bashir	Shaigiya, Ja'aliyin and Danagla (Arab) (Dominant)

Outcome	Country	Date	Leaders	Ethnic groups
Failed coup	Sudan	April 23, 1990	Air-force commander, Maj. Gen. Khalid al-Zayn Ali, the artillery-corps commander, Maj. Gen. Abdul Kader, and the ex-governor of the Eastern Region, Brig. Mohammed Osman Hamed Karar	Shaigiya, Ja'aliyin and Danagla (Arab) (Dominant); Karar was Beja (Powerless)
Successful coup	Togo	January 13, 1963	Sgt. Bodjillo and Sgt. Eyadéma led the coup	Kabré (and related groups) (Powerless)
Successful coup	Togo	January 13, 1967	Lt. Col. Étienne Gnassingbé Eyadéma, chief of staff, and the Togolese Army	Kabré (and related groups) (Junior Partner)
Failed coup	Togo	August 8, 1970	Noe Kutuklui and Jean-Alexandre Osseyi	Ewe (and related groups) (Powerless)
Failed coup	Togo	October 1, 1991	Troops loyal to Eyadéma, led by Narcisse Djoua	Kabré (and related groups) (Senior Partner)
Failed coup	Togo	October 7–8, 1991	Green beret soldiers of the presidential guard	Kabré (and related groups) (Senior Partner)
Failed coup	Togo	November 27–30, 1991	Army units loyal to former President Eyadéma including the Rapid Intervention Force, presidential guard and 2nd Batallion	Kabré (and related groups) (Senior Partner)
Failed coup	Togo	December 3, 1991	Troops loyal to Eyadéma	Kabré (and related groups) (Senior Partner)
Failed coup	Togo	December 15, 1991	Troops loyal to Eyadéma	Kabré (and related groups) (Senior Partner)

(continued)

TABLE A3.2 *Continued*

Event	Country	Date	Conspirator(s)	Ethnic category (and EPR status) of conspirators at time of event
Successful coup	Uganda	February 24, 1966	Prime Minister Obote, with the support of various police and army elements led by Cdr. Idi Amin Dada	Obote is Langi; Amin is Kakwa—all are northerners (Langi, Acholi, Teso, Madi, Kakwa-Nubian, Lugbara, Alur) (Senior Partner)
Successful coup	Uganda	January 24–25, 1971	Sections of the Army and Police led by Maj. Gen. Haji Idi Amin Dada	Amin is Kakwa; other soldiers involved were West Nilers and Nubians—all are northerners (Langi, Acholi, Madi, Kakwa-Nubian, Lugbara, Alur) (Dominant)
Failed coup	Uganda	July 12, 1971	A section of the Army at Moroto Barracks	Acholi and Langi? (formerly Dominant); northerners (Langi, Acholi, Madi, Kakwa-Nubian, Lugbara, Alur)
Failed coup	Uganda	March 23–24, 1974	Members from the Malire Mechanized Battalion, allegedly led by Brig. Charles Arube	Arube is Kakwa; others involved Lugbara, Far Northwest Nile (Kakwa-Nubian, Madi, Lugbara, Alur) (Dominant)
Failed coup	Uganda	November 11, 1974	Members of Amin's Special Commando Division	Not clear
Failed coup	Uganda	February 16, 1975	Members of the army	Not clear
Failed coup	Uganda	August 1975	Lt. Col. Gori and other officers based at Masaka	Far Northwest Nilers (Madi, Lugbara, Alur) (Powerless)

Failed coup	Uganda	June 10, 1976	Probably elements within the army	Not clear
Failed coup	Uganda	July 1976	Senior army and police officers including Ali Towilli, Superintendent of Police	Kakwa-Nubian (Dominant)
Failed coup	Uganda	June 18, 1977	The leader of the abortive uprising was a senior air-force major, Patrick Kimune, one of Amin's most trusted pilots	Basoga (Discriminated)
Successful rebellion	Uganda	April 11, 1979	Uganda National Liberation Front (UNLF), a coalition of anti-Idi Amin forces, backed by Tanzanian army	Langi/Acholi (Discriminated); Southwesterners (Ankole, Banyoro, Toro, Banyarwanda (Discriminated); Baganda (Discriminated); Teso (Powerless)
Successful coup	Uganda	May 11, 1980	The coup was led by Brig. David Ojok, army chief of staff, a close associate of Obote, and supported by Paulo Muwanga, Yoweri Museveni, and Tito Okello	Muwanga is Baganda (Discriminated); Ojok is Langi; (Dominant); Museveni is Ankole (Discriminated); Okello is Acholi (Dominant)
Successful coup	Uganda	July 27, 1985	The four-and-a-half-year-old government of President Milton Obote was overthrown by elements of the Ugandan military under the leadership of Brig. Basilio Olara-Okello and Lt. Gen. Tito Okello	Okello is Acholi (Dominant)

(continued)

TABLE A3.2 *Continued*

Event	Country	Date	Conspirator(s)	Ethnic category (and EPR status) of conspirators at time of event
Successful rebellion	Uganda	January 26, 1986	National Resistance Movement led by Yoweri Museveni	Southwesteners (Ankole, Banyoro, Toro, Banyarwanda), (Discriminated); Baganda (Discriminated)
Failed coup	Uganda	April 7–11, 1988	200 mutineers of the 19th Artillery Regiment and the 8th Infantry Battalion	Not clear
Failed coup	Zambia	October 16, 1980	Edward Shamwana and Valentine Musakanya	Bemba (Senior Partner)
Failed coup	Zambia	June 30, 1990	Lt. Mwamba Luchembe	Bemba (Senior Partner)
Failed coup	Zambia	October 28, 1997	Capt. Stephen Lungu	Unknown
Failed coup	Zimbabwe	June 24, 1982	The home of Prime Minster Robert Mugabe was attacked by a group of soldiers who had earlier seized weapons and commandeered a truck from army barracks in Harare	Ndebele (Discriminated)

TABLE A3.3 *Ethnicity of Rebel Groups in Sub-Saharan Africa, Independence to 2005*

Country	Civil war	Insurgent group(s)	Ethnicity of groups rebelling	EPR status of groups prior to entry in civil war	Date of entry	Date of exit
Angola	Post-independence	UNITA	Ovimbundu	Independence	1975	2002
Angola	Post-independence	FNLA	Bakongo	Independence	1975	1979
Burundi	Hutu uprising		Hutu	Discriminated	1972	1972
Burundi	Organized massacres on both sides		Hutu	Discriminated	1988	1988
Burundi	Hutu groups vs. government	Palipehutu; CNDD-FDD	Hutu	Junior Partner	1991	2003
CAR	Factional fighting		Yakoma	Junior Partner	1996	1997
Chad	First post-independence war	FROLINAT, Various	Muslim Sahel groups	Powerless	1965	1982
Chad	First post-independence war	FROLINAT, Seconde Armée	Toubou	Powerless	1965	1987
Chad	First post-independence war	FROLINAT, Volcan, CDR	Arab groups	Powerless	1965	1988
Chad	Anti-Habré	MOSANAT	Hadjeray	Discriminated	1990	1990
Chad	Anti-Habré	MPS	Zaghawa-Bideyat	Junior Partner (to Discriminated)	1990	1990
Chad	Habré supporters	MDD	Toubou	Powerless	1991	1992
Chad	Southern groups resisting Déby	CSNPD; FARF	Sara	Junior Partner	1992	1998
Chad		MDJT	Toubou	Powerless	1999	2002

(continued)

TABLE A3.3 *Continued*

Country	Civil war	Insurgent group(s)	Ethnicity of groups rebelling	EPR status of groups prior to entry in civil war	Date of entry	Date of exit
Chad	Eastern Chad conflict	SCUD	Zaghawa-Bideyat	Senior Partner	2005	
Chad	Eastern Chad conflict	RDL, FUCD	Tamas	Powerless	2005	
Chad	Eastern Chad conflict		Arabs	Powerless	2005	
Chad	Eastern Chad conflict		Muslim Sahel Groups	Irrelevant	2005	
Congo	Factional fighting	Cobras	Mbochi	Powerless	1997	1997
Congo	Factional fighting	Cocoyes	Nibolek (Bembe, etc.)	Powerless (prior year was Senior Partner)	1998	1999
Congo	Factional fighting	Ninjas	Bakongo	Powerless (prior year was Junior Partner)	1998	1999
Côte d'Ivoire	Northern conflict	Mouvement Patriotique de Côte d'Ivoire (MPCI) and others	Northerner (Mande and Voltaic/Gur)	Discriminated	2002	2004
DRC	Katanga, Kasai, CNL	Katanga	Lunda-Yeke	Irrelevant	1960	1962
DRC	Katanga, Kasai, CNL	Independent Mining State of South Kasai	Luba Kasai	Irrelevant	1960	1962
DRC	Katanga, Kasai, CNL	CNL	Tetela-Yeke	Irrelevant	1964	1965
DRC	Katanga invasions	FLNC	Lunda-Yeke	Irrelevant	1977	1978

Country	Conflict	Organization	Ethnic group	Power status		
DRC	Overthrow of Moburu	AFDL (Kabila)	Luba-Shaba	Powerless	1996	1997
DRC	Overthrow of Moburu	AFDL (Kabila)	Tutsi-Banyamulenge	Discriminated	1996	1997
DRC	Anti-Kabila	RCD, etc. vs. govt	Tutsi-Banyamulenge	Senior Partner (to Discriminated)	1998	
DRC	Anti-Kabila	Mouvement de liberation du Congo (MLC)	Ngbaka	Powerless	1998	
Ethiopia	Eritrea, Tigray, etc.	Tigray People's Liberation Front	Tigray	Discriminated	1976	1991
Ethiopia	Eritrea, Tigray, etc.	Eritrean Liberation Front	Eritreans (Tigrinya)	Discriminated	1974	1991
Ethiopia	Eritrea, Tigray, etc.	Western Somali Liberation Front	Somali (Ogaden)	Discriminated	1976	1983
Guinea-Bissau	Military faction	Military Junta for the Consolidation of Democracy, Peace and Justice	Balanta	Junior Partner	1998	1999
Liberia	Anti-Doe rebellion	NPFL (Taylor), INPFL (Johnson)	Gio	Discriminated	1989	1996
Liberia	Anti-Doe rebellion	NPFL (Taylor), INPFL (Johnson)	Mano	Discriminated	1989	1996
Liberia	Anti-Taylor resistance	LURD	Mandingo	Discriminated	2000	2003
Liberia	Anti-Taylor resistance	LURD	Krahn (Guere)	Discriminated	2000	2003
Mali	Tuaregs		Whites (Tuareg and Arabs)	Powerless	1989	1994
Mozambique	Post-independence conflict	RENAMO	Shona-Ndau	Powerless	1976	1992

(continued)

TABLE A3.3 *Continued*

Country	Civil war	Insurgent group(s)	Ethnicity of groups rebelling	EPR status of groups prior to entry in civil war	Date of entry	Date of exit
Nigeria	Biafra		Igbo	Regional autonomy	1967	1970
Rwanda	Post-revolution strife	RPF	Tutsi	Discriminated	1962	1965
Rwanda		RPF	Tutsi	Discriminated	1990	1994
Rwanda	Ex-FAR and Interahamwe back to power	Army for the Liberation of Rwanda	Hutu	Discriminated	1997	2002
Senegal	Casamance	MFDC	Diola	Junior Partner	1989	2000
Sierra Leone		RUF, AFRIC, etc.	None			
South Africa		ANC, PAC, Azapo	Zulu	Discriminated	1983	1994
South Africa		ANC, PAC, Azapo	Xhosa	Discriminated	1983	1994
Sudan	Anya	Anyanya	Latoka	Powerless	1963	1972
Sudan	Anya	Anyanya	Azande	Powerless	1963	1972
Sudan	Anya	Anyanya	Bari	Powerless	1963	1972
Sudan	Anya	Anyanya	Other southern groups	Powerless	1963	1972
Sudan	Anya	Anyanya	Dinka	Powerless	1969	1972
Sudan	Anya	Anyanya	Nuer	Powerless	1969	1972
Sudan	SPLA	SPLA, etc.	Dinka	Regional Autonomy	1983	2005

Country	Conflict	Armed group	Group	Status		
Sudan	SPLA	SPLA, etc.	Nuer	Regional Autonomy	1983	2005
Sudan	SPLA	SPLA, etc.	Shilluk	Regional Autonomy	1983	2005
Sudan	SPLA	SPLA, etc.	Other southern groups	Regional Autonomy	1987	2005
Sudan	SPLA	SPLA, etc.	Nuba	Powerless	1987	2005
Sudan	Darfur conflict	SLA	Fur	Powerless	2003	
Sudan	Darfur conflict	SLA, JEM	Other northern groups	Powerless	2003	
Uganda	Overthrow of Idi Amin	UNLA	Baganda	Discriminated	1978	1979
Uganda	Overthrow of Idi Amin	UNLA	Langi/Acholi	Discriminated	1978	1979
Uganda	Overthrow of Idi Amin	UNLA	Southwesterners (Ankole, Banyoro, Toro, Banyarwanda)	Discriminated	1978	1979
Uganda	Anti-Obote Rebellion	NRA, etc.	Southwesterners (Ankole, Banyoro, Toro, Banyarwanda)	Discriminated	1981	1986
Uganda	Anti-Obote rebellion	NRA, etc.	Baganda	Discriminated	1981	1986
Uganda	Northern Uganda conflict	LRA, West Nile, etc.	Langi/Acholi	Discriminated	1986	
Zimbabwe	Independence War	ZANU, ZAPU	Africans	Discriminated	1972	1979
Zimbabwe	Ndebele guer's	Ndebele	Ndebele	Discriminated	1983	1987

References

Aburish, Said K. *Saddam Hussein: The Politics of Revenge*. New York: Bloomsbury, 2000.

Acemoglu, Daron and James A. Robinson. *Economic Origins of Dictatorship and Democracy*. Cambridge: Cambridge University Press, 2006.

Acemoglu, Daron and James A. Robinson *Why Nations Fail: The Origins of Power, Prosperity and Poverty*. New York: Crown Publishers, 2012.

Acemoglu, Daron, Davide Ticchi, and Andrea Vindigni. "Persistence of Civil Wars." Cambridge, Mass.: National Bureau of Economic Research, 2009.

Acemoglu, Daron, Thierry Verdier, and James A. Robinson. "Kleptocracy and Divide-and-Rule: A Model of Personal Rule." *Journal of the European Economic Association*, 2 (2–3) (2004): 162–192.

Achebe, Chinua. *There Was a Country: A Personal History of Biafra*. New York Penguin, 2012.

Africa Watch. *The Forgotten War in Darfur Flares Again*. London: Africa Watch, 1990.

African Rights. *Facing Genocide: The Nuba of Sudan*. London: African Rights, 1995.

African Rights *Rwanda: The Insurgency in the Northwest*. London: African Rights, 1998.

Alier, Abel. *Southern Sudan: Too Many Agreements Dishonoured*. London: Ithaca Press Reading, 1992.

Allen, Chris, Joan Baxter, Michael S. Radu, and Keith Somerville. *Benin, The Congo, Burkina Faso: Politics, Economics and Society*. London and New York: Pinter, 1989.

Arriola, Leonardo R. "Patronage and Political Stability in Africa." *Comparative Political Studies*, 42 (10) (2009): 1339–1362.

Arriola, Leonardo R. and Martha C. Johnson. "Ethnic Politics and Women's Empowerment in Africa: Ministerial Appointments to Executive Cabinets." *American Journal of Political Science*, 58 (2) (2013): 495–510.

Autesserre, Séverine. *The Trouble with the Congo: Local Violence and the Failure of International Peacebuilding*. Cambridge: Cambridge University Press, 2010.

Azam, Jean-Paul. "The Redistributive State and Conflicts in Africa." *Journal of Peace Research*, 38 (4) (2001): 429–444.

Baram, Amatzia. "Neo-tribalism in Iraq: Saddam Hussein's Tribal Policies, 1991–96." *International Journal of Middle East Studies*, 29 (1) (1997): 1–31.

Bates, Robert H. "Modernization, Ethnic Competition, and the Rationality of Politics in Contemporary Africa." In Donald Rothchild and Victor A. Olorunsola, eds., *State Versus Ethnic Claims: African Policy Dilemmas* (pp. 152–171). Boulder, Col.: Westview Press, 1983.

Bates, Robert, Avner Greif, and Smita Singh. "Organizing Violence." *Journal of Conflict Resolution*, 46 (5) (2002): 599–628.

Bayart, Jean-François. *The State in Africa: The Politics of the Belly.* New York: Longman, 1993.

Bayart, Jean-François. *The State in Africa: The Politics of the Belly*, 2nd edn. Cambridge: Polity, 2009.

Beken, Christophe van der. *Unity in Diversity: Federalism as a Mechanism to Accommodate Ethnic Diversity—The Case of Ethiopia.* Berlin: LIT, 2012.

Berkeley, Bill. *Liberia, a Promise Betrayed: A Report on Human Rights.* New York: Lawyers Committee for Human Rights, 1986.

The Graves Are Not Yet Full: Race, Tribe and Power in the Heart of Africa. New York: Basic Books, 2003.

Berman, Bruce. "Ethnicity, Patronage and the African State: The Politics of Uncivil Nationalism." *African Affairs*, 97 (388) (1998): 305–341.

Berman, Eli, Michael Callen, Joseph H. Felter, and Jacob N. Shapiro. "Do Working Men Rebel? Insurgency and Unemployment in Afghanistan, Iraq, and the Philippines." *Journal of Conflict Resolution*, 55 (4) (2011): 496–528.

Biernacki, Patrick and Dan Waldorf. "Snowball Sampling: Problems and Techniques of Chain Referral Sampling." *Sociological Methods and Research*, 10 (2) (1981): 141–163.

Blair, Graeme, C., Christine Fair, Neil Malhotra, and Jacob N. Shapiro. "Poverty and Support for Militant Politics: Evidence from Pakistan." *American Journal of Political Science*, 57 (1) (2013): 30–48.

Blattman, Christopher. "From Violence to Voting: War and Political Participation in Uganda." *American Political Science Review*, 103 (2) (2009): 231–247.

Blattman, Christopher and Edward Miguel. "Civil War." *Journal of Economic Literature*, 48 (1) (2010): 3–57.

Boone, Catherine. *Merchant Capital and the Roots of State Power in Senegal, 1930–1985.* Cambridge: Cambridge University Press, 1992.

Brass, Paul. *Ethnicity and Nationalism: Theory and Comparison.* Newbury Park, Calif.: Sage Publications, 1991.

Bratton, Michael and Nicolas van de Walle. *Democratic Experiments in Africa: Regime Transitions in Comparative Perspective.* Cambridge: Cambridge University Press, 1997.

Bueno de Mesquita, Bruce, James D. Morrow, Randolph M. Siverson, and Alastair Smith. *The Logic of Political Survival.* Cambridge, Mass.: MIT Press, 2003.

Bueno de Mesquita, Bruce and Alastair Smith. *The Dictator's Handbook: Why Bad Behavior Is Almost Always Good Politics.* New York: PublicAffairs, 2011.

Buhaug, Halvard, Kristian Skrede Gleditsch, Helge Holtermann, Gudrun Østby, and Andreas Forø Tollefsen. "It's the Local Economy, Stupid! Geographic Wealth Dispersion and Conflict Outbreak Location." *Journal of Conflict Resolution*, 55 (5) (2011): 814–840.

Burgess, Robin, Remi Jedwab, Edward Miguel, Ameet Morjaria, and Gerard Padró i Miquel. "The Value of Democracy: Evidence from Road Building in Kenya." *American Economic Review*, 105 (6) (2015): 1817–1851.

Burr, J. Millard and Robert O. Collins. *Africa's Thirty Years War: Libya, Chad, and the Sudan, 1963–1993*. Boulder, Col.: Westview Press, 1999.

Carter, David B. and Curtis S. Signorino. "Back to the Future: Modeling Time Dependence in Binary Data." *Political Analysis*, 18 (3) (2010): 271–292.

Caselli, Francesco and Wilbur John Coleman. "On the Theory of Ethnic Conflict." *Journal of the European Economic Association*, 11 (s1) (2013): 161–192.

Cederman, Lars-Erik, Kristian Skrede Gleditsch, and Halvard Buhaug. *Inequality, Grievances, and Civil War*. Cambridge: Cambridge University Press, 2013.

Cederman, Lars-Erik, Nils B. Weidmann, and Kristian Skrede Gleditsch. "Horizontal Inequalities and Ethnonationalist Civil War: A Global Comparison." *American Political Science Review*, 105 (3) (2011): 478–495.

Cederman, Lars-Erik, Andreas Wimmer, and Brian Min. "Why Do Ethnic Groups Rebel? New Data and Analysis." *World Politics*, 62 (1) (2010): 87–119.

Cetinyan, Rupen. "Ethnic Bargaining in the Shadow of Third-Party Intervention." *International Organization*, 56 (3) (2002): 645–677.

Chandra, Kanchan. "Cumulative Findings in the Study of Ethnic Politics." *APSA-CP Newsletter*, 12 (1) (2001): 7–25.

Chandra, Kanchan "What Is Ethnic Identity and Does It Matter?" *Annual Review of Political Science*, 9 (1) (2006): 397–424.

"Introduction." In Kanchan Chandra, ed., *Constructivist Theories of Ethnic Politics* (pp. 1–47). Oxford: Oxford University Press, 2012.

Chazan, Naomi. "Ethnicity and Politics in Ghana." *Political Science Quarterly*, 97 (3) (1982): 461–485.

Chazan, Naomi, Peter Lewis, Robert A. Mortimer, Donald Rothchild, and Stephen John Stedman. *Politics and Society in Contemporary Africa*, 3rd edn. Boulder, Col.: Lynne Rienner, 1999.

Chehabi, H. E. and Juan J. Linz. "A Theory of Sultanism 1: A Type of Nondemocratic Rule." In H. E. Chehabi and Juan J. Linz, eds., *Sultanistic Regimes* (pp. 3–25). Baltimore, Md.: Johns Hopkins University Press, 1998.

Clapham, Christopher. "Clientelism and the State." In Christopher Clapham, ed., *Private Patronage and Public Power: Political Clientelism in the Modern State* (pp. 1–35). New York: St. Martin's Press, 1982.

"The Politics of Failure: Clientelism, Political Instability, and National Integration in Liberia and Sierra Leone." In Christopher Clapham, ed., *Private Patronage and Public Power: Political Clientelism in the Modern State* (pp. 76–92). New York: St. Martin's Press, 1982.

Africa and the International System: The Politics of State Survival. Cambridge: Cambridge University Press, 1996.

Clapham, Christopher., ed. *African Guerrillas*. Bloomington, Ind.: Indiana University Press, 1998.

Clapham, Christopher S., Jeffrey Herbst and Greg Ira Mills, eds. *Big African States.* Johannesburg: Witwatersrand University Press 2006.

Clark, John F. "Explaining Ugandan Intervention in Congo: Evidence and Interpretations." *The Journal of Modern African Studies,* 39 (2) (2001): 261–287.

Cockburn, Patrick. *Muqtada: Muqtada al-Sadr, the Shia Revival, and the Struggle for Iraq.* New York: Scribner, 2008.

Cockett, Richard. *Sudan: Darfur and the Failure of an African State.* New Haven, Conn.: Yale University Press, 2010.

Coghlan, Benjamin, Richard J. Brennan, Pascal Ngoy, David Dofara, Brad Otto, Mark Clements, and Tony Stewart. "Mortality in the Democratic Republic of Congo: A Nationwide Survey." *The Lancet,* 367 (9504) (2006): 44–51.

Cohen, Abner. *Two-Dimensional Man: An Essay on the Anthropology of Power and Symbolism in Complex Society.* Berkeley, Calif.: University of California Press, 1974.

Colgan, Jeff D. "Domestic Revolutionary Leaders and International Conflict." *World Politics,* 65 (4) (2013): 656–690.

Collier, Paul. *The Bottom Billion: Why the Poorest Countries Are Failing and What Can Be Done About It.* Oxford: Oxford University Press, 2007.

Collier, Paul *Wars, Guns, and Votes: Democracy in Dangerous Places.* New York: Harper, 2009.

Collier, Paul, V. L. Elliott, Håvard Hegre, Anke Hoeffler, Marta Reynal-Querol, and Nicholas Sambanis. *Breaking the Conflict Trap: Civil War and Development Policy.* Washington, DC: World Bank 2003.

Collier, Paul and Anke Hoeffler. "Greed and Grievance in Civil War." *Oxford Economic Papers,* 56 (4) (2004): 563–595.

"Grand Extortion: Coup Risk and the Military as a Protection Racket." University of Oxford, 2006.

Collier, Paul, Anke Hoeffler, and Dominic Rohner. "Beyond Greed and Grievance: Feasibility and Civil War." *Oxford Economic Papers,* 61 (1) (2009): 1–27.

Collins, Robert O. *Shadows in the Grass: Britain in the Southern Sudan, 1918–1956.* New Haven, Conn.: Yale University Press, 1983.

A History of Modern Sudan. Cambridge: Cambridge University Press, 2008.

Cooper, Frederick. *Africa since 1940: The Past of the Present.* Cambridge: Cambridge University Press, 2002.

Crost, Benjamin, Joseph Felter, and Patrick Johnston. "Aid under Fire: Development Projects and Civil Conflict." *The American Economic Review,* 104 (6) (2014): 1833–1856.

Cunningham, David E. "Veto Players and Civil War Duration." *American Journal of Political Science,* 50 (4) (2006): 875–892.

Barriers to Peace in Civil War. Cambridge: Cambridge University Press, 2011.

Daly, M. W. *Empire on the Nile: The Anglo-Egyptian Sudan, 1898–1934.* Cambridge: Cambridge University Press, 1986.

Dawisha, Adeed. *Arab Nationalism in the Twentieth Century: From Triumph to Despair.* Princeton, NJ: Princeton University Press, 2003.

de Figueiredo, Jr., Rui, and Barry R. Weingast. "The Rationality of Fear: Political Opportunism and Ethnic Conflict." In Barbara F. Walter and Jack Snyder, eds., *Civil Wars, Insecurity, and Intervention* (pp. 261–302). New York: Columbia University Press, 1999.

De Villers, Gauthier and Jean-Claude Williame. *République Démocratique du Congo: chronique politique d'un entre-deux guerres, octobre 1996–juillet 1998*. Tervuren: Institut Africain, 1998.

de Waal, Alex. "Some Comments on Militias in Contemporary Sudan." In M. W. Daly and Ahmad Alawad Sikainga, eds., *Civil War in the Sudan*. London: British Academic Press, 1993.

de Waal, Alex "Counter-Insurgency on the Cheap." *London Review of Books*, 26 (15) (2004): 25–27.

"The Politics of Destabilisation in the Horn, 1989–2001." In Alex de Waal, ed., *Islamism and Its Enemies in the Horn of Africa* (pp. 182–230). Bloomington, Ind.: Indiana University Press, 2004.

"Tragedy in Darfur." *Boston Review*, October/November 2004.

"Deep Down in Darfur: Nothing Is as We Are Told in Sudan's Killing Fields." *Review of African Political Economy*, 32 (106) (2005): 653–659.

Famine That Kills Darfur, Sudan. Oxford: Oxford University Press, 2005.

"Dollarised." *London Review of Books*, 32 (12) (2010): 20.

"When Kleptocracy Becomes Insolvent: Brute Causes of the Civil War in South Sudan." *African Affairs*, 113 (452) (2014): 347–369.

de Waal, Alex and A. H. Abdel Salam. "Islamism, State Power and Jihad in Sudan." In Alex de Waal, ed., *Islamism and Its Enemies in the Horn of Africa* (pp. 71–113). Bloomington, Ind.: Indiana University Press, 2004.

Decalo, Samuel. "Regionalism, Politics, and the Military in Dahomey." *The Journal of Developing Areas*, 7 (3) (1973): 449–478.

"Chad: The Roots of Centre-Periphery Strife." *African Affairs*, 79 (317) (1980): 491–509.

"Regionalism, Political Decay, and Civil Strife in Chad." *Journal of Modern African Studies*, 18 (1) (1980): 23–56.

Historical Dictionary of Togo. Metuchen, NJ: Scarecrow Press, 1987.

Coups and Army Rule in Africa: Motivations and Constraints, 2nd edn. New Haven, Conn.: Yale University Press, 1990.

Historical Dictionary of Benin, 3rd edn. Lanham, Md.: Scarecrow Press, 1995.

"Benin: First of the New Democracies." In John F. Clark and David E. Gardinier, eds., *Political Reform in Francophone Africa* (pp. 43–61). Boulder, Col.: Westview Press, 1997.

Historical Dictionary of Chad. Lanham, Md.: Scarecrow Press, 1997.

Deng, Francis. *War of Visions: Conflict of Identities in the Sudan*. Washington, DC: Brookings Institution, 1995.

"The Legacy of Slavery." In Francis Mading Deng, ed., *New Sudan in the Making? Essays on a Nation in Painful Search of Itself*. Trenton, NJ: Red Sea Press, 2010.

"Sudan at the Crossroads." In Francis Mading Deng, ed., *New Sudan in the Making? Essays on a Nation in Painful Search of Itself*. Trenton, NJ: Red Sea Press, 2010.

Des Forges, Alison. *"Leave None to Tell the Story"*: *Genocide in Rwanda.* New York: Human Rights Watch, 1999.

Devarajan, Shantayanan and Wolfgang Fengler. "Africa's Economic Boom: Why the Pessimists and the Optimists Are Both Right." *Foreign Affairs*, 92 (3) (2013): 68–81.

Dolo, Emmanuel. *Ethnic Tensions in Liberia's National Identity Crisis: Problems and Possibilities.* Cherry Hill, NJ: Africana Homestead Legacy Publishers, 2007.

Easterly, William and Ross Levine. "Africa's Growth Tragedy: Policies and Ethnic Divisions." *Quarterly Journal of Economics*, 112 (4) (1997): 1203–1250.

Eckstein, Harry. "Case Study and Theory in Political Science." In Nelson W. Polsby and Fred I. Greenstein, eds., *Handbook of Political Science* (pp. 79–138). Reading, Mass.: Addison-Wesley, 1975.

Eggers, Dave. *What Is the What? The Autobiography of Valentino Achak Deng: A Novel.* New York: Random House, 2006.

Eifert, Benn, Edward Miguel, and Daniel N. Posner. "Political Competition and Ethnic Identification in Africa." *American Journal of Political Science*, 54 (2) (2010): 494–510.

El-Affendi, Abdelwahab. *Turabi's Revolution: Islam and Power in Sudan.* London: Grey Seal, 1991.

El-Din, Ahmed Kamal. "Islam and Islamism in Darfur." In Alex de Waal, ed., *War in Darfur and the Search for Peace* (pp. 92–112). Cambridge, Mass.: Harvard University Press, 2007.

Ellis, Stephen. *The Mask of Anarchy: The Destruction of Liberia and the Religious Dimension of an African Civil War.* New York: New York University Press, 1999.

Englebert, Pierre and Rebecca Hummel. "Let's Stick Together: Understanding Africa's Secessionist Deficit." *African Affairs*, 104 (416) (2005): 399–427.

Englebert, Pierre and James Ron. "Primary Commodities and War: Congo-Brazzaville's Ambivalent Resource Curse." *Comparative Politics*, 37 (1) (2004): 61–81.

Enloe, Cynthia H. *Ethnic Soldiers: State Security in Divided Societies.* Athens, Ga.: University of Georgia Press, 1980.

Faksh, Mahmud A. "The Alawi Community of Syria: A New Dominant Political Force." *Middle Eastern Studies*, 20 (2) (1984): 133–153.

Falola, Toyin and Matthew M. Heaton. *A History of Nigeria.* Cambridge: Cambridge University Press, 2008.

Fearon, James D. "Ethnic War as a Commitment Problem." Paper presented at the 1994 Annual Meeting of the American Political Science Association, New York, August 30–September 2, 1995.

"Rationalist Explanations for War." *International Organization*, 49 (3) (1995): 379–414.

"Why Ethnic Politics and 'Pork' Tend to Go Together." In *mimeo.* Stanford University, 1999.

"Ethnic and Cultural Diversity by Country." *Journal of Economic Growth*, 8 (2) (2003): 195–222.

"Why Do Some Civil Wars Last So Much Longer than Others?" *Journal of Peace Research*, 41 (3) (2004): 275–301.

"Governance and Civil War Onset." *World Development Report 2011*, Washington, DC: World Bank, 2010.

Fearon, James D. and David D. Laitin. "Explaining Interethnic Cooperation." *American Political Science Review*, 90 (4) (1996): 715–735.

"Violence and the Social Construction of Ethnic Identities." *International Organization*, 54 (4) (2000): 845–877.

"Ethnicity, Insurgency, and Civil War." *American Political Science Review*, 97 (1) (2003): 75–90.

"Sons of the Soil, Migrants, and Civil War." *World Development*, 39 (2) (2011): 199–211.

Findley, Michael and Peter J. Rudloff. "Combatant Fragmentation and the Dynamics of Civil War." *British Journal of Political Science*, 74 (1) (2012): 1–41.

Flint, Julie, "Beyond 'Janjaweed': Understanding the Militias of Darfur," *Small Arms Survey*, June 2009.

Flint, Julie and Alexander De Waal. *Darfur: A Short History of a Long War*. London: Zed Books, 2005.

Darfur: A New History of a Long War. New York: Zed Books, 2008.

Florea, Adrian. "Where Do We Go from Here? Conceptual, Theoretical, and Methodological Gaps in the Large-N Civil War Research Program1." *International Studies Review*, 14 (1) (2012): 78–98.

Foltz, William J. "Reconstructing the State of Chad." In I. William Zartman, ed., *Collapsed States: The Disintegration and Restoration of Legitimate Authority* (pp. 15–32). Boulder, Col.: Lynne Rienner, 1995.

Franck, Raphaël and Ilia Rainer. "Does the Leader's Ethnicity Matter? Ethnic Favoritism, Education, and Health in Sub-Saharan Africa." *American Political Science Review*, 106 (2) (2012): 294–325.

François, Patrick, Ilia Rainer, and Francesco Trebbi. "How Is Power Shared in Africa?" *Econometrica*, 83 (2) (2015): 465–503.

Gallab, Abdullahi A. *The First Islamist Republic: Development and Disintegration of Islamism in the Sudan*. Burlington, Vt.: Ashgate, 2008.

Garang, John. *John Garang Speaks*, edited by Mansour Khalid (London: KPI Limited, 1987).

Garfinkel, Michelle R., and Stergios Skaperdas. "Conflict without Misperceptions or Incomplete Information: How the Future Matters." *The Journal of Conflict Resolution*, 44 (6) (2000): 793–807.

Geddes, Barbara. *Paradigms and Sand Castles: Theory Building and Research Design in Comparative Politics*. Ann Arbor, Mich.: University of Michigan Press, 2003.

George, Alexander L. and Andrew Bennett. *Case Studies and Theory Development in the Social Sciences*. Cambridge, Mass.: MIT Press, 2005.

Gerring, John. *Case Study Research: Principles and Practices*. Cambridge: Cambridge University Press, 2007.

Ghobarah, Hazem Adam, Paul Huth, and Bruce Russett. "Civil Wars Kill and Maim People . . . Long after the Shooting Stops." *American Political Science Review*, 97 (2) (2003): 189–202.

Gleditsch, Kristian Skrede. "Transnational Dimensions of Civil War." *Journal of Peace Research*, 44 (3) (2007): 293–309.

Gleditsch, Kristian Skrede, and Andrea Ruggeri. "Political Opportunity Structures, Democracy, and Civil War." *Journal of Peace Research*, 47 (3) (2010): 299–310.

Gleditsch, Kristian Skrede, Idean Salehyan, and Kenneth Schultz. "Fighting at Home, Fighting Abroad." *Journal of Conflict Resolution*, 52 (4) (2008): 479–506.

Gleditsch, Nils Petter, Peter Wallensteen, Mikael Eriksson, Margareta Sollenberg, and Håvard Strand. "Armed Conflict, 1946–2001: A New Dataset." *Journal of Peace Research*, 39 (5) (2002): 615–637.

Goemans, Hein and Nikolay Marinov. "Electoral Reversals: The International Community and the Coup d'État" (2011).

Goodwin, Jeff. *No Other Way Out: States and Revolutionary Movements, 1945–1991*. Cambridge: Cambridge University Press, 2001.

Green, Elliott. "On the Size and Shape of African States." *International Studies Quarterly*, 56 (2) (2012): 229–244.

Greenland, Jeremy. "Ethnic Discrimination in Rwanda and Burundi." In Willem Adriaan Veenhoven, ed., *Case Studies on Human Rights and Fundamental Freedoms: A World Survey* (pp. 98–133). The Hague: Martinus Nijhoff, 1976.

Gribbin, Robert E. *In the Aftermath of Genocide: The US Role in Rwanda*. Lincoln, Nebr.: iUniverse, 2005.

Grossman, Herschell I. "A General Equilibrium Model of Insurrections." *The American Economic Review*, 81 (4) (1991): 912–921.

Habyarimana, James, Macartan Humphreys, Daniel N. Posner, and Jeremy M. Weinstein. "Why Does Ethnic Diversity Undermine Public Goods Provision?" *American Political Science Review*, 101 (4) (2007): 709–725.

"Is Ethnic Conflict Inevitable? Parting Ways over Nationalism and Separatism." *Foreign Affairs*, 87 (4) (2008): 138.

"Coethnicity and Trust." In Karen S. Cook, Margaret Levi, and Russell Hardin, eds., *Whom Can We Trust? How Groups, Networks, and Institutions Make Trust Possible* (pp. 42–64). New York: Russell Sage Foundation, 2009.

Coethnicity: Diversity and the Dilemmas of Collective Action. New York: Russell Sage Foundation, 2009.

Hadenius, Axel and Jan Teorell. "Pathways from Authoritarianism." *Journal of Democracy*, 18 (1) (2007): 143–157.

Hale, Henry E. *The Foundations of Ethnic Politics: Separatism of States and Nations in Eurasia and the World*. Cambridge: Cambridge University Press, 2008.

Hamidi, Mohamed E. *The Making of an Islamic Political Leader: Conversations with Hasan Turabi*. Boulder, Col.: Westview Press, 1998.

Hardin, Russell. *One for All: The Logic of Group Conflict*. Princeton, NJ: Princeton University Press, 1995.

Harff, Barbara. "No Lessons Learned from the Holocaust? Assessing Risks of Genocide and Political Mass Murder since 1955." *American Political Science Review*, 97 (1) (2003): 57–73.

Harir, Sharif. "Racism under Islamic Disguise." In Hanne Veber, Jens Dahl, Fiona Wilson, and Espen Waehle, eds., *Never Drink from the Same Cup: Proceedings of the Conference on Indigenous Peoples in Africa.* Copenhagen: IWGIA and the Centre for Development Research, 1993.

"'Arab Belt' versus 'African Belt': Ethnopolitical Conflict in Dar Fur and the Regional Cultural Factors." In Sharif Harir and Terje Tvedt, eds., *Short-Cut to Decay: The Case of the Sudan* (pp. 144–185). Uppsala: Nordiska Afrikainstitutet, 1994.

Hartzell, Caroline A. and Matthew Hoddie. *Crafting Peace: Powersharing Institutions and the Negotiated Settlement of Civil Wars.* University Park, Pa.: Pennsylvania State University Press, 2007.

Hegre, Håvard, Tanja Ellingsen, Scott Gates, and Nils Petter Gleditsch. "Toward a Democratic Civil Peace? Democracy, Political Change, and Civil War, 1816–1992." *American Political Science Review*, 95 (1) (2001): 33–48.

Hegre, Håvard, Gudrun Østby, and Clionadh Raleigh. "Poverty and Civil War Events: A Disaggregated Study of Liberia." *Journal of Conflict Resolution*, 53 (4) (2009): 598–623.

Hegre, Håvard and Nicholas Sambanis. "Sensitivity Analysis of Empirical Results on Civil War Onset." *Journal of Conflict Resolution*, 50 (4) (2006): 508–535.

Helmke, Gretchen and Steven Levitsky. "Informal Institutions and Comparative Politics: A Research Agenda." *Perspectives on Politics*, 2 (4) (2004): 725–740.

Hendrix, Cullen S. "Measuring State Capacity: Theoretical and Empirical Implications for the Study of Civil Conflict." *Journal of Peace Research*, 47 (3) (2010): 273–285.

"Head for the Hills? Rough Terrain, State Capacity, and Civil War Onset." *Civil Wars*, 13 (4) (2011): 345–370.

Herbst, Jeffrey. "War and the State in Africa." *International Security*, 14 (4) (1990): 117–139.

States and Power in Africa: Comparative Lessons in Authority and Control. Princeton, NJ: Princeton University Press, 2000.

Herz, John H. "Rise and Demise of the Territorial State." *World Politics*, 9 (4) (1957): 473–493.

Hill, Richard Leslie. *A Biographical Dictionary of the Sudan.* London: Cass, 1967.

Hironaka, Ann. *Neverending Wars: The International Community, Weak States, and the Perpetuation of Civil War.* Cambridge, Mass.: Harvard University Press, 2005.

Hirsch, John L. *Sierra Leone: Diamonds and the Struggle for Democracy.* Boulder, Col.: Lynne Rienner, 2001.

Hirshleifer, Jack. "Theorizing about Conflict." In Keith Hartley and Sandler Todd, eds., *Handbook of Defense Economics* (pp. 165–189). Amsterdam: Elsevier, 1995.

Hobbes, Thomas. *Leviathan.* Harmondsworth: Penguin, 1986. First published 1651.

Hodler, Roland and Paul A. Raschky. "Regional Favoritism." *The Quarterly Journal of Economics*, 129 (2) (2014): 995–1033.

Holt, P. M. *The Mahdist State in the Sudan, 1881–1898.* Oxford: Clarendon Press, 1958.

Homer-Dixon, Thomas F. *Environment, Scarcity, and Violence.* Princeton, NJ: Princeton University Press, 1999.

Horowitz, Donald L. *Ethnic Groups in Conflict.* Berkeley, Calif.: University of California Press, 1985.

Howe, Herbert M. *Ambiguous Order: Military Forces in African States.* Boulder, Col.: Lynne Rienner, 2001.

Huband, Mark. *The Liberian Civil War.* Portland, Oreg.: Frank Cass, 1998.

Human Rights Watch. *Behind the Red Line: Political Repression in Sudan.* New York: Human Rights Watch, 1996.

Bashing Dissent: Escalating Violence and State Repression in Zimbabwe. New York: Human Rights Watch, 2007.

"One Hundred Ways of Putting Pressure": Violations of Freedom of Expression and Association in Ethiopia. New York: Human Rights Watch, 2010.

La Plaine des morts: le Tchad de Hissène Habré, 1982–1990, New York: Human Rights Watch, 2013.

Humphreys, Macartan and Jeremy M. Weinstein. "Who Fights? The Determinants of Participation in Civil War." *American Journal of Political Science,* 52 (2) (2008): 436–455.

Huntington, Samuel P. *Political Order in Changing Societies.* New Haven, Conn.: Yale University Press, 1968.

Ibrahim, Abd Allah Ali. "A Theology of Modernity: Hasan Turabi and Islamic Renewal in Sudan." *Africa Today,* 46 (3) (1999): 195–222.

Ibrahim, Fouad. "The Zaghawa and the Midob of North Darfur – a Comparison of Migration Behaviour," *GeoJournal* 46 (2) (1998): 135–140.

Idris, Amir H. "Beyond 'African' and 'Arab' in Sudan." In Francis Mading Deng, ed., *New Sudan in the Making? Essays on a Nation in Painful Search of Itself.* Trenton, NJ: Red Sea Press, 2010.

Ingham, Kenneth. *Obote: A Political Biography.* London and New York: Routledge, 1994.

International Crisis Group. *God, Oil and Country: Changing the Logic of War in Sudan.* Brussels: International Crisis Group, 2002.

"Darfur Rising: Sudan's New Crisis," Africa Report, March 25, 2004.

"Unifying Darfur's Rebels: A Prerequisite for Peace," Africa Briefing, October 6, 2005.

"Unchartered Waters: Thinking Through Syria's Dynamics," Middle East Briefing, November 24, 2011.

Jackson, Robert H. and Carl G. Rosberg. *Personal Rule in Black Africa.* Berkeley, Calif.: University of California Press, 1982.

Jervis, Robert. "Cooperation under the Security Dilemma." *World Politics,* 30 (2) (1978): 167–214.

The Meaning of the Nuclear Revolution: Statecraft and the Prospect of Armageddon. Ithaca, NY: Cornell University Press, 1989.

Johnson, Douglas H. *The Root Causes of Sudan's Civil Wars: Peace or Truce.* Oxford: James Currey 2011.

"Briefing: The Crisis in South Sudan." *African Affairs*, 113 (451) (2014): 300–309.

Johnson, Douglas and Gérard Prunier. "The Foundation and Expansion of the Sudan People's Liberation Army." In M. W. Daly and Ahmad Alawad Sikainga, eds., *Civil War in the Sudan* (pp. 117–141). London: British Academic Press, 1993.

Jok, Jok Madut. *War and Slavery in Sudan*. Philadelphia, Pa.: University of Pennsylvania Press, 2001.

Jones, Bruce D. *Peacemaking in Rwanda: The Dynamics of Failure*. Boulder, Col.: Lynne Rienner, 2001.

Jorgensen, Jan Jelmert. *Uganda: A Modern History*. London: Croom Helm, 1981.

Joris, Lieve. *The Rebels' Hour*, translated by Liz Waters. New York: Grove Press, 2008.

Julian Wucherpfennig, Philipp Hunziker, and Lars-Erik Cederman. "Who Inherits the State? Colonial Rule and Postcolonial Conflict," *American Journal of Political Science*, (60)(4) 2016: 882–898.

Justino, Patricia. "War and Poverty." In Michelle R. Garfinkel and Stergios Skaperdas, eds., *The Oxford Handbook of the Economics of Peace and Conflict* (pp. 676–705). Oxford: Oxford University Press, 2012.

Kahneman, Daniel and Shane Frederick. "Representativeness Revisited: Attribute Substitution in Intuitive Judgment." In Mie Augier and James G. March, eds., *Models of a Man: Essays in Memory of Herbert A. Simon*. Cambridge, Mass.: MIT Press, 2004.

Kahneman, Daniel. *Thinking, Fast and Slow*. New York: Farrar, Straus & Giroux, 2011.

Kalyvas, Stathis N. *The Logic of Violence in Civil War*. Cambridge: Cambridge University Press, 2006.

"Civil Wars." In Carles Boix and Susan C. Stokes, eds., *The Oxford Handbook of Comparative Politics* (pp. 416–434). Oxford: Oxford University Press, 2008.

"Promises and Pitfalls of an Emerging Research Program: The Microdynamics of Civil War." In Ian Shapiro, Stathis N. Kalyvas, and Tarek Masoud, eds., *Order, Conflict, and Violence* (pp. 397–421). Cambridge: Cambridge University Press, 2008.

Kalyvas, Stathis N. and Matthew Adam Kocher. "How 'Free' Is Free Riding in Civil Wars? Violence, Insurgency, and the Collective Action Problem." *World Politics*, 59 (2) (2007): 177–216.

Kang, Seonjou and James Meernik. "Civil War Destruction and the Prospects for Economic Growth." *Journal of Politics*, 67 (1) (2005): 88–109.

Karsh, Efraim and Inari Rautsi. *Saddam Hussein: A Political Biography*. New York: Grove Press, 2002.

Kasara, Kimuli. "Tax Me If You Can: Ethnic Geography, Democracy, and the Taxation of Agriculture in Africa." *American Political Science Review*, 101 (1) (2007): 159–172.

Kasozi, A. B. K., Nakanyike Musisi, and James Mukooza Sejjengo. *The Social Origins of Violence in Uganda, 1964–1985*. Montreal: McGill-Queen's University Press, 1994.

Keen, David. *Useful Enemies: When Waging Wars Is More Important than Winning Them*. New Haven, Conn.: Yale University Press, 2012.

Khalid, Mansour. *Nimeiri and the Revolution of Dis-May*. Boston, Mass.: KPI, 1985.
War and Peace in Sudan: A Tale of Two Countries. London and New York: Routledge, 2003.
"Darfur: A Problem within a Wider Problem." In Salah M. Hassan and Carina E. Ray, eds., *Darfur and the Crisis of Governance in Sudan: A Critical Reader* (pp. 35–42). Ithaca, NY: Cornell University Press, 2009.
Kramer, Robert S., Richard Andrew Lobban, and Carolyn Fluehr-Lobban. *Historical Dictionary of the Sudan*. Lanham, Md.: Scarecrow Press, 2013.
Kydd, Andrew H. *Trust and Mistrust in International Relations*. Princeton, NJ: Princeton University Press, 2005.
Lacina, Bethany and Nils Petter Gleditsch. "Monitoring Trends in Global Combat: A New Dataset of Battle Deaths." *European Journal of Population/ Revue européenne de Démographie*, 21 (2) (2005): 145–166.
Lake, David A. and Donald Rothchild. "Containing Fear: The Origins and Management of Ethnic Conflict." *International Security*, 21 (2) (1996): 41–75.
Langer, Arnim. "Horizontal Inequalities and Violent Group Mobilization in Côte d'Ivoire." *Oxford Development Studies*, 33 (1) (2005): 25–45.
Lefevre, Raphaël. *Ashes of Hama: The Muslim Brotherhood in Syria*. Oxford: Oxford University Press, 2013.
Lemarchand, René. "Political Clientelism and Ethnicity in Tropical Africa: Competing Solidarities in Nation-Building." *American Political Science Review*, 66 (1) (1972): 68–90.
Burundi: Ethnic Conflict and Genocide. Cambridge: Cambridge University Press, 1996.
The Dynamics of Violence in Central Africa. Philadelphia, Pa.: University of Pennsylvania Press, 2009.
Leonard, David K. and Scott Straus. *Africa's Stalled Development: International Causes and Cures*. Boulder, Col.: Lynne Rienner, 2003.
Lesch, Ann Mosely. *The Sudan: Contested National Identities*. Bloomington, Ind.: Indiana University Press, 1998.
Lichbach, Mark Irving. *The Rebel's Dilemma*. Ann Arbor, Mich.: University of Michigan Press, 1995.
Lieberman, Evan S. "Nested Analysis as a Mixed-Method Strategy for Comparative Research." *American Political Science Review*, 99 (3) (2005): 435–452.
Lijphart, Arend. "Comparative Politics and the Comparative Method." *American Political Science Review*, 65 (3) (1971): 682–693.
Democracy in Plural Societies: A Comparative Exploration. New Haven, Conn.: Yale University Press, 1977.
Lindemann, Stefan. "Just Another Change of Guard? Broad-Based Politics and Civil War in Museveni's Uganda." *African Affairs*, 110 (440) (2011): 387–416.
Londregan, John B. and Keith T. Poole. "Poverty, the Coup Trap, and the Seizure of Executive Power." *World Politics*, 42 (2) (1990): 151–183.
Luckham, Robin. *The Nigerian Military: A Sociological Analysis of Authority and Revolt, 1960–67*. Cambridge: Cambridge University Press, 1971.
Luttwak, Edward. *Coup d'État: A Practical Handbook*. Harmondsworth: Penguin, 1968.

Lyall, Jason. "Are Coethnics More Effective Counterinsurgents? Evidence from the Second Chechen War." *American Political Science Review*, 104 (1) (2010): 1–20. "Process Tracing, Causal Inference, and Civil War." In Andrew Bennett and Jeffrey T. Checkel, eds., *Process Tracing: From Metaphor to Analytic Tool* (pp. 186–208). Cambridge: Cambridge University Press, 2015.

Mackey, Sandra. *The Reckoning: Iraq and the Legacy of Saddam Hussein.* New York: Norton, 2003.

Maddy-Weitzman, Bruce. *Middle East Contemporary Survey*, vol. XXIV: 2000. Tel Aviv: Moshe Dayan Center for Middle Eastern and African Studies, 2003.

Magaloni, Beatriz. "Credible Powersharing and the Longevity of Authoritarian Rule." *Comparative Political Studies*, 41 (4–5) (2008): 715–741.

Magaloni, Beatriz, Jonathan Chu, and Eric Min Min. "Autocracies of the World, 1950–2012." Stanford University, 2013.

Mamdani, Mahmood. *Citizen and Subject: Contemporary Africa and the Legacy of Late Colonialism.* Princeton, NJ: Princeton University Press, 1996.

When Victims Become Killers: Colonialism, Nativism, and the Genocide in Rwanda. Princeton, NJ: Princeton University Press, 2001.

Saviors and Survivors: Darfur, Politics, and the War on Terror. New York: Doubleday, 2009.

Mararo, Stanislas Bucyalimwe. "Kivu and Ituri in the Congo War: The Roots and Nature of a Linkage." In Stefaan Marysse and Filip Reyntjens, eds., *The Political Economy of the Great Lakes Region in Africa* (pp. 190–222). Basingstoke: Palgrave Macmillan, 2005.

Mason, T. David and Dale A. Krane. "The Political Economy of Death Squads: Toward a Theory of the Impact of State-Sanctioned Terror." *International Studies Quarterly*, 33 (2) (1989): 175–198.

Matthews, Ronald. *African Powder Keg: Revolt and Dissent in Six Emergent Nations.* London: Bodley Head, 1966.

McAdam, Doug. *Political Process and the Development of Black Insurgency, 1930–1970.* Chicago, Ill.: University of Chicago Press, 1982.

McGowan, Patrick J. "African Military Coups d'État, 1956–2001: Frequency, Trends and Distribution." *Journal of Modern African Studies*, 41 (3) (2003): 339–370.

Médard, J. F. "The Underdeveloped State in Tropical Africa: Political Clientelism or Neo-patrimonialism." In Christopher S. Clapham, ed., *Private Patronage and Public Power: Political Clientelism in the Modern State* (pp. 162–192). New York: St. Martin's Press, 1982.

Mehler, Andreas. "Peace and Power Sharing in Africa: A Not So Obvious Relationship." *African Affairs*, 108 (432) (2009): 453–473.

Melander, Erik. "The Geography of Fear: Regional Ethnic Diversity, the Security Dilemma and Ethnic War." *European Journal of International Relations*, 15 (1) (2009): 95–124.

Meredith, Martin. *The Fate of Africa: A History of Fifty Years of Independence.* New York: Public Affairs, 2005.

Middle East Watch. *Endless Torment: The 1991 Uprising in Iraq and Its Aftermath.* New York: Middle East Watch, 1992.

Migdal, Joel S. *Strong Societies and Weak States: State–Society Relations and State Capabilities in the Third World.* Princeton, NJ: Princeton University Press, 1988.

Miguel, Edward. "Tribe or Nation? Nation Building and Public Goods in Kenya versus Tanzania." *World Politics*, 56 (3) (2004): 328–362.

Miguel, Edward, Shanker Satyanath, and Ernest Sergenti. "Economic Shocks and Civil Conflict: An Instrumental Variables Approach." *Journal of Political Economy*, 112 (4) (2004): 725–753.

Muller, Ruhimbika. *Les Banyamulenge entre deux guerres*. Paris: L'Harmattan, 2001.

Murdoch, James C. and Todd Sandler. "Economic Growth, Civil Wars, and Spatial Spillovers." *Journal of Conflict Resolution*, 46 (1) (2002): 91–110.

Ngolet, François. "African and American Connivance in Congo-Zaire." *Africa Today*, 47 (1) (2000): 64–85.

Nhial, A. Agaw Jok, Nur Tawir Kafi, and Eltigani Seisi. "Human Rights Abuses in Sudan." *Review of African Political Economy*, 20 (58) (1993): 110–118.

Niblock, Tim. *Class and Power in Sudan: The Dynamics of Sudanese Politics, 1898–1985*. Albany, NY: State University of New York Press, 1987.

Nolutshungu, Sam C. *Limits of Anarchy: Intervention and State Formation in Chad*. Charlottesville, Va.: University Press of Virginia, 1996.

Norris, Pippa. *Driving Democracy: Do Powersharing Institutions Work?* Cambridge: Cambridge University Press, 2008.

North, Douglass Cecil, John Joseph Wallis, and Barry R. Weingast. *Violence and Social Orders: A Conceptual Framework for Interpreting Recorded Human History*. Cambridge: Cambridge University Press, 2009.

Nunn, Nathan. "The Long-Term Effects of Africa's Slave Trades." *Quarterly Journal of Economics*, 123 (1) (2008): 139–176.

Nunn, Nathan and Leonard Wantchekon. *The Slave Trade and the Origins of Mistrust in Africa*. Cambridge, Mass.: National Bureau of Economic Research, 2009.

Nzongola-Ntalaja, Georges. *The Congo from Leopold to Kabila: A People's History*. London: Zed Books, 2002.

Olson, Mancur. *The Logic of Collective Action: Public Goods and the Theory of Groups*. Cambridge, Mass.: Harvard University Press, 1965.

Omara-Otunnu, Amii. *Politics and the Military in Uganda, 1890–1985*. Basingstoke: Macmillan 1987.

Omorogbe, Eki Yemisi. "A Club of Incumbents? The African Union and Coups d'État." *Vanderbilt Journal of Transnational Law*, 44 (2011): 123–154.

Orth, Richard. "Rwanda's Hutu Extremist Genocidal Insurgency: An Eyewitness Perspective." *Small Wars and Insurgencies*, 12 (1) (2001): 76–109.

Ottaway, Marina and David Ottaway. *Ethiopia: Empire in Revolution*. New York: Africana, 1978.

Padró i Miquel, Gerard. "The Control of Politicians in Divided Societies: The Politics of Fear." *The Review of Economic Studies*, 74 (4) (2007): 1259–1274.

Polloni, Domenico. "Darfur in Pieces," UNDP: Conflict Analysis Tools No. 6, 2005.

Posen, Barry R. "The Security Dilemma and Ethnic Conflict." *Survival: Global Politics and Strategy*, 35 (1) (1993): 27–47.

Posner, Daniel N. "Measuring Ethnic Fractionalization in Africa." *American Journal of Political Science*, 48 (4) (2004): 849–863.

Institutions and Ethnic Politics in Africa. Cambridge: Cambridge University Press, 2005.

Powell, Jonathan M., and Clayton L. Thyne. "Global Instances of Coups from 1950 to 2010: A New Dataset." *Journal of Peace Research*, 48 (2) (2011): 249–259.

Powell, Robert. "War as a Commitment Problem." *International Organization*, 60 (1) (2006): 169–203.

Prunier, Gérard. *The Rwanda Crisis: History of a Genocide*. New York: Columbia University Press, 1995.

Darfur: The Ambiguous Genocide. Ithaca, NY: Cornell University Press, 2005.

From Genocide to Continental War: The "Congolese" Conflict and the Crisis of Contemporary Africa. London: Hurst & Co., 2009.

Putnam, Robert D. "Diplomacy and Domestic Politics: The Logic of Two-Level Games." *International Organization*, 42 (3) (1988): 427–460.

Quinlivan, James T. "Coup-Proofing: Its Practice and Consequences in the Middle East." *International Security*, 24 (2) (1999): 131–165.

Rabushka, Alvin and Kenneth A. Shepsle. *Politics in Plural Societies: A Theory of Democratic Instability*. Columbus, Ohio: Merrill, 1972.

Ray, Subhasish. "The Nonmartial Origins of the 'Martial Races': Ethnicity and Military Service in Ex-British Colonies." *Armed Forces & Society*, 39 (3) (2013): 13.

Reiter, Dan. "Exploding the Powder Keg Myth: Preemptive Wars Almost Never Happen." *International Security*, 20 (2) (1995): 5–34.

Reno, William. *Corruption and State Politics in Sierra Leone*. Cambridge: Cambridge University Press, 1995.

Warlord Politics and African States. Boulder, Col.: Lynne Rienner, 1998.

Reyntjens, Filip. *The Great African War: Congo and Regional Geopolitics, 1996–2006*. Cambridge: Cambridge University Press, 2009.

Ricks, Thomas E. *Fiasco: The American Military Adventure in Iraq*. New York: Penguin, 2006.

Roessler, Philip. "The Enemy Within: Personal Rule, Coups, and Civil War in Africa." *World Politics*, 63 (2) (2011): 300–346.

Roessler, Philip and David Ohls. "Self-Enforcing Powersharing in Weak States," College of William and Mary, 2016.

Roessler, Philip, and Harry Verhoeven. *Why Comrades Go to War: Liberation Politics and the Outbreak of Africa's Deadliest Conflict*. London: Hurst Publishers, 2016.

Ronen, Dov. *Dahomey: Between Tradition and Modernity*. Ithaca, NY: Cornell University Press, 1975.

Roth, Guenther. "Personal Rulership, Patrimonialism, and Empire-Building in the New States." *World Politics*, 20 (2) (1968): 194–206.

Rothchild, Donald. "State-Ethnic Relations in Middle Africa." In Gwendolen Margaret Carter and Patrick O'Meara, eds., *African Independence: The First Twenty-Five Years* (pp. 71–96). Bloomington, Ind.: Indiana University Press 1985.

"Hegemonial Exchange: An Alternative Model for Managing Conflict in Middle Africa." In Dennis L. Thomson and Dov Ronen, eds., *Ethnicity, Politics and Development* (pp. 65–104). Boulder, Col.: Lynne Rienner, 1986.

"Ethnic Bargaining and State Breakdown in Africa." *Nationalism and Ethnic Politics*, 1 (1) (1995): 54–72.

Managing Ethnic Conflict in Africa: Pressures and Incentives for Cooperation. Washington, DC: Brookings Institution Press, 1997.

Rothchild, Donald and Michael W. Foley. "African States and the Politics of Inclusive Coalitions." In Donald Rothchild and Naomi Chazan, eds., *The Precarious Balance: State and Society in Africa* (pp. 149–171). Boulder, Col.: Westview Press, 1988.

Rothschild, Joseph. *Ethnopolitics: A Conceptual Framework.* New York: Columbia University Press, 1981.

Ryle, John. "Disaster in Darfur," *The New York Review of Books*, August 12, 2004.

Saideman, Stephen M. "Is Pandora's Box Half Empty or Half Full? The Limited Virulence of Secessionism and the Domestic Sources of Disintegration" In David A. Lake and Donald Rothchild, eds., *The International Spread of Ethnic Conflict* (pp. 3–32). Princeton, NJ: Princeton University Press, 1998.

Salehyan, Idean. "Transnational Rebels: Neighboring States as Sanctuary for Rebel Groups." *World Politics*, 59 (2) (2007): 217–242.

Rebels without Borders: Transnational Insurgencies in World Politics. Ithaca, NY: Cornell University Press, 2009.

"The Delegation of War to Rebel Organizations." *Journal of Conflict Resolution*, 54 (3) (2010): 493–515.

Salehyan, Idean and Kristian Skrede Gleditsch. "Refugees and the Spread of Civil War." *International Organization*, 60 (April 2006): 335–366.

Sambanis, Nicholas. "A Review of Recent Advances and Future Directions in the Quantitative Literature on Civil War." *Defence and Peace Economics*, 13 (3) (2002): 215–243.

"What Is Civil War?" *Journal of Conflict Resolution*, 48 (6) (2004): 814–858.

Sambanis, Nicholas and Moses Shayo. "Social Identification and Ethnic Conflict." *American Political Science Review*, 107 (2) (2013): 294–325.

Samset, Ingrid. "Conflict of Interests or Interests in Conflict? Diamonds and War in the DRC." *Review of African Political Economy*, 29 (93–94) (2002): 463–480.

Sandbrook, Richard and Judith Barker. *The Politics of Africa's Economic Stagnation.* Cambridge: Cambridge University Press, 1985.

Schatzberg, Michael G. *Political Legitimacy in Middle Africa: Father, Family, Food.* Bloomington, Ind.: Indiana University Press, 2001.

Schultz, Kenneth A. "The Enforcement Problem in Coercive Bargaining: Interstate Conflict over Rebel Support in Civil Wars." *International Organization*, 64 (2) (2010): 281–312.

Schweller, Randall L. "The Logic and Illogic of the Security Dilemma and Contemporary Realism: A Response to Wagner's Critique." *International Theory*, 2 (2) (2010): 288–305.

Sharkey, Heather J. *Living with Colonialism: Nationalism and Culture in the Anglo-Egyptian Sudan.* Berkeley, Calif.: University of California Press, 2003.

Shayo, Moses. "A Model of Social Identity with an Application to Political Economy: Nation, Class, and Redistribution." *American Political Science Review*, 103 (2) (2009): 147–174.

Shinn, David H. "Addis Ababa Agreement: Was It Destined to Fail and Are There Lessons for the Current Sudan Peace Process?" *Annales d'Ethiopie*, 20 (2004): 239–259.

Singh, Naunihal. *Seizing Power: The Strategic Logic of Military Coups*. Baltimore, Md.: Johns Hopkins University Press, 2014.

Siollun, Max. *Oil, Politics and Violence: Nigeria's Military Coup Culture (1966–1976)*. New York: Algora, 2009.

Smock, David R., and Audrey C. Smock. *The Politics of Pluralism: A Comparative Study of Lebanon and Ghana*. Cambridge: Cambridge University Press, 1975.

Snyder, Richard. "Paths Out of Sultanistic Regimes: Combining Structural and Voluntarist Perspectives." In H. E. Chehabi and Juan J. Linz, eds., *Sultanistic Regimes* (pp. 49–81). Baltimore, Md.: Johns Hopkins University, 1998.

Stearns, Jason K. *Dancing in the Glory of Monsters: The Collapse of the Congo and the Great War of Africa*. New York: Public Affairs, 2011.

Stewart, Frances. *Horizontal Inequalities and Conflict: Understanding Group Violence in Multiethnic Societies*. New York: Palgrave Macmillan, 2008.

Straus, Scott. *The Order of Genocide: Race, Power, and War in Rwanda*. Ithaca, NY: Cornell University Press, 2006.

"'Destroy Them to Save Us': Theories of Genocide and the Logics of Political Violence." *Terrorism and Political Violence*, 24 (4) (2012): 544–560.

Svolik, Milan W. *The Politics of Authoritarian Rule*. Cambridge: Cambridge University Press, 2012.

Tansey, Ois. "Process Tracing and Elite Interviewing: A Case for Non-Probability Sampling." *PS: Political Science and Politics*, 40 (4) (2007): 765–772.

Tarrow, Sidney G. *Power in Movement: Social Movements, Collective Action, and Politics*. Cambridge: Cambridge University Press, 1994.

"Inside Insurgencies: Politics and Violence in an Age of Civil War." *Perspectives on Politics*, 5 (3) (2007): 587–600.

Thomson, Alex. *An Introduction to African Politics*. London and New York: Routledge, 2011.

Tilly, Charles. *From Mobilization to Revolution*. Reading, Mass.: Addison-Wesley, 1978.

Tiruneh, Andargachew. *The Ethiopian Revolution, 1974–1987: A Transformation from an Aristocratic to a Totalitarian Autocracy*. Cambridge: Cambridge University Press, 1993.

Toft, Monica Duffy. *The Geography of Ethnic Violence: Identity, Interests, and the Indivisibility of Territory*. Princeton, NJ: Princeton University Press, 2003.

United Nations, *Final Report of the Panel of Experts on the Illegal Exploitation of Natural Resources and Other Forms of Wealth of the Democratic Republic of the Congo*, New York: UNSC, 2002.

Utas, Mats, ed. *African Conflicts and Informal Power: Big Men and Networks*. London: Zed Books, 2012.

Uvin, Peter. "Ethnicity and Power in Burundi and Rwanda: Different Paths to Mass Violence." *Comparative Politics*, 31 (3) (1999): 253–271.

Valentino, Benjamin, Paul Huth, and Dylan Balch-Lindsay. "'Draining the Sea': Mass Killing and Guerrilla Warfare." *International Organization*, 58 (2) (2004): 375–407.

Villers, Gauthier de, and Willame Jean-Claude. *République Démocratique du Congo: chronique politique d'un entre-deux-guerres, octobre 1996–juillet 1998.* Paris: L'Harmattan, 1999.

Vlassenroot, Koen. "Citizenship, Identity Formation and Conflict in South Kivu: The Case of the Banyamulenge." *Review of African Political Economy,* 29 (93) (2002): 499–516.

Vreeland, James Raymond. "The Effect of Political Regime on Civil War: Unpacking Anocracy." *Journal of Conflict Resolution,* 52 (3) (2008): 401–425.

Walter, Barbara F. *Committing to Peace: The Successful Settlement of Civil Wars.* Princeton, NJ: Princeton University Press, 2002.

Reputation and Civil War: Why Separatist Conflicts Are So Violent. Cambridge: Cambridge University Press, 2009.

Warburg, Gabriel. *Islam, Sectarianism, and Politics in Sudan since the Mahdiyya.* Madison, Wisc.: University of Wisconsin Press, 2003.

Weber, Max. *Economy and Society,* 3 vols. New York: Bedminster Press, 1968.

Weeks, Jessica L. "Strongmen and Straw Men: Authoritarian Regimes and the Initiation of International Conflict." *American Political Science Review,* 106 (2) (2012): 326–347.

Weidmann, Nils B. "Geography as Motivation and Opportunity: Group Concentration and Ethnic Conflict." *Journal of Conflict Resolution,* 53 (4) (2009): 526–543.

Weinstein, Jeremy M. *Inside Rebellion: The Politics of Insurgent Violence.* Cambridge: Cambridge University Press, 2007.

Wendt, Alexander. "Anarchy Is What States Make of It: The Social Construction of Power Politics." *International Organization,* 46 (2) (1992): 391–425.

Wimmer, Andreas. *Waves of War: Nationalism, State Formation, and Ethnic Exclusion in the Modern World.* Cambridge: Cambridge University Press, 2013.

Wimmer, Andreas, Lars-Erik Cederman, and Brian Min. "Ethnic Politics and Armed Conflict: A Configurational Analysis of a New Global Dataset." *American Sociological Review,* 74 (1) (2009): 316–337.

Wonkeryor, Edward Lama. *Liberia Military Dictatorship: A Fiasco "Revolution."* Chicago, Ill.: Strugglers' Community Press, 1985.

Wood, Elisabeth Jean. *Insurgent Collective Action and Civil War in El Salvador.* Cambridge: Cambridge University Press, 2003.

"The Social Processes of Civil War: The Wartime Transformation of Social Networks." *Annual Review of Political Science,* 11 (1) (2008): 539–561.

Woodward, Peter. *Sudan, 1898–1989: The Unstable State.* Boulder, Col.: Lynne Rienner, 1990.

"Sudan: Islamic Radicals in Power." In John L. Esposito, ed., *Political Islam: Revolution, Radicalism, or Reform?* (pp. 95–114). Boulder, Col.: Lynne Rienner, 1997.

World Bank. *Sudan: Stabilization and Reconstruction,* vol. I. Washington, DC: World Bank, 2003.

Sudan: Stabilization and Reconstruction, vol. II: *Statistical Appendices.* Washington, DC: World Bank, 2003.

Wright, Lawrence. *The Looming Tower: Al-Qaeda and the Road to 9/11.* New York: Vintage Books, 2007.

Wrong, Michela. "The Emperor Mobutu." *Transition*, 81/82 (2000): 92–112.
It's Our Turn to Eat: The Story of a Kenyan Whistle-Blower. New York: Harper, 2009.
Wucherpfennig, Julian, Philipp Hunizker, and Lars-Erik Cederman. "Who Inherits the State? Colonial Rule and Post-Colonial Conflict." Paper presented at Annual Meeting of the American Political Science Association, New Orleans, 2012.
Wucherpfennig, Julian, Philipp Hunziker, and Lars-Erik Cederman, "Who Inherits the State? Colonial Rule and Postcolonial Conflict," *American Journal of Political Science*, 60 (4) (2016): 882–898.
Wucherpfennig, Julian, Nils B. Weidmann, Luc Girardin, Lars-Erik Cederman, and Andreas Wimmer. "Politically Relevant Ethnic Groups across Space and Time: Introducing the Geoepr Dataset." *Conflict Management and Peace Science*, 28 (5) (2011): 423–437.
Young, Crawford. "The African Colonial State and Its Political Legacy." In Donald Rothchild and Naomi Chazan, eds., *The Precarious Balance: State and Society in Africa* (pp. 25–66). Boulder, Col.: Westview Press, 1988.
The African Colonial State in Comparative Perspective. New Haven, Conn.: Yale University Press, 1994.
Young, John. *The Fate of Sudan: The Origins and Consequences of a Flawed Peace Process*. New York: Zed Books, 2012.

Index